HOW LINCOLN LEARNED TO READ

Twelve Great Americans and the Educations That Made Them

Daniel Wolff

BLOOMSBURY

New York Berlin London

Published by Bloomsbury USA, New York

All papers used by Bloomsbury USA are natural, recyclable products
made from wood grown in well-managed forests. The manufacturing
processes conform to the environmental regulations of the country of origin.

LIBRARY OF CONGRESS CATALOGING-IN-PUBLICATION DATA

Wolff, Daniel.
How Lincoln learned to read : twelve great Americans and the educations
that made them / Daniel Wolff.—1st U.S. ed.
p. cm.
Includes bibliographical references and index.
ISBN-13: 978-1-59691-290-8 (hardcover)
ISBN-10: 1-59691-290-1 (hardcover)
1. Education—United States—History.   2. United States—Biography.
I. Title.

LA205.W65 2009
370.973—dc22
2008024695

First published by Bloomsbury USA in 2009
This paperback edition published in 2010

Paperback ISBN: 978-1-60819-037-9

3   5   7   9   10   8   6   4

Typeset by Westchester Book Group
Printed in the United States of America by Quad/Graphics Fairfield

Praise for *How Lincoln L*

"A keyhole view into the country's first two centuries . . . *How Lincoln Learned to Read* reinforces the notion that the nation's inherent rebellious streak has served it well. 'To believe your own thought,' as Emerson wrote in his famous essay 'Self-Reliance,' 'that is genius.' Poor, unconnected people such as Elvis, he writes, 'were supposed to harden into a category, to disappear.' That they sometimes don't—that they sometimes find hope—well, that's a story worth retelling."
—***Boston Globe***

"A riveting, original examination of education inside and outside the classroom . . . [These] stories attest that learning doesn't just happen in a schoolhouse, and life itself may well be the most effective teacher of the most important lessons. Well thought-out, well-argued and thoroughly engaging."
—***Kirkus Reviews*** **(starred review)**

"Though his formal education was scanty, the young George Washington was described by an admiring neighbor as a boy who would go to school all his life. In this remarkably original group portrait of similar strivers, Daniel Wolff redefines the phrase 'education for life.' His classrooms range from a printer's shop in colonial Boston to the Pentecostal church attended by Gladys Presley's boy Elvis. Looming above them all is the unschooled Lincoln, whose capacity for self-education will both shape and justify a brutal war for human possibility. *How Lincoln Learned to Read* might just as well be titled *How Lincoln Learned to Lead.*"
—**Richard Norton Smith, author of *Patriarch***

"Learning is a mysterious miracle, and in this set of interconnected essays, Daniel Wolff tries to illuminate that process by looking deeply into how some iconic Americans . . . metabolized their experiences in and out of the classroom. 'How do we learn what we need to know?' asks Wolff. To answer that question, he delves deeply into the letters, diaries and autobiographies of these wildly different characters, thematically connected as ones who never let school—or lack thereof—get in the way of education."

—Chicago Tribune

"From Abe Lincoln's obsession with books and newspapers to Elvis' fascination with movies and their soundtracks, Wolff ties these varied biographies together with common historical threads, discerning how each was able to surmount difficulties and make his or her mark . . . Enriched by historical details of the Civil War and world wars, the Great Depression, and the rise of unions, and backed by extensive primary sources, Wolff's essays provide enlightening glimpses into the often-serendipitous process of education."   —Booklist

"[Wolff's] essays remind us that greatness in America can bubble up just about anywhere, and that even the great have trouble understanding the ingredients of their own success."

—Wilson Quarterly

"This extended essay, in the form of a dozen entertaining profiles of great Americans—an unexpected cross-section, from Ben Franklin to Elvis Presley—provides an unusual look at the varieties of educational experience that shaped these groundbreakers."

—Publishers Weekly (starred review)

"*How Lincoln Learned to Read* is the fascinating, largely untold story of the early educations of some of America's most compelling leaders. A wonderful storyteller, Daniel Wolff leads us down a path that ultimately brings us back to Henry Adams's most fundamental question: What part of education is useful and what is not? There has probably never been a point in our nation's history when the answer to that question was more important."

—Arne Duncan, U.S. Secretary of Education

CONTENTS

PROLOGUE: THE PRESENT

Imagine a playground at dusk. A bunch of kids are running around, tired after a long day but still having fun. Their parents and babysitters, guardians and grandparents are sitting nearby, talking.

The conversation begins with grades and homework. Whose kid is flunking; whose is in advanced math; who got which teacher.

At some point, it goes from how the kids are doing to how the school is doing. Whether it's a good one; whether it's working.

And that turns into a familiar, almost inevitable argument. What are they teaching kids these days? What *should* they be teaching? It's the argument about standards and discipline and homework: the one that ends up on the cover of newsmagazines.

"When I was a kid," somebody begins, and there are groans in the half-dark. "Uh-oh! Here we go!"

People start talking about their school days. Maybe one woman remembers being part of the push to improve the science curriculum back in the cold war. Then a guy describes his eighth-grade shop class. This one was taught something called "phonics" because the country decided Johnny couldn't read. And that one dropped out: had to work nights, always did badly on the tests.

Then a funny thing happens.

As they continue to swap stories, somebody mentions a great-aunt who showed him how to cook. Someone else tells about the time she and a buddy trained pigeons. Somebody tries to talk about being in the war. The definition of education broadens, opens up to include a whole range of lessons and a lot of different kinds of teachers.

"What part of education has . . . turned out to be useful and what not." That's how Henry Adams framed the question early in the twentieth century. He remembered playing with other kids out in the fields of Quincy, Massachusetts: he learned something there. And when he was in his father's library listening to grown-ups talk about abolition. And on his trip as a teenager down into the slave-holding states of the South. He includes his parents among his early teachers, also his siblings and grandparents. He tells a story about refusing to go to school one day, age six, and how his grandfather took him by the hand and walked him there without saying a word. The lesson, Adams decides, was in the old man's "intelligent silence."

School itself Adams calls "time thrown away." The private academies he went to concentrated on Greek and Latin. He considered that useless: subjects you had to study to show you'd gotten an upper-class education but of no practical value. Harvard was four more "wasted" years. "The man of sixty," he writes, "can generally see what he needed in life, and in Henry Adams's opinion it was not school." He lived through an era of astonishing industrialization— where monopolies began to control vast stretches of the economy, and inventions like the electric dynamo transformed notions of power and possibility. That was the stuff he thought he should have been prepared to understand.

In the dusk of the playground, Adams offers a kind of model, a guide to asking the question. *The Education of Henry Adams* tries to focus on useful knowledge and winnow out the rest. Plus, it makes clear that to describe how and what we learn is to talk about the forces of history. It's a way to tell the story of the democracy.

The conversation on the playground turns out to be an old one: older than the nation. "After God had carried us safe to New England," reads a pamphlet from 1642, "and we had built our houses, provided necessaries for our livelihood, rear'd convenient places for God's worship, and settled the Civil Government: One of the next things we longed for, and looked after was to advance Learning, and perpetuate it to Posterity."

Hasn't each generation had this longing to advance Learning—and this argument about the best way to do it? And hasn't the answer they've come up with affected how the next generation has asked the question?

Say we start at the founding of the republic. And pick an American who helps define how we think of ourselves, helps define what and how we've learned. Ask Henry Adams's question: what part of your education was useful and what not? Limit it to what we now call the school years—ages five to eighteen—but use the broad definition of learning that includes what happens both in and outside the classroom. Let them answer in their own words: from autobiographies, letters, notes. Then, move forward to the next period of time, and ask another person. And so on.

The stories will skip around, of course. To different parts of the country, different circumstances. But maybe they'll also build on each other and form a kind of history. How we've defined and redefined knowledge. How we've decided who should have access to which knowledge and why. How we've tried to perpetuate it, to pass it on.

In the end, maybe this history will help tell us who we, as a country, think we are. Or more accurately, who we want to be when we grow up. Because isn't any history of American knowledge, by definition, a history of expectations, of preparing for the future, of hope?

How do we learn what we need to know?

BEN

Your eight-year-old spends a year in school and then—for reasons that aren't totally clear—leaves. You send him to a tutor and, after a year, that ends, too. Age ten, he's done with formal schooling. Instead, he starts learning the family business . . . and hates it. He threatens to run away and go to sea. You walk him around the city, showing him various trades: carpenters, bricklayers, ironworkers. You decide he should try your nephew's business: manufacturing and sharpening knives. He lasts about three days.

Finally, out of options, you send your now twelve-year-old across town to live with his older brother and learn to be a printer. It takes some persuading, but you get him to sign an agreement to stay for nine years. He lasts a little more than five. Then—angry at his brother and in trouble with the law—he breaks the contract and sneaks out of town. Not quite eighteen, he slips onto a ship and disappears.

Outlined like this, it's the education of a problem child: inconsistent, directionless, contrary. He doesn't seem to want to fit in anywhere. Yet it turns out to be the start of a classic rags-to-riches story: one of America's earliest. And this education becomes a national prototype of how we learn the things we need to know. Generations have returned to the image of this runaway, Benjamin Franklin, arriving in colonial Philadelphia: hungry, broke, wandering the streets with some cheap loaves of bread under his arm—and on his way to becoming author, inventor, scientist, diplomat, founding father. The details come from Franklin himself, who takes care in his autobiography to be "particular in this Description" in order to show how little he started with and how far he came through what he calls his "self-education."

That's the point of his autobiography, which is written as a kind of template, or, as one commentator puts it, a self-help book. Franklin started it when he was in his mid-sixties. "Having emerg'd from the Poverty and Obscurity in which I was born and bred," he explains, "to a State of Affluence and some Degree of Reputation in the World," he figures his life might be "fit to be imitated." He goes on to tell his story in this slightly bemused voice, often funny, humble (or pretending to be), but always calculating. By the time the manuscript was published, he'd helped lead his country to independence. So, the middle-aged narrator with his paunch and his reading glasses is looking back at a boy who's going to help foment rebellion. As a guide to education, *The Autobiography of Benjamin Franklin* is a dropout's prescription that the key to success is . . . dropping out.

The reason Ben's father decides to send him to school at all—in an era when most kids didn't go—is, Franklin says, his "early Readiness in learning to read." It "must have been very early," he points out parenthetically, "as I do not remember when I could not read." His parents' friends, he adds, took this as a sign that he'd grow up to be a scholar. But the story of the-boy-who-could-always-read leaves out the question of who taught him. His father, Josiah, came from a line of educated artisans. Ben's great-grandfather was thrown in an English prison for writing offensive poetry; his grandfather loved reading and writing; one of his uncles wrote poetry and kept a selection of transcribed sermons. All these men worked with their hands; all of them learned to read and write.

Ben's mother, Abiah, was the child of a part-time schoolmaster, Peter Folger. Folger had arrived in Boston in 1635, when the city was only five years old. He'd moved to Martha's Vineyard and then become one of the ten original landowners on the island of Nantucket. He farmed and worked as a surveyor, but he also ran a missionary school, trying to convert the native Wampanoags, teaching them to speak and read English. His son, Abiah's brother, became a Nantucket schoolmaster. So, Ben's mother was probably literate, too, and raised to appreciate the value of an education.

Both the Franklins and the Folgers were Puritans. In their rebellion against the Anglican Church, Puritan ministers and their congregants were constantly reading the Holy Word, combing its every detail and debating interpretations. "All things are conveyed to us in a Logical way," preached Samuel Willard, the Franklin family's pastor at Boston's South Church, "and bear some stamp of reason upon them . . . *[W]ithout Knowledge*," he emphasized, "the mind of Man cannot be *good*, and . . . a people are *destroyed* for lack of Knowledge." As a result, seventeenth-century New England was a particularly literate colony with one university graduate per every forty families: a higher ratio than in old England. By 1680, 98 percent of Massachusetts men who were asked to sign documents could read and write, and over 60 percent of the women.

The boy, then, grows up in a house where the parents are always reading and his siblings are in various stages of learning how to. When Josiah Franklin arrived in Boston in 1683, he already had two children with his first wife, and they'd have five more. Widowed in 1689, the thirty-one-year-old quickly married Abiah, twenty-two, and they went on to have ten more kids. Ben, born in 1706, was their eighth. At that point, there were probably four older siblings at home: a twelve-, nine-, seven-, and three-year-old. The house had an upstairs for sleeping, but everything else happened in a twenty-foot-wide ground-floor room. There, with a big fireplace and a pair of windows looking out on the street, they worked, cooked, ate, and read. If Ben couldn't remember how he learned, it was probably because his early years were saturated with it: a regular buzz of words broken only when they crossed the street to go to the South Church and hear sermons on the importance of the Scripture.

Boston was an outpost at the edge of an enormous continent. It took four to six weeks for a ship to cross over from England, so the colony had to be largely self-reliant. Back when his father arrived, the settlement consisted of about six thousand people, including, on average, one Negro slave per home. It was a port, busy and densely inhabited, with small dark houses packed closely together and open sewers running down the center of each street. England produced most of its manufactured goods, and outlying farms provided fresh food. By the time Ben was growing up, nearby forests had been lumbered out, and the wood for heating and construction was mostly shipped in from Maine. The infant mortality rate was 50 percent, and the town was periodically swept by disastrous fires and even more disastrous epidemics.

In a colony whose first priority was survival, most education amounted to job training. "My elder Brothers," Ben writes in his autobiography, "were all put Apprentices to different Trades." When a boy was somewhere around ten, he was bound to a master craftsman. Under English law, he signed a contract where the master would house, feed, clothe, and train the apprentice for seven years. Often the training was kept in the family to make sure trade secrets stayed that way. So, back in England, Ben's father had been apprenticed at age nine to his older brother, a silk dyer. At the end of their contract, apprentices created what was known as their "master piece": practical proof that the education had worked. Then, the various guilds monitored to make sure the quality of the product stayed high and the number of craftsmen low. That was true in England anyway, but Boston was a new world. When Ben's father arrived, for example, he discovered that silk was a luxury in Massachusetts and switched trades, something he wouldn't have been allowed to do in the old country. He started making candles and soap.

Josiah Franklin believed in the apprentice system: a tradition of vocational education that guaranteed you'd make a relatively good living. He taught his son John the family business. And sent James to England to learn how to be a printer. The point of education in the Franklin family was to provide security, not adventure—to offer answers, not ask questions.

The-boy-who-could-always-read was Josiah Franklin's tenth son, known as the "tithe" because a good Puritan tithed that child to the church. By the time Ben was born, Josiah had done well enough to buy a bigger house. He was adding to the family income by taking in lodgers. And he held a position of responsibility at the South Church, often consulting on important decisions. They waited till the boy was eight, and there were only two younger sisters left at home. Then Josiah, fifty-six, and Abiah, forty-seven, decided that Ben, their "bookish" boy, would get the education that prepared him to become a Puritan minister.

It was, in its own way, an ambitious move. In colonial Boston, slaves, indentured servants, and unskilled laborers "hovered on the edge of poverty." Above them were tradesmen like Josiah Franklin: in a class Ben would later refer to as the "Leather Apron" men. Then came doctors, lawyers, government officials, and ministers. Merchants were the wealthiest class in the port town. But even though the richest tenth of the population owned two fifths of all Boston's property, merchants were thought of as being a little suspect: they didn't make anything except money. The most prestigious citizens in the colony were the educated. In setting his eight-year-old on the path to become a minister, Josiah was aiming for the top.

The route was clear enough. First, you entered your boy at the Boston Latin School. That prepared him to enter Harvard College. And that gave him the qualifications to become a preacher. Boston Latin had been founded in 1635 as a free, public school: the colony's first. The city's most influential minister, the Reverend Cotton Mather, had gone there, and his son was a student when Ben arrived. Boston Latin was open to all white males who wanted to block the "ould deluder, Satan" by gaining the "ability to read and understand the principles of religion and the capital lawes of the country." Its curriculum centered on Latin and Greek, the better to discern "ye true sense & meaning of ye original [Scripture]." And its teachers had to be approved by the town's ministers. Consider it the start of our public school system, and Boston Latin sets the precedent for an education that firmly marries church and state. It taught what's been called the four Rs: reading, writing, 'rithmetic, and religion.

Ben only had a short walk to school: a two-story, forty-foot-long building that held a hundred boys. He sat with the other students his age on benches, lined three rows deep against the wall. The schoolmaster, Dr. Nathaniel Williams, was thirty-nine years old, a fellow parishioner at South Church "enclining to Fatness; His Countenance Fresh and Comely." After graduating Harvard, he'd gone on to two years of missionary work in the West Indies. Dr. Williams and his assistant, Edward Wigglesworth, did all the teaching.

The seven-year program was almost all rote learning. A student's first three years were spent memorizing rules of Latin syntax, vocabulary, and Cato's moral precepts. In addition, one eight-year-old reported, the master "put our class upon turning Aesop's Fables into Latin verse." In their fourth year, Dr. Williams wrote, the students translate Erasmus "if their capacities allow" and memorize Ovid, "which is recited by heart on the usual time of fryday afternoon." Students were supposed to sit quietly on their hard benches, stand to recite their memorized passages, and neatly copy their Latin sentences. "Tutors be strict; but yet be gentle, too," Reverend Mather rhymed in his eulogy to the founder of Boston Latin. "Don't by fierce cruelties fair hopes undo." Ben's teacher doesn't seem to have resorted to fierce cruelties, though with two adults in charge of a hundred boys of varying ages and abilities, it must have been tempting. Dr. Williams taught with what the town's selectmen called a "Tedious and burthensome methode." As a result, there seems to have been a fairly constant level of disruption. School reports were full of complaints about tardiness, students playing "hookey," gambling, bad language, and the shooting of popguns. Dr. Williams told one reverend-to-be, "[Y]ou are so full of play that you hinder your classmates." He could have been talking about Ben.

In his autobiography, Franklin says he excelled at Latin, rising to the top of his first-year class, then being skipped a grade so he could jump to third-year studies when he returned. Except he didn't return. He says his father withdrew him because of "the Expence of a College Education . . . and the mean Living many so educated were afterwards able to obtain." But that doesn't seem like it could have been the case. Boston Latin was free, and Harvard regularly provided scholarships for the sons of tradesmen. As to making a decent living, Josiah Franklin must have known all along where this education led. Maybe, as some have argued, it was Benjamin's lack of "piety" that made Boston Latin the wrong choice. But it's hard to know what that translates into for an eight-year-old: popguns and bad language? "I was generally a Leader among the Boys," he writes, "and sometimes led them into Scrapes."

He leaves Latin. And his father promptly enrolls him in what was known as a "writing school." There were eight of these in the city. Ben's was run by George Brownell and his wife out of their home, just a couple of blocks from the Franklins'. That his father sent him here makes the explanations for leaving Latin even less believable. Josiah Franklin had to pay for this education, and it's not clear how it would help his son make a living. Compared with Latin, Brownells was somewhere between an elementary and a finishing school. Ben was taught penmanship, spelling, "cyphering," and composition. The girls (Brownells was coed) were instructed in music, dancing, quilting, and embroidery. The curriculum was different from Latin's, but the teaching method was about the same. Writing was a "constant drill." In arithmetic, Mr. Brownell would pose a problem from his textbook (the only one in the room) and have the whole class work on a solution. When someone got it right, the rest of the students copied down the answer. Ben failed the subject, despite what he calls Mr. Brownell's "mild encouraging Methods." And after a year, he left. At ten years old, he'd come to the end of his formal schooling.

He'd been singled out, put on the fast track, and then fallen (or been taken) off. Looking back, the middle-aged author of the *Autobiography* deliberately leaves the impression that he could have gone this route and succeeded. And he would retain some of the characteristics of this near-education. He made fun of authors who dropped Latin phrases into their writing to show they'd been schooled—but he did it for the rest of his life. The difference, per the *Autobiography*, was that he'd educated himself. And that may have been the most important thing he learned from his brief time in school. He'd gotten a taste of the approved educational route, and he wouldn't be taking it. If he was going to be considered an educated man, he'd have to earn his own credentials: invent himself. And that, he'd go on to argue, only made sense: a new kind of education for a new world.

"At Ten Years old," he writes, "I was taken home to assist my Father in his Business." The year before, his half-brother Josiah Jr., the adventurous one, had been lost at sea. And John, trained in the candle and soap business, had gotten married and moved to Rhode Island. So the bookish boy was designated to take his place and become an apprentice tallow maker, known in England as the noxious trade.

It started with chunks of animal fat. His father got them at the slaughterhouse, then, after cutting away whatever meat remained, chopped the fat into bits and dumped it into the big iron pot that hung in the fireplace. For the better part of an hour, it boiled there, constantly stirred with a long wooden spoon. The pot was then hauled off the fire and left to cool till the melted fat could be strained off. More water got added, and the mixture returned to the fireplace, where it was kept at a low boil for another four hours. The smell in the room must have been constant, as well as the heat and the sheen of grease over everything. After a day of cooling (and while another batch bubbled over the fire), the ingredients would have separated: the meat and gristle reduced to a kind of jelly on the bottom, fatty water in the middle, and on top, a disk of tallow. The process was not only noxious to be around, but the home factory presented all kinds of dangers. One of Josiah and Abiah's children, Ebenezer, had drowned in a "Tub of Suds" at the age of sixteen months.

Ben mostly worked at the finishing end. He was too small for the heavy business of rendering. Instead, he cut lengths of twisted cotton for wicks. These he made into candles either by dipping them, over and over again, into the vats of melted tallow, or by laying them into molds, which he then filled with the hot tallow and had to make sure stayed filled as they cooled. He worked fourteen-hour days, side by side with his father. He also waited on customers and ran errands, every day but the Sabbath. That, starting at sunset Saturday night, was spent in church, listening to the long sermons.

Often, his father made a point of having dinner guests "and always took care to start some ingenious or useful Topic of Discourse, which might tend to improve the Minds of his Children." Typically, Ben and his little sisters wouldn't have been allowed to join in. Sometimes after dinner his father would take out his violin and play psalms and sing in his "clear pleasing Voice." But more often, the evenings were dedicated to studying the scriptures and praying. Wouldn't it be a "Saving of time," Ben supposedly asked his father, if they just said one grace? As the others prayed, the boy's mind would wander. He'd gaze at the big, greasy maps of the world that hung near the table. It's how, he says, he taught himself geography. Right outside, just down the road from the room full of boiling fat and prayers, ships came and went from those very lands. No wonder the boy dreamed of being a sailor.

That wasn't going to happen; the Franklins had already lost one son at sea. But after a couple of years, it must have been clear that their youngest was never going to be a candle maker. Not a happy one, anyway. By the age that kids today enter middle school, he'd spent two years in the classroom and two years with hot tallow. The former had established that he wasn't on track for what we'd call a white-collar job. The latter seems to have convinced his parents that, if he was going to follow a trade, it would have to be something at least minimally more interesting than his father's.

Josiah started taking his son on tours of the city. Boston's streets were full of men at work: smithies banging anvils, carpenters planing beams, masons shaping rocks into walls. "It has ever since," Franklin wrote, "been a Pleasure to me to see good Workmen handle their Tools." The hierarchy of trades put tallow makers among the least skilled, blacksmiths and carpenters a notch up, then silversmiths and printers. By the time father and son were making their tour, Boston's population had grown to around eleven thousand. Its economy was booming, helped by the construction of a big new wharf. Wages were double those in London, although the number of poor was also rising, as were the prices of basic commodities like wheat. What all of Boston shared—Leather Apron men and clergy,

Harvard students and housewives—was being subject to a distant king. The royal governor controlled trade, and loyalty to the crown kept bumping up against the colonists' own best interests. During Ben's short lifetime, taxes had quadrupled. When a leading member of the South Church tried to set up a private bank, a royal decree squashed it. Boston was still half a century from revolution, but in the 1720s, as one historian describes it, "almost every problem and conflict . . . erupted violently, nearly destroying the townspeople's traditional values." Here was his father insisting he find a safe, dependable trade, even as the royal governor explained to Bostonians: "You have no rights but not to be sold for slaves."

Ben describes his father as having "solid Judgment in prudential Matters, both in private and publick affairs." The prudential thing to do, Josiah Franklin decided, was to send his boy off to learn the cutlery business from an older cousin. Except the cousin didn't want to abide by the standard agreement: he wanted to be paid to take on an apprentice. And so, Ben writes, "I was taken home again."

It's here, in the sequence of the autobiography, that Franklin starts talking about reading. The twelve-year-old is back with his family, back to the smell of melting fat, back listening to his father's prayers and running his father's errands. He finds his refuge in books.

He says his first love was *The Pilgrim's Progress.* John Bunyan's clear, direct style helped turn the book's moral lessons into a kind of adventure story. Franklin says he devoured it, then spent what little money he had to buy the whole series of Bunyan's works. When he was done, he sold these to get popular histories of England that featured "wonders, rareties, and curiosities." He also went through his father's small library, even though it was mostly religious tracts. Alongside the Reverend Mather's "Essays to do good," he found Plutarch's *Lives* and Daniel Defoe's social criticism. There were certain advantages to living at home, including an abundance of candles, a relative luxury in Boston. At night, the boy could sit in a corner and use that flickering light to disappear. Into history. Into the details of arguments. Into adventure.

He says it was this "Bookish Inclination" that made his father finally decide the boy should try being a printer. Ben's twenty-one-year-old brother, James, was back from England and had set up one of only four presses in Boston. But, Franklin writes, "I stood out some time." Printing was better than boiling beef fat, but it was still keeping shop. Reading his books and wandering Boston's wharves had convinced him that what he needed to know could only be found elsewhere. He was going to be a sailor. If his father wouldn't let him, he'd run away. Freedom and action were what counted. Wasn't that why his father had left England? Wasn't that the spirit of the colony, the lesson to be learned from this city of immigrants?

"I stood out some time." You can picture the twelve-year-old digging in his heels. And his father's reaction? We aren't told, but it must have been something about being practical. And obedient. All Franklin writes is that he "at last was persuaded." He signed an indentured contract that bound him to his brother without pay—apprentice to master—until the boy turned twenty-one. It was like signing up for middle school, high school, and college, all with a single instructor teaching a single subject.

Printing was a skilled trade, but it had its own drudgery. Especially for an apprentice, who started out doing the most basic jobs: sweeping up, fetching water, keeping the equipment clean, making sure there was wood for the fire. Eventually, he'd advance to where cleanup included replacing type when a job was done. Pulling the used font from the forms and returning it to the type case, he learned where each letter and spacing was kept. The idea was that someday he'd be able to do the reverse: stand with the composing stick in his left hand and, eyes on the text, pull the type without looking. But that would come later. Before he got to compose, he had to learn how to boil lampblack to make ink. And then how to soak small leather balls in the ink till they were saturated and then beat them against the typeface till it was dark enough to print. And before he did that, he had to learn how to make the balls: scraping the hair off bits of leather, softening the material by soaking it in urine, then sewing the scraps together. As he advanced, an apprentice was allowed to moisten the paper so it would accept ink, and, if he was strong enough, to work the press, which meant throwing his weight against the handle and imprinting the carefully laid-out type one sheet at a time.

Mostly, an apprentice picked up his trade by watching. You didn't ask questions; you didn't get demonstrations; there wasn't time for that. If, while you were cleaning up around the press, you learned a little about how it worked, well, that was fine. As long as it didn't interfere with business. In Ben's case, it didn't help that his master was his brother. And the difference in age must have made it even tougher: a twenty-one-year-old trying to start a new business, depending on and ordering around a twelve-year-old. "[M]y brother was passionate," Franklin writes in his autobiography, "and had often beaten me, which I took extreamly amiss." Part of a standard apprentice's contract was the promise to serve his master faithfully and "his lawful commands everywhere gladly do." The "gladly" doesn't seem to have applied here. Still, Franklin says he quickly became proficient and "a useful Hand to my Brother."

The *Autobiography* skips over what he learned and how. His apprenticeship not only gave him a trade, but an identity, so that years later, when he was a famous author, diplomat, and scientist, he still signed his name, "Benjamin Franklin, Printer." But here, without even breaking the paragraph, he goes from saying he'd become a "useful Hand" to talking about what he was reading at the time. He'd been apprenticed to become a printer, but his unofficial goal was to learn how to read and use the language.

As he put it, he aimed to become "a tolerable English writer, of which," he adds, "I was extremely ambitious." He wasn't going to become a minister via Boston Latin, or a gentleman by way of a writing school. And it looked like he'd never lead his life of adventure at sea. No, the son was going to end up the tradesman his father wanted. But a tradesman with extreme ambition. Looking back on his adolescence, he singles out "Prose Writing" as "a principal Means of my Advancement." This aspect of his education, he goes on to explain in detail.

Books were hard to come by in colonial Boston, but the printing trade was a good one to be in. He'd borrow a volume from a bookseller's apprentice, read it that night, and be sure to get it back in the morning in pristine condition. He'd read on his lunch break, sometimes instead of lunch, and when customers saw him, they'd offer to loan him books. It made for a haphazard curriculum, but there were advantages to that. He read for pleasure, letting his curiosity and ambition lead him.

The first writing he tried was poetry, age thirteen or so. His brother, getting wind of it, put him to work composing ballads about local events. Once they'd been printed up, Ben got sent out on the street to hawk them. Barely a teenager, he was getting his writing in print and selling it. He says it "flatter'd [his] Vanity." But his father soon pointed out that "Verse-makers were generally Beggars." Ben shifted to prose.

Again, his father criticized the result, this time because they lacked "elegance of Expression." Ben says he "grew more attentive to the *Manner* in Writing, and determined to endeavor at Improvement." He set himself a rigorous curriculum. He'd take apart published essays and then put them back together, using his own words. It was a little like replacing typeface: a methodical, craftsman's approach. Again, there's no one to teach him, no direct instruction. He says he happened to find a grammar book that mentioned Socrates and soon was experimenting with the classic method, trying on the voice of "the humble Enquirer and Doubter." He found he could win arguments this way, asking a series of small, apparently innocent questions. It was a little embarrassing how well it worked, "drawing People even of superior Knowledge into Concessions." He says he eventually dropped the method but kept the habit of expressing himself "in Terms of modest Diffidence." He also held on to the role of the Doubter.

The teenager started reading the leading religious skeptics of his day. All around him, the Puritan world began and ended with the Divine Being. God's presence in the Holy Word was why children were taught to read. His absence in the women of nearby Salem was why, the decade before Ben was born, they were brought to trial as witches. Ben doesn't doubt that there's a God, but his reading of the "deists" convinces him that the Lord isn't actively involved in human affairs. In his own words, Ben begins "evading" church, using the time for more study. He admires John Locke's "An Essay Concerning Human Understanding." Locke's championing of natural reason as the ultimate judge of and guide to knowledge fits Ben's self-education: his one-boy school based on asking questions, on what he doesn't and needs to know. Admitting a profound "Ignorance in Figures," for example, he plows through an arithmetic text and then a book on navigation.

The *Autobiography* emphasizes how independent this education is: a boy finding his own way, skipping meals and sneaking time to pore over books. As a middle-aged author, Franklin draws his young self learning not just outside the system but basically without any help. But it isn't all that solitary. His father critiques his writing, his brother publishes it; he tries out his arguments on friends, they loan him books. And though he trusts his natural reason to lead him to what he needs to know, he tests it by seeing if his knowledge works in the world.

So, in his ambition to be a tolerable English writer, he needed readers. In the summer of 1721, when he was fifteen and a half, his brother began publishing the *New England Courant*, the fourth newspaper to appear in America and the first independent one. In a city full of controversy, split over its loyalties both to the king and the church, James Franklin's *Courant* set out to appeal to the skeptical, sophisticated, and irreverent. At first, Ben just helped with printing and delivering. But within a year his prose would be appearing on the front page.

The *Courant*'s opening salvo was aimed at Reverend Mather and, through him, the Puritan Church. The occasion was a smallpox epidemic that would eventually kill nine hundred Boston residents, about one in every seven. Reverend Mather was for inoculating the population: a still new and largely untested approach. He'd learned about the technique from one of his slaves, whom the reverend called "a pretty Intelligent Fellow." The *Courant*, on the other hand, maintained that giving people even a small dose of a lethal disease was irresponsible. Its argument was based less on science than on establishing the paper as anti-church. The clergy supported inoculation, so the *Courant* was against it.

James Franklin had launched his paper in an era of increasing political tension. Elisha Cooke Jr., son of a wealthy doctor and landowner, had begun challenging British control of the local government. He wanted Bostonians to be able to print more currency and establish their own banks. And with the money he made through his virtual monopoly of the lumber industry, he had the funds to back his opinions. Starting in 1719, Cooke handpicked anti-British candidates to run for office, and soon his backroom "Caucus" could all but guarantee their success. It amounted to Boston's first political machine. Cooke's slates were reelected better than 80 percent of the time, one establishment replacing another. But the new one was homegrown and part of a larger move toward independence.

The *Courant* attracted a core group of doctors, writers, and merchants, many of them Harvard graduates. They were mostly Anglicans and different from the Leather Apron crowd in most other ways, too. Reverend Mather labeled them the "Hell-Fire Club," out to "debauch and corrupt the minds and Manners of New England." Their conversations in James Franklin's print shop must have been wide-ranging, contemptuous of common opinion, and above all, witty. Modeling themselves on the writers in the British paper the *Spectator*, members of the Hell-Fire Club preferred to attack authority by mocking it. Over in the corner, taking all this in, was the teenage apprentice.

But he would no more have been allowed to join in these debates than in his father's dinner table conversations. He didn't have the credentials. He hadn't gone to Harvard or even made it out of Boston Latin. He was a six-foot-tall, broad-shouldered kid in a dirty apron, working the handle of the press or bent over a book during his lunch break. As to getting his writing in the paper, there was the annoying reality that his brother was the publisher. As Franklin put it, "[he] would object to printing any Thing of mine . . . if he knew it to be mine." The *Courant* was the local publication most likely to accept Ben's liberal views—and it was right there—but he couldn't use it to test his prose style. Not under his own name anyway. If he was going to have a voice, it would have to be someone else's.

Many of the writers around him published under pseudonyms. "Zechariah Hearwell," for example, contributed to the *Courant*. And that approach was modeled on the pieces signed "Jack Modish" in the *Spectator*. In the repressive atmosphere, there was a tradition of disguising your identity or publishing anonymously; it allowed for something like freedom of speech. In Ben's case, it would also hide the fact that the little brother of the publisher was submitting work. And it would disguise how much schooling the author did or didn't have. So, in the spring of 1722, the sixteen-year-old apprentice slipped the first of more than a dozen letters under the door of his brother's print shop. It was signed "Silence Dogood," in mockery of Reverend Mather's "Essays to do good."

The first piece opens by pointing out that people tend to judge writing based on who wrote it: "*poor* or *rich*, *old* or *young*, a *Schollar* or a *Leather Apron Man*." So, Ben will dedicate this letter and the next two to establishing Silence Dogood's character. He's set out not just to write under an assumed name but to create a particular perspective. His Dogood is a woman: the middle-aged widow of a country minister. She's openly, even proudly, unschooled. She says she's picked up a little book learning by reading through her late husband's library: an outsider's self-education a lot like Ben's. The reader doesn't expect her to be sophisticated, and part of the running joke is how her lack of schooling lets her see colonial life that much more clearly. Smart, funny, down-to-earth, it's a comic voice that lets Ben's satire stay in the realm of good clean fun, and at the same time, slash that much deeper. The sixteen-year-old is soon enjoying what he calls the "exquisite Pleasure" of hearing people praise the letters without knowing who wrote them.

Once her character is established, the first subject Silence Dogood lays into is education. She announces that she has a minister boarding at her house, and he'll help her "beautify" her writing with an occasional sentence in the "learned languages" so as to make it "fashionable, and pleasing to those who do not understand it." Ben slips the needle in quietly, with almost nonchalant accuracy. And that's just the beginning. In letters that appear every couple of weeks, he'll take apart a wide range of the colony's pretensions, all with a kind of mock innocence.

The next target is Harvard. If Ben had gone on at Boston Latin, he would have been a freshman by now: in a Harvard class of forty, about half of whom would end up Puritan ministers. Instead, he has Silence Dogood wondering if she should send her son to "that famous Seminary of Learning." She has a dream about the place. She dreams that Harvard students aren't there to learn but because their parents can afford it; that the main reason they want to be ministers is the promise of an easy and comfortable living; and that once they graduate—basically uneducated but with a diploma that guarantees their futures—they end up plagiarizing their Sunday sermons. In Widow Dogood's dream, Harvard is a kind of finishing school; its students learn "little more than how to carry themselves handsomely, and enter a Room genteely." "Dunces and Blockheads," they end up "*e'en just* as ignorant as ever." If it sounds like a brutal attack, Ben manages to launch it obliquely, in the carefully worked-out voice of Silence Dogood—and adds another layer of protection by veiling it all in a dream that the widow doesn't quite understand. In his autobiography, Franklin will call the Silence Dogood letters his "Performances." They are that.

The next letter goes on to another aspect of education. "What has a Woman done," Dogood asks, "to forfeit the Priviledge of being taught?" They learn to read, she says, "and perhaps to write their Names, or so, and that is the Heigth of a Woman's Education." Ben is applying his studies here, putting words from Daniel Defoe's essays into the widow's mouth. She goes on to blame men for keeping women ignorant, "maintaining us in idleness." In the letters that follow, the apprentice fires away at everything from Boston's hypocrisy about things sexual to the lack of separation between church and state. He has his widow mock hoopskirts, Puritan pride ("Even those who nourish it in themselves, hate to see it in others") and New England's funereal poetry, which throws in Latin phrases as "garnish." One of Silence Dogood's reoccurring themes is a person's right to think through an issue and state an opinion. She takes her fellow do-gooders to task for letting themselves be silenced, giving up their freedoms to the "blind Zealots among every Denomination of Christians."

In July 1722, as the *Courant* is publishing Ben's eighth letter, its independent thinking lands it in trouble. James Franklin is accused of criticizing "His Majesty's Government," as well as "the Ministry, Churches and College." He's hauled off to jail, and Ben becomes temporary manager of the paper. He writes a response to the censorship that's signed "Silence Dogood" but barely bothers to sustain her character. Instead, the letter quotes at length from a British essay defending "Freedom of Thought [and] Freedom of Speech, which is the Right of every Man." It denounces "Ministers" who help "cook up Tyranny." The next letter attacks religious hypocrites who "ruin their Country for God's sake." Silence Dogood, in her anger, has lost both her distinctive voice and her sense of humor.

When James gets out of jail and the paper returns to something like normal, so does the widow. She proposes a club to support those "punish'd with their Virginity until old Age." She observes how drunks suddenly become experts on all kinds of topics thanks to the "liberal Education of a little vivifying *Punch*." But it's a brief lull. In early 1723, the House of Representatives accuses the *Courant* of perverting the Holy Scriptures, and a judge calls the newspaper "a High Affront to this Government." James Franklin has to go into hiding. And Silence Dogood disappears, too. If the letters began as a test of Ben's self-education—a kind of clever high school thesis performed in public—the stakes have gotten considerably higher.

Around this time, the seventeen-year-old publicly reveals that he is Silence Dogood. "I began to be considered a little more by my Brother's Acquaintance, and in a manner that did not quite please him." For his next published piece, Ben keeps the tongue-in-cheek sarcasm but drops the widow's character. "Rules for the *New England Courant*" appears as an anonymous letter to the editor. It acidly recommends that the paper try to stay "inoffensive" and "pleasant." It shouldn't mock religion or ministers, who are, after all, "the *Best of Men*." And it shouldn't make fun of people's moral shortcomings. In other words, to keep out of trouble, the *Courant* should stay stupid. It's the kind of advice a master might give an apprentice. Or a husband a wife. Or a teacher a student: follow the rules and don't ask questions. Ben's voice is biting, barely controlled. He's mimicking what Boston's ruling class routinely told people like the Franklins—and what England told its colony.

By joining "State" with "Steeple," as Ben's brother rhymed in the *Courant*, the government aimed "to blind the People." Knowledge was supposed to stay with "the Clergy and the Judges," not "in the Heads of common Drudges." Wasn't that the point of this carefully controlled colonial society? Silence Dogood mocked and James Franklin's newspaper attacked a system that believed in keeping most folks ignorant. Under that arrangement, an inquiring, unrestrained education amounted to an act of treason.

Ben, almost eighteen, was once again being listed as the publisher of the *Courant* so his brother could avoid "the Censor of the Assembly." In the *Autobiography*, Franklin calls it "a very flimsy Scheme," but it kept the business afloat. Boston was a city in turmoil. "Most of the traditional institutions of reason and restraint," as one historian puts it, "were divided, confused or discredited. Hatred for things England had reached new heights. The town and the province were on the brink of rebellion, and everyone knew it." A decade later, when the colony had backed down and reentered an uneasy truce with England, Franklin would maintain that the point of his self-education was simply to learn the craft. "There is scarce any Accomplishment more necessary to a Man of Sense," he'd write, "then that of *Writing well* in his Mother Tongue." But in the heat of his literary apprenticeship, as he was composing his master piece—the Dogood letters and the other articles in the *Courant*—he was after more than just writing well.

Franklin's education had always been vocational, aimed at practical ends. To earn a living as a printer often meant you had to be publisher and writer, providing content for the presses. He'd learned the way an apprentice learned: hands-on, taking prose apart and putting it back together again. He'd had to pursue his studies haphazardly, but he'd used what books he'd found as methodically as he could. From the comparatively simple moral adventures of *The Pilgrim's Progress*, he'd worked up to the skepticism of John Locke. He'd learned how to write clearly and construct a logical argument. And he'd developed a style, making up for a lack of poetic ability with a sly sense of humor and developing the condensed, pointed edge of the aphorism. Finally, he'd discovered that one way to survive in the midst of controversy was to attack from behind the carefully designed mask of an invented character.

At about the age a student today would graduate from high school, Ben graduates Boston. In the *Autobiography*, he explains that he was still fighting with brother James and hints that his success as Silence Dogood hadn't helped the situation. It must have been hard to contemplate four more years as an apprentice. Plus, he'd given his "Rulers some Rubs," Franklin says, and they'd begun to consider him "in an unfavorable Light." His graduation consists of breaking his contract with his brother and his word to his parents. He slips out of town in secret. If the *Autobiography* paints him arriving in Philadelphia as a freeman—independent, adventurous, a skilled craftsman—he could also be seen as a kid on the lam, hungry and alone.

Decades later, he'd claim that he was talked into writing the *Autobiography*: a friend convinced him that his life story offered "a noble rule and example of *self-education* . . . the education of a wise man." The noble rule and example wasn't so much that he'd taught himself, but that he'd found his own way to what he needed to know. Because this is also the story of a social education, shaped by his parents and siblings, his friends and fellow apprentices, the crowd of writers at the *Courant*, and his audience of readers. What's more, the dropout defined himself at least in part by what he dropped out of: picking up skills at Boston Latin and the writing school, learning a trade in the apprentice system—a trade he'd use as a kind of safe harbor from which he could read, write, argue. In fact, as an adult, Franklin ends up a champion of schools and schooling. In his "Proposals Relating to the Education of Youth in Pensilvania," he'll dream of an academy that plays down the rote learning of Latin and Greek in favor of "useful Knowledge . . . introduc'd to Advantage, and with Pleasure to the Student." It's how he'd learned, except no one had introduced his knowledge to him; he'd fought for it. By the time he writes the "Proposals," he's in his forties and interested in founding institutions (specifically the University of Pennsylvania) that would perpetuate a kind of controlled, ongoing rebellion.

Because that's finally what he'd studied: not just writing tolerable prose or constructing a solid argument, but rebellion. Take a look at his spotty history, and there's a consistent theme: if an institution isn't useful, doesn't teach what you need to know, you have a right to leave. The teenager who arrives in Philadelphia and walks the streets with his loaves of bread is a product of rebellion. He's left the church and then made fun of it. He's criticized His Majesty's government and argued that the freedom to do so is a fundamental right. He's dropped out of school, broken his apprenticeship, and run away from family and home. The writing style he's developed, including the satire and the invented characters, is a method particularly suited to speaking out against old institutions.

Just before leaving Boston, in his next-to-last piece for the *Courant*, Ben writes as one Timothy Wagstaff. Under that pseudonym, he lashes out at the enemies of the paper: people who think religion should have a "gloomy Soul, and a dejected Countenance." Who criticize *Courant* writers for having "things *serious* and *comical* inserted in the same Paper." Who are, as he sums it up, in favor of "cutting or stretching all Men to their own Standard of Thinking." That standardization is what he'd fought and mocked and would continue to through various other characters, including the impoverished, henpecked Poor Richard of his annual almanac. "Most of the learning in use," Richard says, "is of no great use." Instead, education ought to help people question politics and religion and any other institution in the new country.

Eventually, signing himself "A TRADESMAN of Philadelphia," he'd call for the right of his fellow citizens to take up arms. And in the same voice of a simple, middle-class burgher stating the obvious, he'd help lead them toward revolution. Franklin became famous for taking on the protective cover of a "common dunce." It helped him ask the obvious and experiment with the unknown, but he also wore his beaver hat and his printer's apron as a kind of sign that knowledge ought to be accessible to everyone. Decades later—when he was representing his new nation in France—this acting out of the bumpkin character only irritated his fellow delegate John Adams. "His whole life," Adams wrote, "has been one continued insult to good manners and to decency." Or, to put it another way, it was a life that insulted the status quo. And, as told in the *Autobiography*, it became one of the models for how Americans learn. "A learned blockhead," as Poor Richard put it, "is a greater blockhead than an ignorant one."

NABBY

A couple of decades after Ben Franklin snuck out of Boston—and just a dozen miles from that city—Abigail Smith was born. "Nabby" arrived in the world with a whole set of advantages that the tallow maker's son never had and at least one disadvantage. She was female.

It was a disadvantage, anyway, when it came to schooling. Nabby's America, on the verge of its battle for independence, assumed its daughters didn't need formal education. A girl was going to grow up to be a wife and a mother. So, almost all her instruction could and did take place at home. If she happened to live in an area with a writing school like Brownells, where Franklin had gone—and she could afford it—she might be taught basic literacy skills as well as music and dance. Or, she might pick up those skills at a "dame's school," reciting the alphabet as she did her needlework. But an education in history or Greek, Socrates or Shakespeare, was for boys only. Here's how Nabby put it: "Every assistance and advantage which can be procured is afforded to the Sons, whilst the daughters are wholly neglected in point of Literature."

Except it's hard to believe the person who wrote this sentence had been wholly neglected. Look at its parallel construction—the way it turns around at the word "whilst"—and the clear, confident language. Maybe the author hasn't been formally educated, but she's managed to become literate and then some. How? And why?

Why does a daughter need to know about Literature with a capital L? What world did she dream of entering?

Nabby's grandfather had started as a butcher's apprentice in Charlestown, Massachusetts, and risen to become a member of Boston's wealthiest class. His route was the one Ben Franklin had fantasized about. William Smith Sr. had gone from the life of a Leather Apron man to sea, eventually becoming a ship's captain. He'd then parlayed that into a career as a merchant: the new, slightly disreputable class that prospered by trading with England. One of his sons had followed him into business. The other, Nabby's father, was sent to Harvard to become a minister. Less rebellious than Franklin and with a lot more money, William Smith Jr. had dutifully gone down the proscribed educational path and come out, age eighteen, with a Harvard degree. He may not have been one of the "Dunces and Blockheads" from Silence Dogood's dream, but he didn't have much intellectual ambition.

He was twenty-seven before he was ordained the Reverend William Smith. It was 1734, and he'd moved out of Boston to become the minister in the small town of Weymouth, the oldest community in the Massachusetts Bay Colony. Founded in the 1620s, Weymouth was a quiet, agricultural village of about two thousand. Its families were almost all descendants of early Puritans: living on land first cleared and farmed a hundred years earlier, content to stay put. As one of Nabby's sisters would write, the town had "never been distinguished, unless for its Inactivity." Boston was about ten miles away, but that took a while on horseback over rough roads. And once you got there, the city was noisy and crowded, full of new immigrants and new ideas. People tended to stay in Weymouth. Four years after becoming the minister, Reverend Smith bought a parsonage and farm. He'd remain there the rest of his life.

When he was thirty-three, the reverend married Elizabeth Quincy, eighteen, the daughter of Colonel John Quincy. The colonel was head of the leading family in nearby Braintree—which would eventually be renamed for him. Elected year after year as speaker for the town meeting, he was also the justice of the peace and representative to the Massachusetts legislature. The Quincy family said it could trace its ancestry back to a forefather present at the signing of the Magna Carta. They've been described as among "the most noted of the most respected class of their day." Plus, the colonel had married well. Nabby's grandmother was the daughter of a well-known Puritan minister, tying the couple to the highest ranks of the religious establishment. Elizabeth Quincy had grown up at Mount Wollaston, their seaside estate. She not only brought Reverend Smith a sizable dowry but arrived in Weymouth with an old-money, upper-class vision of what a woman needed to know.

Nabby was the Smiths' second child, three years younger than her sister Mary. Both were thin and frail, often sick. But where the oldest was an obedient girl, determined to please, Nabby would describe her own disposition as "volatile, giddy." Comparing herself with Mary, she'd write how "a thread would govern one, a cable would be necessary for the other." Soon, there was a younger brother and then another sister. They were all raised in the parsonage.

Reverend Smith was a conservative minister. He carefully wrote out his sermon each week, structuring it the way he'd learned at Harvard, then read it twice during the daylong Sunday service. If this predictable ritual could get a little dull for the congregation (which always included the reverend's wife and children), it must also have been comforting, with its familiar pace and quiet faith. But outside the little Weymouth church and all across New England, that comfort was being challenged. During Nabby's childhood, a religious revival swept through the colonies. The First Great Awakening had believers standing in the aisles and testifying to a new birth of Christ's spirit. Faith, the rabble-rousing preachers proclaimed, was feeling: a passion that touched you and changed you. Anyone could know it, not just people who studied Latin and Greek. The Great Awakening rebelled against Puritan traditions, as the Puritans had once rebelled against the Anglican Church. Three decades before Massachusetts declared independence, its churches shook with this democratic, grassroots movement.

Not in Weymouth. The Reverend Smith didn't see the need for radical change. As a respected leader, respected partly because of his education, he raised his children to follow tradition—and to stay away from the common people. Nabby's sister would describe their upbringing as "totally secluded." As the minister's family, they were expected to set an example. And being descendants of the Quincys only increased their prestige and separation. What the Smith girls needed to know was distinctly different from most of Weymouth's daughters.

Weymouth was a farming town. As a woman on a colonial New England farm, your life was largely defined by chores. You woke before first light and put wood on the banked fires. Then you went out to the shed and milked the cows, hauled the full buckets back indoors, set aside a few pans to make cheese and butter. As you heated up last night's leftovers for your family's breakfast, you started cooking the new day's food. Bread needed to be baked; butter churned, salted, and packed away; beer (the staple beverage) brewed. While your husband worked in the fields, you had to tend the garden: it was woman's work to plant, weed, and harvest vegetables. It was also woman's work to feed and water the chickens, collect the eggs, and on special occasions, slaughter a hen. As it was woman's work to take care of the calving, make sausage, put up preserves, and take the grist to the mill.

Clothing was a whole other responsibility. Women sheared the sheep in the spring, then cleaned the wool of twigs and burrs, scoured it, and dyed it in big vats. The indigo (blue) color and madder (red) were imported. For other shades, a woman had to learn which native flowers and berries produced what. After the dyed wool had dried, you carded it, taking a little bit at a time and working it between two toothed paddles until it was fine enough to spin. Days were spent at the spinning wheel, turning it with your right hand while you fed the yarn with your left. When you'd wound forty strands of thread onto a fifty-four-inch reel, you had a hank. Seven hanks made a skein. Six skeins were considered a solid day's work. An equally long process went into making linen out of flax.

For manufactured goods, including blankets, napkins, sheets, and aprons, the colonies had always relied on England. But between when Ben Franklin and Nabby Smith were born, basic weaving in America had shifted from being an apprenticed trade controlled by men to another unpaid chore women did at home. Standard farmhouse furniture had come to include a seven-foot loom, as wide and long as a double bed. You sat on its bench with your feet pumping, your hands throwing the wooden shuttle back and forth, and if you were good at it and worked hard, you could turn out about three yards of heavy wool cloth in a day. Which then had to be cut and sewn. Plus, there were socks to be knit, needlework, and embroidery. Of course, it all needed to be washed and dried, folded and mended. And then there was the house to keep clean, the yard to sweep. An anonymous writer in a newspaper of the day outlined what a colonial girl needed to know:

Teach her what's useful, not to shun deluding;
To roast, to toast, to boil and mix a pudding;
To knit, to spin, to sew, to make or mend;
To scrub, to rub, to earn & not to spend.

It was a curriculum taught by and for women: mothers, grandmothers, aunts, and older sisters. It wasn't called an apprenticeship—no guild, no master piece—but that's what it was most like. As soon as a girl could walk, she began learning how to help with the daily chores: holding the reel of thread for her mother, working her own miniature loom. By the time she was four, a girl was expected to be able to knit basic stockings and mittens; by six, spin flax. By eight, most girls were helping take care of their younger sisters and brothers.

The Puritan belief that a Christian should be able to read the Bible applied to girls as well. Typically, mothers taught daughters, also passing on a little basic arithmetic. That's if the mother was literate. Girls brought up to be farmer's wives—and most girls were— had to know how to manage a household: keep track of supplies and expenses, bargain with the tradesmen, deal with the itinerant laborers needed at harvest. About half the white women in America knew how to read by the time of independence (compared with 90 percent of white men). Silence Dogood's reason why men kept women ignorant—to maintain them in idleness—starts to look like a whole other level of satire: most colonial women weren't maintained and had little to no idleness.

A woman's job description dictated how much she needed to be literate. Women couldn't vote, and the vast majority didn't own any property. Under British law, a wife's status and authority were derived from her husband. "Wives are part of the house and family," as an author declared in 1712, "and ought to be under a husband's government." Daughters were raised to marry. Courtships often began before you were a teenager, and while there might be flirtation and romance, the final agreement was supposed to be negotiated by the two sets of parents. For families like the Quincys, marriage was, among other things, a financial merger and the primary way property got passed on. Meanwhile, the gap between the colony's rich and poor kept growing larger. By Nabby's day, more and more daughters had no dowries. They were marrying without their parents' consent or not marrying at all. By 1750, almost 40 percent of pregnancies occurred outside of wedlock.

Having babies was a woman's main job. Nabby would one day joke: "I begin to think population a very important Branch in the American Manufactorys." Ben Franklin was his father's tenth son. Colonel Quincy's wife, Elizabeth, had their first child when she was twenty and a family of five by the time she was thirty-four. Nabby's mother had four children by the time she was twenty-four. And Nabby would start when she was twenty-one and have five pregnancies in seven years. Most women went through childbirth without a doctor. Trained physicians were expensive and only called in extreme cases. Instead, girls were taught a variety of folk medicines and cures. Nabby, for example, believed in herb baths and recommended a poultice of white bread or chamomile flowers to fight a cold. With infant mortality at 50 percent, women were expected to know how to deal with death, the same way they had the responsibility to tend to the elderly and the infirm.

Finally, the standard curriculum for a girl included learning how to please—or, at least work with—a husband. If she was under his government, she was also his economic partner. "No man ever prospered in the world," Nabby would one day write, "without the consent and cooperation of his wife." Colonial marriage wasn't anything like an equal arrangement, but a couple had to figure out a division of labor that worked. Again, that depended on the nature of the labor. Nabby's future husband, for example, characterized the best qualities of a woman as "Kindness, softness, Tenderness." Nabby would one day declare "that women, in general, have more delicate sensations than men," an attribute girls of her class were taught to cultivate. She thought she might have learned this lesson too well, that she was a child marked by "too much sensibility."

Nabby's mother set up the Smith parsonage a lot like Mount Wollaston, where she'd been raised. Elizabeth Quincy Smith had grown up with servants and slaves. So had Reverend Smith. So would Nabby. If anything, by the time Nabby came of age, a woman in her position had more cheap labor available to do the chores. Land was starting to run out in New England. Between 1700 and 1750, the population had climbed from roughly a hundred thousand to four hundred thousand. The typical size of a farm had decreased by a third since the days of the first settlers. And New England soil was producing less. The colonists "mined the land rather than farmed it": clear-cutting the forests, planting the same crops in the same fields year after year, losing the best topsoil to erosion. Older settlements, like Weymouth and Braintree, were starting to be used up. As the hardscrabble existence of a small farmer got even harder, sons and daughters began heading into the city to find work. Or, they became tenants, working for the large landowners. Or, they had to make a living as servants. Reverend Smith had bought the Weymouth parsonage with inherited money and went on to buy another farm in Lincoln and still another in Medford, probably with the help of his wife's dowry. What made it possible for men like the reverend to manage multiple operations was cheap, available labor. As local farms failed, there were that many more field hands, caretakers, maids. While Nabby's education included the basics of cooking and sewing, a Smith girl didn't need to know how to milk a cow; she needed to know how to run a household where the cows got milked.

Nabby grew up with at least two slaves: Tom and Pheby. Pheby, a young girl, was "treated as a family member," according to one author. Except, of course, she worked for the family. And wasn't paid. And wasn't free to leave. As an adult, Nabby would oppose slavery, pointing out the contradictions of the American Revolution: "[We] fight ourselves for what we are daily robbing and plundering from those who have as good a right to freedom as we have." But Pheby was only given her freedom after Reverend Smith died—and when Massachusetts was officially abolishing slavery. Even then, a person in Nabby's position kept indentured servants: she'd write her sister about a "very clever black Boy of 15 who has lived with me a year and is bound to me till he is 21." And she adds, "I had rather have black than white help, as they will be more like to agree."

America, as Nabby saw it, had "none so immensely rich as to Lord it over us, neither any so abjectly poor as to suffer for the necessaries of life provided they will use the means." Compared with England, that may have been true. But in her era, one out of six colonialists lived in bondage, and part of Nabby's education was learning how to manage the help. In the month before she got married, she was writing her fiancé about which servant to hire. "[One] has been recommended to me as a clever Girl and a neat one . . . She was bred in the Family of one of our substantial Farmers." In the end, the young couple settled on a black maid, trained by the groom's mother. And a quarter century later, Nabby would be supervising what she characterized as "a pretty good Housekeeper, a tolerable footman, a middling cook, an indifferent steward, and a vixen of a House maid."

Nabby was taught early on that with these advantages came obligations. While the reverend instructed his daughter not to speak ill of others, Mrs. Smith took it a step further: "We should never wait to be requested to do a kind office, an act of love." Freed from the typical chores of a farmer's daughter, Nabby was expected to help tend to Weymouth's needy. Along with their mother, the Smith girls would make regular visits to comfort the sick, bring a meal to the hungry, help care for the children of the poor. After Nabby got old enough to visit Boston, she'd write with horror how "[t]he poorer sort of children are wholly neglected, and left to range the Streets without Schools, without Business, given up to all Evil." In her village, she'd learned to make sure that sort of thing didn't happen.

But Nabby's privileges didn't extend to her own formal education. "I was never sent to any school," she writes. "Female education in the best families went no further than writing and arithmetic, in some few and rare instances music and dancing." Ben Franklin thrived on his haphazard, spotty self-education: it helped him find holes in the orthodoxy of his times. But Nabby missed what she couldn't have: "I regret the trifling narrow contracted Education of the Females of my own country." Especially compared with the men. Her future husband, for example, went off to a dame school when he was six or so. There, the students each had a hornbook: a piece of wood four inches by two inches. Beneath a protective, see-through layer of horn was a piece of paper with the alphabet, some simple syllables, and the Lord's Prayer. The dame would have her students recite their hornbook lessons in unison, loud and clear, then listen for any deviation in the chorus. She'd use the same method once they graduated to *The New England Primer*: an eighty-page booklet that included simple rhymes, moral lessons, and prayers.

The Smiths could easily have afforded private school. But as sister Mary wrote, the girls stayed in the parsonage under "the necessity of keeping us from scenes of dissipation and frivolity." No popguns and bad language for the reverend's daughters. At age twenty, Nabby would admit to a basic "unacquaintedness with the World." What education she got happened apart from her peers and the booming schoolhouse. She'd come to recognize some advantages to that. When it came time to educate her own seven-year-old, she'd send him to a tutor rather than the town school. Children, she'd write, should be "unaccustomed to such examples as would tend to corrupt the purity of their words and actions that they may chill with horrour at the sound of an oath, and blush with indignation at an obscene expression." While her formal education might have been trifling and narrow, it also kept her pure.

She was homeschooled. Her teachers were relatives and family-approved friends. Her mother provided most of her practical and moral training: how to be the reverend's daughter and the manager of an upper-class household. Instead of dame school, she was sent off for extended visits with her grandparents, the Quincys. Like Franklin, Nabby was bookish, and the Colonel and Mrs. Quincy indulged her: she was given free run of the Mount Wollaston library. "I frequently think they made a more durable impression upon my mind," Nabby would write years later, "than those which I received from my own parents." She remembered her grandmother as "wise and just . . . [Her] lively, cheerful disposition animated all around her whilst she edified all by her unaffected piety." For her part, Grandma Quincy liked to say of Nabby, "Wild colts make the best horses."

How wild could this frail, secluded girl have been? Nabby's word for it was "volatile." She had this insatiable interest in literature and ideas and ended up spending hours bent over her grandfather's books. It led her to form her own opinions and, even more, to step right up in mixed company and express them—confidently and often. It verged on unladylike behavior, but instead of trying to break her, Grandma Quincy offered a kind of gentle encouragement. She used, as Nabby put it, "the happy method of mixing instruction and amusement." Like Franklin, Nabby learned best when it was fun. But Nabby gives more credit to her teachers than Franklin ever did. She acknowledges her grandmother as the one who encouraged her to think. Years later, she'd say of her own son: "Little Tom . . . learns fast now he has got a school master." She thought instruction was key and sounds like she's reminiscing about her visits to Mount Wollaston when, as a grown-up, she describes how the ideal instructor ought to have "a peculiar easy manner of communicating his Ideas to Youth, and the Goodness of his Heart, and the purity of his morals without an affected austerity must have a happy Effect upon the minds of Pupils."

Nabby wanders her grandfather's library with more access to books and more leisure time to pursue them than most people in the colony. At home, her father lets her browse his collection, too, and Reverend Smith even teaches his daughter "a little smattering" of French. She manages to keep up on the issues of the day both in Weymouth and Braintree. Nabby's sister recalled the girls sitting in the shadows of the main room, listening to Colonel Quincy and other local leaders discuss "valuable ideas." Both households had a steady stream of visitors. Inns and lodging houses were considered common; a gentleman traveler got letters of introduction and stayed at other gentlemen's homes. In a sense, then, Nabby's education came to her.

Richard Cranch, born in England, started visiting the Smith parsonage when he was twenty-nine. Mary was fourteen, Nabby eleven: both finished with what amounted to their elementary education. Mary was just reaching the age of courtship; Nabby still the wild little girl. Tall and charming, Cranch always seemed to be, as a friend wrote, "swallowed up in the raptures." He tried to make a living as a watch repairman, and later, a farmer, but neither very successfully. His real interest was theology. He'd worked out his own system of making prophecies based on the scriptures. To the two girls, he must have been a strange piece of exotica, washed ashore in quiet Weymouth. Cranch was interested in the soul not so much like Puritans were—as a battleground to fight Satan—but in a romantic, ethereal way. Nabby remembered him telling the adolescent girls how "the true female characteristic consisted not in the tincture of the skin or a fine set of features [but] beyond the exterior form." He was, however, interested enough in the exterior form to court and, seven years later, to marry sister Mary.

Cranch adored books. "He it was," Nabby writes, "who taught me to Love the poets and put into my hands, Milton, Pope, and Thompson, and Shakespeare, he it was who taught me to relish and distinguish their merits." To relish and distinguish: it sounds like Grandmother Quincy "mixing instruction and amusement." Cranch introduced Nabby to the writings of Samuel Richardson, who would become her favorite novelist. Nabby says she became "passionately fond of all his works," including his first and most widely read novel, *Pamela; or, Virtue Rewarded*. Published four years before Nabby was born, *Pamela* was written as a series of letters from "a Beautiful Young Damsel" to her parents. The damsel is a servant;

her young master tries to seduce her. She resists, and her virtue is rewarded when master marries maid. *Pamela* was a page-turner, immensely popular especially among women readers. Richardson says his goal was "to Divert and Entertain, and at the same time to Instruct and Improve the Minds of the YOUTH of both Sexes." For Nabby, the books must have raised the possibility that day-to-day events in little towns like Weymouth might be the stuff of a larger, exciting story. And that a woman's life could be part of that drama.

She was constantly discussing literature and ideas in what amounted to an informal class. It drew from a select circle of educated, socially acceptable friends. The doctor in Weymouth, Cotton Tufts, was her father's nephew and married Lucy Quincy, Nabby's aunt. The year Cranch started visiting the parsonage, Tufts was twenty-three, well-read and witty. When she wrote her "Unkle Tufts," Nabby would drop quotes from Pope: the kind of literary garnish Franklin had made fun of—and practiced. Nabby's circle loaned each other books, discussed poetry, referred to themselves (in the fashion of the day) using mythological pseudonyms. Her girlfriends included Calliope, Arpasia, Aurelia. Entering what we'd think of as her middle school years, Nabby called herself Diana. In the course of a single paragraph, her letters might quote from *King Lear*, *Macbeth*, and *A Midsummer Night's Dream*. And she'd rely on these kinds of literary allusions her whole life. Describing the first time she met George Washington, she'd write: "Those lines of Dryden instantly occurd to me, 'Mark his Majestick fabrick!'" When the British burned Charleston during the Revolutionary War, she turned to Shakespeare: "Extremity is the trier of Spirits."

It was a kind of hothouse education: protected, a little inbred, its goal these elaborate literary blooms. "How soon must Society grow insipid and conversation wearisome," Nabby's sister wrote, "unless it is enlivened by a taste for literature." Books gave a teenager in sleepy, rural Weymouth something to talk about. They also taught what it might mean to be sophisticated. Writing about the literature Cranch introduced her to, Nabby would later claim, "whatever I possest of delicacy of sentiment, or refinement, taste, in my early and juvenile days, I ascribe to the perusal of those Books." She also believed Richardson's novels, for example, could "dispose the mind to receive and relish every good and benevolent principle." She used what she read—from poetry to history—like she used the Bible: to comfort and guide. In her early thirties, when a friend dies in the Revolutionary War, Nabby writes her husband about it first in patriotic terms—"[He] fell gloriously fighting for his Country"—then in suitably religious terms: "God is a refuge for us." Then, she quotes from the romantic British poet William Collins: "How sleep the Brave who sink to rest // By all their country's wishes blest!"

No surprise, then, if her suitor and eventual husband had to be well-read. When they first met, Nabby was fourteen, John Adams nine years older. Adams was a friend of Cranch's: a short, chubby, opinionated young man. He'd graduated Harvard, taught school for a couple of years, and then returned to his hometown of Braintree to practice law: a respectable profession, though not as prestigious as reverend or doctor. The first thing he noticed about Nabby, he says, was her wit: flashing and still wild. Adams was the newcomer, a twenty-three-year-old entering an ongoing conversation with Cranch, thirty-two, Unkle Tufts at twenty-seven, and the two precocious teenage girls. Adams had more formal education than Nabby: at her age, he was preparing for Harvard's entrance exams with a private tutor. But the newcomer doesn't seem to have been as quick with or as interested in the literary banter. He was a property owner, after all, with responsibilities: "middle class," as one of his grandsons would put it, where Nabby was "descended from so many of the shining lights of the colony."

Adams's diary entry about the Smith girls wonders: "[A]re fondness and Wit compatible?" Nabby was quick, but Adams thought she lacked "Tenderness." He didn't become a regular visitor to the household until three years later. By then, if his letters are any gauge, he'd learned to play the literary games, addressing the now seventeen-year-old Nabby as Diana. But his attraction was also physical. Instead of books, his letters drop references to her "sweetly blowing" breath and their kisses: "two or three Millions." In fact, he teases her about how much time she spends reading. In a flirtatious letter listing her supposed faults, Adams pretends to be upset that she's pigeon-toed, doesn't play cards well, crosses her legs, and blushes too much. The blushing he attributes to her "Country Life and Education"; at seventeen, she still hasn't seen much of the world and is shocked—or pretends to be—by its crudeness. Instead, she's stayed inside—in the library—and Adams claims the "Fault" of her bad posture "is the Effect and Consequence of another, still more inexcusable in a Lady. I mean an Habit of Reading, Writing and Thinking. But both the Cause and the Effect ought to be repented and amended as soon as possible."

You can hear the joke between them: Adams mocking the typical male perspective (which may also have been his own) that a woman should be attractive and ignorant. And Nabby mocks right back, taking on the tone of the dutiful, empty-headed bachelorette: "[T]o appear agreeable in the Eyes of Lysander," she writes, using her Shakespearean nickname for Adams, "has been for Years past, and still is the height of my ambition." But it's a joke with an edgy undercurrent. In fact, her ambition reaches considerably further. This is, by now, a well-read young woman who has her own opinions and no plans to squash them. And she's smart enough to realize that could lead to trouble. As she writes a friend, "[I]t is a most dangerous thing for a female to be distinguished for any qualification beyond the rest of her sex."

Her beau sounds as if he's just teasing when he asks her to repent her literary habits: Adams's letter reads like a satire of a typical Puritan sermon. But jump forward to when they're married and have a daughter. Nabby will insist the girl ought to have the kind of classical schooling Nabby was never allowed. Adams answers, "[Y]ou must not tell many people of it, for it is scarcely reputable for young ladies to understand Latin and Greek." Another joke? Maybe. But here's Adams on the education of their fourteen-year-old daughter: "I hope your Attention will be fixed chiefly upon those Virtues and Accomplishments, which contribute the most to qualify Women to act their Parts well in the various Relations of Life, those of Daughter, Sister, Wife, Mother, Friend." In other words, Latin and Greek have nothing to do with what a woman needs to know.

Nabby didn't openly dispute those roles or try to change them.

But she believed that how well she performed them depended, in part, on this habit of hers: of reading, writing, and thinking. As a daughter (and granddaughter), Nabby had entered the adult world through the library; it was one of the ways she'd learned what grown-ups cared about and how they talked. As a sister, she'd maintain a constant stream of letters back and forth to Mary and Betsy: writing not only kept them in touch; it helped bind the Smith family together. As to her role as wife, literature had helped get her the part. In her circle, it was key to the courtship process. She spotted Adams as an educated suitor; he saw a young woman comfortable among people who read and discussed books. And as much as it helped bring the lovers together, Nabby's literary habits would do even more to keep the marriage working.

A young lawyer in colonial New England had to travel the circuit, visiting the various regional courts. Adams called it "a continual Scaene of Fatigue, Vexation, Labor and Anxiety." It regularly kept him away from home. And his absences only got longer when he became a representative to the legislature, then to the Constitutional Conventions, and later still, to the governments of Europe on behalf of the new United States. Letters were the way Nabby and her husband stayed in touch. In her grandfather's library, she couldn't have known how often her future husband would be away. But the eighteenth century was the golden age of letter writing, and Nabby—like her sisters and her friends—did know that she was going to do a lot of her communicating with pen and paper.

"*Style* I never studied," she claimed later in life, insisting her prose was simply "the spontaneous effusions of friendship." But in the letters that have been saved (a couple thousand), you can see her rejecting ornate sentence structure for what she called "natural ease" and "simplicity." "[T]'is a pleasure for me to write," she says just before she gets married, when she's composing almost daily letters to her fiancé. She mentions how she doesn't "feel as great restraint" when she writes and how it can be "a relief to my mind to drop some of my sorrows through my pen." Her subjects range from business and family to the politics of the day to how lonesome she gets. Though she often apologizes for her spelling and punctu-

ation and will eventually ask that her letters be burnt ("I have not
any ambition to be in print"), her prose is passionate and exact:
well enough made to transmit her crackling intelligence centuries
later.

The page was a place where she could be herself without always
having to act her role as wife and mother. She cherished its privacy
and freedom. Take her letter of August 1776. With her husband
down in Philadelphia working to draft a declaration of independence, she goes to Boston to have the family inoculated against
smallpox (by then, a fairly common procedure). She stays with an
aunt and is given what she calls a little "closet" in the house. It's got
a bookshelf and a desk to "write all my Letters and keep my papers
unmollested by any one." If Franklin set a model for self-education,
the pleasure Nabby expresses here is an almost eerie anticipation of
women's private, underground educations: "I do not covet my
Neighbours Goods, but . . . I always had a fancy for a closet with a
window which I could more peculiarly call my own."

One of the things she learns—and maybe that means she taught
herself—is that women and men are equals. Or should be. In a letter
written when she's nineteen, she compares her heart—that "cabinet"—
with her suitor's: "I have often been tempted to believe, that they were
both cast in the same mould, only with this difference, that yours was
made with a harder mettle, and therefore is less liable to an impression." Both have, she suspects, "an eaquil quantity of Steel." A dozen
years later, she's grown fiercer. As her husband is busy declaring the
nation's independence, she composes what will become a famous letter calling on him to "Remember the Ladies." She asks, in general,
"that some more liberal plan might be laid and executed for the Benefit of the rising Generation, and that our new constitution may be
distinguished for Learning and Virtue." More specifically, she argues,
"Men of Sense in all Ages abhor those customs which treat us only as
the vassals of your Sex." Particularly "mortifying" is "when a woman
possessed of a common share of understanding considers the difference of Education between the male and female Sex, even in those
families where Education is attended to."

Nabby argues that this difference in education is impractical.

Whether or not an American child went to school (and at the time, most didn't), their first teacher was almost certainly their mother. "If much depends as is allowed upon the early Education of youth and the first principals which are instilld take the deepest root," then it only made sense for society to educate women. "If we mean to have Heroes, Statesmen and Philosophers, we should have learned women."

She isn't attacking the system of higher education and privilege, the way Silence Dogood did. After all, Nabby was the daughter of a respected minister. And she'd marry a young lawyer from a good family. Yes, Adams would fight for American independence, and Nabby was, if anything, even more committed to the ideas of the revolution. But in an era of upheaval, with her country declaring it had become necessary to assume "separate and equal station" among the world's powers, Nabby doesn't talk about women getting out from under the government of men. She accepts the traditional roles. "Nature," she'll write, "has assigned to each sex its particular duties and sphere of action." But, she writes, "If you complain of neglect of Education in sons, What shall I say with regard to daughters, who every day experience the want of it." She uses herself as Exhibit A. "With regard to the Education of my own children, I find myself soon out of my debth, and destitute and deficient in every part of Education." At the end of this passionate argument, she writes her husband, "Excuse me, my pen has run away with me." Indeed.

Abigail Adams was thirty-two when she composed this letter. It's a month after the Declaration of Independence is made public, read aloud to cheering crowds in cities across New England. She's been married a dozen years and has an eleven-year-old daughter and three sons: nine, six, and four. The Revolutionary War is about to change her role and test her education, test whether she really has learned what she needs to know.

The couple was used to being separated. When her husband would go away on business for a few weeks, he'd instruct her about supervising the hands, keeping the hay protected, even the right mix of creek mud and dung to make fertilizer. By 1774, Adams had become a multiproperty owner like Reverend Smith: he'd bought his father's homestead and another farm in Braintree. Now, heading off to the first Constitutional Congress, he leaves his wife in charge of the operation, asking her to give her attention to "the Family, the stock, the Farm, the Dairy. Let every Article of Expence which can possibly be spared be retrench'd."

It's after the battle of Lexington and Concord, when her husband is in Philadelphia for months at a time, that Nabby recognizes her job has shifted. She's still her children's teacher, though her sons and daughters have reached an age where, as she writes, "a Mothers care becomes less necessary and a fathers more important." They're ready to learn more than basic reading, writing, and arithmetic, and with her husband away, it's up to her to decide whether to send them to a dame's school, or hire tutors, or keep them at home. But more than that, she has to assume the man's role as the full-time and long-term overseer of what she considers her husband's "private affairs." She now has "not only to pay attention to my own in door domestic affairs," she writes, "but to every thing without, about our little farm, etc." Adams writes Nabby that she's a "Heroine" for doing all this. She answers, "I take the best care I am capable," then confesses to not knowing what to do with the boys since the war has closed all schools.

Battles are being fought less than ten miles from the farm. One day she climbs a nearby hill and reports that the sound of the cannons is "an incessant Roar." With most of the men off fighting, Braintree is largely undefended. And as the wife of a leading American politician, Mrs. John Adams offers a particularly tempting target for the British. "Perhaps the very next letter I write will inform you that I am driven away from our yet quiet cottage." Her eldest son, John Quincy, remembers how it felt like they were "liable every hour of the day and of the night to be butchered in cold blood, or taken into Boston as hostages." Isolated, thrown back on her own resources, Nabby starts signing her letters to her husband, "Hermitta."

She keeps insisting she isn't prepared for this. Her protected, literary education hasn't taught her the skills for keeping the farm out of debt, the family together, the long-distance marriage working. But the facts speak otherwise. And soon she admits, with some pride, that she's learning how to handle it: "I shall be quite a Farmeriss an other year." Her faith helps her through. She takes comfort from her books. And she's come out of her hours alone in the libraries with an iron sense of purpose. After Adams returns home for a few months, she finds herself pregnant, again. And alone, again. She sits down one summer night to write her husband about the rising prices and how the "Hay will be plenty but your Farm wants manure." She's had strange shaking fits, which her friends say are just the "Vapors"—but she knows otherwise. She knows their child is stillborn. As she'll put it, later, "[I was] perfectly sensible of its discease as I ever before was of its existence." But in this letter to her husband, on the eve of giving birth to what she knows will be a dead child, she only pauses between the reports on hay and manure to note that she's beginning to feel the first contractions.

By Nabby's calculations, the couple has had the "happiness" of living in the same house "not more than half" of their married life. Across the colonies, the war leaves many women alone and with new responsibilities. But where other couples reunite afterward, John Adams's diplomatic duties will extend their separation to a decade. For Nabby, it's often overwhelming. "O Why was I born with so much Sensibility," she'll write her husband and eldest son, both in France, "and why possessing it have I so often been call'd to struggle with it?" Women, she declares, "are formed to experience more exquisite Sensations than is the lot of your Sex. More tender and susceptible by Nature." Again, it's a traditional view of the difference between the genders, and she shows no sign of wanting to change that. Her vision of what will happen when her husband finally comes back is everyone returning to their original roles: "Our Boys shall go into the Field and work with you, and my Girl shall stay in the House and assist me."

But there's some playacting going on here. The same way there is when John Adams keeps writing he's going to quit politics, come home, and be a simple farmer. There was no going back. For Nabby, learning how to supervise help and run the house had expanded into managing the farms. She's applied what basic math

she'd learned to balancing the family budget. "Debts are my abhor-
rence," she writes her husband, and manages to pay off the ones he'd
fallen into. In the period of inflation that followed independence–
when goods from England were rare and sold at a premium–John
Adams regularly shipped Abigail quantities of hard-to-get items like
tea and ribbons. The merchant's granddaughter then cut deals to sell
them in the markets of Boston. At the same time, she was in charge
of a series of real estate transactions, buying up farms around Braintree and in Vermont.

The war had expanded the uses of her literary education, too. As
the fighting ground on, letters were often delayed a month or more,
and many never got through. Official news of how the Boston campaign was going was sketchy at best. Nabby became a kind of military reporter to her husband, filling him in on the movement of
troops, the number of dead, the suffering of the civilian population.
He'd pass the information on to his fellow delegates in Philadelphia.
"I have more particulars from you than anyone else," he wrote.
"Pray keep me informed." He discussed military strategy with her,
and as the political crisis deepened, she began to read more history.
After Ticonderoga fell, she quoted at length from the strategies that
had helped Carthage defeat Rome. And urging the delegates in
Philadelphia to have the courage of their convictions, she reminded
her husband that the fall of Sparta had come from "an excessive love
of peace."

The prose style she'd studied for what seemed like frivolous
reasons–to compose witty, flirtatious letters–ends up helping hold
her family together. The written word is how she stays in touch
with her husband–sharing not just their business affairs but her
worries, passions, loneliness, and anger. Her sisters, meanwhile,
haven't prospered the way she has. Mary's marriage to the impractical Cranch has left her in near poverty, taking in boarders to
make ends meet. As John Adams becomes the nation's second president, the First Lady maintains ties with her relatives through
funny, gossipy, down-to-earth letters. Eventually, her narrative skill
and sharp eye will make her letters a prime source of history. She
claimed to have no literary ambition, but had this been a secret goal

all along? Sitting alone in her grandfather's library, feeding her habit, had she dreamed of something like this? If not of being so close to political events, then of a world where her opinion and how she expressed it made a difference?

"I must study Politicks and War," John Adams wrote his wife from Paris, "that my sons may have liberty to study Mathematicks and Philosophy. My sons," he went on, "ought to study Mathematicks and Philosophy, Geography, natural History, Naval Architecture, navigation, Commerce and Agriculture in order to give their Children a right to study Painting, Poetry, Musick, Architecture, Statuary, Tapestry and Porcelaine." It's a sequence of gradually developing leisure and peace, where American education eventually frees men to focus on the sorts of things upper-class women have traditionally learned. Nabby doesn't contradict her husband, but hasn't she learned a different lesson? She's had to fight for her education. So will her daughters. So will their daughters. And what they'll need to know—if Nabby's experience is any measure—may include Poetry and Porcelaine but will end up being defined by Politicks and War.

ANDY

The man who defeated Nabby's son John Quincy Adams for the presidency of the United States was an ignorant, vengeful, backwoods autocrat. He didn't know history or political science or even basic grammar. And his only regular reading, besides the Bible, was the daily paper.

That, anyway, is how his opponents saw him. For them, Andrew Jackson's victory signaled the end of the era when education mattered, when America was run by an East Coast aristocracy that went to Harvard and knew Latin. Instead, this frontier president ran and won as a man of the people. "The planter, the farmer, the mechanic and the laborer," Jackson declared, "these classes of society . . . are the bone and sinew of the country." Their enemy—his enemy—was "the moneyed interest."

Okay. Except Jackson had plenty of money. And he didn't make it by getting his hands dirty. At twenty-one, he'd arrived in Tennessee as a young lawyer and would wind up owning one of the largest, most successful cotton plantations in the state—as well as 150 slaves. He campaigned as an outsider, but when he came east in 1828 to assume the presidency, Washington society found him surprisingly elegant. Not a Harvard gentleman—certainly not an Adams—but a gentleman nonetheless. He'd gotten a different kind of education; call it Southern or Western. It hadn't taught him a trade or left him particularly fond of books. He'd learned most of what he'd needed to know in a sparsely populated backcountry, among immigrants, and in the midst of war. And he considered the real test of his knowledge to be, not talk, but action.

The Jacksons were Irish. At least, that's what they were called once they got to America. Both sides of Andy's family were actually descendants of the Lowlander Scots, transplanted by the English to Northern Ireland in the beginning of the eighteenth century. The Lowlanders were supposed to subdue the native Irish and stabilize the colony for its British owners. Grandfather Hugh Jackson had been a linen merchant near Ulster. Andy's grandparents on his mother's side, the Hutchinsons, were also in the linen trade and had done well. But in Ireland, no Jackson or Hutchinson had the right to own land: they were all tenants. And the British lords systematically fined and shut down their Presbyterian churches.

The first wave of Scots-Irish came to the American colonies starting around 1710, when British trade restrictions effectively closed the market for Ulster wool. Ten years later, when Ben Franklin was a young apprentice, the Irish famine started to push more immigrants toward America. By 1740, with hundreds of thousands dying of starvation, the migration became an exodus. A quarter million Scots-Irish had reached the new world by 1780.

Once they arrived, many Lowlanders were pulled toward the Southern colonies that were desperately seeking what they called "substantial people." "Substantial" meant white. In 1724, blacks in South Carolina outnumbered whites three to one, and the area was the largest importer of African slaves in North America. They were shipped in to work the huge rice and indigo plantations along the coast. For the owners, the resulting profits were tremendous, but so were the dangers. In the decade Andrew Jackson was born, there were ten times more Africans in the region than white males over sixteen. If—and many Carolinians thought it was when—the slaves rebelled, the whites wouldn't have a chance. Inland, meanwhile, the Cherokee and other tribes blocked expansion west by stubbornly holding on to their hunting grounds. Between war with the Indians and the threat of a slave uprising, the British colonial authorities were looking for any and all white settlers, even Presbyterians. The crown granted one company 120,000 acres on the condition that it was settled by British subjects. Starting in 1761, South Carolina offered individual immigrant families "bounties": free land, tax exempt, and it even threw in some basic farming tools.

Once again, the Scots-Irish were brought in to stabilize a royal colony. And once again, they were treated as second-class citizens. Plantation owners already claimed the rich, rice-growing land on the coast; their prosperity had helped make Charlestown (as it was called then) one of the economic and intellectual centers of the South. No, the "bounty Irish" were being offered land in the Piedmont out on the colony's western border. It was hill country: thick forests broken by creeks and rivers. Families arrived, staked out as much property as they thought they could clear, and threw up a cabin. Most settlers couldn't afford slaves; they got by planting some corn and letting a few cows and hogs graze in the woods. Immigrants started to stream in, especially after a series of raids in the mid-1760s led to the starvation and elimination of the Cherokee. "There is scarce any history either ancient or modern," wrote a South Carolina gazette in 1768, "which affords an account of such a rapid and sudden increase of inhabitants in a back frontier country." That was the cleaned-up version. The way an Anglican minister put it that same year, South Carolina was offering bounties to bring over "ignorant, mean, worthless, beggarly Irish Presbyterians, the scum of the earth and refuse of mankind."

Include among that scum, Andrew Jackson Sr., his wife, Betty Hutchinson Jackson, and their sons: Hugh, two years old, and Robert, less than a year. They arrived in 1765 and settled in a community known as the Waxhaws. About sixty-five miles square, straddling the (disputed) border between North and South Carolina, it was a frontier settlement south of Charlotte, "an inconsiderable place," and north of Camden, a tiny trading village. There were about sixty families when the Jacksons arrived; most of them spoke with an Ulster brogue. All six of Mrs. Jackson's sisters had already settled in the area. So, James Crawford and Jane Hutchinson Crawford moved in next to Robert Crawford, and there was a Hutchinson sister a mile east and another a mile farther on.

If the settlement sounded and looked a little like the old country—and the settlers were still British subjects—the difference was that a family could own its section of land. They weren't tenants. And they could practice their religion. The Jackson family claimed some two hundred acres about a dozen miles from the Presbyterian church. It was a considerable spread—the average farm was about fifty acres—and they hadn't taken a bounty, so they must have arrived with some money. That first year, Andrew Jackson Sr. cut down enough of the ancient trees to build a cabin. Typically, these had a door, a window, and a single room with a low-ceilinged sleeping loft upstairs. A fence was set up around a dirt yard. And a field was cleared to plant corn and flax. They may have gotten in one crop, but in the early spring of their second year, Jackson died. That left his widow with two small boys; plus, she was pregnant. A third son was born in March of 1767, and she named him after his late father.

They moved in with Mrs. Jackson's older sister, Jane Crawford. The Crawfords had four sons, and Jane, an invalid, needed help raising them. It meant seven boys about a dozen years apart packed into the sleeping loft. The arrangement would last almost a decade, with Andy, the youngest, growing up among cousins who felt like brothers. The Crawfords were more prosperous than most in the area: owned several hundred acres and some slaves to help work them. Andy's mother supervised most of the cooking and the other chores; she'd arrived from Ireland with a reputation as an expert at spinning flax. James Crawford had his own skills. He was a well-known moonshiner with a large still out by the creek. Whiskey and brandy were as good as money in the Piedmont, and drinking was one of the few amusements in a life of subsistence farming, deer hunting, and the occasional trip to the market in Camden.

As far as the British were concerned, the settlers along the North and South Carolina border amounted to "persons of motley national origins." They were there as a buffer. The Catawba, who had lived where the immigrants now farmed, had been resettled on a reservation, but the war with the Cherokee was still fresh in people's minds. And there was always the threat of a slave uprising. The royal government saw no need to provide an education for people like the Jacksons and Crawfords: how much does a wall of defense need to know? Technically, of course, they were white people, but what was considered civilization existed mainly on the coast. That's where the plantation owners and merchants built their town houses, decorated them with imported wallpaper, used linens monogrammed with the family's coat of arms. Charleston's elite were mostly loyalists, Church of England. They sent their children back to London for schooling. And they controlled the colonial government. To qualify as a member of the Commons House, you had to own at least five hundred acres or ten slaves. Less than 5 percent of the population passed that standard, and why would they worry about the well-being or education of the other 95 percent?

No, all the backcountry settlers really needed to know was to fight on the side of the white man. The Waxhaws had no representative government and no local courts. The year Andy was born, thieves and horse rustlers were making raids all through the area, turning it into "a kind of sanctuary allowed to Criminals and Vagabonds." Four thousand residents signed a petition asking the royal government to establish a system of law. Meanwhile, local vigilante groups known as Regulators sprang up both to keep order and to protest high taxes. The British treated it like a peasant uprising. They dispatched troops and soon put down the disturbance. Afterward, some settlers left the Piedmont, and many of those who stayed nursed a hatred for the royal government and its "civilized" supporters on the coast.

The Waxhaws set up its own isolated, Presbyterian civilization. The Reverend William Richardson had arrived about six years before the Jackson family. In a settlement of cabins, he had a two-story building and owned a number of slaves. He was also educated, reading Greek, Latin, and Hebrew and keeping the only library of any size for miles around. Out in that backcountry of whiskey stills and horse rustlers, the reverend held "literary evenings" with his wife, Agnes, "high-spirited, talented and beautiful."

The reverend believed his duties included educating his congregation. As well as delivering regular sermons, he'd go house to house and quiz the children on the Westminster Larger Catechism: over a hundred questions and answers to be memorized and recited aloud. It opened by asking about the "chief and highest end of man," and after providing the answer ("to glorify God"), went on to explain everything from original sin and its punishments to the creation of angels. Andy would have begun memorizing the sequence almost as soon as he could speak. It was a preschool education without doubts: the word of God providing both the problems and the solutions. While he was getting the catechism down cold, his mother would have taught him how to read. Between 70 and 80 percent of the Ulster Irish settlers were literate, mostly for the same reason Puritans had been: to study the scripture.

Andy barely got the advantage of Reverend Richardson's teaching. A couple of months after the boy turned four, the reverend was found dead, a bridle wrapped around his neck. The apparent suicide was attributed to melancholy; it must have shaken the small community to its core. Their intellectual and religious leader had apparently failed to find comfort in either his faith or reason. When the reverend's widow remarried a little too quickly for local comfort, the Waxhaws reverted to an Old World tradition. They dug up the reverend's skull and made the widow touch it. Then, they waited. If the skull bled, the widow would have been found guilty of murder. Reverend Richardson had preached the power of the Holy Word and the value of education, but the immigrants had brought another set of beliefs with them. A boy learned those, too.

Andy's mother was part of what higher culture the Waxhaws had. Her relatives owned slaves; she was friends with the widow Richardson. And she valued learning. She sent all three of her sons to the local school, about a mile from James Crawford's place. It looked a lot like all the other cabins in the pine woods, except it boomed with the sound of kids reciting from their hornbooks. Andy entered at kindergarten age and stayed three years. That is, he probably went for four or five months of each year, starting after harvest time and leaving for planting. His other education was on the Crawford farm.

The workday schedule and the division of labor in the Waxhaws were a lot like on a typical New England farm. Andy's mother was in charge of the household, tending to both her own children and her invalid sister's. The man of the house, James, spent the day working and overseeing in the cornfields. All summer, the boys helped hoe weeds: hot, itchy, monotonous work. Andy preferred the stables, where he started to learn about horses: a favorite subject of frontier debate and study. At night, men and boys gathered around the still down by the creek. They were there to make sure the mash fermented slowly enough and "the worm"—a spiral of copper tubing—stayed at the right temperature for distillation. Of course, the product had to be sampled, too. Picture Andy sitting at the edge of the fire with his cousins and brothers, listening to the talk about women and horses and fighting: learning.

When Andy was in the equivalent of second or third grade, news arrived about the battle at Lexington and Concord. It was a long ways off. Still, North Carolina declared "the cause of Boston is the cause of all." And Mecklenburg County (its border just across the road from James Crawford's farm) proudly pronounced its citizens "a free and independent people." During the summer of 1776, the war came closer. The British under Lord Cornwallis tried and failed to take Charleston. Andy's brother Hugh, barely a teenager, planned to join the fighting as soon as he could, and Robert wouldn't be far behind. That's when Mrs. Jackson decided Andy, her nine-year-old, would become a minister.

As with Ben Franklin's family, the decision was both pious and ambitious. It meant Andy would join the educated elite. He'd need to know Greek and Latin and have to leave the Waxhaws, at least for his training. The local model for how this worked was Reverend Richardson's nephew and namesake, William Richardson Davie. His parents had arrived in the Waxhaws the year before the Jacksons and settled on bounty land. Reverend Richardson, childless, had tutored his sister's son to one day take over the Waxhaws pulpit. Davie was fifteen when the reverend committed suicide; the teenager inherited his uncle's library. The will also provided for the boy to study at a private college in Charlotte. It stipulated that one of the reverend's slaves, referred to only as Joe, would have his wages garnished for four years to pay the tuition.

The Jacksons found their own equivalent of a rich uncle. James Crawford was as close as Andy came to a father. His brother, Robert, was one of the wealthiest men in the area. At age nine, Andy moved into "Uncle" Robert Crawford's home and started attending an all-boys' academy that ran at the Waxhaws meetinghouse. The academy was a backcountry version of Boston Latin. It had the same curriculum of Latin texts and the same basic teaching technique: repetition. The farm boys in their loose-fitting clothes and floppy hats recited their lessons, while the teacher—in knee britches, stockings, and a tricornered hat—stood up front and listened for mistakes. It must have been an odd, almost surreal scene. Out in the piney woods, a couple hundred miles from "civilization" and with a revolutionary war looming on the horizon, the kids were drilled dawn to dusk in what Andy would later call "the dead languages." There was no nearby place to apply these skills, no obvious reason to learn them. What drove Andy was his mother's ambition. He never did learn much Latin, and his spelling would later be called "grotesque." Still, he stuck with it for three years, getting more formal schooling than most kids in the Waxhaws, or, for that matter, beyond. He'd never become a reverend, but, like Franklin, he seems to have held on to the sense that he'd been singled out for something different, better.

Andy stayed in school even after the British brought the war deeper into the south. In late 1778, the royal strategy shifted the front to Georgia and the Carolinas partly on the theory the English army would find more support among Southern sympathizers than it had in New England. With some thirteen thousand soldiers and five warships, the British captured Savannah; the next spring, they were once again threatening Charleston. When some of that city's wealthy residents retreated inland for safety, they set up an academy for their children and hired away Andy's teacher to run it: an indication that the boy had been getting a pretty sophisticated, upper-class education. Though the only instructor was now gone, Mrs. Jackson and the other parents persisted. There were about a dozen students in the Waxhaws Academy: one of the oldest was made the instructor, and school went on. This in a subsistence economy, during wartime.

Meanwhile, Andy's move from James's to Robert Crawford's place had changed his out-of-school education, too. You can see the difference in the Crawfords' social positions by their roles in the war. Where James would serve as a foot soldier in the militia, Robert would start as a captain and end up a major. Andy was now living in a two-story house almost as imposing as the late Reverend Richardson's. It was set on the main road to Camden, and the same rules of hospitality applied here as in Nabby Smith's New England. "Travelers with any pretensions to respectability," an eighteenth-century chronicler of the Carolinas wrote, "seldom stop at the wretched taverns; but custom sanctions their freely calling at the planter's residence." Robert Crawford was the closest the region came to landed gentry, and his house was a regular stopping place—including, years later, for George Washington. Robert Crawford, in his forties when Andy came to live with him, had the means to entertain in style. Travelers were served fine food off good silver, their horses tended to, and their rooms prepared, all by Crawford's slaves.

For Andy, it was a whole new curriculum. Where James Crawford probably came in from the fields, washed up, and ate supper in his work clothes, Robert most likely changed for dinner, appearing in the britches and stockings of a gentleman. Where James went out to the still after eating, Robert sat on the porch with his guests and had drinks served. And while the conversation in both places was about women and horses and fighting, on Robert Crawford's porch the women were ladies in hoop skirts and plumed hats; the horses were thoroughbreds, bred to race; and the fighting included duels of honor. Andy, just entering his adolescence, heard how a gentleman gambled and paid off his debts. He learned how to prepare a rooster for a cockfight: one of the chief upper-class entertainments. "Take and give him some Pickle Beef Cut fine 3 times a Day," he instructs in a twelve-year-old's handwriting, "and give him sweet Milk Instead of water to Drink." The visitors might have come to Robert Crawford's porch from far away, but their talk must have made the possibilities of another life sound near. The boy was learning the proper way to behave if—no, when—he got there.

The siege of Charleston failed in early 1779. The British retreated back toward Savannah, chased by the Southern Continental Army. Andy's brother Hugh was part of the pursuit, under the command of Reverend Richardson's nephew, W. R. Davie. He'd decided not to enter the church and was now Lieutenant Davie. That June, his small cavalry detachment fought a battle at a place called Stono Ferry. Davie led a force of a hundred Carolinians to within sixty yards of British defenses. A couple of hours of intense, close-range shooting followed. Davie was badly wounded; Andy's sixteen-year-old brother survived unscathed, only to die a few days later of heat exhaustion. He was buried in the graveyard not far from the academy where Andy was still reciting his Latin declensions.

That December, the British attacked Charleston again, and this time, succeeded. The city surrendered in May of 1780 in what's been called the largest single American loss of the war. The royal army immediately set out to subdue the rest of the state. Two weeks after the fall of Charleston, a rumor reached the Waxhaws that a force of royal cavalry was approaching down Camden Road. Andy, his brother Robert, and his Crawford cousins hid and watched the enemy, led by Lieutenant Colonel Banastre Tarleton, ride slowly by. "Tarleton passed within a hundred yards of where I was," Andy would remember years later. "I could have shot him."

Instead, "Bloody" Tarleton launched what became known as the Massacre at the Waxhaws. Charging his cavalry "with the horrid yells of infuriated demons," Tarleton captured some three hundred American troops. The British commander claimed that the patriots kept firing even after raising the white flag. What followed was carnage. "I have," Tarleton reported later, "cut 170 Off'rs and Men to pieces." According to survivors, fifteen minutes after the last American had fallen, Tarleton's troops were still slicing at lifeless bodies, pitchforking the top layer out of the way to get at those below. The Waxhaws Massacre would set the precedent for how the frontier war was fought: without rules or mercy.

After the battle, the wounded were carried to the meetinghouse. It was a sweltering summer day, and the floor was soon covered with the dead and dying. Andy and his mother moved among them trying to help, but there wasn't much to be done. As Andy remembered it, "None of the men had less than three or four, and some as many as thirteen gashes." It signaled the end of his elementary education: his classroom had become a morgue.

If his formal education had seemed impractical before—something he stayed with mostly because his mother wanted him to—it now made no sense. He'd spent three years at common school, four more at the academy. He was literate, could write a fairly good hand, and had picked up some basic grammar and arithmetic. For the next year and a half, he'd study war.

According to some historians of the period, it was "romantic partisan warfare, full of midnight marches, sudden surprises, and desperate hand-to-hand combat." Bands of irregulars fought hit-and-run battles, hiding in the thick forests and swamps, harassing the British. The leader of one South Carolina unit, Francis Marion, became famous as the Swamp Fox; his equivalent in the Piedmont was W. R. Davie. But there was nothing romantic about the Waxhaws Massacre. And in the fighting that followed, the clear moral universe of the Westminster catechism disappeared. What had been a cluster of Irish immigrants, each on a separate farm but all trying to survive, became a deadly landscape of shifting loyalties.

Soon after the massacre, Bloody Tarleton returned to the Waxhaws. He set up camp and ordered locals to come in and sign oaths of allegiance to the crown. In return, as Andy recalled years later, they'd receive "written protections." Some signed willingly. Some signed to save their farms, then spent the rest of the war fighting underground. "It was evident," Tarleton wrote, ". . . that the counties of Mecklenburg and Rohan were more hostile to England than any other in America." Many of the local men refused to sign, going off to fight for the American army under Thomas Sumter, leaving their wives and children to take care of the farms.

That summer of 1780, Andy rode with Lieutenant Davie's unit to Hanging Rock, South Carolina, not far from the Waxhaws. The dawn raid was designed as a diversion to allow Sumter's forces to attack elsewhere. It was a battle of volunteers, neighbor against neighbor, no British soldiers involved. Davie's eighty men included Uncle Robert Crawford as well as Andy's former schoolmate/teacher at the academy and, perhaps, Andy's sixteen-year-old brother. Their target was a farmhouse where three companies of loyalists had bunked down. While his big brother would have been allowed to fight at Hanging Rock, Andy was three years younger. He and the other boys his age stayed back in the shadows of a ravine; along with some slaves, they took care of the horses. Davie wrote that his riflemen, "not distinguishable from the Loyalists," slipped right past the sentries. When the sleeping, surprised troops rushed out of the farmhouse, the patriots trapped them against a staked fence and, in Davie's words, "literally cut them to pieces."

Andy didn't see the fighting, but he saw the results. He probably helped round up the sixty captured horses and collect the hundred or so muskets strewn among the bodies. And he may have watched, afterward, as the patriots got drunk instead of chasing whatever survivors were left. According to the traditional, romantic vision of war, it taught a young man a code of honor as moral, in its own way, as any he learned in church. But Hanging Rock was about deception. It was about neighbors able to sneak up on neighbors because they were "not distinguishable" in how they dressed or talked. And then slashing at each other in a blind rage. That summer at a similar battle, a seventeen-year-old American soldier wrote: "the poor Tories . . . lay in heaps on all sides, while the groans of the wounded were heard in every direction. I could not help turning away . . . with horror and, though exulting in victory, could not refrain from shedding tears." Was that Andy's reaction? Or did the thirteen-year-old yearn to be part of it?

A week after Hanging Rock and about twenty miles away, the main British forces under General Cornwallis routed the Revolutionary Army. Blame fell on both the outmatched American commanders and the local volunteer militia, which broke ranks and fled. By early September, the British controlled South Carolina and were pressing a "full-scale invasion" into North Carolina. The main army's route took it through the Waxhaws, where Cornwallis made his headquarters at the finest house in the area: Robert Crawford's. He stayed two weeks, "fattening his Horses," according to an American witness, "and Carrying off every article valuable to our Army." Meanwhile, he ordered that all farms suspected of housing patriots be "uniformly" burnt to the ground. Already, as Lieutenant Davie wrote, the "continual devastation of warfare [had left] many of the plantations intirely deserted."

Andy, his mother, and one of her sister's families joined the stream of refugees heading north. At some point, he must have gotten separated from the others because, years later, a woman would recall talking with a gangly boy. He wore a wide-brimmed yellow hat and was riding past her farm alone.

"Where you from?"

"From below."

"Where are you going?"

"Above."

"Who are you for?"

"The Congress."

"What are you doing below?"

"Oh, we are popping them still."

"What's your name?"

"Andrew Jackson."

It's the terse, careful dialogue of wartime: the thirteen-year-old boy and a fourteen-year-old farm girl trying to cope with a world collapsing around them. Eventually, the Jacksons found their way to Guilford Courthouse, North Carolina, another small Irish settlement. Andy spent his time there helping with farm chores, listening to war news, watching the adults around him try to fight off despair. "The enemy seems determined," the governor of South Carolina wrote that winter, ". . . to break every man's spirit, if they cannot ruin him."

General Nathaniel Greene, put in charge of the southern wing of the Continental Army, described Andy's people—the backcountry Carolina fighters—as "bold and daring." In comparison, he wrote, "the people upon the sea-shore are sickly and but indifferent." The army as a whole he found "wretched beyond description," many of them hungry and barely clothed. Plus, there weren't enough of them to defeat the British in a face-to-face battle. Instead, Greene ordered a series of strategic retreats, luring Cornwallis into chasing the Americans toward the northern coast. For the Jacksons, it meant the occupying army left their hometown, and the family returned to the Waxhaws early in 1781. But it didn't mean the end of fighting. If anything, the backcountry warfare grew fiercer. "[T]he Whigs and Tories," General Greene wrote, "pursue each other with little less than savage fury."

Fury was a lot of what Andy learned. The Piedmont had been plundered beyond recognition: houses burnt, storehouses raided, the remaining cattle and corn, according to Davie, "not sufficient for the wants of the Refugee families." In that barren landscape, locals rode out at night looking for revenge. They'd attack with hunting rifles or knives, whatever was at hand, then slip back into the woods or hide out at sympathizers' farms. It wasn't clear whom to trust or, for that matter, whom you were fighting. Andy and his brother often rode with their surrogate father, James Crawford, until one day—pinned down by crossfire and shooting at figures they could barely see—Crawford took a bullet. He died a week later. "The friends of American liberty," one local woman would recall, "were hunted like deer."

On April 10, 1781, a band of rebels gathered outside the Waxhaws meetinghouse, Andy's former classroom. British regulars got wind of the meeting, and Andy, just fourteen, barely managed to escape. He and his brother Robert hid in the woods while the meetinghouse was torched. The next morning, they rode to the farm of one of their Crawford cousins; British forces showed up soon afterward. Both boys were captured. While the royal troops were looting the house, their commanding officer ordered Andy to kneel and clean his boots. It's an indication of how personal the fighting was, and how irrational: the uniformed British commander going out of his way to humiliate a backcountry Irish teenager. Andy refused; the officer slashed at him. "The sword reached my head," Jackson would recall in old age, "& has left a mark there as durable as the scull, as well as on the fingers." Robert also refused and also got cut.

For the next two days, the British marched their prisoners toward Camden, treating them, as Andy later wrote, "harshly & inhumanely." When they arrived, the only substantial building left in town was the three-story jail. There, the teenage Jackson boys were locked up with 250 other prisoners of war, many of them sick with smallpox, all of them hungry and cold.

Andy had spent four or five months riding with the rebels, living by his wits, learning how to fight and retreat, how to blend into the landscape during the day and emerge at night to test his courage and fury. It had been an education picked up on the run, tested every night. Now, that education ended. Separated from his brother, told that all prisoners would soon be hung, Andy spent two weeks in the cramped, infected jail. "I frequently heard them groaning in the agonies of death," he would write of his fellow prisoners, "and no regard was paid to them."

By this time, Cornwallis had given up chasing Greene, realizing that each "victory" was further weakening the British army. Instead, he headed toward Wilmington and his supply lines. That left Greene free to reconquer South Carolina and Georgia. Late that April, on a sandy ridge overlooking the Camden jail, fourteen hundred of Greene's soldiers fought nine hundred loyalists. This time the local militia held, but the enlisted men refused to fight, and Greene had to retreat. Andy watched it all through a peephole he'd made in a boarded-up window. It was the closest he'd get to the kind of traditional battlefield that they wrote about in history books.

Three days later, the Jackson brothers were included in a prisoner trade: thirteen British for seven Waxhaws men. As he walked the forty miles home through a pouring rain, Andy felt the first shivers of what would turn out to be smallpox. It would kill his brother Robert within days. Andy barely hung on, spending a month delirious with a high fever and open sores. He then came down with malaria: more chills and fever.

By early summer, he was finally on the mend. With the British forces in retreat, Mrs. Jackson decided to leave her last surviving child at Robert Crawford's and make the two-hundred-mile trip to

Charleston. Her sister Jane's orphaned sons were being held there in prison ships, along with other Waxhaws men; she and the Reverend Richardson's widow and some other local women would try to negotiate their release. Years later, Andy described the conversation he had with his mother before she left. He called her words "the only capital I had to start my life." She reminded him of lessons she'd already taught him: "In this world you will have to make your own way. To do that you must have friends. You can make friends by being honest, and you can keep them by being steadfast." That's how he remembered it, anyway: a lesson in loyalty and honor. "Avoid quarrels as long as you can without yielding to imposition. But sustain your manhood always." There was more— about being grateful for kindnesses, about respecting himself and defending his good name—and then she was gone. That July, one of the Crawford boys straggled back to the Waxhaws. He brought Andy the news that his mother had contracted typhus and been buried in an unmarked grave.

"I, at first, could not believe it," Jackson wrote later. "When I finally realized the truth I was utterly alone." Robert Crawford took him in. Or, rather, let the fourteen-year-old stay in the household where he'd been living, off and on, for the last five years. If anything, the war had made Uncle Robert even more prosperous. As one descendent put it, the Major "became rich during and after the Revolution." Taking advantage of the disruptions and shortages, he'd become the area's leading merchant. His place was picked as the local supply depot for General Greene's army, maybe by W. R. Davie, who was put in charge of the commissary around this time. The Crawford farm saw a constant flow of soldiers and supplies, military contracts to be doled out, favors to be called in. The last major battle in the South took place near Charleston that September. The next census would show Robert Crawford heading a household of eleven and owning fifteen slaves.

Andy, still recovering, worked at Crawford's "public station" as a clerk, but didn't last long. He quarreled with the militia captain in charge. It was over "some reason, I forget now what," Jackson wrote in his old age, "merely a difficulty between a pompous man and a sassy boy." He may have forgotten the difficulty, but he remembered the reason: it was a matter of honor. "I had arrived at the age to know my rights, and although weak and feeble from disease, I had courage to defend them, and if he attempted anything of that kind I would most assuredly Send him to the other world." An Irish orphan with a dent in his skull from a British sword, he may not have looked like a gentleman, but he expected to be treated like one. And if combat and defeat and prison had taught him nothing else, it had taught him that you fought for your rights; you took action. Other men may have come away from the war committed to peace, determined to go back and farm for the rest of their lives; Andy wasn't one of them. Looking back on his adolescence, Jackson proudly described a teenager who would "most assuredly" kill over an insult. He'd learned to draw a line and give a warning; he'd learned that any further negotiating was a sign of weakness.

After Andy's quarrel with the militia captain, Major Crawford sent his charge away. He placed the boy in what amounted to an apprenticeship at a local farm. Andy spent six quiet months mostly learning about horses and saddle making. "I think I would have made a pretty good saddler," he reflected years later. But his mother had dreamed of him becoming a gentleman, not a Leather Apron man. And though he was the sole heir to his father's two hundred acres, he hadn't been raised to be a farmer either. There's a story from around this time of Andy helping his cousin build a house. Mid-job, he supposedly threw down his ax "and swore that he was never made to hew logs."

Instead, he'd come to believe that he was made to live the life he saw at Uncle Robert's. Cornwallis had surrendered at Yorktown that fall of 1781, but the British still occupied Charleston. Many of the city's wealthy families retreated inland for safety, and Andy suddenly found himself around young people "addicted" to horse racing and cockfights. The sons of Lowland plantation owners liked to gamble for high stakes and took pride in their style, win or lose. With the country still reeling from the revolution, an observer of the gentry noted: "Instead of Politics the general Topick of Conversation in this place is Horse, a Subject tho apparently perfectly understood and repeatedly talked over seems never to be exhausted." Now, in their midst appeared this six-foot-tall, sandy-haired teenager with a brogue. He knew horses and was a fierce competitor, with the temper and presence to match. He couldn't have exactly fit in with the sophisticated city crowd, but he would have made an impression. And learned.

That winter, after the British had decamped, Major Crawford made the four-day trip down to Charleston to take care of postwar business. He took Andy with him. They arrived in a city emerging from three years of occupation. Before the war, it had a population of about twelve thousand, half of them blacks. An elite of about a thousand had controlled 75 percent of the wealth. Many of these had been British supporters. Now, though the legislators welcomed the rich families back (the legislature, after all, had always been controlled by major landowners), not everyone was so forgiving. According to a local paper, "A spirit had gone forth among the lower Class of people to drive away certain persons whom they call Tories." There were riots and murders and houses were torched. Public meetings called for the expulsion of British sympathizers. Andy, who arrived in the midst of this "bitter class antagonism," would have followed the lead of his mentor. Major Crawford traveled in the upper circles of Charleston society; his daughter would marry into one of its richest families. Andy probably took part in the elegant hunt clubs that were functioning once again and the winter calendar of concerts and balls. He learned how to bet at the city's racetracks, dress for a minuet, dine at a formal table.

Whether Andy got an inheritance when his mother died, was supported by Major Crawford, or made his money gambling, he managed to run with a fast crowd. He'd later tell the story of a dice game in a Charleston tavern. One of the players bet two hundred pounds against all Andy owned: his horse. "My calculation was that, if a loser in the game, I would give the landlord my saddle and bridle, as far as they would go toward the payment of his bill, ask a credit for the balance, and walk away from the city." Jackson never talked much about his youth, but he must have liked the figure he cut in this story: from his devil-may-care, bet-it-all bravado to his willingness to pay up and walk away to the fine touch that all he had at the time was invested in a horse. It's a story about what he thought he needed to know in the wide-open, postwar years. Not the Leather Apron practicality of Franklin, or the management skills of Abigail Adams, but a style that would mark him as a gentleman: someone willing to take a risk, who liked the thrill of action. He threw the dice and won.

When Andy returned from the big city to the Waxhaws, it was caught up in what one historian calls a "postwar rampage." "Dislocated whites" were grabbing land and "snatching slaves at will." In some ways, it was a throwback to the vigilante movement of the Regulators, with some of the same basic demands. Soldiers returning to their ruined farms believed they'd fought not just for independence but for justice. They wanted as much say in the new government as the elite. The elite felt otherwise. Their party, the Federalist Party, worked to keep the coastal plantation owners in power. Their support of a strong central government was a way to maintain order and fight what they saw as radical land grabs. Andrew Jackson would one day defeat the Federalist candidate John Quincy Adams by running as a champion of the common man, the "bone and sinew" of the country. Now, coming home to finish the equivalent of his high school education, he had a chance to take sides. He could defend the farmers' rights, join with the kind of men who'd gathered around Uncle James's still. Or, he could side with Uncle Robert and the visitors sipping drinks on his porch. He doesn't appear to have hesitated.

The local model for a gentleman's education was W. R. Davie's. After the garnished wages of Reverend Richardson's slave had paid his way through private school, Davie had gone up to Princeton, New Jersey, and graduated from the Presbyterian college there. He'd then studied law in Salisbury, North Carolina. His role in the revolution had earned him the reputation as "one of those cool, quick men who apply master-wit to the art of war." Davie's hit-and-run, guerrilla style depended on his connections among his fellow backcountry Scots-Irish: they'd housed and fed and fought with him. But if Davie was one of Andy's models, the boy had to notice that the hero of the Waxhaws didn't stay after the war: he moved east, closer to the center of power on the coast. Still in his mid-twenties, Davie established a profitable law practice among the state's gentry. That's where he found his clients, and that's whom he went on to represent as a member of the Federalist Party at the Constitutional Convention. Eventually, he'd become governor of North Carolina.

Uncle Robert followed this basic model for the education of the other orphaned former prisoner of war in his care: Andy's cousin Will. In the fall of 1782, he sent the boy to Salisbury to study law under the same man who'd taught Davie, Spruce Macay. With the newly independent Carolinas rewriting their legal codes, lawyers were in demand. And with the frontier pushing west, the smart ones had a chance to make a fortune off border disputes and real estate deals. The possibilities drew Andy back into school. As dislocated farmers rampaged through the countryside, he enrolled at the Bethel Academy, where he brushed up on his English, Latin grammar, and handwriting. If this sort of study had once seemed dull, conjugating verbs in a dead language was now a means to a practical end: a requirement for studying law.

To support himself, the seventeen-year-old taught at a local school, appraised horses, and at one point, took a trip to Salisbury to sell some of Robert Crawford's slaves. While in town, he probably saw his cousin Will, who was spending his days copying documents, studying Blackstone's *Commentaries*, and filing papers for Lawyer Macay. Hard to believe any of that looked too interesting to Andy. But Macay may have. He'd gone to Princeton, too, then married a prominent judge's daughter, and been the state attorney for the past five years. He'd become one of the richest men in the area. Macay owned a dozen horses, some twenty slaves, and thousands of acres, and he moved among the most influential men in the South. To work in his office was to get an education in power politics.

After his brush-up term at the academy, Andy moved in with Will. He'd just turned eighteen, and it marked the end of his early education. He'd have to wait a year before he could actually clerk for Macay. And he'd be twenty before he was admitted to the bar. Then he'd practice in a series of law offices and travel the circuit court, staying in roadside taverns, gambling, drinking. "Aw, I was a raw lad then," Jackson recalled, "but I did my best." There's the story of Andy and Will and some other law students tossing their whiskey glasses into the fireplace after a night of partying. Then they decided that wasn't enough. They trashed their landlord's table, his chairs, the bed and the curtains, and then set them all on fire. Like the story of the dice game, this one's about learning a certain style and a certain definition of freedom: studying privilege.

The earliest extant letter of Jackson's is from this time. It shows the man his education had produced, combining the thin skin of the immigrant, his mother's ambitions for him, and the quick leap to violence that the war had helped teach.

> When a man's feelings and character are injured he ought to Seek aspeedy redress; . . . My character you injured; and further you have Insulted me in the presence of a court and larg audianc. I therefore call upon you as a gentleman to give me Satisfaction for the Same . . . for it is consistent with the character of a gentleman when he Injures a man to make aspedy reparation: therefore I hope you will not fail in meeting me this day from 4.
>
> Andrew Jackson

It doesn't have the spelling or the grammar of a gentleman—this son of the Waxhaws would never quite achieve that—or the easy, nonchalant confidence of someone born with money. No, it's a challenge to duel written by a man who—as his mother had predicted—was making his own way with the help of his friends. Jackson wrote the note as he was headed west to become the public prosecutor for a frontier district beyond the Waxhaws. It was a plum job he'd gotten through one of Macay's law clerks: early proof that it was who, not what, he knew that mattered. And all the more reason to be willing to kill anyone who injured his character.

In a way, what Jackson needed to learn was how to break with the past. He'd use his knowledge—from gauging horse flesh to con-jugating Latin verbs—to help leave his immigrant community be-hind. Moving west into what would become Tennessee gave him a chance to start fresh. He'd work as a prosecutor, mostly for the "propertied classes," often getting paid in real estate. During a period characterized as "one of the biggest and most successful land grabs in American history"—not by small farmers but by well-funded real estate investors—Jackson would end up with one of the region's largest plantations. His wealth and connections helped get him ap-pointed a major general in the militia. And like W. R. Davie, he'd make his political reputation through the military. Jackson would lead the campaign to eradicate the remaining Indian tribes in the Deep South: a bloodier slaughter than Bloody Tarleton ever led. That earned him his command at the Battle of New Orleans, where he became a national hero in what would be called the second American Revolution. That, in turn, would lead to the presidency.

After he got to Tennessee, Jackson barely communicated with his relatives and former friends. Later, as one historian writes, "[he] an-swered their inquiries in a tone that discouraged further correspon-dence." He was, after all, a reinvented man: not a farm kid with an Irish brogue but a lawyer graduating into the propertied class. Just a month after leaving the Carolinas behind, he celebrated this gradua-tion in the traditional way. He bought his first female slave.

BELLE

Belle was maybe born in 1797.

If she had a last name, it might have been Hardenbergh.

Her birth date and name—and her education, for that matter—were considered of no importance. She was probably born on Johannes Hardenbergh's farm, which lay about a hundred miles up the Hudson River from New York City. A century earlier, Hardenbergh's ancestor had been granted a huge patent—nearly two million acres—to settle in what was then called the New Netherlands. So, Johannes Hardenbergh had inherited real estate and political power. He'd been a colonel in the Revolutionary War and served as a member of the assembly and then the state legislature. He owned several miles of land along the Wallkill River. He also owned seven human beings.

Belle's father and mother were known by their Dutch-African names: Bomefree and Mau-mau Bett. Belle would describe them as models of "faithfulness, docility, and respectful behavior," which made them what might be called successful. That is, within the system of slavery, they succeeded in surviving into their forties, knowing where most of their children were, and remaining in the service of a single, wealthy family. To do as well, their newborn daughter would have to learn the rules of the institution and the white people who ran it. Belle's main school would be slavery.

It wasn't Southern slavery like Andrew Jackson eventually practiced: a plantation with miles of flat cotton fields, hundreds of black workers, and a few white overseers in a mansion. This was Northern slavery, and more specifically, Northern Dutch slavery. The West India Company had started bringing Africans up the Hudson some 170 years before Belle was born. The geography was a little like the Waxhaws: hilly, with thick forests and fertile river bottoms. There was no mass crop or need for mass labor. But Dutch settlers wanted slaves. Owners of the large patroon estates, like the Hardenberghs, had more land than they could work. Meanwhile, the majority of settlers made their living in the fur trade and maintained small subsistence farms. They'd buy a male slave to help clear land, plant and harvest wheat, keep track of the livestock. Black women mostly did household chores from spinning wool to taking care of the children.

On average, Dutch families in the area owned one to four slaves. "Despite their unequal relationship," one historian writes, "masters and slaves worked together at the same tasks, lived together in the same house, and celebrated the Dutch holidays together on terms of easy familiarity." Belle needed to know—and would quickly learn—there was nothing easy about it. But slavery in the Hudson River valley did produce a kind of integration. There was a saying in Kingston, near where Belle was born: "Every other white man a Negro, and every other house a barn." Blacks were allowed to testify in court, and during the wars against the Indians, carry weapons. Still, they were property. And from the masters' perspective, they existed to serve. "Life was leisurely," says a history of these Dutch villages, "slaves numerous, and hired help worked from sunup to sundown." To put that another way, life was leisurely *because* slaves were numerous.

When the British took over the New Netherlands, they made the slave laws harsher and expanded the trade into a booming business. The number of blacks in New York rose from a little over two thousand in 1700 to more than nine thousand adults by 1746. Most of these were in Manhattan, which soon had more slaves than any other American city besides Charleston. Other centers included

Albany and, midway between the two, Ulster County, where Belle was born. By the Revolutionary War, there were almost two thousand slaves in Ulster alone. Twenty years later, when Bomefree and Mau-mau Bett had their baby girl, there were almost three thousand. They were scattered in little towns like Hurley, where the Hardenberghs lived: still primarily Dutch-speaking and agricultural. Because owners here valued trained domestics, most of their slaves were bought already "seasoned" from Barbados and Jamaica. In New York City, on the other hand, traders dealt directly with Africa, and between 1750 and 1770, demand was so high that the west coast of that continent was nearly depopulated. At the New Jersey port of Perth Amboy, unsold slaves were kept in makeshift pens, and after a certain period of time, could be bought at "distress prices." Blacks soon made up 12 percent of New York State's population.

Belle's parents had been born during this glut period. Given that they only spoke Dutch—and never seem to have told her stories about Africa or the Caribbean—they may have been Hudson Valley natives. Colonel Hardenbergh had gotten married in 1751; his family included some of the largest slave owners in the region; it was customary to give slaves as wedding presents. That may have been how he came to own Bomefree and Mau-mau Bett. When the colonel died just a couple years after Belle was born, his son Charles inherited the couple. Because Belle and her brother Peter were just toddlers, they were allowed to stay with their parents.

One of the first lessons Belle had to learn was that a slave family remained a family at the whim of its master. Belle was probably her parents' tenth child; all the rest had been disappeared. In the cellar where Charles Hardenbergh housed his slaves, Belle's mother tried to explain. Belle remembered light filtering through the floorboards over their heads, a pine knot burning on the dirt floor, her mother's voice. The last two children were taken just before Belle was born. The boy was five, the girl three, it was winter: a sleigh had pulled up to Colonel Hardenbergh's house. The children were called, resisted briefly, then were loaded in the sleigh and driven away. It was a brief, brutal story. Belle's mother told it both as a memorial to the departed and as a lesson. This was the system they lived under; every black child needed to know.

In fact, Dutch owners considered children a kind of flaw in that system. Eventually, of course, they grew up to be free labor, but they were nearly useless till they were eight or nine. Worse than useless really, because their mother had to take care of them, which meant her productivity fell off. Plus, the babies had to be housed and fed: a cost with no immediate benefit. The rule of thumb was that male slaves in their twenties were the most valuable; women were worth 20 to 40 percent less; a ten-year-old brought another 20 percent less than that; and infants fetched next to nothing. The problem, from the owner's point of view, was that slaves kept having babies. Some of the houses in the Hudson Valley looked, as one observer put it, like "overstocked hives." The solution was to get rid of the young early.

Belle learned how to walk in the Hardenbergh cellar and to speak a kind of countrified, Low Dutch. A tin dipper was a *blikke*; a grandmother, a *grootje*, and a kid with a lot of questions, *krankie*. She also learned, by following her mother around, the basics of how to keep house. Homes in Ulster County were often built out of local sandstone or granite. The interior walls were plastered, and part of a female slave's duty was to keep them sparkling white. The tile hearths needed to be swept. Wood floors were covered with a light coating of sand, and black domestics were expected to change that weekly, clearing out the old and spreading the new in pleasing, geometric patterns. There was that much more work in a big place, like the Hardenberghs', which also served as a hotel. Not to mention the milking, the spinning and weaving, and the tending to children.

Mau-mau Bett would have looked after the Hardenberghs' two boys and two girls, all under ten, as well as Belle and Peter. The Dutch had a tradition of presenting their children with infant slaves: personal attendants who spent all day with their small masters, almost as if they were equal. Three-year-old Belle's role may have been something like that: the half-dozen children in the Hardenbergh house thrown together for large parts of the day, then the black ones taken down to the basement to sleep. It was a complicated, daily lesson in status—one of many. For example, Belle would have watched Mau-mau wash and feed and generally act as a parent to the Hardenbergh children. "Astonishing" is how one eighteenth-century observer described slave mothers in Hudson Valley households: "what liberty of speech was allowed to those [of] them who were active and prudent. They [could] chide, reprove and impostulate in a manner that we would not endure from our hired servants." And then an eight-year-old Hardenbergh could turn around and give Belle's mother an order, and she'd have to obey.

Belle's parents served Charles Hardenbergh six days of the week. On Sundays, they had what the Dutch called "half-freedom." Under this tradition, loyal slaves were rewarded with the use of a small plot of land and these off-hours to farm it. Belle's family raised tobacco, corn, and flax on the side of a mountain. They could sell their crops for extra food and clothing, most of which went to the kids. The arrangement worked to the master's advantage, of course: the Hardenberghs retained ownership of the land, meanwhile cutting down the overhead of keeping slaves. Still, if it wasn't actually half-freedom, it must have given Belle a taste.

Like most slaves in Ulster County, Belle's family never went to church. Around the time of Belle's birth, the Dutch Reformed denomination had declared there was "no difference between bond and free, but all are one with Christ." Theoretically that meant a baptized slave had the same status in church as a free white person. The catch was that newborns could only be baptized in the Dutch Reformed Church if their parents had been. And to convert, Belle's parents would have had to pass through a course of study that included memorizing the Heidelberg Catechism and reading various hymns, psalms, and prayers. Bomefree and Mau-mau Bett were illiterate.

Down in New York City and up near Albany, a missionary group called the Society for the Propagation of the Gospel in Foreign Parts tried to teach slaves to read so they could become one with Christ. But owners mostly resented it: an educated slave was liable to be trouble. Plus, the missionary society was British, trying to make converts to the Anglican Church. So, Dutch owners like the Hardenberghs stayed away from it. The "easy familiarity" of the slave system in Ulster County didn't include teaching black people to read or write. Belle would never learn.

When she was almost nine, Charles Hardenbergh died. For the human beings he owned, it was the end of a world. Belle's mother knew she'd lose what remained of her family. She wept; she went back over the loss of her other children; and she turned religious. As the surviving Hardenberghs decided what to do with their slaves, Mau-mau Bett told her daughter: "[T]here is a God who hears and sees you."

"A *God*, mau-mau! Where does he live?"

"He lives in the sky . . . and when you are beaten, or cruelly treated, or fall into any trouble, you must ask help of him, and he will always hear and help you."

The stars and the moon, Mau-mau Bett went on, are the same "that look down upon your brothers and sisters, and which they see as they look up to them, though they are ever so far away from us, and each other." This sky god had the power to connect a family, even when it was forced to live apart.

It wasn't the Heidelberg Catechism. And Mau-mau Bett didn't teach from the Bible. That belonged to the white world and the church black people never entered. No, this was a personal god, powerful, and if you were a slave in a small white-dominated community, secret.

In the South, the death of the master often led to what abolitionists called the "terrible auction." That had once been true in New York: Belle would have gone on the block with the rest of Hardenbergh's possessions. But by now, 1804, something called "gradual abolition" had begun. Slave auctions in New York State had all but disappeared. When one took place, it "usually attracted more critics than buyers." The institution that had shaped Belle, that she had been forced to study under, was slowly disappearing.

What had Abigail Adams said? "[We] fight ourselves for what we are daily robbing and plundering from those who have as good a right to freedom as we have." The Revolutionary War had been a chance to end those contradictions. Vermont had abolished slavery in 1777; Pennsylvania, Massachusetts, Connecticut, and Rhode Island had followed. But in New York, it was big business. Thirty years before Belle was born, the majority of the delegates to the New York Constitutional Convention had declared their opposition to slavery—but couldn't agree on how to dismantle it. The answer turned out to be bit by bit. New York wouldn't ban its slave trade until a dozen years after the Declaration of Independence. And it took another decade for the state to pass a manumission act. By then, immigrants like the Scots-Irish were doing some of the menial labor Africans once had. Whites had to be paid, but not much—and there were no housing or feeding costs. Slavery in New York didn't disappear with a triumphant stroke of the pen; it was erased slowly, when and if it made economic sense.

So, Belle was educated in a system that was being phased out. She grew up under a state law that said a girl born into slavery after 1799 would become free when she turned twenty-five, a boy at twenty-eight. That meant that just as an owner's human inventory reached maximum market value, it became worthless to him. But only if it stayed in New York. The state had banned the exportation of slaves, but owners found ways around that, and Negroes scheduled to be freed were often sold to Southern owners. That helps explain the drop in New York's black population from about 8 percent in the 1790s to less than 3 percent by 1830.

When Charles Hardenbergh died, Belle's father was in his late fifties. That was way past prime and made it impractical to pass Bomefree on to other family members: his upkeep would cost more than he was worth. The Hardenberghs could have turned him out and kept Mau-mau Bett, still a useful worker. Maybe splitting up the old couple seemed cruel. Maybe the Hardenberghs figured that, separated from her husband, Mau-mau Bett would be too resentful to be of much use. Whatever the reasons, they decided the pair would go with the house. Belle's mother would be freed, providing she looked after her husband, and the new owners agreed that the couple could continue to live in the basement, picking up whatever work they could find.

Nine-year-old Belle, on the other hand, was old enough to be worth something. She'd had some domestic training, seemed fit, and was likely to grow up to be a large, strong, valuable woman. Plus, she'd retain her value. Belle was born before the 1799 cutoff date on the state's gradual manumissions act. That meant that, even if the system was being phased out, the purchaser would be buying a slave-for-life. The Hardenberghs offered her along with some sheep, and the package fetched a hundred dollars. A good wagon at the time was worth about forty.

Until now, Belle's education—how she'd received it, anyway—hadn't been all that different from Nabby Smith's. One learned to give orders, one to take them, but neither girl could go to school. They were taught at home, at their mother's knee. Now, as Belle ended what amounted to her grade school, she was about to lose that. But the curriculum—what she needed to know—would hardly change at all. The education of a slave remained a hard, fixed thing. Meanwhile, the nation was trying to figure out who should be responsible for teaching its enfranchised voters—free white males—and what that education was for.

About forty miles south of where Belle grew up, in the Hudson River town of Newburgh at the end of the Revolutionary War, a young schoolteacher named Noah Webster happened to listen in on some soldiers as they were getting ready to be mustered out of the American army. What Webster heard was cacophony: Dutch, French, German, Swedish, various dialects of English, and what he called "the gargled grunts of Philadelphia Negroes." He said it left him with "extreme depression & gloomy forebodings." How could the United States ever really be united if its citizens spoke and spelled and wrote differently? Webster, a Yale graduate, set out to compose an American grammar book. "*Now* is the time," he declared, "and *this* the country in which we may expect success in attempting changes to language, science, and government. Let us then seize the moment and establish a national language as well as a national government."

Webster's first schoolbook appeared in the early 1780s. Riding a wave of patriotism (and its author's tireless promotion), Webster's grammar soon replaced the *New England Primer* as the standard classroom text. By the time Belle was born, it was second only to the Bible as the bestselling book in America. Webster believed the old way of learning how to read and write—using the scriptures as a model—resulted in an archaic style. Instead, his famous blue-backed speller included prose examples by famous Americans. That way, students would be taught not only a modern national language but a sense of patriotism. Americans had passed from being colonists to citizens of rebellious states, but the next step—the sense of belonging to a nation—still needed to be learned. "Begin with the infant in his cradle," it said on Webster's title page, "let the first word he lisps be Washington."

Mother or older sister might teach that first lisp. But after that, Webster thought, there had to be a more dependable, uniform system. "In our American republic," Webster wrote, "where government is in the hands of the people, knowledge should be universally diffused by means of public schools." Soon after the Revolutionary War, the New York State Legislature began debating how to do this. The issue rose at the same time and from some of the same fundamental questions as the debate over abolition: what did it mean that all people were created equal? In 1795, the legislature finally authorized state money to fund education, as well as the right of local governments to establish taxes for its continuing support. But it was no easy sell. Not only was public education costly, but many Americans cherished their regional differences. In Albany, for example, when Webster delivered his speech on national language and schooling, it was met with a stony silence. "The Dutch," he wrote, "have no taste for the English language." Plus, families with money could fend for their own. Wasn't this idea of a public education system really a kind of charity, aimed at the poor? And what did the poor need to know? They'd gotten along without much schooling up till now. When Belle was three, the New York legislature reversed course and ended its common school funding.

The argument that got the movement going again wasn't so much the nation's need for literacy or a unifying patriotism, but for obedience. What made a republic successful, Noah Webster wrote, was "a singular machinery . . . which takes the child as soon as he can speak, checks his natural independence and passions, makes him subordinate to superior age, to the laws of the state, to town and parochial institutions." It was like religion: a child had to be taught to answer to a higher authority. So, Webster included in his textbook something he called the Federal Catechism. "What are the defects of democracy?" children were taught to ask. "Tumults and disorder," they'd recite, brought on by the unfortunate fact that "a multitude is often rash."

And who were most often rash and disobedient? The poor. "The mendicant parent," as the governor of New York put it, "bequeaths his squalid poverty to his offspring." That's why the poor needed to go to school. More specifically, that's why the rich needed to pay for the poor to go to school. The year before Belle was sold away from her family, some of the most "distinguished" families in the city established a volunteer charity called the New York Free School Society. The society believed that "evil must be corrected at its source, and that education was the sovereign prescription." It set up schools to turn urchins into orderly members of the democracy. Their method of instruction was a new one, developed in England. Several hundred students sat in a big assembly hall. Monitors came to the front, where a master teacher told them what the next lesson would be. Then the monitors (picked from the older students) would go back and teach their section. When enough time had passed for the lesson to be absorbed, the sections would take turns trooping forward and reciting to the head teacher. It was mass education, the big hall echoing with simultaneous instruction and the sound of kids being marched up and back. Never mind what the mendicant students thought, the rich sponsors hailed the new system as "a blessing sent down from heaven to redeem the poor."

Webster was an abolitionist. He included in his grammar book his belief that Americans faced the choice "of either acknowledging the rights of your Negroes, or of surrendering your own." But if and when Negroes got their rights, most were going to pass directly from slavery into poverty—and add to the problems facing the new country. Again, charitable institutions sprang up. The elite founders of the New York Manumission Society included Alexander Hamilton and John Jay. In the late eighteenth century, the society had begun setting up African Free Schools in New York City. Their goal: to "rescue the minds of the descendants of Africa" and to make them "quiet and orderly citizens." It's possible that if Belle had been free, and living in the city—and sponsored by a well-off family—she might have ended up in one of these schools. But the odds were against that. During her childhood, the African Free Schools served fewer than five hundred students a year.

At the same time, more than a million people in America were being educated to be slaves. When Belle's family was yanked out from under her, that was the singular machinery she was supposed to fall into. Only now, slavery would stop teaching her through her family and start giving its lessons directly: blunt and undiluted. As Belle put it when she was sold to her new owner: "*Now, the war begun.*"

Slaves reflected their owner's status, and John Neely was a step down economically. He owned a store just outside Kingston and a small farm. Plus, he and his wife spoke only English. "If they sent me for a frying-pan," Belle recalled, "not knowing what they meant, perhaps I carried them the pot-hooks and trammels. Then, oh! how angry mistress would be with me!" It was a harsher kind of slavery than the nine-year-old was used to, and there seemed to be no learning how to get it right. Belle was often beaten. In the barn one Sunday morning, her master whipped her with a bundle of hot rods until the blood ran. She'd carry the scars the rest of her life.

Half a century later, Belle faced a crowd of white hecklers and asked them if they had a reason to hate colored people. Because, she'd go on, when God asks her why she hates whites, "I have got my answer ready." And she'd drop the top of her blouse to reveal the crisscross of scars. But if Neely's beatings taught her hatred, it wasn't against all whites. Not, anyway, to the same degree. She saw her treatment by the Hardenberghs, for example, as less cruel than illogical. How could they house their slaves in the cellar, treat them like livestock, and also expect them to act like humans? She'd eventually forgive another master, explaining his behavior as a product of the system, recounting with joy his late realization that "slavery was the wickedest thing in the world." As a black person in America,

Belle knew her life depended on learning how to make these distinctions between white people. It was a crucial part of her education. "Simple and artless" is how a white acquaintance would one day describe the grown-up Belle. "[But] her eye will see your heart and apprehend your motives, almost like God's." It wasn't godlike or some sixth sense; it was a skill learned out of necessity. And in later years, Belle would be proud of it, contrasting it with her illiteracy: "I don't read such small stuff as letters, I read men and nations."

Now the nine-year-old in the Neely household knew she needed help. A few months after her sale, Belle says she began to "beg God" to send her father to her. Soon, he came, and Belle saw it as a kind of miracle: proof that prayer worked. It may also have been an example of how communication worked in the underground black community. Though families were separated and kept in relative isolation on Ulster County farms, slaves managed to stay in touch. It was abbreviated, often secretive contact, but Belle, for example, says she eventually got to know at least six of her ten brothers and sisters. Slaves could meet in town while running errands, at the grist or the saw mill, along the roads. They could get permission to visit on Sundays. And if they couldn't see each other, they passed messages along the grapevine. As soon as Belle's father saw how bad things were, he started working this network. Not long afterward, word having mysteriously passed from slave to slave to master to master, a local fisherman appeared at the Neelys and bought Belle. If she believed he'd been sent "in answer to her prayer," it also taught that there was a system within the system of slavery. That with the right connections, tugged just so, blacks could influence a white-run institution.

Belle's purchase by the fisherman, Martimus Schryver, was, at best, a sideways move economically. With the Hardenberghs, she'd been fed and clothed relatively well. With the Neelys, on the other hand, she complained of suffering "*terribly—terribly*" from the cold. Belle described the Schryvers as "rude, uneducated . . . but kind." They owned a large "unimproved" farm a little closer to the Hudson River than the Neelys' place and earned their living fishing and running a small inn. At least they spoke Dutch so Belle had a better idea what was expected of her. It was, in her words, "a wild, out-of-door kind of lief."

Belle spent the equivalent of her middle school years owned by the Schryvers. She'd become a tall, powerful girl with a straight posture and a deep voice. Her new owners couldn't afford just a domestic; they had her carry the day's catch from the shore to the inn, go into the woods and collect the herbs and roots to brew beer, hoe the corn, and occasionally cross Roundout Creek to pick up a gallon of liquor or molasses at the Strand, Kingston's commercial center. This "wild" life included her first experience as a semi-independent adult in a city. While Kingston was no longer the state capital, it was still the county seat, with an imposing Dutch Reformed Church and one of the state's oldest private schools.

Belle says that part of what she learned in these years was how to curse and smoke and drink. Plus, she got her first taste of a certain kind of nightlife. As a grown woman, Belle often sang a tune called "Washington's Ball," which she said she first heard at the Schryvers' inn. She'd stand outside and watch the white people dance: the ladies in high-crowned caps and starched dresses, the men in their tight britches. "The President's March," as it was also known, was the hit of the day: a jaunty, paradelike tune composed in the early 1790s. Later, when lyrics were added, it became widely popular as "Hail Columbia." The preteen Belle not only learned the tune but developed a rich, deep singing voice.

By Belle's count, she managed to get away from the Schryvers and visit her parents in the cellar of the old Hardenbergh hotel "three or four times." Free but without any means of support, they survived by hiring themselves out for general work. Bomefree, for example, was too old to help with the harvest but might rake behind the carts. And as they aged, they depended more and more on charity. Neighbors baked them a loaf of bread or let them come by and pick apples. When Belle was about thirteen, Mau-mau Bett, the younger and more independent of the two, died. Belle and her brother Peter were allowed to attend the funeral. After that, her father started wandering among the descendants of Colonel Hardenbergh, finding shelter where and when he could. He was lame and losing his sight. Belle tried to keep track of him and visit when she could, or he'd come to see her. But about the time her mother died and her father began drifting from place to place, Belle was sold again.

At thirteen, nearly six feet tall, experienced in both house- and fieldwork, Belle brought a good price. Her next stop—her high school—was ten miles south, on a farm overlooking the Hudson in the town of New Paltz. An "isolated, conservative, tightly-knit farming community," New Paltz had been founded by French Huguenots. It consisted of about twenty buildings, including a couple of stores, a church, and a schoolhouse. Slavery had always been part of its social fabric: a family with any means bought a girl to help with housework and child rearing, which is why New Paltz had more female slaves than male. Belle's new owner, John Dumont, was just starting a family that would eventually include nine children. He employed at least two white servants and Belle made his fourth slave. But Dumont had purchased her to do more than cook and watch the children. "*That* wench," he's quoted as saying, "is better to me than a *man*—for she will do a good family's washing in the night, and be ready in the morning to go into the field, where she will do as much at raking and binding as my best hands."

The year she was sold, New York passed a statute requiring owners to teach slave children how to read the Bible. But at thirteen, Belle was too old to be affected by the law. The Dumont children recalled, "[I]t seemed almost impossible to teach her anything." It's not clear what they meant. More and more complex chores? The family spoke English and said Belle picked that up "with much difficulty"; she'd always speak with a thick Dutch accent. Slavery continued to be Belle's main school.

John Dumont had been raised in a slave-owning family—which meant he was probably brought up on a day-to-day basis by a black woman like Mau-mau Bett. His wife, on the other hand, had grown up with hired help. Mrs. Dumont was no abolitionist but, like Noah Webster, felt "the labor of slaves . . . less productive than that of freemen." The disagreement played out in how the couple treated its domestic help. The white servants, in Belle's words, kept trying "to *grind her down*." The kitchen girl, Kate, for example, waited until Belle went out to do the milking one morning, then slipped ashes into Mrs. Dumont's breakfast potatoes. When the missus saw their "dirty, dingy look," she blamed Belle and told her husband, "[I]t is the way *all* her work is done." The punishment could have been severe. As slavery in New York slowly disappeared, this kind of grinding-down became more common: working-class whites in competition with and resenting blacks. Out in the world, it tended to be the Federalist Party—the educated elite—who started African Free Schools and sided with the Negroes. And so, in this miniature battle of the Dumont kitchen, it was the head of the house, John Dumont, who uncovered the ashes trick. He absolved Belle and "muttered something which sounded very like an oath" in his wife's presence.

The lesson was as subtle and contradictory as the bond between master and slave. Asked if Dumont beat her, Belle would answer, "Oh, yes, he sometimes whipped me soundly, though never cruelly. And the most severe whipping he ever gave me was because *I* was cruel to a cat." Again, Belle is distinguishing between owners, between sadism and what she makes sound like discipline. In the school of slavery, the arrangement was always unequal: the teacher, after all, owned the student. But given the possibilities, Dumont produced something like loyalty and affection in Belle. She remembers how her fellow slaves taunted her as a "*white folks' nigger*" because she worked so hard for her master, sometimes staying up several nights in a row.

Belle was determined to be the kind of faithful, obedient slave her parents had been. Why? In her own words: "It made me true to my God." Nineteenth-century abolitionists would interpret this to mean that "it helped form in her a character that loved truth." In other words, within a degrading system, Belle learned a moral code—and, so, stayed something like clean and pure. That may have been, but it also seems more complicated than that. Later in life, as a free woman, she'd choose to visit John Dumont. She'd turn to him for advice. She'd even come back and tend the dying Mrs. Dumont.

To some, this was evidence that Belle had somehow received a

Christian education in charity and forgiveness. One writer has Belle exclaiming, "Lord, Lord, I can love *even de white folks!*" (The Southern accent added, apparently, because that's how slaves were supposed to talk.) But Belle passed into adolescence having had little to no contact with an organized church. In fact, she'd later declare that she never heard a preacher or went to a meeting, couldn't read the Bible, and never had it read to her. All of which was fairly typical: by 1800, only fifty thousand of the one million slaves in America were Christians. No, what Belle says is her behavior as the Dumonts' faithful slave made her true to *her* God. And, she could have added, she found that God in *her* church, the one she built by hand.

It was out on a small island in one of Ulster County's creeks, on a point of land where the willows grew thick. There, Belle constructed a "circular arched alcove" by weaving together the branches. In private, unseen and unheard, she began to talk to God on a daily basis: the God her mother had told her about. It may be more accurate to say she began to bargain with Him. If He gave her what she wanted, she'd "pay him by being very good." All fine in theory, except being good within the rules of slavery meant turning into what her fellow slaves called a "white folks' nigger." The contradictions were impossible and constant: to obey her master (or Master) was to suppress and betray her own spirit. No wonder she went off into the willows and tried to talk her way through it.

In the end, Belle wasn't very good at being good. She says she "yielded to all her temptations." It wasn't just that she cursed, or drank, or smoked, though that was part of it. The fundamental "sin," the one she couldn't shake, seems to have been that she enjoyed black folks and black culture.

To understand why this might fall under the category of yielding to temptation, it helps to jump ahead a little. Belle would be twenty by the time New York State finally passed an emancipation act that affected her. And it was still a gradual one: she wouldn't be a legally free woman until she was thirty. So, she'd strike a deal with John Dumont to let her go a year early if she was "faithful." When the time finally came, he'd break his promise. Betrayed, she'd walk off his farm: an escaped slave. But a few months later, she'd decide to return. Why? Belle says she "looked back into Egypt," and it seemed "so pleasant there." Specifically, the springtime holiday she called "Pingster" was about to happen, and she imagined "all her former companions enjoying their freedom for at least a little space, as well as their wonted convivialities, and in her heart she longed to be with them."

In Belle's growing-up, the Dutch celebration of Pentecost—Pinkster—was the highlight of the African-American year. For a week each spring, as the Hudson Valley's azaleas bloomed, the Dutch let their slaves have their own "frolic." In New York City, blacks from as far as forty miles away would gather in the parks. Up in Albany, a carnival village would be set up, complete with sideshows and food booths, applejack and hard cider, fiddlers and drummers. During the course of Pinkster week, a king or chief would be elected and have a grand procession through the crowd, a lot like today's Mardi Gras or Carnival. Watching "the darkies" celebrate, a white observer noted: "The dances were the original Congo dances . . . As a general thing, the music consisted of a sort of drum, or instrument constructed out of a box with sheepskin heads . . . accompanied by singing some queer African air." Pinkster struck whites as queer because it didn't teach English traditions, or Irish, or the new, patriotic American traditions. "The features that distinguished a Pinkster frolic from the usual scenes at fairs, and other merry-makings," James Fenimore Cooper wrote, ". . . were of African origin." There was the shakedown: a dance done on a five-foot-long wooden shingle, the beat produced by the crowd hitting their thighs and pounding their heels. There was another dance called the jug, and an unnamed one so "indecent," so "sexually provocative," that a commentator noted, "at last the white visitors shunned being present."

The year after the Dumonts bought Belle, the Albany council had tried to shut down the local celebration because of "boisterous rioting and drunkenness." The very fact of Negroes congregating worried some slave owners, especially as the push for emancipation gathered strength and the number of runaways increased. In Belle's neighborhood, New Paltz's property owners formed the Society of

Negroes Unsettled: a kind of white posse organized to catch and return escapees. Some believed Pinkster only made the situation
worse. When you see the Pinkster King, as a white observer put it,
crowned and leading hundreds of others in mass drumming and
dancing, "[T]hen you'll see // A slave whose soul was always free."
Frederick Douglass, on the other hand, thought these holidays
"among the most effective means, in the hands of the slaveholder,
in keeping down the spirit of insurrection." Whether you resented
Pinkster as a safety valve or cherished it as a way to learn how freedom felt, it was distinctly and proudly African-American.

Belle loved it. At Pinkster, she could celebrate, show off, be sexy
and funny: what white people called indecent. One of the Dumont
daughters would later recall Belle as "an excellent dancer and a
good singer, having a pleasant voice, rich and powerful." Pinkster
was a rare chance to use those talents. It was the opposite of going
into the bushes alone, and every spring she'd feel the pull and yield
to temptation.

When she was about seventeen, the tall thin teenager fell in love.
Robert was owned by a disapproving neighbor, who wanted his
slave to breed in-house. Though he was ordered to stop visiting the
Dumonts, Robert kept sneaking over. Somewhere in this period,
Belle had her first child (and maybe her second). Then Robert was
caught at Belle's place and beaten by his owner. He never visited
again and died not long afterward.

Meanwhile, Belle's father, Bomefree, had been passed among
the Hardenberghs, staying a few weeks at one house, then walking
the roads of Ulster County to find another. Belle had twice gotten
permission to visit him. Blind, all but crippled, and alone, Bomefree
was, in Belle's words, "a poor old man" who "cried aloud like a
child," convinced that "*God* had done it all." Now, with her baby in
her arms, Belle went to where she'd heard, via the slave network,
that her father was staying. It was a twelve-mile walk, and when she
arrived, he was gone: on to the next temporary shelter. She never
saw him again. He froze to death, alone, in a shack in the woods.

Slavery was designed to destroy family. To make itself the only
institution that mattered. So, a slave learned that to establish any-

thing like a home amounted to an act of defiance: a way of undermining the system that held you captive. In those terms, Belle graduated when she was eighteen. That's when she married another Dumont slave called Thomas. He was considerably older, with two previous wives. According to one of the Dumont children, "Tom's version of the affair was that they had merely been out on a frolic together and had agreed to live together as man and wife." By "frolic" does she mean Pinkster? Do we picture the older man attracted to the girl with the deep voice, pounding her heels and doing the shakedown? Belle claimed the courtship ended with a ceremony, making it a legal marriage. Whether legal or not, it amounted to an act of independence. Five years earlier, New York State had passed a law recognizing slave marriages, legitimatizing children of such marriages, and prohibiting owners from separating husbands and wives. By marrying, Belle had entered an institution that—theoretically, anyway—slavery couldn't touch.

She'd end up having four children with Thomas, three of whom survived infancy: two daughters and a son. "[I] never could take any one of dem up and say, 'my child,'" she was quoted as saying, ". . . unless it was when no one could see me." That was probably because the Dumonts, like many owners, continued to treat slaves as they always had, disregarding the new abolition laws. Opposition was particularly strong in Ulster County, where the Dutch still considered themselves a people apart: what was this American government to tell them how to manage their property? New York's abolition law technically freed Belle's children on July 4, 1827. But even if the Dumonts followed it, they could keep the children of their slaves as indentured servants: Belle's eldest till she was twenty-five, the others till they were twenty-one.

So, Belle still faced the kind of family breakup that Mau-mau Bett had taught her about; she still needed the lessons she'd learned sitting by the fire in the Hardenbergh basement. And Belle taught her children from the same curriculum. Years later, her eldest would recall how Belle "used to sit with her children on the floor in their cabin on the Dumont farm, before a fire place, with a pine knot for light, and mend her clothing, and talk with them." But if the talk was still about surviving slavery, Belle reached for a different conclusion. "This was [her] dream," her daughter recalled: "She told the children that some day they would have a home of their own, and that the family would all be together."

Belle knew she couldn't hold her family together under slavery. Her six-year-old son had already been taken from her illegally, sold, and shipped to Alabama. But she could, maybe, reunite them if she could get away from the Dumonts. She had no idea how she'd support herself out there and must have known she couldn't make it with all her children in tow. So, when Belle walked off the Dumonts' farm—"I did not *run* away; I walked away by day-light"—she took her baby, a one-year-old, and left her husband and the girls behind.

Her education had been under slavery; now the test was to survive freedom. For the first year or so, she'd stay in Ulster County, doing domestic work for subsistence wages. And she was lucky to get it. One observer of the Hudson Valley's freed blacks noted: "[They] lead the life of Indians, cultivating a little mays but living chiefly in the woods . . . unable to bring up their families." Slavery taught the opposite of independence. It taught that you needed a master to make decisions for you, that you couldn't possibly live outside the system. Some owners simply sent their freed slaves directly to the poorhouse. But Belle had managed to graduate from that school not only determined, but stubbornly self-confident. She'd even go to court and—in an extraordinary assertion of her rights—fight and win the case to get her son back.

By then, she'd joined the Methodist Church. While the Dutch Reformed God maintained a dignified distance from believers, Methodists spoke more directly to theirs: He seemed more like the one Mau-mau Bett had believed in. And that seemed especially true after the Second Great Awakening started sweeping through New York. Like the first revivals during Nabby Smith's childhood, this awakening was also a kind of democratic rebellion, challenging established religion and featuring evangelical services led by itinerant preachers. The born-again spirit offered Belle a chance to worship in integrated crowds that treated her something like an equal. But even more than that, in the late-night, open-air Methodist meetings, Belle recognized a Christianity that looked a lot like Pinkster. "Ring shouts" after the regular services featured black people dancing in huge circles and singing. Instead of songs read out of hymnbooks, theirs were invented on the spot, from the spirit. These "spirituals," as one historian points out, came "dangerously near to being dance turns in the style of slave jubilee melodies." That wouldn't have seemed dangerous to Belle.

By this time, New York City had become the largest single community of free blacks in the western hemisphere. In her independence and newly found religion, Belle moved down there along with her two sons. She kept house for a series of white "Methodist perfectionists," attended the Zion African Church, and then briefly joined an upstate religious commune. She'd soon return to the city and spend another decade working as a domestic.

"What happened to the Negro in New York after emancipation," writes one historian, "forms one of the darkest chapters in the history of the state." Attacked by working-class mobs, excluded from many skilled jobs, deprived of the right to vote, African-Americans had escaped slavery only to enter a society with no place for them— except as the target of white rage. Belle would work hard for years and end up with almost no savings: as far from her dream of family as ever. "[S]he came to the conclusion that she had been taking part in a great drama, which was, in itself, but one great system of robbery and wrong." It felt like she'd gone from one kind of enslavement to another.

Once again, Belle decided to walk. On Pinkster day, 1843, she crossed from Manhattan to Brooklyn and started toward the rising sun, determined to become an itinerant preacher. In her new life, she'd take the name Sojourner, and eventually, Sojourner Truth.

If slavery had taught her that she was first and foremost a slave, now she'd flip that around and use it for her own, not some master's, profit. "With the exception of her children," a biographer writes, "Truth's close associates during her adult life were middle-class white people of education." It's how she made her living. Addressing abolitionist meetings, often the only black person there, she stood out—in the words of her fellow ex-slave Fredrick Douglass—as "a genuine specimen of the uncultured negro . . . a strange compound of wit and wisdom, of wild enthusiasm and flint-like common sense . . . Her quaint speeches easily gave her an audience."

They might have been quaint, but her speeches were also funny and pointed. She played off the crowd's fascination with and fear of Negroes, holding herself up—her scars, her intelligence—as evidence of another culture, the one slavery produced. And she did more than just speak. Sojourner Truth was known for mesmerizing halls full of abolitionists, feminists, and spiritualists with her "still more remarkable talent for singing." Solo, unaccompanied, she'd perform Methodist hymns in a "strange cracked voice." She'd also offer songs she'd made up, often taking the lyrics from abolitionist publications. So, the tune of "John Brown's Body" would become "We Are the Valiant Soldiers," and Stephen Foster's "Oh! Susanna" would turn into "I'm on My Way to Canada." In the magazine profile that would eventually establish Sojourner Truth as a national figure, Harriet Beecher Stowe, the author of *Uncle Tom's Cabin*, wrote:

> She sang with the strong barbaric accent of the native African, and with those indescribable upward turns and those deep gutturals which give such a wild, peculiar power to the negro singing—but above all, with such an overwhelming energy of personal appropriation that the hymn seemed to be fused in the furnace of her feelings and come out recrystallized as a production of her own.

Belle, of course, wasn't a barbarian or a native African. She was an American-born slave, and this peculiar power she fused was the power of an African-American. It was the product of what she'd learned inside slavery: the ability to read her masters, the skills she'd developed at Pinkster, her religious self-education. From those, Belle forged Sojourner Truth. And Sojourner Truth—with income from lectures and her autobiography—would eventually pay off the mortgage on a house. There, Belle would finally reunite the surviving members of her family.

To Harriet Beecher Stowe, Sojourner Truth was one of those

"grandly formed human beings, that have come to us cramped, scarred, maimed, out of the prison-house of bondage. One longs to know," the abolitionist continues, "what such beings might have become if suffered to unfold and expand under the kindly developing influences of education." But to get to what Belle might have been, Stowe jumps past what she was. She might have unfolded differently under Noah Webster's common school system, or some other kindly education, but she learned what she needed to know as a slave. And that experience would remain part of American knowledge, indelible, passed on to both black and white.

One of Sojourner Truth's proudest moments—and a cornerstone of her legend—was her meeting at the White House with the man she called "the great and good" Abraham Lincoln. In her lectures and autobiography, Sojourner Truth would emphasize the honor of having the president of the United States receive a Negro woman in his office. What she left out was how he received her. Relaxed and funny with his white visitors, Lincoln tensed up when he turned to the colored woman. He called her "Aunty," an eye-witness reported, "as he would his washerwoman."

ABE

Abraham Lincoln was shot and killed by Indians.

He was out sowing newly cleared fields when it happened, and his three sons saw him fall. One ran for help, another gunned down the native, and the youngest—eight years old—sat in the freshly turned dirt and watched his father die.

The eight-year-old grew up and made sure his children heard about the killing. According to the dead man's grandson and namesake, it was "the legend more strongly than all others imprinted upon my mind and memory."

The death was used to explain why the family's fortunes had fallen. But it also taught a larger lesson: a warning about pioneer life, how all their work to tame the wilderness and plant a civilization could be erased in an instant. For the grandson, the legend turned out, finally, to be about education. "Owing to my father being left an orphan . . ." he'd write, "in poverty, and in a new country, he became a wholly uneducated man." And the grandson was determined to change that, to break the frontier cycle of poverty, of constantly seeking new land, of sowing seed and reaping death.

When the Shawnee cut down Abraham Lincoln, he was standing on a twelve-hundred-acre piece of land that he considered his property. Trace back how he came by it, and you find a pattern. Samuel Lincoln, born in England, lands in Massachusetts in 1637. A weaver in the old country, he becomes a prosperous merchant, the kind that formed a new upper class by the time Ben Franklin was growing up. Samuel's son stays near his birthplace, but the grandson moves down to New Jersey, where he establishes himself among the economic and social elite. The next generation pushes on to Pennsylvania's western frontier, out by the Allegheny Mountains, where Mordecai Lincoln Jr. becomes a wealthy landowner. His son heads farther south and west into Virginia, and in the sixth generation, Abraham Lincoln is killed in what would become the state of Kentucky. It's the classic, early-American pioneer route: along the Alleghenies into the Shenandoah Valley and then through the Cumberland Gap, each time reaching for the new frontier.

Maybe, as some historians have suggested, the explanation was an inexplicable romantic need, a "yearning for the wilderness and distant places." But the pioneers also kept moving because they had to. Many were forced out by wealthy landowners or because of their religious beliefs. And as early as Nabby Smith's time, Americans tended to mine the land more than farm it. They'd clear a field of its old-growth forest, plow the rich dirt, and then plant corn crop after corn crop till the earth was exhausted. Erosion would set in, the creeks would turn muddy, and it was time to leave. Sure, there was the pull of new, cheap acreage just over the next range of mountains, but there was also this push: that to stay where you were was often, quite literally, to lose ground. During the colonial era, only one out of five men *didn't* move in his lifetime.

And the reason they could start fresh, again and again, was because western land kept becoming "free." There was a pattern to this, too, and Abraham Lincoln dying in his field was part of it. The British had designated everything beyond the Appalachians as Indian Territory: the Native Americans would hunt there, supplying the fur trade, while the colonialists would stay east and farm. It was Benjamin Franklin who, in 1766, told the British House of Commons that fur was "not an American interest. The people of America are chiefly farmers and planters." Franklin argued that what Americans needed was land. Eventually, the crown agreed to buy, and the Iroquois agreed to sell. The problem was that the Iroquois didn't own, or control, or even use the land they handed over. It was the Shawnee and other tribes that hunted what would become West Virginia and Kentucky. They were who suffered when men like Daniel Boone promoted the newly opened frontier. Boone reported buffalo "more frequent than I have seen cattle in the settlements, browsing on the leaves of cane, or cropping the herbage in these extensive plains." The forests were huge, he added: yellow poplar, oak, chestnut, and walnut. Families who arrived too late in the season to build cabins sometimes wintered over in the gigantic, hollowed-out trunks.

The Shawnee not only hunted in the Kentucky region, but they were used to planting maize and tobacco there in the spring and coming back for the fall harvest. Their resistance to the colonial settlers became known as the "Forest Wars," which raged, on and off, for fifty years. When America declared independence, it also declared that the Indian border drawn by the British was no longer in effect. Franklin, John Adams, and the rest of the Continental Congress announced that pioneers could now settle all the way to the Ohio River. There were massive land purchases by North Carolinians and Virginians (George Washington was a major speculator in the Ohio Valley), followed by retaliatory Indian raids.

Abraham Lincoln ended up in a freshly plowed field in Kentucky because the Virginia General Assembly had offered enormous tracts of "waste and unappropriated lands" at bargain prices, often with full credit. A year after Boone led over a hundred settlers through the Cumberland Gap, Grandfather Lincoln bought two tracts northeast of what would become Louisville. When he, his wife, and their five children arrived, the Forest Wars were about to intensify. The twenty thousand immigrants pouring into the Ohio Valley, plus those already squatting across the Ohio River, gave, as General Washington put it, "great discomfort to the Indians." The Shawnee, along with other tribes, fought a war of small raids: bands sniping at the settlers, then retreating back into the woods. Neither side recognized the other's borders; both claimed the land in the names of their gods; both fought to preserve their culture; and at this point, both cultures might be described as semi-nomadic.

One traveler, arriving in Kentucky within a year of the Lincolns, called the frontier "a gloomy thing . . . [N]ot a soul was then settled on the Ohio between Wheeling and Louisville, a space of five or six hundred miles . . . [and] in all Beargrass settlement not a soul was in safety but by being in a fort." Danger from the various tribes was constant: in May of 1786, when Abraham fell in his field, he joined a total of some two thousand settlers who would be killed during the decade.

After her husband's death, Bathsheba Lincoln moved her children south, closer to other settlements. Thomas, the eight-year-old who had watched his father die, grew up helping his brothers and sisters with farm work and doing odd jobs for relatives. He was apprenticed to a joiner, and by the time he was eighteen, was helping build a mill in Elizabethtown. With the money he earned as a frontier carpenter, as well as his share of his father's estate, he bought (at age twenty-five) a 238-acre farm where he, his mother, and one of his married sisters lived.

Thomas's son would describe him as "a wandering laboring boy" who "never did more in the way of writing than to bunglingly write his name." But at least Thomas could read and write. And he had a trade that brought in good money. He was respectable enough to be asked to serve on juries in Elizabethtown and had the savvy to build a flatboat, carry produce down the Ohio to New Orleans, and return with a good profit. After he married, he kept the farm for his mother and moved into Elizabethtown, where he had two building lots. And when his first child, Sarah, was born, he bought another farm. By 1809, when his son Abe was born, the thirty-one-year-old Thomas Lincoln owned a total of almost 350 acres. Measured by his real estate holdings—and in a barter economy that was how wealth was gauged—he was near the top 15th percentile of property owners in Hardin County. Painting him as a wholly uneducated, wandering, laboring boy was his son's way, years later, of shading the picture for effect.

What Thomas Lincoln didn't have was formal schooling, but he married it. Nancy Hanks had more exposure to books than many women of the time. She'd been raised from the age of seven by a well-off aunt and uncle, owners of some six thousand acres and at least two slaves. The elderly guardians "reared and educated" Nancy and one of her cousins, who lived in relative comfort and, according to a relative, "went to school together." How much schooling isn't clear, but when Thomas Lincoln, her next-door neighbor, married Nancy, he chose a woman who valued literacy. One biographer says Nancy taught Thomas how to sound his way through the Bible. Abe would describe his mother as "highly intellectual by nature [with] a strong memory [and] acute judgment."

On the frontier, the primary purpose of reading was still religious. Kentucky's settlers were overwhelmingly Baptist; a church had been founded near Elizabethtown the year before the Lincolns arrived. Thomas and Nancy were swept up in the Second Great Awakening that had also shaped Sojourner Truth's faith. They joined a back-to-the-Bible, fundamentalist denomination called the Separate Baptists. Services featured "strong gestures and tears and altar calls, during which the preacher left the platform and went through the congregation exhorting sinners to be saved." The Separate Baptists were anti-slavery and pro-integration: three of the eighteen founding members of the Elizabethtown Baptist church were "colored." Persecuted and driven out of Virginia by the Anglicans, Separate Baptists sought the truth not in the church but the Good Book. That's what the preacher held in one hand as he stormed through the congregation; that's what he turned to when the flood of inspiration slowed a little. Like the early Puritans and the Scots-Irish on Andy Jackson's frontier, the Baptists pushing west carried the American tradition that you needed to learn to read because you needed to read the Bible.

The first home Thomas and Nancy's son remembered was their 230-acre Knob Creek farm, set back in a valley west of Elizabethtown. Moving there when the boy was two, the family started attending the Little Mount Baptist Church. Meanwhile, in their cabin, Nancy Hanks Lincoln regularly read the Bible aloud to her husband and children. How Lincoln learned to read was how most kids did during that time: from his mom, at home.

When he was six, the boy began his formal education. There was a private academy in Elizabethtown, but that was too far away and too expensive. And there wouldn't be a functioning public school system in Kentucky for another two decades. Instead, small communities like Knob Creek found their own way: "[W]herever a cluster of cabins appeared—schools were established, presided over by teachers who sometimes knew little more than their pupils." Abe and his older sister walked a couple of miles to learn from a neighbor and fellow parishioner.

While places like New York City were beginning to develop mass schooling for the urban poor, on the frontier the basic formula had hardly changed since Franklin's time. In the winter months, after the harvest and before sowing, Sarah and Abe went to what was known as an ABC, or "blab," school: reciting, working on their handwriting, copying down arithmetic, all in a multi-age gaggle of neighborhood kids. They worked with a revised speller that dated back to the 1740s. Lincoln would later dismiss this education as inconsequential, but it was more than most kids got. Even two decades later, only about 20 percent of Kentucky's school-age children actually attended. There was a monthly fee, and many parents didn't see the need. The Lincolns did, partly as good Baptists, and their children studied with at least two teachers while they lived at Knob Creek. But the parents probably also saw a practical need for a formal education. After all, Thomas Lincoln's lack of access to book learning was one of the reasons he was being forced out of the state.

When Grandfather Lincoln arrived in the Kentucky region, there were fewer than seventy-five thousand settlers. That number had climbed past four hundred thousand by the time Abe was born and would be close to 565,000 by 1820. The in-rush had been haphazard: a first-come, first-serve land grab that didn't pay much attention to deeds or surveys. Thomas Lincoln had lost thirty-eight acres from his original farm because the survey hadn't been recorded correctly; his next property had ended up in litigation; and the family had been forced off the farm where Abe was born because of a flaw in the title. The Lincolns weren't alone in this: almost half Kentucky's pioneers ended up losing land due to bad surveys and faulty titles. Elizabethtown, the county seat, became a legal center: three stores, three or four blacksmiths, and twenty-two lawyers. The legal disputes not only brought in regular fees but built political careers. Three of Elizabethtown's attorneys became senators, two governors, and James Buchanan ended up president. It's the path Andrew Jackson had taken to power. Now, Abe's father found himself on the other end of the equation.

To Thomas Lincoln, as one commentator puts it, "it seemed that [the lawyers] were all working for the rich, slave holding planters." He'd impressed on his young son that the family had lost its wealth and status because of a long-ago Indian attack. Now, he was losing more than six hundred acres because other, richer citizens could afford to hire men with book learning, men who knew how to work the law. On Abe's seventh birthday, a suit was filed that claimed Thomas Lincoln's Knob Creek farm was actually part of an inheritance belonging to a family in Philadelphia.

Faced with a fight he couldn't win, Thomas continued a family tradition: he moved west. "This removal was partly on account of slavery," Abe would explain years later, "but chiefly on account of the difficulty in land titles in Kentucky." The two explanations were linked. When the Lincolns moved to Knob Creek, there were almost as many slaves in Hardin County as white people. If Abe's father wanted to sell his crops or livestock at market, he had to compete directly with men who had all the advantages of slave labor. It was mostly these men who amassed the wealth; they ended up with the land. While the Lincolns' church preached against slavery as a moral wrong, Thomas Lincoln's son grew up witnessing how it was also economically unfair. "Slave states," as Abe put it years later, "are places for poor white people to remove from."

The solution was just over the Ohio River. There, the United States government had declared the vast Northwest Territory slave-free and open to settlers. It's where the Shawnee and other tribes had retreated when forced out of Kentucky, but the year Abe was born, there had been another land transfer. Again, a small group of tribesmen had claimed title, this time to some three million acres. Again, the U.S. government took possession. The deal was cut by the governor of the newly formed Indiana Territory, William

Henry Harrison. And the Shawnee leader who stepped forward to express his tribe's fury was a forty-year-old chief known as Tekamthi, or the Celestial Panther; the settlers called him Tecumseh. "You are continually driving the red people," Tecumseh told Harrison, "[and will] at last drive them in to the great lake where they can't stand or work." Harrison's response was to send survey teams into the new territory. Tecumseh began traveling through the western frontier, organizing a Native American federation to hold the line against the white settlers. The summer Abe was three, most whites in the Northwest Territory were living in fortified stockades, as Tecumseh's federation effectively controlled the region. Then Harrison led Kentucky's militia into what historians have called the "first American Civil War": a hundred thousand Native Americans (along with British troops) versus a million settler Americans west of the Alleghenies. This War of 1812 was fought on a number of fronts: three years after Tecumseh was killed in a skirmish in Upper Canada, General Andrew Jackson led his troops to victory in the Battle of New Orleans. With each victory, the frontier shifted west—and the settlers moved in.

Two winters after Tecumseh's death, Thomas Lincoln built a flatboat, floated down the Ohio River, and hiked inland to a small settlement on Little Pigeon Creek. By now, 1815, the federal government was selling land in the territories for two dollars an acre, with generous credit and long-term tax abatements. The United States was determined that Indiana wasn't going to have survey and title troubles like Kentucky had. The territory was cleanly divided into townships, six miles square, with each township then measured out into thirty-six equal sections (one of which was supposed to be set aside for a public school). Thomas laid claim to a quarter of a section: 160 acres. He didn't have title yet, but the following fall he'd get up to Vincennes, the capital, and legally register his holding. Though the land was still undeveloped wilderness, in some ways this new start was a move *toward* law and order.

Abe would live in Little Pigeon Creek from the age of seven until he was nineteen. There, he'd get his pioneer education, learning what was needed to survive, to establish a community, to make sure the wilderness was civilized.

When the Lincoln family had made the two-week, hundred-mile trip across the river from Kentucky, they came out at the end of a rough forest road. This was their quarter section, although there was no sign of the neatly laid-out subdivision lines. Instead, they faced an almost impenetrable tangle of thickets, grapevines, and huge trees. The surveyor of this particular section noted that a mile of its timber had been "destroyed by fire"; the rest was medium-growth hazel overshadowed by hundred-foot oak and hickory. "[A] vast forest" is how Dennis Hanks, Abe's cousin, described it: "I will jest Say to you that it was the Brushes Cuntry that I have Ever Seen in any New Cuntry . . . all Kinds of under groth Spice wod . . . Shewmake Dogwood grape Vines Matted together So that as the old Saying goes you could Drive a Butcher knife up to the Handle in it."

Although this was "New Cuntry" to the settlers, they kept stumbling into evidence that it was actually old. Now and then, especially down by the Ohio River, they'd come upon massive mounds of earth arranged in various complicated, geometric shapes, their exact purpose and age unknown. The area was secured now, but eerie. And most of it so flat and overgrown that one traveler found it depressing: "[I]t is seldom that a view of two hundred yards in extent can be caught in Indiana." The seven-year-old boy saw it as "a wild region, with many bears and other wild animals, still in the woods." As soon as they arrived, his father put an ax in his hands. "[F]rom that till within his twenty-third year," Abe would write of himself, "he was almost constantly handling that most useful instrument—less, of course, in plowing and harvesting season." The ax was the first tool because, as Abe put it, "the clearing away of surplus was the great task ahead."

Surplus. That's what the giant trees were. Remove them, and the land began to match the surveyor's clean lines. So, the Lincolns spent their first days building a cabin out of the logs. And then settled in for the winter, living off game Thomas killed, felling the hardwoods, slashing the undergrowth, burning and yanking out stumps and roots to where, by the first spring, they'd opened six acres and were ready to plow.

They weren't totally alone. There were seven other families in the Little Pigeon Creek area. That meant some help with cabin building and other cooperative ventures. In June, after the first corn had been planted, Thomas joined in building a Baptist church about a mile and a half from their cabin. Thirty thousand people had slipped into the new territory by the time Tecumseh was killed; the population doubled in the next four years. By the Lincolns' second winter, Indiana had enough people to apply to become a state. According to its constitution, there was supposed to be a system of free public education, starting with district schools and extending through university, but it was all on paper. The first priority was clearing the land, draining the marshes, laying roads. There wouldn't be any free schools in Indiana for more than three decades. And no school for Abe in the near future.

After officially registering his land, Thomas Lincoln invited his wife's aunt, Elizabeth Sparrow, her husband, and their ward, nineteen-year-old Dennis Hanks, to come to Indiana. Land disputes had forced the Sparrows out, too, and the area around Little Pigeon Creek was becoming an "enclave of transplanted Kentuckians." Early that winter of 1818, Spencer County was created. A log courthouse and jail were put up in Hanging Rock (later known as Rockport), a trading town on the Ohio River. Soon, the Lincolns would have ten acres in corn, five in wheat, and two in oats. They kept cows and pigs; they tanned their own leather; and Abe's mother spun cloth to make pants and shirts. There was even a mill a few miles away where they could grind their grain.

The trips to the mill offered a rare chance to see other people, exchange jokes, and share news. Eight-year-old Abe often went; that winter he scared everyone when the mill horse kicked him, and he was "apparently killed for a time." Still, he'd later recall these trips into society as giving him "the greatest pleasure of his boyhood days." The rest of his time was mostly consumed by chores: long hours clearing brush and putting up rail fences. The

Indiana forest, as one traveler described it, was still "just penetrated in places by backwoods settlers who are half hunters, half farmers."

The hunting half was a big part of a pioneer education: learning the woods, how to track and shoot. But it wasn't what Abe wanted to know, and he made that clear. "A few days before the completion of his eighth year," he'd tell his biographer, he shot and killed a wild turkey. And then made a vow: "He has never since pulled a trigger on any larger game." It was an early declaration of independence. Though Thomas Lincoln raised food and supplemented his income with carpentry work, he still had to hunt to feed his family. All the settlers did. To opt out of that as the equivalent of a fourth grader was to make a statement. To go on and stick by the vow was to declare, on a daily basis, that your interest and education were aimed elsewhere. And then to tell the story as an adult—an adult who famously didn't talk much about his childhood—was to underline the importance of the decision. He wasn't going to be a hunter-farmer. He was headed away from the forest, toward town.

That spring of 1818, building lots went up for sale in Rockport, and a justice court was established. But the Lincolns were still just an accident away from seeing all they had go back to wilderness. One day that fall, Elizabeth Sparrow's husband felt suddenly dizzy. Nausea followed and then an intense thirst, and the Lincolns recognized what was known as milk sickness. The settlers weren't aware of the cause (their cows eating a plant called poison snakeroot), but they knew the effect. Thomas Sparrow was dead within a week. His wife followed a few days later. And a week after that, Abe's mother, Nancy Hanks Lincoln, died.

It left eleven-and-a-half-year-old Sarah as the woman of the house: to cook and clean and sew. And it left her little brother in an almost all-male world: working under his father's direction, his only company the nineteen-year-old Dennis Hanks. Before his mother's death, he'd been spending most of his time in the fields. But at least he came home in the evening to the voice of his mother reading aloud or helping him with his figures. Now, the hunter-farmer was the only culture around. One biographer calls that next year the hardest in the boy's life.

Without Nancy Lincoln, the frontier operation barely functioned and didn't make much sense. As Dennis Hanks put it, "We lived the same as Indians, 'ceptin we took an interest in politics and religion." The settlers had come to establish civilization, but now this little outpost—a father, a teenager, and two kids—barely qualified. Even a ten-year-old boy could see that. Especially a ten-year-old boy. Thirteen months after his wife's death, Thomas left his children and Dennis in the forest and went back to Kentucky. When he returned to the clearing, he had a new wife, her three children, and a wagonload of her goods that included bedclothes, kitchenware, and books.

Sally Bush was the daughter of a prosperous man who owned a few thousand acres in Kentucky and had run the Hardin County jail (where Thomas Lincoln had once worked). The dowry she'd brought to her first marriage had been a sizable five hundred acres. Though she seems to have gone through most of her inheritance, the woman who arrived with Thomas Lincoln in Pigeon Creek came from a substantial background. The wagon full of furniture suggested as much; the books confirmed it. She brought John Bunyan's *Pilgrim's Progress*, Daniel Defoe's *Robinson Crusoe*, and *Aesop's Fables*, among others. If she read them, she had more schooling than many women. If, on the other hand, Sally Bush Lincoln was illiterate (as some claim), bringing books was a signal of the kind of civilization she hoped to plant in what she called this "desolate" region. Ten years younger than Thomas Lincoln, she energized the log cabin that winter of 1819: cleaning, whitewashing, making new clothes for the children. And sending them all to school.

Abe turned eleven that February and began a growth spurt that would leave him a good half foot taller than most adult men. It had been four years since he and his sister had been in a classroom. His brief Kentucky education already amounted to more than most children got, but now Abe would spend three of the next five winters in school. Sally Bush Lincoln "made a way for him to attend," as one biographer puts it—and to be with books. He was extraordinarily hungry for it, and during what amounted to his middle school years, he fed.

That first winter, he went to a one-room school about a mile and a half from the farm. Typically, these had a dirt floor, a constantly burning fireplace at one end of the room, and a single window covered with greased paper to keep out the wind. The boy's teacher was Andrew Crawford, a thirty-five-year-old justice of the peace. School cost the parents a couple of dollars per student per semester: a sizable commitment for the combined Lincoln-Bush family of five children. In return, the kids studied spelling, read the Bible aloud, and, according to one fellow student, were taught etiquette: how to enter a parlor, open the door for a lady, frame a polite answer to a question posed in polite society. Like Andy Jackson learning Latin in the Waxhaws, this was training for a world the students might never see.

There were now nine families with forty-nine children within a mile of the Lincoln farm: enough to make the school viable. Soon, that would increase to fifty families, almost all from Kentucky. The surveyor's lines were filling in. Spencer County replaced its log jail and courthouse with brick structures, and Indiana's overall population approached 150,000.

Abe skipped school the winter of his twelfth year, probably because he was needed on the farm. By now, the Lincolns were working about forty acres. But book learning had become essential to him. He'd later declare the ability to read and write the one true mark of civilization: "[To it] we owe everything which distinguishes us from savages. Take it from us, and the Bible, all history, all science, all government, all commerce, and nearly all social intercourse, go with it." Literacy, the boy decided, was the crucial distinction between white society and red. And books, he resolved, were what would distinguish this southern Indiana boy. It became a kind of corollary to his earlier vow: he wouldn't hunt; he would read.

"Diligent for knowledge" is how his stepmother described him. His stepsister was a little more pointed: "Abe was not Energetic Except in one thing—he was active & persistent in learning—read Everything he Could." And Dennis Hanks was blunt: "Lincoln was lazy—a very lazy man—He was always reading—scribbling—writing—Ciphering—writing Poetry, etc. etc."

His parents were mostly good about it. Thomas Lincoln, his wife recalled, "could read a little [and because] he himself felt the uses and necessities of education, [he wanted] his boy Abraham to learn & encouraged him to do it in all ways he could." But the stepmother was the one who felt strongly about it: "I induced my husband to permit Abe to read and study at home as well as at school . . . [W]e took particular care when he was reading not to disturb him—would let him read on and on till he quit on his own accord." The boy immersed himself in her books, rereading them, memorizing passages for the way they sounded, or the wisdom, or the jokes. It was, by all reports, an intense, single-minded education.

Why?

Why go contrary to the frontier life, separate himself from the other kids, get labeled lazy? What exactly was the hunger? And what was the point of his education?

Years later, he was asked something along these lines. It was about his ability at public speaking, "this unusual power of 'putting things.' No man has it by nature alone. What," the fifty-one-year-old Lincoln was asked, "has your education been?"

"I can say this," he answered, "that among my earliest recollections, I remember how, when a mere child, I used to get irritated when anybody talked to me in a way I could not understand. I don't think I ever got angry at any thing else in my life. But that always disturbed my temper and has ever since."

It was *not* knowing that got to him. Having people talk over his head. Being left out of the conversation.

"I can remember going to my little bedroom, after hearing the neighbor's talk, of an evening, with my father, and spending no small part of the night walking up and down, and trying to make out what was the exact meaning of some of their, to me, dark sayings. I could not sleep, though I often tried to, when I got on such a little hunt after an idea, until I had caught it."

Like tracking an animal. He'd sworn off that, but there was this: this hunt for ideas.

"[A]nd when I thought I had got it, I was not satisfied until I had repeated it over and over, until I had put it in language plain enough, as I thought, for any boy I knew to comprehend. This was a kind of passion with me, and it has stuck by me."

It was more than just catching the idea. He needed to put it back into language: to be able to share it. The hunt started with being left out of the conversation and wasn't over till he'd brought this dark thing—this idea—into the community. That was his passion. And that led to a specific kind of education.

School was part of it. He was back during the winter of his thirteenth year, studying with a new teacher. He may have stayed in class as long as six months this time. And he also read at home. His stepmother had brought a copy of Noah Webster's grammar and a couple of anthologies: *Lessons in Elocution* and Murray's *English Reader*. The elocution lessons were divided into reading and speaking sections and included poems by Shakespeare, Milton, Pope, and Gray. In a region without many libraries, it gave a portable sampling of classic literature. And it emphasized the idea that being able to "put things" in public was part of learning. Sally Bush Lincoln recalled how the boy "made speeches such as interested him" and which would so distract and amuse the boys around him, that "his father had to make him quit sometimes."

Murray's *English Reader* sampled world literature, too, with an explicit moral purpose: "promoting piety and virtue" and placing "religion in the most amiable light." By the time he was fourteen, Abe was a sexton at the Little Pigeon Baptist Church, but it seems to have meant more to him as a social occasion and a paying job than as religious training. Per his stepmother, he never took the Bible to be "the revelation of God." But he liked the way the preacher would "read his text and preach and pound." The boy got to where he could mimic the sermons "word for word," fascinated by the rhetoric, the rise and fall of persuasion.

In that sense, there was little difference between a sermon, a tall tale, and a dirty joke—and the boy performed them all. According to one author, Abe had, "from an early age, a notorious fountain of tasteless stories." The lanky kid in the badly fitting clothes could attract a crowd by reciting the poetry of Robert Burns, or telling the one about "Governor Tickner his city bread son & his Negro Bob." One friend thought Abe's "Great passion for dirty Stories" came from "his Early training by the Hanks Boys" and that later, as an adult, "he commenced a different train of thought and Studdie." But his pleasure in telling tales, dirty and clean, on the stump and off, was lifelong. He didn't so much lose his fascination with a punch line as extend its application. The myth of Lincoln, as one scholar puts it, is the guy who scribbled the Gettysburg Address spontaneously on the back of an envelope: "a democratic muse unacquainted with the library." The reality was a boy who had started studying how to turn a phrase early on, in school and out.

As a teenager, Abe worked for neighbors, cutting cord wood and making fences, the wages going back to his family. "I was raised to farm work" was his description. To make a rail fence, he took that most useful instrument, the ax, and chopped down young ash or oak or walnut: saplings maybe ten feet tall and four inches across. Then he limbed them and, with a maul, drove iron wedges into the green trunks till they split in quarter sections. Then he'd build a fence, as the settlers put it, "horse high, bull strong, pig tight." A good worker could drop a hundred trees a day, sunrise to sunset, and produce four hundred feet of rails. For that, the young rail-splitter made twenty-five cents. It was work he was raised to: his present, and, supposedly his future.

He fought it. Go through the reminiscences collected from neighbors, and time after time they picture him bent over a book: whether out in the fields, at home by firelight, or riding to the mill. "He worked for me," one farmer recalled, "but was always reading and thinking. I used to get mad at him for it. I say he was awful lazy . . . He said to me one day that his father taught him to work; but never taught him how to love it." It's a joke with an edge. What Thomas Lincoln had helped teach his son to love was books: a lesson the father may have regretted. Notes from an interview with Dennis Hanks, anyway, seem to confirm that: "Mr. Lincoln—Abs father—often said had to pull the old sow up to the trough—when speaking of Abes reading & how he got to it, then and now he had to pull her away."

The boy wasn't about to be pulled away. He'd work through whatever books he could lay his hands on, copying down lines that interested or confused him. Then, his stepmother recalled, he'd test them out loud, "always bringing them to me and reading them. He would ask my opinion of what he read, and often explained things to me in his plain and simple language." Later, he'd tell a biographer, "I catch the idea by two senses, for when I read aloud I *hear* what is read and see it . . . and I remember it better." If anything, the teenager grew more intense about his education. "He must understand everything," Sally remembered, "even to the smallest thing—minutely and exactly, he would then repeat it over to himself again and again—some times in one form and then in an other and when it was fixed in his mind to suit him he . . . never lost that fact or his understanding of it." How Lincoln learned to read at this level was also at home: slowly, out loud, often before an audience.

His last winter in school was when he was fifteen. Azel Dorsey was Abe's most trained teacher, especially good in math. Dorsey was the first treasurer of Spencer County. He taught simple and compound interest, fractions, geometry, multiplication and division, as well as reading and writing. The teenager took to math as another way to talk about order, to hunt meaning and make it plain to others. A few years later, he'd expand on these basic skills to become a surveyor, laying grids across the wilderness.

Abe's formal schooling ended there. He'd later say all of it "did not amount to one year." But for a pioneer education, five winters of attendance—spanning ages six to sixteen—was considerable. Now, he'd spend the equivalent of his high school years testing what he'd learned and adding new skills. Near the crossroads that led down to Rockport, James Gentry ran a local store. Abe got a job there. The store didn't amount to more than a "small stock of goods," but it meant the boy could get his hands on the *Sangamon Journal*, the *Louisville Journal*, and the *St. Louis Republican*, among others. By this time, there were sixteen newspapers being published in Indiana alone.

Between waiting on customers, he would have read about the controversial presidential election of 1824. Because Andrew Jackson received the most popular votes but not a majority of the electoral ones, the decision was thrown into the House of Representatives. Three days before Abe's sixteenth birthday, John Quincy Adams was named president. General Jackson called it the stolen election, and in Indiana, where the military hero was the overwhelming favorite, the outcome seemed to confirm an elite New England prejudice against frontiersmen. The teenager in the corner store wasn't so sure. He didn't like Jackson's support of slavery. Maybe, more important, he wasn't convinced by Jackson's position that a little government was a little too much. Power at the federal level, General Jackson claimed, was "an engine for the support of the few at the expense of the many." It destroyed that pioneer spirit of independence and individuality.

The Indiana boy pored over what was happening, nationally and locally, to where a friend and early biographer would claim, "Mr. Lincoln's education was almost entirely a newspaper one." He compared what he read to what he saw around him: the frontier's pressing need for improvements like roads, canals, railroads. Settlers could continue to do what the Lincolns had always done: consume and discard land, then push west. But one day the frontier had to end. And then people would need to know how to stay where they were. As Abe would one day lecture his stepbrother: "What can you do in Missouri better than here? . . . If you intend to work, there is no better place than right where you are; if you do not intend to go to work, you can not get along any where. Squirming & crawling about from place to place can do no good."

The lanky teenager reading papers in the local store was only about five years from his first run for office. At twenty-three, he'd campaign on a platform that championed "the public utility of internal improvements." If people were going to stop squirming, were going to develop from pioneer to resident, they'd have to agree on shared goals and pool their resources to accomplish them. Lincoln was heading toward his eventual definition of government: "a combination of the people of a country to effect certain objects by joint effort. The legitimate object of government is to do for a community of people, whatever they need to have done, but can not do, at all, or can not so well do, for themselves."

One thing he decided they couldn't do as well on their own was schooling. Education, he'd declare during his first run for office, is "the most important subject which we as a people can be engaged in." Every man, he thought, ought to receive "at least, a moderate [one]" so that "he may duly appreciate the value of our free institutions . . . to say nothing of the advantages and satisfaction to be derived from all being able to read the scriptures." Finally, sounding like a student of Noah Webster, he saw education as a way to make "morality, sobriety, enterprise and industry . . . much more general than at present." He'd done a lot of his learning outside school, but he saw a public education system as key to establishing order and civilization. By the time the boy was working at the Gentry store, the rich Indiana topsoil was already beginning to blow away. If windbreaks and crop rotation were what settlers needed to stop erosion, school was what they needed to hold on to their social institutions.

The summer of his seventeenth year, Abe lived down near Rockport, where he helped run a ferry service on the Ohio River. As well as poling passengers over and back, he plowed his boss's fields, slaughtered his hogs, and split rails in what he'd later call "the roughest work a young man could be made to do." The teenager on his way to becoming a politician also found time to visit local courtrooms, read *The Revised Laws of Indiana*, and study "our free institutions." He'd already found patriotic heroes in Noah Webster's primer; around this time, he delved deeper by borrowing popular biographies of Franklin and Washington. "I recollect thinking then," he'd write, "boy even though I was, that there must have been something more than common that those men struggled for." One day, he ferried two travelers out to catch a steamboat, and from high above him on the railing, they each tossed down a fifty-cent piece. "I could scarcely believe my eyes as I picked up the money . . . The world seemed wider and fairer before me." That was part of what he was struggling for: to enter a world of steamboats and industry, where men had money in their pockets and made it with a pen, not an ax.

It's tempting to call this his graduation: seventeen, the coins in his hand, his education behind him and the world ahead. He already knew how to hunt down an idea, stubbornly and tirelessly. He'd go on to drill himself in English grammar, learn surveying, and eventually study and practice the law. He'd leave the gloomy frontier behind and become one of those educated men who knew how to work the system, the kind landowners hired, the kind his father could never afford. But this doesn't quite count as his graduation from Little Pigeon Creek. He'll return for two more years, adding a last phase to his education.

There's a clue to what he still needed to know in the newspapers he was busy reading. "Every school boy in the Union," the *Indiana Centinel* editorialized, "now knows Tecumseh was a great man." Calling him "a statesman, a warrior and a patriot," the paper went on: "[Tecumseh's] greatness was his own, unassisted by the science or the aids of education." It must have been a startling lesson for Abe: as if the Lincoln family legend was gradually being rewritten. The Shawnee who had shot his grandfather was becoming the hero, admired because he *wasn't* civilized, for his *lack* of education. As the wilderness was plowed under, as the nation voted for Andrew Jackson, the Indian killer, it embraced Tecumseh as a symbol of what had been lost. For a boy fascinated with politics, the lesson was worth some study. In effect, he needed to know how an educated man appealed to those who believed in the uneducated, the self-made, the natural.

He'd already learned some of the necessary skills in Little Pigeon Creek. He could look up from reading a biography of Washington and tell a long, crowd-pleasing, dirty joke. In fact, the biographies helped teach him the technique. The most popular life of Washington, for example, emphasized how the father of the country had "no chance of ever rising in the world but by his own merit." It painted Washington as a typical American with a blab school education; he learned the four Rs but nothing so upper class as

Latin. The new nation grew its own heroes; formal schooling struck many as elitist and vaguely British.

By this time, Franklin's *Autobiography* had emerged as the classic model for American self-education, and the boy read it more than once. In his own first attempt at autobiography, Lincoln would describe his education with one word: "defective." Later, he'd expand a little. Where he grew up, there were "some schools, so called; but no qualification was ever required of a teacher beyond 'readin, writin, and ciperin' to the Rule of Three. If a straggler supposed to understand latin happened to sojourn in the neighborhood, he was looked upon as a wizzard. There was absolutely nothing to excite ambition for education. Of course, when I came of age I did not know much," Lincoln concluded, adding, "I have not been to school since."

One historian calls Lincoln's image as an unschooled rail-splitter a "performance" that amounted to "high art." During his lifetime, observers regularly noted that his success from "such restricted and unpromising opportunities . . . will always be a matter of wonder to the American people." The "log cabin myth," as it's been called, confirmed not only Lincoln's genius but the country's. As one of his contemporaries put it, "[N]one but a government like ours could produce such a man." When Abe was nineteen, he watched the power of this appeal help Andy Jackson come back and defeat the incumbent, President Adams. And when he was thirty, he'd see it work for that other Indian fighter, William Henry Harrison. The man who defeated Tecumseh had grown up the rich son of a plantation owner. But he'd get elected president by polishing the image of "a plain, simple backwoodsman content to sit rocking on the porch of his log cabin, and thinking long, homely thoughts about old-fashioned frontier virtues."

Lincoln would establish his own credentials as an Indian fighter by enlisting in the Black Hawk War (though he never saw action). And he'd learn how to emphasize how plain his boyhood had been. Asked to supply a biography when running for president, he'd declare it "a great piece of folly to attempt to make anything out of me or my early life. It can all be condensed in to a single sentence, and that sentence you will find in Gray's *Elegy*, 'The short and simple annals of the poor.' " By then, he'd mastered his approach. He'd learned how to present himself as a common, unschooled man—and do it while quoting poetry: Franklin's old trick of dropping citations even as he ridiculed the practice. And instead of stopping at the single sentence, Lincoln would then go on to provide a narrative that underlined his lack of schooling: "He was never in a college or academy as a student, and never inside of a college or academy till since he had a law license. What he has in the way of education he has picked up."

This "picked up" education ends on the same river where, fifty-cent pieces in hand, he'd imagined the wider world. It's a couple years later. He's nineteen, and instead of a skiff, he's in a sixty-five-foot flatboat. His only sister, Sarah, has died in childbirth; he's been living in the Little Pigeon Creek cabin with just his father, stepmother, and one stepbrother. James Gentry, owner of the corner store, has offered him a chance to take this flatboat down to New Orleans to trade produce. There, he'll visit his first big city and have his first look at mass slavery: black people chained together for auction, "as I have never seen them in Kentucky." Pushing away from Rockport, he's leaving his pioneer education and the depressing wilderness behind. From now on, he'll spend more time in a landscape of courthouses, banks, and libraries.

"[I]t is universally admitted," the governor of Indiana declares around this time, "that the earth was designed for improvement and tillage"; that's why "civilized communities" have the right to appropriate the land of "uncultivated savages." And as the flatboat catches the current and spins downriver, there's the result: the bustling town of Rockport built on limestone cliffs that were once a Native American burial site. Here's what learning and progress can lead to: a permanent improvement, built by joint effort.

As the teenager pushes off, as he graduates, does he take one last look at the Indiana riverbank? If so, he probably sees what one history of the area describes as a common sight on this stretch of shoreline. From the limestone cliffs beneath the county seat, "[n]umerous skeletons are being constantly disclosed by the action of the river. Thighbones, skulls with teeth and the heavier bones well-preserved are often . . . partially revealed . . . or washed . . . wholly out."

THOCMETONY

Picture a little domed schoolhouse: no more than a tent, really, made of thatched grasses tied to a willow frame. It's floating just above the desert in western Nevada and out of it come peals of laughter.

Inside, the forty-year-old instructor, Sarah Winnemucca Hopkins, has been teaching a couple of dozen Paiute children basic English. When she says "down," they all drop to the sandy ground. When she says "up," they grab the willow framing and lift the entire structure into the air, then dissolve into giggles.

This is the Peabody Indian School: the culmination of Sarah's education. Or, rather, of her two educations. It's named after Elizabeth Peabody, a woman then in her eighties whom the novelist Henry James described as "the last survivor of New England's heroic age." Peabody had been a key figure in Boston's transcendentalist circle, friend to Ralph Waldo Emerson, first publisher of Thoreau's "Essay on Civil Disobedience," an abolitionist, and an educational reformer who helped lead the successful movement to establish kindergartens in the United States.

It was Peabody who had arranged for Sarah to lecture throughout the Northeast as Princess Winnemucca: a full-blooded Northern Paiute dressed in beaded buckskin, a gold crown on her head, and an embroidered cupid dangling from her waist. "Oh, for shame!" she'd tell her New England audiences. "You who are educated by a

Christian government in the art of war . . . Yes, you who call your-selves the great civilization . . . I am crying out to you for justice,— yes, pleading for the far-off plains of the West, for the dusky mourner."

And it was Peabody—with the help of her equally distinguished sister, Mary Peabody Mann—who had gotten Sarah to write her au-tobiography: *Life Among the Piutes: Their Wrongs and Claims.* The book and the lectures had helped turn Princess Winnemucca into a na-tional spokeswoman for Native American rights. "In the history of the Indians," the San Francisco *Morning Call* wrote, "she and Poca-hontas will be the principal female characters."

But the Peabody Indian School was the great dream. Run not on a reservation but on Sarah's brother's farm in Lovelock, Nevada, it would integrate the Paiutes into white civilization *and* preserve Indian culture. "A few years ago," Sarah wrote the parents of her students, "you owned this great country; today the white man owns it all, and you own nothing. Do you know what did it? Edu-cation. You see the miles and miles of railroad, the locomotive, the Mint in Carson where they make money. Education has done it all," she continued. "Now, what it has done for one man it will do for another."

The Peabody Indian School was the western outpost of a battle the New England sisters had been fighting since before Sarah was born. Elizabeth Peabody had taught at Boston's first "open" school, encouraging students' creativity, opposing what she called the "steam-engine system" of cramming them with facts. Mary Peabody had married the leader of the national movement to create free com-mon schools, Horace Mann. Mann believed education was "the great equalizer . . . the balance-wheel of the social machinery." It would, "by enlarging the cultivated class or caste . . . do more than all things else to obliterate factitious distinctions in society."

In 1837, in the midst of a national economic crisis, the Massa-chusetts State Board of Education had appointed Horace Mann its secretary. By then, farms in the Northeast had begun to disappear. In their place came factories and industrialization, as Massachu-setts took over England's manufacturing role. Huge linen mills had sprung up to process Southern cotton. While farm families left for the West, immigrants rushed in to take the factory jobs. By the end of the 1840s, Irish workers had helped increase the state's population by some 30 percent. "In Horace Mann's lifetime," as one observer put it, "Massachusetts had acquired a proletariat."

It wasn't an easy acquisition. Just before he took office with the Board of Ed, Mann witnessed what he called "a riot of almost unheard-of atrocity" between the old-guard Protestants and the new Boston Irish. Somehow, Mann argued, these low-paid, badly housed foreigners needed to be incorporated into the American dream. His solution was a lot like the one Noah Webster had proposed down in New York: to establish common schools that taught, in Mann's words, the "common virtues" and the "common basis of our political faith." Education was the way to turn the relationship between the classes from "antagonistic" to "fraternal." Even those who disagreed had begun to see the practical advantages of state-run education. Workers who went to school, as one factory owner told Mann, had "a higher and better state of morals, [were] more orderly and respectful in their deportment, and more ready to comply with the wholesome and necessary regulations of an establishment."

By the time Sarah Winnemucca was a toddler, half the states in the union had common schools, with 45 percent of America's children attending. The nation was pursuing Horace Mann's motto "*Train up a child in the way he should go, and when he is old he will not depart from it.*" Elizabeth Peabody believed in a gentler, more transcendental way of reaching the same goal: "When a child has been led to enjoy his intellectual life, in any way, and then is made to observe whence his enjoyment has arisen, he can feel and understand the argument of duty."

There it is: the floating school. The giggling pleasures of learning would lead children to what they needed to know: the argument of duty. If it could work for Irish immigrants, why couldn't it work for Northern Paiute? Princess Winnemucca was the test case and the model. If the school did its job—if it floated—it confirmed that she'd learned what she needed to know. As she wrote Mrs.

Peabody: "I attribute the successes of my school not to my being a scholar and a good teacher but because I am my own Interpreter, and my heart is in my work." The key, then, was being able to stand in both civilizations—to learn this specific, capitalized role of Interpreter.

It began as an education in survival.

The Great Basin, where the Paiute had lived since A.D. 1000, consists of two hundred thousand square miles of arid, mountainous land. The prevailing westerly winds come off the Pacific Ocean and leave what moisture they carry in the Sierra Nevada. East of there, the smaller mountains of the Great Basin might get two feet of rain a year. In the desert valleys, it's more like eight inches, and summer temperatures often reach a hundred degrees. Runoff from the mountains and natural springs help feed what rivers there are, all of which dry out and disappear in the gray-green landscape of sagebrush and sand. The river now known as the Truckee starts at Lake Tahoe and flows down through Reno till it ends about forty miles away at Pyramid Lake. The one called the Humboldt River comes from the east—from the direction of Salt Lake City—and ends in the dry lands at Humboldt Sink, where Sarah was born around 1844. Except she wasn't Sarah then, or Princess Winnemucca; she was Thocmetony, "shell flower."

Across the Great Basin, each band of a hundred or so Paiute identified itself by the food in its region. So, around Humboldt Sink was the ground squirrel band; another lived primarily off jackrabbits; and at the 350-foot-deep Pyramid Lake, there was a spring run of sucker fish—*Chasmistes cujus*, or cuiui—which gave Thocmetony's band its name. The Paiute's constant search for protein meant they migrated in a fairly predictable pattern. It was this cycle that made up the core curriculum of Thocmetony's first education: learning where, when, and how to find enough food to survive.

Since Thocmetony was born at the Humboldt Sink, it was probably in August. That's when her band was down near the shallow marshes, living off the small red buck berries that grew there. Her mother would have walked through the thorny thickets, knocking the branches and catching the berries in a carefully woven basket. Her children—two boys and a girl—would have been with the pregnant woman, eating the tart berries as they walked. Most of the harvest, she'd take back to camp, where she'd press some through a small woven sieve to make a sugarless sauce and sun-dry the rest for the coming winter. During the days, her husband hunted robins and the other birds that came for the berries—or the bobcats that came for the birds. At night, when great horned owls called in the brush, the old women would tell their ghost stories. Those weren't owls; they were demons! They flew through the night carrying the kind of big, conical baskets all Paiute women traveled with, except the owl demons' baskets had a spike at the bottom so they could skewer and eat bad little children. And which were those? The ones who cried or made too much noise. The Paiute depended on stealth and patience to find food; they began teaching their children the value of stillness early on.

After Thocmetony's birth, her father, Winnemucca, would have stopped hunting and stayed home for the good part of a month to let Tuboitonie, her mother, rest. Then it was time for the piñon harvest. These small, almost see-through pine nuts could only be found high up in the mountains. When scouts came back with the first of the year's crop, the band would have an all-night dance. They'd move in a tight circle, shoulder to shoulder, singing and praying for a big harvest. One of the grandmothers would scatter some of the nuts outside the circle because, as one anthropologist has put it, "the Indian believed that whenever they took something from the earth they were obliged to give back something in return." Survival in the desert was too tenuous not to believe: in prayer, luck, spirits—whatever might help you get through the coming winter.

Thocmetony would eventually learn the complicated, communal skill of harvesting and preparing the piñons. That first year, she probably went into the mountains wrapped in a rabbit-skin blanket and tied with soft, buckskin thongs to a little willow cradle. Once they got up into the forest, the men climbed the scrubby pines and shook down the cones. Extended families of cousins and in-laws walked through this rain, helping to fill the women's baskets. It was social, intense, dawn-to-dusk work. In a good year, a family tried to put away a thousand pounds of pine nuts, each no bigger than an olive pit.

During those first few years, the baby would roll naked on a bed of pine needles or teeth on a peeled stick. But soon Thocmetony's grandmothers and aunts would begin to show her how to use the tiny nuts. The making of piñon soup was a woman's skill and duty. In a broad winnowing tray, you gently roasted the nuts by bouncing them together with hot coals. Then you cracked the hulls, grinding them with a smooth, cylindrical rock. Scooping the mixture back into the tray, you separated out the nuts by blowing or letting the wind hit at just the right angle to carry off the hulls. After roasting the nuts again, you winnowed one more time and then ground the meat into a fine, creamy-gray flour. The flour was stored till it was time to add water and whatever protein could be found—bits of bird or squirrel, a handful of ants—to make a thick, nutritious soup.

In November, after the piñon harvest, the band headed back down into the desert for the rabbit hunt. The men wove hemp stalks into hundreds of feet of netting, which was then strung among the sagebrush. The women and children marched across the desert, driving the rabbits into the mesh. There were feasts then, while the women dried and stored the surplus for winter. The Paiute wore only a piece of hide at their waists, adding rabbit-pelt blankets to protect them against the cold. It took a hundred skins to make an adult's blanket, forty to make a child's.

Before the snows started, the cuiui band would set up camp by Pyramid Lake. Most of the year, as they traveled, Thocmetony's family lived in temporary shelters, pulling together the branches of sagebrush to get out of the wind and sun. At Pyramid, the women built more-permanent structures, erecting a willow pole frame and covering the small dome with cattail mats. Thocmetony spent her winters in one of these shelters, a *karnee*: the smoke from a small fire escaping through the hole in the top of its dome, her mother weaving willow baskets and preparing meals, her father out hunting small rodents or trying his luck with the antelope herds. If he could bring in enough meat, and if the women had packed away enough nuts and dried fish and berries, they'd survive to see the spring.

Sometimes you came back to the same karnee the next winter and rethatched it; sometimes you started over from scratch. Home, after all, wasn't a building. Home was larger than that: the whole shifting landscape of desert, river, and mountain as the band cycled through it.

Mid-February, the ground squirrels came out of hibernation and were hunted with bow and arrow. By March, birds began arriving from the south: Canada geese, mallards, curlews, killdeer. The call of the huge flocks signaled spring. Women waded out into the cold waters, yanked out the first pale cattail shoots, and fed them to their children, who waited on shore in their rabbit-skin blankets. Once the ground thawed, old and young dug for roots and nibbled seeds from the few bushes on the sand hills. They'd search the shore for duck and goose eggs, while the men hunted from small reed boats.

April and May were when the cuiui and the cutthroat trout ran. In a good year, the men speared fish by the hundreds, tossing them up on the banks for the women to split and clean with sharp rocks. Huge bonfires burned along the shore, and everyone gorged themselves: the fat, greasy children toddling around camp, the women exchanging a winter's worth of news, the gulls fighting for what little the Paiutes threw out. Stacks of cuiui were dried and stored away in nearby caves.

In June and July, the hard-shelled seeds of the wild rice had to be threshed, singed, and husked. Pollen from the cattails, mixed with water, could be baked into dry cakes: supplies for the long treks across the desert. And then it would be August again, and time to push through the thorns for the buck berries. It was a regular cycle, adjusted a little each year depending on where and when food was available. Archaeological digs in the caves around Pyramid Lake show a stable population of Native Americans lived on this same basic diet for some three thousand years.

Thocmetony's hands-on education had begun as soon as she

could walk. Her classroom was the family camp; her first teachers probably her aunts and grandmothers; and the curriculum traditional. "Basically," as one anthropologist has put it, "women worked with plants, clothing and children."

In this education, the "argument of duty" was clear: you needed to know certain things to survive. Along with that came a set of values. There was no sense, for example, in accumulating possessions: dragging them along only lowered your chances of finding food. A particularly well-shaped grinding rock might be stuck in the branches of a piñon tree for next year, but most of what you had was disposable. You learned to weave a quick, light basket to carry home duck eggs, then threw it in the fire when you got back to camp. At the end of your life, whatever you owned was burned along with your body.

While some Paiute had specialized skills—Thocmetony's father organized antelope hunts, for example—it was mostly a common school education to prepare you for the common search for food. Paiute society reflected that: there was no chief. A council of men and women made the occasional group decision, but mostly the families fanned out across the desert, each fending for itself. You depended on other members of your band to get you through the lean times, sharing caches of fish or nuts, with the understanding that the generosity might be returned the next winter. And there were shared activities like the rabbit hunt. But the main unit was the immediate family: parents and offspring. "They not only take care of their children together," Thocmetony wrote of Paiute husbands and wives, "but they do everything together; and when they grow blind, which I am sorry to say is very common, for the smoke they live in destroys their eyes at last, they take sweet care of one another."

The Paiute didn't fight many large-scale battles; in her life, Thocmetony saw only one war dance. Each band tended to stay in its traditional region, coming together when there was a bonanza like a fish run or a rabbit hunt, otherwise avoiding contact and conflict. In Kentucky, the Shawnee the Lincolns confronted had regular skirmishes with other tribes; it's how young men proved themselves.

The Paiute's subsistence living didn't leave much room for that. A boy earned his manhood through a kill, but of an animal, not an enemy.

There were, of course, disputes: petty jealousies, quarrels between lovers, various competitions. One of the Paiute's great pleasures was gambling—at the piñon harvest, for example, when there was enough food and time to relax. Families bet against families, sometimes bands against bands, with hours spent dickering over the blankets and baskets and beads that each side anted up. Then, two players were picked. One did the hiding: a stick in each hand, one plain, one ornamented. The other tried to guess which was which. Meanwhile, the crowd would be singing and beating on logs to distract the players. It was a game of savvy and luck: something like the endless search for food in the desert. And the pleasure seems to have been in the playing. "Winners were never congratulated," one expert states, "nor were losers ever consoled"—which may have been a function of what was won and lost: ephemeral possessions.

Eighteen years before Thocmetony was born, back when her mother and father were kids, the first white man came into the Great Basin: a trapper looking to expand the fur trade west. Two years later, an expedition by the British Hudson's Bay Company "discovered" the river region that would be Thocmetony's birthplace. When her parents were not yet teenagers, another party of white men came through claiming to be trappers. But the United States Army captain on this expedition had "made arrangements to collect information" to help expand the U.S. frontier west. When the party came upon a group of "smiling, prancing, high-stepping Paiutes," they surrounded them and opened fire, killing thirty-nine. The next spring, on their way back past the Humboldt Sink, they killed fourteen more. Though the desert was next to worthless for farming and trapping, settlers had to pass through to get to Oregon and California. The Indians were seen as a potential threat—and expendable. As one of the early traders put it, they were "a groupe of the lowest & most degraded of all the savage hords of the west . . . All they had in the world was some dried rabbit-meat."

In 1844, the year Thocmetony was born, John Charles Frémont

led his second expedition out of Missouri looking for a river route to California. Coming down out of the arid mountains, the explorers happened on a dark green lake that "broke upon our eyes like the ocean." Around the lake (which Frémont would name Pyramid), he found "poor-looking Indians . . . still in the elementary state of families, living in deserts, with no other occupation than the mere animal search for food." Frémont didn't shoot them, but his guide, Kit Carson, paid forty dollars to buy an adolescent boy as his slave. When Frémont got back east, his account of California's natural wealth, of this strange desert where the rivers never reached the sea, and of the primitive "Asiatic" Indian bands became a bestseller. It helped bolster President James Polk in his "fixed determination to acquire California."

But there still wasn't a decent trail over the Sierra Nevada. Settlers followed the Humboldt River west till it dried up, then had to abandon their wagons—and kill their livestock—amid the "awful piles and hills of black, hard, basaltic rocks." They crossed the mountains on foot with what they could carry. In October, two months after Thocmetony was born, a wagon train led by Elisha Stevens arrived at the Humboldt Sink. There, they found a camp of hundreds of Indians they called Diggers because they were rooting around looking for plants and insects. "Indolent and degraded," according to the white men, this was almost certainly Thocmetony's band. The pioneers faced forty miles of desert and then the mountains. "Finally," they recorded, "an old Indian was found." He drew maps in the sand indicating a river to the west. The Stevens party took him as "guide and hostage," and he helped them become the first settlers from the east to bring wagons into California. They called their guide Captain Truckee—because they assumed the Paiute had captains and because he kept saying something that sounded like "truckee" (and turned out to be Paiute for "all right" or "okay"). He was Thocmetony's grandfather.

Truckee came back from California convinced these visitors were his "white brothers." When Frémont's next expedition turned into the United States' occupation and conquest of the West, Truckee went along. It may have shaken him to see how Americans treated other tribes. At Sutter's Fort, the large trading post on the Sacramento River, local Indians were first taught "fear and respect," then made to "do all the drudgery." But Truckee came away from the Mexican War carrying a signed letter of commendation, the first guns the Paiute owned, and tales of beautiful clothes, big cities, and giant ships. He knew enough English to sing "The Star-Spangled Banner." And he was convinced that the Paiute had to adjust to the coming of the settlers the same way they adjusted to changes in the annual fish run or the piñon crop. It was a matter of survival.

Thocmetony's father saw it differently. While Truckee was away in California, Winnemucca had the same dream three nights in a row: a vision. "I looked North and South and East and West, and saw nothing but dust, and I heard a great weeping. I saw women crying, and I also saw my men shot down by the white people . . . I saw it as if it was real . . . [T]o avoid bloodshed," Winnemucca concluded, "we must all go back to the mountains during the summer." Here was the alternative: to keep completely separate from the new culture. To risk starvation by staying in the mountains even when the buck berries were ripe. Both survival strategies were risky, and the choice divided the band. But in Thocmetony's family, it was personal. To adapt or avoid was to choose between grandfather and father.

Many Paiute chose avoidance. But that became more and more difficult. By the time the Mexican War was over and the United States had officially taken control of Nevada, Brigham Young had led some four thousand Mormons to Salt Lake City on the east of the Paiute range. Truckee's pass through the mountains was now known as Donner's Pass, after the party that had tried to get through it in the winter of 1846. Like the Lincolns, the Donners had started their family migration in North Carolina, moved to Kentucky and then Indiana, and had even lived in Springfield, Illinois, when Abe was getting his career started there. But the Donners had decided to continue on to the promise of California. Their horrific end—snowbound in Truckee's pass, forced to turn to cannibalism—was known to everyone in the area. It confirmed the Paiute's worst fears. Thocmetony's father had always said the settlers looked like huge owls, with "hair on their faces, and . . . white eyes." The story of the Donner party served as proof: these were boogiemen, owl demons.

So, most Paiute tried to stay away. When Thocmetony was around five, she was in a group of foraging women and children that discovered it had wandered near a wagon train. Everyone ran. But the little girl couldn't move very fast, and her mother was slowed down by having to carry Thocmetony's baby sister. The Paiute had a traditional strategy to cope with this kind of situation: they hid their children. "Let us bury our girls," Thocmetony's aunt suggested, "or we shall all be killed and eaten up." The adults quickly dug two holes, placed the girls up to their necks in the sand, stuck sagebrush around their heads to keep off the sun, and promising to be back at dusk, ran for their lives. The children had been trained to stay still, to blend into the desert. "Oh, can any one imagine my feelings," Thocmetony wrote years later, "*buried alive*, thinking every minute that I was to be unburied and eaten up by the people that my grandfather loved so much?"

Any hope that the Paiute could just stay out of the settlers' way ended that summer of 1849. Up until then, the migration west had been more push than pull. The national economy had been struggling for a dozen years, since the crisis of 1837. Over-industrialization, crop failures, and land speculation had led to banks reneging on their notes. A third of New York City's working class was left unemployed, prices shot up, and there was no effective federal brake on the inflation partly because President Andrew Jackson, in his less-government campaign, had done away with the Bank of the United States. The downward spiral continued through the 1840s, helping to push more and more wagon trains west. Then in early 1848, just as the economy started to recover, gold was discovered at Sutter's mill. About two thousand people had tried to cross the Nevada desert the year the Donner party was lost; after gold was found in California, twenty thousand "forty-niners" left Missouri—in the month of April alone. The banks of the Humboldt River became a rutted, primitive highway. As Thocmetony turned six, a survey of the desert where the river ended found over a thousand dead mules, nearly four thousand dead cattle, and 953 graves.

The next spring, when Thocmetony was about the age of a second grader, members of a wagon train killed her uncle, Truckee's son, and five other Paiute. Truckee refused to seek revenge. Weeping, he urged the Paiute to learn more about the white people's ways. And that fall, he insisted that his extended family make the trip to California with him. Thocmetony's father refused, but her mother agreed to go. And Truckee was determined his granddaughter would, too. It was, he believed, the only way she could learn what she needed to know.

The little girl resisted with everything she had. Like all Paiute children, she'd been trained to obey and never cry. Now she kicked, scratched, bit, wept. Even as the band of thirty started off, she begged her mother to "go back to father—let us not go with grandpa, for he is bad." Truckee was gentle but firm. His granddaughter was his "sweetheart . . . dying for fear of my white brothers." She'd see the truth. But when the seven-year-old came close to her first white man, she screamed. "Oh, mother, the owls!"

What seems to have attracted and fascinated Thocmetony from the beginning was what these owls possessed: their things. Early in the trip, her grandfather gave her a tin cup and explained what it was. When they got to Stockton, a bustling town of twenty-five hundred, the little girl couldn't sleep in her excitement over seeing her first steamboat. And she gorged on their cake made with something white and sweet. Still, the sight of settlers made her tremble.

The turning point came when she got a bad case of poison oak. Delirious with fever, Thocmetony lay on her rabbit-skin blanket day after day, her eyes too swollen to see. "At last some one came that had a voice like an angel," she recalled. Day after day, she kept hearing the angel's voice: "Poor little girl, it is too bad!" Or, rather, she heard soothing sounds that she later learned were words. When she was well enough to see her nurse: "The first thing she did she put her beautiful white hand on my forehead. I looked at her; she was, indeed, a beautiful angel." Truckee explained that this "white sister," who had once lost a little girl around Thocmetony's age, had been visiting daily, bringing medicine. "So," Thocmetony writes, "I came to love the white people." And with the owl demons transformed into angels, she wanted to enter their kingdom. Thocmetony immediately set out to learn English. Her grandfather translated what the angel had called her, and they became her first words: "poor little girl." Call it the start of her second education.

She didn't convert completely or instantaneously. That winter, the family stayed in California at a ferry crossing on the San Joaquin River. While her grandfather grazed livestock up in the foothills of the Sierra, he left the women and children behind "to learn," in Truckee's words, "how to work and cook." As Thocmetony was taught how a white woman kept house, she remained fascinated by their stuff: chairs and tables, cups and cooking pots. But California's gold rush was overwhelmingly male, from the prospectors to the workers at the ferry landing. And most of these men considered Paiute "squaws" suitable for only two things, one of which was housekeeping. "The men whom my grandpa called his brothers," Thocmetony writes, "would come into our camp and ask my mother to give our [older] sister to them." Her mother managed to keep them off. But along with English and cooking, Thocmetony was learning this reality, too. Years later, she'd announce that the real subject of her autobiography was "wrongs and claims." In it, she'd quote what her mother decided after living among the settlers: "They are not people; they have no thoughts, no mind, no love."

In the spring, Truckee's band returned to the Great Basin. There, they found the Paiute dead and dying. Asiatic cholera had spread from Sacramento through the mining camps into the karnees. The epidemic would cut the Northern Paiute population in half. Again, Thocmetony's father and grandfather had opposing explanations. Her father swore the settlers had poisoned the Humboldt River. "I cannot," Truckee said, "and will not believe my white brothers would do such a thing." Again, Thocmetony had to choose which lesson to learn.

The next four or five years—the rest of her elementary education—was taken up with traditional Paiute schooling. As she went from girl to teenager, she learned where to find seeds and roots, how to clean and dry fish, the best way to build shelter, and during the long winters, the art of weaving various kinds of willow baskets. Years later, Mary Peabody Mann would have the romantic notion that one day there would be a "fair exchange": in return for learning to read and write, Indians would teach whites their vast "knowledge of nature." But even as she learned the old skills, Thocmetony must have known—all the Paiute came to know—it barely made sense. She was getting an education in a way of life that had gone on for thousands of years and was ending in the span of her childhood.

Long lines of wagon trains now passed through the desert each summer. Their livestock ate all the wild rice; their drivers harvested the cattail for fodder. Stops along the California trail had turned into trading posts and were now becoming small towns. Mormon Station became Genoa; Eagle Station became Carson City. The piñon trees began to disappear, cut down for log cabins. Though the Paiute had horses by now, they couldn't compete with the guns and traps of white hunters; there was less and less game to get them through the brutal freeze of winter. The arrival of the white "Emigrant," as an agent for the Bureau of Indian Affairs reported, had so reduced the Paiute's subsistence economy that the natives only had a few, bad options: "They cannot hunt upon the territories of other tribes, except at the risk of their lives. They must therefore steal or starve."

Or adapt. That was the path, anyway, that Truckee continued to believe in. By the mid-1850s, there were still no more than two hundred white residents in what would one day be Nevada. Paiute picked off stray cattle as the emigrants passed through, did odd jobs at the trading posts, bartered trout for bread, and managed to survive. The settlers wanted to negotiate a treaty where the whites would go to the leader of the Paiute with their grievances and vice versa. Except the Paiute bands didn't have official leaders. Finally giving in, Thocmetony's father agreed to be called Chief Winnemucca and signed the treaty.

Truckee pushed his family to adapt even more. When

Thocmetony reached adolescence, her grandfather got her and her younger sister work in the little town of Genoa. Thocmetony writes that they were hired as "playmates" for an eight-year-old white girl, Lizzie Ormsby. Most likely, the term was used the same way it had been with Sojourner Truth. In return for room and board and the chance to learn English, the Indian playmates cooked, cleaned, and cared for the children. According to a California newspaper of the time, the well-mannered Paiute made the "best servants in America."

For her middle school years, then, Thocmetony transferred to a whole other kind of education. Her employer, William Ormsby, was a forty-niner who had left his family in Pennsylvania to join a wagon train west. Arriving in Sacramento, he'd helped establish the city's first private mint: using a sledgehammer on freshly dug ore to strike ten-dollar gold pieces. Two years later, he owned a ranch in the Russian River valley. Major Ormsby, as he was now calling himself, returned east to collect his family. He must have had a moneymaking scheme because he came back with a party of settlers and a hundred fine-boned Kentucky thoroughbreds. By the time he reached Salt Lake, only one horse was alive. And in a cemetery in Woods Cross, Utah, a grave marker dated 1851 reads, "Olive Cynthia Ormsby, Died March"—probably the major's infant daughter.

Six years later, when Thocmetony and her sister joined the household, the major was an ambitious speculator. Genoa consisted of about twenty houses and a hundred white people, all living behind a ten-foot-high stockade. The Ormsbys occupied a former tin shop, which is where Thocmetony found her new angel. Mrs. Ormsby was a very white-skinned, dark-haired, twenty-nine-year-old, who dressed in long, elegant gowns. She wanted her surviving daughter to know about the finer things and would eventually commission an oil portrait of her posing by a carved upholstered chair on an ornate rug. Without a school in Genoa, it was Mrs. Ormsby who taught her child how to read and write and behave like a lady—with the Indian "playmates" picking up what they could. "[W]e learned the English language very fast," Thocmetony would write, "for they were very kind to us." It was probably here that she started being called Sarah.

As this second education took hold, Sarah found herself between civilizations. On the one hand, the fourteen-year-old girl was getting invited to local dances to "make up the set." She was pretty, with bright eyes and a good figure, and she had Mrs. Ormsby as an example of how to behave. Soon, she became a minor celebrity in the frontier towns: Miss Sarah Winnemucca, the Paiute Princess. On the other hand, she was and would always remain an Indian. While she was living in Genoa, two white traders were murdered in the High Sierra. The killers tried to make it look like "the red devils" had done it, with arrows clumsily stuck into bullet wounds. Major Ormsby ordered the arrest of three natives, who were killed the next day by a lynch mob. When Sarah protested, even the kind Mrs. Ormsby maintained, "[M]y husband knows what he is doing."

As Sarah started the equivalent of her first year in high school, the Bureau of Indian Affairs began to "make some geographical explorations with a view of selecting suitable reservations." Major John Wesley Powell, the explorer of the Grand Canyon, was also the bureau's agent for the Southern Paiute. "Indians are begging for land," he wrote. "They say, fix it so that we can stay here, and so white men can not take this land from us and we can get a living for ourselves." Meanwhile, from the settlers' point of view, keeping the Diggers in one spot, instead of continually crisscrossing the Great Basin, would make development that much easier. And development—civilization—was the point. The Ormsbys, for example, bought building lots in newly laid-out Carson City, named for Frémont's former scout. It was still mostly sagebrush and sand, but the promoters said it was going to be the future capital of the future state of Nevada. The plan called for a big central plaza, and the Ormsbys bought right across from it.

The winter of 1858 was long and harsh, especially for the estimated sixteen hundred Paiute living near what Sarah referred to as "our Pine-nut mountains." That January, as the Indians fought starvation, prospectors began finding flecks of high-quality gold near Carson City. There was a rush on the area that spring. And then in the summer, word started to spread that the thick blue mud the prospectors were shoveling out of their gold mines was mostly silver. The Comstock Lode turned out to be five miles wide, twenty-five hundred feet deep, and worth three thousand dollars a ton. By the fall, as an agent for the Bureau of Indian Affairs put it, there was "a general stampede."

The first arrivals lived in tents, but there weren't enough to go around. Men started burrowing into the mountainside till it was dotted with smokestacks. The area saw its second straight tough winter, and a newspaper reported, "The Indians in Truckee Meadows are freezing and starving to death by scores." Settlers offered food, but many Paiute refused, convinced it had to be poison. In November 1859, the federal government set aside two tracts of land for Indian reservations: one southeast of Carson City on the Walker River and one that included Pyramid Lake. But many settlers continued to graze their cattle and plant crops inside the boundaries. Unable to forage, Indians on the reservation had to depend on the Bureau of Indian Affairs to provide food, which its agents commonly withheld and sold at a profit. Years later, when anthropologists collected oral histories from the Paiute in western Nevada, they reported that nearly all "portrayed white men as cannibals both of land and of the body."

Sarah was still trying to navigate between the two cultures. After leaving the Ormsbys, she started living in various mining towns. Here, she established a pattern that would continue the rest of her life. She'd get temporary work in the white economy—as a maid or a laundress—then return to the Paiute for the piñon harvest or the spring fish run. "I would rather be with my people," she eventually wrote, "but not to live with them as they live." While some of that came from her attraction to the white culture, it was also because there was no longer a way to live as a Paiute. It had proved fatal.

When Sarah was around fifteen, a traveler on the Humboldt River reported: "[a] strange but interesting woman visited our camp. She was a full blood Piute Indian woman, highly intelligent and educated and talked the English language fluently. She ate breakfast with me and became so interested in our conversation that she offered to travel with me, across the desert to Carson Valley. Her name was Sarah Winnemucca." It's hard to tell what role Truckee's grand-daughter is playing here. Is she guide to the white man? Camp follower? Interpreter? Whatever she does for him, the teenager has attached herself to the party and is presumably getting three meals a day. How else was she supposed to survive?

As soon as the weather broke that spring of 1860, the prospectors came out of their caves, and a rush of new arrivals crossed over from California. Soon, there would be six thousand white people in the Great Basin, making the Paiute, for the first time, a minority. The exploding population needed lumber for cabins, mills, and mine timbers: the demand was an estimated twenty thousand board feet a day. Soon, the pine nut mountains had been stripped. Sawdust clogged the Carson and Truckee rivers: banks of it, like sandbars, polluted the water and blocked the fish run.

As the Paiute gathered that May at Pyramid Lake, a messenger arrived. He brought the news, in Sarah's words, that "[t]wo little girls about twelve years old went out in the woods to dig roots, and did not come back." Their trails "led up to the house of two traders named Williams." It was the nightmare that Sarah's sister had barely escaped, that all Paiute women feared when they made contact with white culture. An Indian search party arrived at the traders' cabin and were told the girls hadn't been seen. They pushed in, and down in a crawl space, the girls' father found his children "lying on a little bed with their mouths tied up with rags. When my people saw their condition," Sarah writes, "they at once killed both brothers and set fire to the house."

Sarah's two worlds now crash together. Her own Major Ormsby leads the retaliatory strike. As his squad of a hundred or so men approached Pyramid Lake, the Paiute ambush them, killing more than seventy, including Ormsby. A month later, 750 militiamen arrive from California. Among them is John Ormsby, who discovers his brother's "badly mutilated" corpse and has it buried with full military honors. Depending on the source, the militia goes on to kill 4, or 40, or 140 Paiute.

Sarah probably retreated north into the Oregon desert with her father's band. There was sporadic violence in the Great Basin but never an open rebellion like Tecumseh had led; the Paiute were slowly and inevitably cornered. By the end of the summer, Sarah was back in the mountains of western Nevada, not far from the Comstock Lode, where her grandfather was dying.

Truckee's death marks the close of an era—and the end of Sarah's childhood education. She's about to turn sixteen. In a way, her grandfather's plan had worked. His granddaughter, his sweetheart, had gone from being terrified of the white owls to speaking fluent English. She was already one of the leading interpreters among the Northern Paiute, and on his deathbed, Truckee tried to get her even more schooling. He sent for a frontiersman named Snyder, a "dear beloved white brother," and made him promise to take Sarah and her sister to San Jose. There, Truckee said, a group of Belgian nuns had "promised to teach my two little girls." After this last request, Truckee turned to Sarah's father, Winnemucca. "[D]o your duty as I have done to your people and to your white brothers," he insisted. And then he died. "I crept up to him," Sarah wrote, years later. "I knelt beside him, and took his dear old face in my hands, and looked at him quite a while. I could not speak. I felt the world growing cold; everything seemed dark. The great light had gone out."

Truckee wanted his possessions burnt in the traditional Paiute ceremony, but he also instructed that a cross be placed on his grave. Sarah and her sister went to San Jose, but after three weeks, the white parents at the missionary school objected to their children sharing a classroom with Indians, and the girls had to leave.

On the way back to the Great Basin, Sarah would marry Truckee's white brother, Snyder: the first of her four marriages, three of which would be to white men. Far to the east, Lincoln had been elected president, the South had seceded from the union, and a war had begun. Apparently the nation was fighting over whether people who were considered non-white should also be considered citizens. In October 1864, Lincoln would declare Nevada a state, slave-free.

By then, Sarah would be making a living as Princess Winnemucca, part of a vaudeville show that toured the local mining towns. She'd come on right after the minstrel act and perform *tableaux vivants*: "The Coyote Dance" and "Taking a Scalp." The performances were no more accurate than her buckskin costume or gold crown, but they played to the audience's idea of the noble, doomed savage. Eventually, this would evolve into the lectures that made her famous: "eloquent," as the papers wrote, "pathetic, tragical at times . . . a spontaneous flow [that told] . . . the story of her race."

When violence flared between settlers and Paiute, Sarah would act as an interpreter for the U.S. Army. She'd stay from time to time on the reservations, sometimes working as a teacher's assistant. But like 90 percent of the Northern Paiute, she mostly lived elsewhere, believing the reservations encouraged a "listless dependency." In her first letter to the newspapers, published when she was twenty-six, she'd write, "If this is the kind of civilization awaiting us on the reserves . . . it is much preferable to live in the mountains and drag out an existence in our native manner."

But she couldn't do that either. She'd keep coming back into town, working as a matron at a hospital or a washerwoman. Sometimes, she'd sell native handicrafts to the whites. Sometimes, she'd join the other Paiute and beg at the train stations. Because of her marriage to a white man, her father would refuse to speak to her. And because her role as interpreter had made her the messenger for one too many false promises, many Paiute would come to distrust her. "We were only ashamed," she wrote, "because we came and told them lies which the white people had told us." Eventually, with the Peabody sisters as her patrons, she'd meet presidents and generals and speak in major cities across the country. But afterward, at age forty, she'd be back on the Pyramid Lake reservation, eating pine nuts and fish. On the one hand, she was furious at the Bureau of Indian Affairs: "Every one connected with the agency is wholly devoid of conscience." On the other, she felt betrayed and unappreciated by her own people: "[As the Paiute] are not disposed to stand by me in the fight, I shall relinquish it. As they will not help themselves, no one can help them . . . I have laboured to give my race a voice in the affairs of the nation, but they prefer to be slaves so let it be."

Then comes the dream of the floating school. She must have known it was an illusion, as impossible as the role of interpreter. But despite everything, she believes. This strange object, hovering above the horizon, exists in defiance of the sanctioned, federally funded Indian schools of the day. They were designed to take children from the Western tribes and move them to Eastern boarding schools, like Carlisle, where they'd be taught to forget the old traditions. As a Carlisle commencement speaker told the students: "You cannot become truly American citizens, industrious, intelligent, cultured, civilized until the INDIAN within you is DEAD."

Sarah's floating school fought that, trying to keep the traditional ways alive. But she also saw the future. "These are the days of civilization," Sarah told her Paiute parents. "We must all be good, sober and industrious and follow the example of our white brothers. We must become educated and give our children an education." It's Truckee's idea. And Horace Mann's: school as the great equalizer, society's balance wheel.

It floats for a year, then two. Visitors come to see the little Indian girls in their Mother Hubbard dresses, writing their names on the blackboard and reciting the days of the week. One observer admits she had to "rudely stare . . . when these seemingly ragged and un-tutored beings began singing *gospel hymns* with precise melody, accurate time, and distinct pronunciation."

And then, after four years, it's over. The Peabody Indian School is located on Sarah's brother's farm, and the nearby settlers resent the idea of a Paiute farmer. They let their cattle graze on his land; they cut off his access to the irrigation ditch. When the wheat harvest comes in, Sarah's white husband absconds with the profits. But more than that, her own people don't believe in this dream of education. An apocalyptic religion springs up among the Paiute. It promises that if they dance and pray long enough, the ghosts of the dead will rise, take back the world from the white people, and kill all Indians who speak English. Sarah calls the ghost dance religion "nonsense," but her students start to leave. Maybe schools work somewhere else, for other outsiders, making them civilized, teaching them how to survive. But the Paiute look at the model before them—the education of Thocmetony, the interpreter—and find it easier to believe in the return of the ancestors. The giggling and gospel singing end. The floating school drifts to the ground, closes. Two years later, Sarah's dead.

HENRY

"from seven on," Henry Ford wrote in a scribbled, uncorrected note to himself, "i had a mechanical turn." He was jotting down entries like these in little unlined books to try to make sense of his past, his education. How had he become Henry Ford?

"i made water wheels and steam engines."

Dearborn, Michigan was farming country: rich soil just eight miles west of Detroit. An ancient lake bottom, it still had a tendency to flood, so the farmers—like Henry's father, William—dug drainage and irrigation ditches. In one of these, Henry set up his first waterwheel.

"then at School," he went on, "where we drove a coffee grinder and ground Clay, which was verry Slow." The waterwheel was hooked through a system of wires and homemade drive rods to a coffee grinder that one of the boys (Henry?) must have appropriated from home. The serious first graders bent over the contraption, feeding it clay, adjusting the machinery. The payoff wasn't the end product—ground dirt, or if you put in gravel, sparks—but seeing the power transferred, seeing water work.

The grinder was too slow to stay fun. So, Henry notes, "then i got a ten gallon can made a furnace of Clay and brick bats Made turbine steam engine." The project was collaborative: "about ten of my school mates would go to the RR and pick up Cake to burn." Someone (Henry?) organized the boys to scavenge along the railroad tracks and keep the furnace fed with coal. Ford's sketch shows what looks like a popgun attached to the top as an exhaust and a tin pinwheel. The machine was set up by the fence in the corner of the school yard. "we never got over ten lbs of steam tho turbine ran very fast–three thousand RPM." This was a big improvement: fire, steam, and a humming pinwheel.

"the boiler finally blew up and scalded three of us, and i carry a scar on my cheeks today." Ford wrote this years later, as an internationally famous tycoon, a hero of the new industrial America. "it set the fence on fire and raised ned in general." Beneath the sketch of the steam engine, he adds the final proof of the machine's power: "Blew a piece thru my lip and a piece hit Robert Blake in the stomach–abdomen and put him *out*."

That's how he learned. That's how he became Henry Ford. At but not in school. In an essay called "Self-reliance" that Ford would read and reread as a kind of inspirational primer, Ralph Waldo Emerson wrote, "There is a time in every man's education when he arrives at the conviction . . . that imitation is suicide." That's how it happened, Ford explained to himself. He'd discovered what he needed to know not by being taught, by imitation, but by trial and error. Self-education. Experimentation. Enjoying–as much as anything–the stunning, explosive lessons of failure. "There is an immense amount to be learned," he wrote, "simply by tinkering."

Some biographers say Henry Ford was named for his father's younger brother: the one who left for the California gold rush and never came back. Others say it was his father's immigrant cousin: the Henry Ford who stayed in Dearborn and played in the fife and drum band. Either way, the boy was named after a member of the last generation of American settlers: the group that finished defining and then started filling in the nation's borders. This Henry was born July 30, 1863, only a few weeks after the Battle of Gettysburg. There, Detroit's Twenty-fourth Michigan Regiment sustained the largest loss of any Northern unit in the Civil War. Henry wasn't four months old when President Lincoln declared those deaths had not been in vain but would mark a "new birth of democracy." The recovering, reunited nation was about to launch the greatest industrial surge in its history.

Henry's father, William, had come over from Ireland in 1847: the twenty-year-old son of a tenant farmer. Like Andrew Jackson's family, the Fords settled in an already established community of friends and relatives. William's uncles had helped pioneer the region fifteen years earlier, and there were Fords on farms all around Dearborn. The town boasted a school, an improved plank road to Detroit, and—the era's true indicator of prosperity—a stop on the railroad line. With the help of relatives, Henry's grandfather immediately cleared and planted a farm. His son William brought in some extra cash as a carpenter with the Michigan Central, which was laying track toward Chicago. Although William was interested in the railroad and machinery in general, the duty of an eldest son lay with his father on the farm. And he believed in the argument of duty.

According to Henry's sister, he also believed that "the great miracle of America" was that a man "was his own boss" and "could own the land upon which he lived and worked." In his early thirties, William Ford and his brother purchased the family farm. The immigrant son became a prosperous, upstanding member of the community, sitting on local school boards and juries. Henry's father's ideal was as old as the nation: that the successful pursuit of happiness ended with the independent farmer; that was the model democratic citizen. William Ford was, in Abe Lincoln's words, the settler who stopped squirming and prospered. And he made a point of passing the lesson on to his offspring. "We children," Henry's sister wrote, "grew up with those memories of the pioneers . . . as our guide."

But if Henry's father is the measure, then the great miracle of America included marrying well. One of the largest land-holding families in the area lived near the Ford farm. Patrick O'Hearn had come from Ireland as a soldier in the British army, gone AWOL, and ended up marrying a well-off widow a dozen years his senior. Childless, they'd adopted a girl called Mary Litogot. William Ford had started working as a handyman over at the O'Hearn place when he was in his mid-twenties and Mary was ten or so. He watched her grow up and graduate from the local Scotch Settlement School, then married her. The newlyweds moved in with her parents. Then, with the O'Hearns' help, they built an eleven-room house for the extended family. Henry was born there, and that year the elderly O'-Hearns began deeding their property over to William.

As a result, Henry grew up in relative prosperity on a ninety-one-acre farm. The Fords raised grain and hay, bred sheep and cows, and kept both a peach and an apple orchard. Henry's childhood unfolded in a two-story white house surrounded by shade trees. Across the road were the orchards and the fenced-in vegetable garden and the cow barn. Stretching off into the distance, the wheat fields ended at a dark green windbreak: the last reminder of the virgin forest that had been cleared a generation before. This was where and how an American boy was supposed to grow up. As Emerson put it in his journal, "The farm the farm is the right school."

The right school for what?

Henry would later say, "for sanity of mind." But the country's economy was headed away from the vegetable garden and the cow barn. The year Henry was born, Michigan was still a patchwork of family farms loosely connected by a total of about eight hundred miles of railroad. By the time he was forty, it would be crisscrossed with ten thousand more miles of track. Lumber helped drive the expansion. Midwestern cities like Detroit and Chicago were adding acres of housing each year; whole towns were rising on the Western prairie, where trees were in short supply; and Eastern states had so depleted their forests that they had to find imports if they were going to keep building. Michigan, meanwhile, had what seemed like an inexhaustible supply of timber, especially white pine.

The problem was cutting it, milling it, and getting it to market. Two years before the California gold rush, Michigan shipped east its first load of boards finished on a steam-driven mill. The rig must have looked like an enlarged version of Henry's school yard turbine: an engine off one of the Great Lakes' steamboats had been

refitted to power big circular blades. While the gold rush was drawing men west, profits from that bonanza turned out to be worth an
estimated billion dollars *less* than what Michigan's lumber industry
generated. By 1854, Saginaw was milling sixty million board feet of
pine. And by the time Henry was six, Michigan would be the leading source of lumber in the nation and would stay the leader for the
next thirty years.

Lumber needed railroads to get to market. Railroads helped turn
Detroit into an industrial center. In 1853, the city manufactured the
first freight cars built west of the Alleghenies. In the two decades after Henry was born, Detroit's Michigan Car Company churned out
nearly fifty thousand railroad cars at one of the largest factories in
the nation. And the trains hauled other resources. Beneath the white
pines, Michigan discovered huge iron ore and copper ranges. Starting in 1860, copper became Detroit's biggest export. The Detroit
and Lake Superior Copper Company built the largest smelter in the
world; nearby Wyandotte constructed the first Bessemer steel plant
in America. The year before Henry's birth, a hundred fifteen thousand tons of ore shipped out of the city. By the next year, that figure
had more than doubled. Soon, floating drydocks, shipyards, and repair shops lined the Detroit River. Here, locals designed and built
massive iron ore boats, their turbines dwarfing anything used by the
railroads. A boy growing up in Dearborn lived on the outskirts of
the future, a half-day's walk from what was about to happen. No
wonder the kids in Henry's school yard wanted to tinker with steam
engines.

"My mother always said," Ford wrote, "I was a born mechanic."
Mary Litogot O'Hearn Ford had grown up on a farm. Though
she'd gone to school and enjoyed reading, her duties as a housewife
weren't that different from what had been expected in Abigail
Adams's day. She was in charge of the cooking, washing, cleaning,
sewing, weaving, gardening, and the making of soap and candles.
She had help from hired hands and maids, but she still managed
the house while taking care of her main job: having and raising children. After Henry was born in 1863, his mother gave birth every

two years for the next decade: John, Margaret, Jane, William Jr., and Robert. As soon as one could walk across the parlor, the next took over the crib in her bedroom.

In Henry's words, "My mother taught me how to work." Or, as sister Margaret put it: "Mother believed in doing things and getting things done. She was systematic and orderly and thorough, and she demanded that from us." A person's duty might be "hard and disagreeable and painful"; all the more reason to do it. She taught Henry that "the highest duty in the world" was what she called "service." A good Episcopalian, Mary Ford defined "service" as work done for others without thought of reward. You can picture the young, bright-eyed woman driving the lesson home as she diapered one child and read to another. "[I]f we couldn't be happy here in this house," her son remembered her teaching, "we'd never be happy anywhere else." The religion part never took with Henry: "I went to Sunday school sometimes but I never thought it amounted to much." But as an adult, he claimed Mary Ford's moral teachings as his primary lesson: "I have tried to live my life as my mother would have wished."

"Could read all the first reader before I started school," Henry scribbled in one of his autobiographical notes. His mother tutored him in *McGuffey's First Eclectic Reader*, the standard curriculum in the region. McGuffey's readers were like Noah Webster's but written for the inhabitants of the new Midwestern towns. *O* was for *ox*, *V* for *vine*, and *Y* for *yoke*. William McGuffey was an ordained Presbyterian minister and a "theological and pedagogical conservative." He declared his illustrated lessons "aimed to combine *simplicity* with *sense*, *elegance* with *simplicity*, and PIETY with both." Between 1836, when the first edition came out, and 1920, an estimated one hundred twenty million copies were sold.

So, when Henry went off to school in January 1871, it was a fairly seamless transition. The seven-year-old continued the McGuffey curriculum that his mother had begun and went to the same school she'd once attended. The old wooden building had been replaced by a brick one with modern glass windows, but it was still run much the same way. For that matter, Henry's one-room schoolhouse had hardly changed from the dame schools of Nabby Smith's era, or the blab schools of Lincoln's. A single teacher supervised thirty to forty-five students, ages six to sixteen. The day began with a song or a prayer, then proceeded through spelling, reading, writing, and arithmetic lessons, with kids (two to a desk) standing to recite aloud. "[T]here wasn't any set schedule," as Henry's sister remembered it. "It depended on the mood of the teacher."

Michigan had tried, early on, to set up a standardized educational system. Like Indiana and Illinois and other states that came out of the Northwest Ordinance, it dedicated proceeds from the sale of one of each township's thirty-six sections to finance public schooling. "Religion, morality and knowledge, being necessary to good government," the ordinance had declared, "and the happiness of mankind, schools and the means of education shall forever be encouraged." Michigan had pushed even further. Its 1835 constitution made it the first state to establish a superintendent of public instruction and a state-controlled school fund. That superintendent immediately went east to study Horace Mann's model and came back convinced that Michigan needed a centralized system with trained teachers and mandatory attendance. "If children, as is generally conceded, belong to the republic," he wrote, "then it is obviously the duty of the state to see to it that they are properly trained, instructed, and educated."

Part of the goal of public education was still to Americanize immigrants; as late as 1850, half of Detroit was foreign-born. But it was also to Americanize Americans: to properly train the republic's children, whoever they were and wherever they were born. Henry Ford would one day call this the "democratic conception . . . to make men equal." By the time Henry was born, the state was running over four thousand school districts, and 75 percent of its kids between four and eighteen attended. The year Henry entered his first classroom, Michigan made attendance compulsory for at least three months. And by the time he'd finished his second year, the Michigan Supreme Court had set a national precedent by ruling that local districts could use public money to run high schools. American democracy would provide a free education for (almost) all. And unlike Europe, which set up one track for the working class and one for the university-bound, America would have a single, equal system. That, anyway, was the stated goal.

Henry's school, like most in Michigan, opened in the winter after harvest and closed a few months later when planting began. And like most, it was a one-room schoolhouse run at the whim of an untrained teacher. It followed what amounted to a standardized curriculum: the McGuffey readers. For children like Henry who were born "immediately succeeding the pioneer period," as one expert writes, "the influence of McGuffey may well have been greater than that of any other writer or statesman in the West." As a grown-up, Henry Ford could recite a line from a McGuffey reader and expect friends to recite the next, even though they'd gone to different schools in different states during different years.

Students moved through the palm-sized McGuffey readers at their own rate. The vocabulary got progressively harder, but the object of the exercise stayed the same: to instill a moral code. So, the first primer ended with a lesson about "a lit-tle boy, not tall-er than the ta-ble." (McGuffey taught pronunciation and spelling as well as reading.) On his way to school, which "he was not fond of," he gets distracted and ends up being "ver-y late." The lesson ends with a question: "Do you think a good boy will do as this boy did?" In the *Second Reader* (the one Henry began in school) a boy breaks the window of a "rich merchant," decides to come clean and pay for it, and "in a few years, he became the merchant's partner, and is now rich."

Later in life, these readers became almost a fetish for Ford. He'd tell *Good Housekeeping* magazine that the generations "that grew up on McGuffey did better in common sense and common honesty." He'd accumulate one of the largest private collections of readers in the world, purchase and rebuild William McGuffey's birthplace as a museum, and finance model schools that used facsimiles of McGuffey's 1857 edition. In Ford's words, these books deserved to be the cornerstone of an American child's education because "the McGuffey Readers taught industry and morality."

They may have, but if you listen to his classmates' testimony (and his own), Henry was the boy-not-fond-of-school. "We used to need extra discipline" is how one friend remembers what it was like to sit next to Henry. "When a boy got in trouble," Ford recalled, "he was brought up front and placed on the 'mourners bench' directly under the teacher's eye. You could get a good view of the stove from that location, and I sat there so much of the time that it was indelibly impressed on my memory." It may be that Ford is embellishing a little here: polishing his image as someone who stood out, who realized early on that imitation was suicide. But if grammar was what he was supposed to learn, he may well have been a kid who never paid much attention in class. As a twenty-three-year-old, he begins a letter to his wife-to-be: "Dear Clara, I again take the pleasure of writing you a few lines. It seems like a year since i seen you. It don't seem mutch like cutter rideing to night does it but I guess we will have some more sleighing." Ford's famous statement, "History is bunk," underlined his disdain for book learning in general. In his mid-fifties, he'd identify Benedict Arnold as "a writer, I think" and testified at a libel trial: "I don't like to read books; they mess up my mind."

What he liked was machinery. The same year Henry went off to school, he saw his first pocket watch. One of the German farmhands showed it to the seven-year-old: flipped open the back and revealed a world of gears and wheels. Here was a thing that ran on its own, that was calibrated to perform the same task again and again, that did work for you. You could learn how to fix one of these, even build your own. And the way you learned was by touch: by taking it apart and turning the pieces in your hands till you knew them in three dimensions. It was a different kind of knowledge from books. And once your hands knew how these gears and springs worked, they could unlock basic principles of motion and power. It was a common thing, a pocket watch, but it opened a whole universe.

William Ford often brought his oldest son into Detroit. Business took him there—the city now held almost eighty thousand people and dominated the local economy—but it was also fun: to watch the ships dock and the flurry of trains come and go. Once when they stopped at a roundhouse, an engineer named Tommy Garrett

(Henry would remember the man's name seventy years later) took the time to explain to the seven-year-old the basic workings of a steam engine: the valve that let steam into the chamber, how the pressure drove the piston, how another valve let the steam out. Back on the Dearborn farm, Henry set his mother's teapot on the back of his sled and pushed it around the yard, pretending he had an engine.

This was what he needed to know. He'd have to learn it on his own because school didn't teach machines. His father let him have a little workspace out in one of the barns, which the boy stocked with mostly handmade tools. Looking in through the window of a factory in Detroit, he'd seen how files were made: scoring metal so it would rasp other metal. Then he'd gone home and made his own and used them to file his mother's knitting needles down into screwdrivers. He traded marbles with his schoolmates for clock wheels, or would give one of his father's German farmhands a penny to buy gears from a jewelry shop, also in Detroit. The city was the mother of machinery: a great intersection of repair shops and lathes, steam engines and foundries. It's where he could get the stuff he needed to learn.

"I was always tinkering with wheels," he wrote later. "My father used to give me Caesar." Maybe that was true, although William Ford seems to have been as interested in machinery and progress as any mid-nineteenth-century American. In 1876, he'd make a cross-country trip to Philadelphia's Centennial Exposition to see its forty-foot-tall engines, its narrow-gauge railroads, and its experimental machinery that ran off the internal combustion of gasoline. But the father's priorities were clear: his eldest son's first duty was the farm. School had to fit into that schedule and so did tinkering.

Trouble was that—like Andy Jackson and Abe Lincoln—Henry hated farmwork. One of the Fords' hands would later describe the boy as the "laziest bugger on the face of the earth!" Where Lincoln got called lazy because he was always reading, for Henry it was sneaking off to "watch a threshing machine work." Farming might be noble; it might be what his father and mother and McGuffey held up as righteous work; but to Henry, following "many a weary mile behind a mule" amounted to "drudgery." It made no sense to clear and plow, plant and water, get out under an August sun, all for a field of corn. "[C]onsidering the results," he concluded, "there was too much work on the place." Farms were badly designed, inefficient: "Power is utilized to the least possible degree."

So, he'd sneak off. By the time he was twelve, he was finding his own way into Detroit: walking, hitching a ride on a farm wagon, sometimes coming back on the freights, getting home at two and three in the morning. To be in the city during those years was not only to see machinery, but to see what machinery was doing to the economy. While the economic surge from the Civil War had helped end the extended panic of 1837, another had begun in 1873. Banks, speculating on the expansion of railroads and other new technologies, had overextended and collapsed. Eighteen thousand businesses failed in two years. Owners reacted by cutting wages, often as much as 40 percent. Unemployment nationally had gone to 14 percent and was still rising. Workers reacted with protests and stoppages. The tinder points were precisely where industrialization had taken hold: in the mines and the mills and on the railroads. Three hundred policemen were called to quell disturbances on the Michigan Central; across the country, workers ran locomotives into roundhouses and refused to continue service until pay scales improved.

But pay stayed low, and an attempt to organize a national labor union around the eight-hour day and living wages was crushed. The once-booming manufacturing city that the adolescent slipped in and out of was filled with men looking for work. According to the newspapers and the Sunday sermons, the problem wasn't the fault of mechanization—or of industry in general—"but a breakdown in character, in the old American traits of making-out and making do." As if the solution could be found in the McGuffey readers.

Henry's notes about his childhood education don't mention the unemployed. He seems to have kept his focus on machinery. "I always had a pocket full of trinkets—nuts, washers, and odds and ends." He thought of it as his private education: almost a secret.

When he became a tycoon, Ford reconstructed the house he grew up in, including a hidden workbench that he used late at night and could slip under the bed if he heard anyone coming. His sister Margaret claimed the workbench had always been downstairs in plain view. But the way Ford remembered it, his education had been a private thing, solitary. Never mind school, or the panic of 1873, or his family. It was a boy and his tools and the way gears transferred power.

The spring before Henry turned thirteen, his mother died in childbirth. William Ford got Henry's aunt to move in and look after the kids. The farm stayed prosperous, but, in Henry's words, "The house was like a watch without a mainspring."

Later that empty summer, Henry and his father were driving their horse and buggy down a farm road when they came upon a vision. It had wheels the height of a man and a steam vent twice that high. It was loud and gave off smoke and sparks. When its drive belt was engaged to the back wheel, it rolled ponderously over the ground. And when that same power was hitched to a thresher or a saw, the farm changed: some of the drudgery disappeared. "In July 1876. The first portable engine came in our part of the country," Ford scratched in one of his autobiographical notes: "it was owned by Mr Fred Reden. it was a 10 H.P. N&S of Battle Creek Mich." Years later, in his office at the Ford Motor Company, he'd keep a big photograph of a similar engine mounted over his desk. He always believed the July meeting was one of the turning points in his education.

"Mr Reden Let me fire and run the engine many times that and the next year. He was a good and kind man." To operate a Nicholas and Shephard portable engine, you had to maintain just the right pressure, playing with the intake and outtake, and keep correcting tension on the drive belt. The boy had known since he was seven that he had a mechanical turn of mind. Now, driving Mr. Reden's steamroller slowly across the fields, he came to a more specific revelation. "That showed me that I was by instinct an Engineer."

Maybe it should be counted as two revelations. The first was that, as a teenager, he was capable of running something of this size and power. He was an Engineer—with a capital *E*—able to control a machine and make it work for others. The second revelation was that he had this skill by instinct.

He understood the principle of the steam engine—could build little ones and sketch them on scraps of paper—and that was important. It would eventually be a key part of his methodology: "I draw a plan and work out every detail on the plan before starting to build." But when Mr. Reden let him run the Nicholas and Shephard that summer, Henry did it by feel. It's how he learned, and it's how he'd go on to earn his living. Before he started manufacturing cars, he'd have jobs (in chronological order) operating a neighbor's steam engine, troubleshooting Westinghouse engines, and supervising three big dynamos at the Edison Illuminating Company—all, if his own stories are to believed, by touch. In a typical story, "He walked around the balky engine once or twice and maybe fussed with it a little bit. Then he walked up to the throttle, turned on the steam, and away it went." And as a car designer, while Ford could and did read a blueprint, he preferred working from a life-size model. That way, he could run his hands over the body and listen to the engine. In fact, he distrusted theories and men with degrees. "The moment one gets into the 'expert' state of mind, a great number of things become impossible," he'd write. He believed the best mechanics and engineers had what Emerson called, "this primary wisdom . . . Intuition."

Henry spent his middle school years developing this aptitude. "The first watch I fixed," he scribbled in one of his notes, "was after Sunday shool Albert Hutchings came out of the Gardner House With a big watch chain on his vest. I wanted to see it—it was stoped I worked in it and saw what was wrong."

He didn't work on it; he worked *in* it: immersed, feeling his way. Watches made perfect study guides: to the mechanically minded, they offered a sort of universal language. In America's early days, clocks had been handmade by skilled craftsmen. Around 1820, a small Connecticut factory started applying for patents on what amounted to a machine to make these machines. Soon, manufacturers were stamping out wheels and clock faces. By 1850, a single factory in New Haven could turn out 130,000 clocks a year. Along with guns, clocks were one of the first American-made products to use interchangeable parts, and Henry could see the advantages. For one thing, it made them relatively cheap: the cost driven down by being able to hire low-paid, unskilled laborers to run the punch machines.

For another, mass production made repair easier. When Henry used a ground-down shingle nail to pry open the back of Albert's pocket watch, he recognized the world he found there. He'd studied it in other watches; it was a kind of standardized curriculum. He saw that the roller jewel had "overbanked"; some jolt must have kicked it out of its setting. That meant the central lever wasn't advancing the gear that turned the minute and hour hands. Another advantage to interchangeable parts was that if something had been broken, Henry might have had the replacement in his own collection—or could have gotten it from Detroit. But in this case, all he needed was the tweezers he'd made out of one of his mother's corset stays. He dropped the jewel back in place. The watch ran.

Soon, other friends were giving him repairs. He'd tinker at his workbench at night or behind his textbook at school. After all, it was here—in the watches—that he was doing his real studying. Henry said his father used to get angry with him for doing the work for free, but Henry leapt at the chance to take a watch apart. Looking back on it years later, he wrote: "Machines are to mechanics what books are to a writer. He gets ideas from them and if he has any brain he will apply those ideas."

First, though, he had to understand. With Albert's watch, he'd later admit, "I really did not know what made it overbank." He could spot the problem but not the cause. "Three years later, I learned more." That's when he would come back and, even though Albert's watch was running fine, pry it open again, seat the lever in plaster, and add "just a bit of solder" so the jewel couldn't vibrate out of place. What had made him return to the problem? Henry said it was "this rude, simple, primitive power which we call 'stick-to-it-iveness.'" It wasn't enough to learn how to run machinery and fix it; he had to understand how to prevent the problem. Because that meant he knew it—knew the ideas behind it—and could apply those ideas to designing new machines.

By the time he was fifteen, Henry believed he "could do almost anything in watch repairing." In the meantime, he studied other machines, whenever and wherever he could. One Sunday, instead of going to church, he went to investigate the steam engine at a nearby sawmill. "It seemed to me," he'd write, "that a Sunday without work at my machines was so much time given utterly to waste." In fact, Sundays were particularly good for learning because most people went to church—and that left a lot of Dearborn's equipment lying around idle and unattended. He was curious about how this particular engine's slide valve worked. It was a Fulton, made right in Detroit, but the only way to understand it was to take it apart. He'd removed the heavy, central cylinder, set it on a pile of sawdust, and stretched his right arm up into the cavity to feel the valve (you couldn't see in there; it had to be by touch), when the cylinder "tiped over and caught my arm," he wrote: "dug for ½ Hr to get out." He finally pulled away enough sawdust for the cylinder to roll off him—and put his arm right back in to feel for the valve. It's another story about stick-to-it-iveness, but it also shows how desperate he was to get access to engines. In terms of his education, it was time to make a choice: either keep studying the few machines he could find in Dearborn or go to Detroit where they were made.

At sixteen, most kids were done with school anyway. Henry felt he'd learned what he could there: some appreciation for reading, writing, and arithmetic; some social skills; and the basic McGuffey lesson in "industry and morality." Beyond that, he didn't see much point. "An educated man is not one whose memory is trained to carry a few dates in history," he'd declare, "he is one who can accomplish things." That was true American knowledge, and Henry went out looking for a "true education . . . gained through the discipline of life." He didn't reject formal schooling outright, but it couldn't take him where he needed to go. "Modern industry," he'd write, "requires a degree of ability and skill which neither early quitting of school nor long continuance at school provides."

The way Henry told the story, he snuck off the farm one day

without his father's approval. He portrayed himself as a kind of rebel who broke from the family and carved his own way in the city. But William Ford already knew that his eldest son wasn't about to do his duty to the farm. "Henry worries me," his father wrote. "He doesn't seem to settle down and I don't know what's going to become of him." His father seems to have arranged Henry's first lodging in Detroit: at an aunt's house. And it was years before Henry gave up the security his family offered. He'd return to the farm every fall to help with the harvest. And in his mid-twenties, he'd support his new bride by lumbering a piece of Dearborn property given to him by his father. What he did break with—and early on—was this idea that success meant settling down and growing things. "I never had any particular love for the farm," he wrote. "It was the mother on the farm I loved."

So, the five-feet-eight, thin-boned, wide-faced seventeen-year-old finds work in a Detroit factory. Call it his late high school education. His first job is with nineteen hundred other workers turning out railroad cars at the city's largest manufacturing establishment, the thirty-acre Michigan Car Company. He starts at $1.10 a day, on the high side for an apprentice—almost as if he'd managed to skip a grade. For a clue to how that might have happened, look at the way he approached his employers later in life. Here's Ford, age twenty-eight, walking into the Edison Illuminating Company:

"Who's in charge here?"

"I am. What can I do for you?"

"I'm an engineer. Have you any work I can do?"

"How much do you know about the work?"

"I know as much as anyone my age."

If he did bluff his way into the job, it helps explain why he only lasted a week. "I went to Detroit Dec 1, 1879," he scribbles. "To carshop 6 days Got into trouble babbiting a box Will tell." He never did tell, but babbiting a box—lining it with soft, white metal—requires some experience. It must have seemed simple enough to Henry: you pour molten metal into a form. But all the old babbit has to be removed first and the new solution kept mixed, or the process doesn't take. And the box has to be completely dry: the slightest moisture and the hot metal can explode. All dross has to be skimmed off the top before the pour; the form needs to be slightly warmed; and the liquid has to flow steadily up and over the mold so any impurities spill off. Henry may have known as much as anyone his age, but how much babbitting had he done in Dearborn? When the first Sunday came, his career at Michigan Car Company was over.

His father set him up in his next job. By this time, 1880, the economy was on the upswing. Detroit was home to over nine hundred manufacturing enterprises, churning out more than thirty million dollars' worth of product. Mechanization had allowed businesses to consolidate; there were fewer steel and iron mills, for example, but they'd almost doubled their production. At the same time, there was a network of smaller companies turning out parts, figuring out faster ways to make their products, experimenting with new technologies. Henry's father found him work with James Flower & Brothers, run by a family who sometimes bought their produce out at the Fords' farm. Master machinists and engineers, trained in England, the Flower brothers advertised as "*Manufacturers of The Celebrated 'Flower' Patent Stop Valve* and FIRE HYDRANT." They'd started their shop in 1852 and survived three decades by being responsive to Detroit's rapidly changing economic needs. Their old, three-story brick building contained a foundry, turned out "every description of brass work," and housed a dealership in iron pipe and fittings. "They manufactured everything in the line of brass and iron," one of Henry's co-workers recalled: "globe and gate valves, gongs, steam-whistles, fire hydrants, and valves for water pipes . . . They made so many different articles that they had to have all kinds of machines, large and small lathes and drill presses."

If machines were Henry's books, here was a library. But he'd mostly have to browse it by himself. Though Flower & Brothers was a lot smaller and more personal than Michigan Car, he still wouldn't receive much direct training. That kind of apprenticeship had been disappearing since Ben Franklin's day, and by Henry's time, it was pretty much gone. In England, for example, the Flower brothers had been trained in the traditional way to complete their master pieces and become knowledgeable in all aspects of the craft. With that kind of education, a skilled machinist typically made about 60 percent more than the average wage earner. But apprentices like Henry, writes a contemporary observer, "receive little or no instruction except when the foreman or some journeyman takes a particular interest and goes out of his way to teach the 'cubs.'" Instead of learning to be an all-round mechanic, Henry worked at a milling machine, putting hexagons on brass valves. It was repetitive, specialized, solitary work and reflected a relatively new phase of American industrialization. "The master had become the boss," as one study puts it, "craftsmanship had become work." Henry was being taught to be a cog in the machinery of mass production.

At Flower & Brothers, he'd gone back to base wages, $2.50 a week. He worked ten hours a day, every day but Sunday. (To cover room and board, he worked nights in his apartment, cleaning and repairing watches.) A description of a foundry in those days called it "an inferno of smoke, flame, and coruscations." Mechanics' work was considered "coarse and brutal." The finishing floor where Henry milled valves was badly lit and poorly ventilated, the air thick with fine metal dust. One of his co-workers remembered how the low-ceilinged brass shop was "awfully hot in the summer." That's when Henry quit, after nine months on the job. He was back on the family farm in time for harvest.

The way he explained it, the Flower brothers "showed us how to do a few things very well. That's why I changed; so that I could learn more about different things." Which he did. But in a way, the larger lesson was how little he needed to learn. There was no reason to be a master craftsman. By now, manufacturing techniques—from gigs to copy lathes—were making it so "a farmboy [could] turn out work as good as a first-class mechanic." Detroit had a growing network of specialized molders and machinists, upholsterers and bicycle manufacturers. What a teenager with ambition needed to know was how to make the most of that situation. When Ford eventually produced his first prototype car, he didn't make all the parts: he got the seat from one shop, springs from another, the balance wheel cast at a third. And when his Model A went into production in 1903, essential components—the engine, axle, and transmission—were all contracted out. Part of what he learned in the Flower Brothers' sweaty brass shop was that he didn't need to be inside the machinery; he needed to learn how to be outside, running it.

That fall, he continued his education at the Dry Dock Engine Works. In his autobiography, he skips right over his first year in Detroit—the job he didn't hold and the one his father helped him get—and makes it look like he snuck straight off the farm to Engine Works. That might be because he considered his two years there the climax of his schooling. The place had one of the best-equipped machine shops in the city. It also offered what amounted to an advanced class in business management.

By now, the east side of the Detroit River had become an industrial strip of interrelated marine businesses. The Engine Works had prospered by offering a wide range of services from steam engines to propeller wheels to mining machinery. "Particular attention is given to steamboat repairs and ship works," says an 1870 advertisement. A decade later, when Henry arrived, it was specializing in building marine engines and had started work on its first compound, two-cylinder model. A two-cylinder engine recycled the spent steam from one chamber to power another; an innovation that had only become possible after engineers had figured out how to build heavyweight, high-pressure boilers. Making the huge machines was a slow, labor-intensive process; Engine Works turned out between seven and nine a year.

During Henry's time there, more than half these engines went into ships built by a single company: Detroit Dry Dock. It, in turn, was supplying the Detroit and Cleveland Navigation Company, controlled by James McMillan. McMillan also owned the Michigan Car Company, Henry's first employer. In fact, McMillan owned a lot of Detroit. A director of banks, railroad tycoon, philanthropist, and eventually, U.S. senator, McMillan was the city's embodiment of the Horatio Alger dream. "[N]o man in the history of Detroit in his time," wrote a business magazine, "caused more day's wages to be paid, more millions of product to be fabricated, or more workingmen's homes to be reared." While Henry was at Engine Works,

McMillan was busy opening northern Michigan to development. Detroit Dry Dock built him two giant passenger ships that initiated service from Detroit to the Upper Peninsula, as well as the year-round ferries his company ran at the Straits of Mackinac. All these ships were powered by engines built at Henry's shop, and all were designed by a young marine engineer, Frank Kirby.

It was Kirby who captured Henry's imagination. The son of a boat builder over in Saginaw, Kirby had been sponsored by one of his father's wealthy East Coast customers, who had arranged for the fifteen-year-old to study engineering at New York's Cooper Institute and work in the Brooklyn shipyards. He returned to become Michigan's leading designer of steel-hulled ships. In 1878, his thousand-ton *City of Detroit* was the first of thirteen enormous and elegant side-wheelers built for McMillan's passenger line. He also designed tugboats, ice-breaking ferries, and in 1881, the first of what would become the characteristic Great Lakes ship: the metal-hulled freighter.

As well as a mechanical turn of mind, Kirby had a business sense. When Henry arrived at the Engine Works, it was still owned by its founding partners. Over the next four years, Kirby became its single largest stockholder. He also bought shares in McMillan's ship building operation. By the 1890s, with Kirby as a key player, McMillan would end up with a single, integrated operation: his company ordered the ships, his company built them, and his company provided the steam engines.

For two years, then, the teenager in the machine shop had a front-row seat at the creation of a new business model: a model that grew out of ever-increasing mechanization. Craftsmen had already turned into specialized subcontractors. If you gathered the subcontractors under one roof, it cost more initially but you gained power and control. In this case, McMillan was the financier, but Frank Kirby combined the roles of engineer, designer, manager, and owner. He ran the manufacturing process, from dreaming up a machine through production to sales. The famous contemporary example of this kind of practical entrepreneur was Thomas Edison. During these apprentice Detroit years, Edison became Henry's ultimate hero: "a new combination," Ford would write, ". . . a scientist but also he was a man of extraordinary common sense." Edison would one day return the compliment, calling Ford a "natural mechanic" who was also a "natural businessman." Ford made it look natural; in fact, he worked hard learning both these skills. "Almost anyone can think up an idea," he'd write. "The thing that counts is developing it into a practical product." Years later, over the Romanesque pillars of his engineering laboratory in Dearborn, Ford carved Edison's name alongside Galileo, Newton, and, yes, Kirby.

Henry studied Frank Kirby from a distance; he only caught an occasional glimpse of the designer at Engine Works. The boy's day-to-day education took place on the shop floor with his co-workers. A photograph shows Henry as one of the youngest in a group of fifty or so white men, ranging from old-timers with full beards to boys with smooth adolescent faces. It's a ready-looking crew with their boots, long shop jackets, and leather caps. As skilled craftsmen, many earned above-average wages. Young apprentices "were encouraged to think for themselves," as one study puts it, ". . . to become entrepreneurs and to rise, like Horatio Alger's characters." It was like the story in McGuffey: if you worked hard and told the truth, you could end up partners with a rich merchant. Like Frank Kirby. Or you might end up James McMillan himself!

That was the dream. But in reality, few Detroit workers could save any money. Most lived from paycheck to paycheck, working ten-hour shifts. Many were laid off in the winter. And the odds of moving into management were slim: 80 percent of Detroit's skilled craftsmen stayed in blue-collar jobs. Machine shops like Henry's were known for having lots of German and British workers, many of whom had come from the old-world, trade union tradition. In fact, about 90 percent of the city's workers were either foreign-born or, like Henry, children of a foreign-born parent. For many, the logical response to low wages and lack of opportunity was to organize.

Labor newspapers started appearing in Detroit. One called the *Socialist* advocated a "cooperative commonwealth with workingmen their own employees." German-born cigar makers helped found the Workingmen's Party of the United States. By 1880, Detroit was not only the headquarters of the national Socialist Labor Party but had elected one of its members to the city council. That same year—Henry's first at Engine Works—Detroit's branch of the Knights of Labor boasted fifteen hundred members and would have thirteen thousand within five years. Instead of encouraging apprentices to dream of being entrepreneurs, the Knights' motto was, "An injury to one is the concern of all." And their definition of who was part of the labor movement included not only the men on the shop floors but "the clerk, the school teacher . . . [and] the worst paid, most abused and illy appreciated of all toilers—women."

From this perspective, the Horatio Alger idea was bunk. "No wage worker ever has or ever can become a millionaire by honest labor," a Detroit agitator wrote. "The first step towards the accumulation of a million is to cease to earn a living and go into the business of skimming others." One way the unions saw workers getting skimmed was through mechanization: management used it to eliminate skilled jobs and cut wages. As a Knights of Labor speaker put it: " 'Labor-saving' machinery, to be truly such, should save—not starve—the producing classes."

Henry agreed with at least part of that. By the time he left the Engine Works in the summer of 1882, his goal was to build machines that would improve the average man's life. He dreamed of inventing a tractor along the lines of Mr. Reden's steamroller. "Man minus the machine is a slave," he'd write (especially, he thought, when it came to farming). "Man plus the machine is a free man."

But he didn't agree that his fellow workers could or should lead the way. The Knights of Labor pointed out that Jesus was a carpenter: "He is not less because He worked, neither are you." Maybe not, but Henry looked around the shop floor and concluded that "the vast majority of men want to stay put. They want to be led." He'd eventually take that logic even further, calling it "self-evident that a majority of people in the world are not mentally—even if they are physically—capable of making a good living." The *Communist Manifesto*, written a dozen years before Henry was born, called on workers of the world to unite. But that wasn't how Henry saw progress happening. It was "modern industry," he'd write, "[that was] gradually lifting the worker and the world." And, he'd add, there was "something sacred about big business which provides a living for hundred and thousands."

What his education had taught him was that the world was divided into two groups: "men who work with their hands," as he put it, and men like Frank Kirby and Thomas Edison: "larger men who give the leadership to the community." Henry was determined to become one of the larger men.

How?

Partially through tinkering: fourteen years of it, after leaving Engine Works and before test-driving his first gasoline-powered car. But there was also the ability to lead, and he came to believe that part couldn't be taught. "Where is the master," as Emerson put it in Ford's favorite essay, "Self-reliance," "who could have instructed Franklin, or Washington, or Bacon, or Newton? Every great man is unique." It was a question of stick-to-it-iveness and faith. "To believe your own thought," Emerson went on, "to believe that what is true for you in your private heart is true for all men,—that is genius." Ford's proof would come in the marketplace, with the Model T. He'd listen to his private heart, build a "universal car"—known as the farmer's car—and end up with a corporate empire.

His success would be held up as a modern Horatio Alger story, but that didn't sit right with Ford. He kept trying to explain what had happened, how he'd learned what he'd needed to know. He scribbled notes about his childhood machines. He evoked his mother's early lesson: "[W]hen one serves for the sake of service . . . then money abundantly takes care of itself." Still, it was obvious that abundance only came to some, that hard work wasn't necessarily rewarded. In fact, Ford would admit that "repetitive labor"—milling hexagons at Flower & Brothers—had been "terrifying" to him. "To other minds," he went on, "perhaps I might say to the majority of minds, repetitive operations hold no terrors."

That, finally, was the conclusion he reached: "The average worker, I'm sorry to say . . . wants a job in which he does not have to think." He'd build his empire on that premise: huge factories where workers mass-produced a great man's idea. This was the sacred future—and the duty of the state was to prepare the majority for those jobs. All men might have the right to life, liberty, and the pursuit of happiness. "[But] most certainly all men are not equal," the grown-up Henry would declare, "and any democratic conception which strives to make men equal is only an effort to block progress."

WILLIE

Willie Du Bois was the light-skinned Negro who lived by the tracks.

His father left town right after he was born, never to be seen again. His single mother—crippled on her left side from a stroke—worked every once in a while on a local farm, took in borders to help pay the rent, and accepted "unobtrusive charity." That's how Willie put it. He'd also write that they "must often have been near the edge of poverty. Yet I was not hungry or in lack of suitable clothes, or made to feel unfortunate."

It was small-town poverty, cushioned by what Willie called the "great clan" of his mother's extended family. But it was more than just the fifty or so black people; the white citizens looked after them, too: "took her and me into a sort of overseeing custody." At least that's the way he remembered it: a little American town of four thousand where racial distinctions didn't mean that much—and economic differences didn't either. "A town of middle-class people" is how he'd describe it, where almost everyone worked for a living. And almost anyone with enough ambition and ability could get ahead. That was a shared article of faith—the democratic conception, as Henry Ford put it—and Willie believed. True, in his part of western Massachusetts, most of the Negroes were laborers or maids, but Willie was taught an explanation for that. "If others of my family, of my colored kin," he wrote, "had stayed in school instead of quitting early for small jobs, they could have risen to equal whites. On this my mother quietly insisted."

Willie became the Negro who went to school.

He loved it. Small, not very athletic, he started at age six, walking from their cheap rental by the tracks down a lane to the school yard where a big chokecherry tree grew. It shaded two buildings: one wood, one brick. Willie started in the wooden one, the elementary school. The town had put up its first schoolhouse around when Nabby Smith was born: more than a century before he entered the current structure. And that, in turn, had been built some twenty-odd years ago, in 1851, when Massachusetts had made education mandatory for six- to twelve-year-olds.

So, he was taking part in an accepted and well-established public institution. At nine each morning, the fifty or so students began with a short devotion and song. What followed he called a simple curriculum: "reading, writing, and arithmetic; grammar, geography and history." At noon, there was an hour's lunch break, then back till four: "each day, five days a week, ten months a year." Willie makes it sound rudimentary, and in many ways it was. "We learned the alphabet, we were drilled vigorously on the multiplication tables, and we drew accurate maps. We could spell correctly and read with understanding." But that was more training and more time in school than many children received in the 1870s. Especially colored children.

"My schoolmates," Willie noted, "were inevitably white." That he could even attend an integrated school was a result of having been born in what might be called Horace Mann's Massachusetts. If he'd lived in the South—and if he'd managed to go to school at all—it would have been the colored one. And he probably would have left it without even basic skills. Instead, he was part of the "Massachusetts theory" of education that Mann and supporters like the Peabody sisters had fought for: free public school for all so that all could have "an equal chance for earning."

At first, Willie's town of Great Barrington had balked at the concept—especially at its cost. In the 1840s, the town allocated twice as much of its budget to preachers as to its schools. Then came Mann's reform effort. A Great Barrington special school com-

mittee made a point of declaring how his "name in connection with
education in Massachusetts will ever be greatly remembered." It
was Mann's statewide overhaul, the committee acknowledged, that
had helped bring about "a very great improvement in the schools."
There'd been a falling off during the Civil War: buildings had "de-
teriorated," the quality of teaching had gone downhill, parents had
sent their children "for a shorter term," and school spirit as a whole
had grown "lower and ruder." But since the war, Great Barrington
and Massachusetts in general had made a concerted effort to revitalize public education. Willie's teachers, for example—mostly older
women and "inevitably white American Protestants"—had gone
through two years of training in state-run "normal schools" that
Mann had helped institute.

Willie recalled it as an "education according to the preconceptions
of the late nineteenth century . . . [a] long and rather severe discipline
in the three R's." His first teacher at Centre Primary, Miss Mary
Cross, used a traditional mode of instruction: having her students
stand, then beating time while they recited from their readers. She'd
also quiz them individually, and Willie became one of her favorites.
He answered questions (in his own estimation) "glibly and usually
correctly because I studied hard." Great Barrington used a graduated
series of uniform writing books so the pupils could get, in the local
school committee's words, "some fixed habits of writing." Willie applied himself: "[T]he spelling and grammar of the English language,
the usage in phrase became deeply grounded and second nature to
me at an early age."

By the time he'd been in school three years, the regional Great
Barrington school district consisted of twenty-one buildings that
served 859 students. This was supported by a tax of about two dollars per citizen. Education now accounted for more than a third of
the total town budget, considerably more than the next most expensive item, "Highway and Bridges." Still, Willie remembered how
every year a local farmer—"the dirtiest old man I ever saw . . . fat
and greasy"—would stand up in town meeting and launch a "fierce
attack" on how his tax money was being wasted on public education. Hadn't he grown up here—and his father and his father's

father—and done just fine without formal schooling? What were these kids being educated for, anyway? "The farm the farm" was the best school.

Every year, the town listened politely and then went ahead and passed the budget. For one thing, people knew the era of the farm was over. Willie only had to look at his mother's family to see the change. The Burghardts had been in the Great Barrington area for two hundred years. Tom Burghardt had been, like Belle, the slave of a Dutch family in the Hudson River valley. After winning his freedom by fighting in the Revolutionary War, Tom and his Bantu wife had started what Willie called "a mighty family." For three generations, Burghardts had lived on small farms in the Great Barrington area. But by Willie's time, as he wrote, "The bits of land were too small to support the great families born on them." Properties had been divided and redivided and worked for too long. Plus, there was the competition from inexpensive produce grown in the Midwest. The year before Willie entered school, he and his mother and grandmother had to move into town. It marked the end of an era. New England had begun catering to summer visitors and patriotic tourists, and some members of the mighty Burghardt family took jobs as waiters and cooks. Others moved out of the area completely, headed into the big cities to look for industrial work.

This shift in the economy was one of the reasons the town didn't pay much attention to Ol' Greasy's annual attack. Changing times demanded changes in education. By 1873, Massachusetts was the most industrialized state in the nation. Massive red brick mills lined the rivers in places like Fall River, Adams, Lawrence. Lowell, the City of Spindles, had jumped from a population of twenty-five hundred in 1826 to eighteen thousand a decade later—and by 1870, it had topped forty thousand. The displaced Burghardts wouldn't have headed for Lowell: Negroes weren't allowed to work in the mills. But Negro labor had created them. Southern slavery had produced the cotton that Northern states turned into cloth. One U.S. senator called the arrangement an "unholy union . . . between the cotton planters and fleshmongers of Louisiana and Mississippi and the cotton spinners and traffickers of New England—between the lords of the lash and the lords of the loom."

Industrialization affected even little towns like Great Barrington. "I was born by a golden river," Willie would write, and then add, ". . . golden because of the woolen and paper waste that soiled it." The first mill had gone up on the Housatonic in 1824; a quarter century later, when the railroad came through, investors refitted these factories and added new ones. By the time Willie was in elementary school, while the town still had over two hundred farms, the value of its manufactured goods was more than double its agricultural products. There was an ironworks, a big paper mill, and the five-hundred-foot-long Monument Mills—for many years, the town's largest employer and taxpayer.

Despite Willie's memory that Great Barrington was uniformly middle class, it had its own lords of the loom. Parley Russell, who inherited Monument Mills, was also a director of the local bank and ran the water company. Willie was playmates with his son, Louis, a "frail, good-hearted, but slow-witted" boy, who—like many of the wealthiest children—didn't go to public school but was home-tutored. Willie got periodic invitations to cross the tracks and climb the hill to the Russell mansion, "one of the most imposing in the village." The bright Negro boy and the slow white boy played in the great halls and ate snacks prepared by Irish maids. Was this part of the town's overseeing custody? Willie wasn't a slave playmate the way Belle had been, or the child's servant like Thocmetony, but he wasn't an equal either.

At the other end of the social scale, Great Barrington's industries had produced what Willie described as "a mass of Irish peasants." They were, he wrote, "herded in slum areas in the upper part of the town surrounding the mills." He didn't know much about them; they were "set aside from the community of long-standing." And most of them didn't go to public school either. The mill kids often lacked decent clothes. Many of them started working in the factories as soon as state law allowed—which was age ten. Willie considered their poverty different from what he and his mother experienced: foreign, separate, industrial. It was assumed they'd end up in the kind of jobs Henry Ford had described: where you weren't asked or expected to think.

Monument Mills was famous for its Marseilles bedspreads. While they were made to look handmade, the days of Granny doing needlework in front of the fireplace had gone with the family farm. Instead, the intricate spreads were produced on a machine called the Jacquard loom. By Willie's day, Monument had almost seventy of these and turned out 330,000 spreads a year. A designer would create a pattern of, say, flowers and vines, often copied from a wallpaper catalog. Once the pattern had been transferred to graph paper, a cutter used a stamping machine to punch the code for this design onto heavy, five-by-eighteen-inch cards. The cards then rotated through the Jacquard loom, which often had to read hundreds of them to complete a pattern. It was like a player piano roll, or an early version of computer software. Programmed, the looms executed a series of precise moves and turned out the same bedspread, over and over again.

Photographs of Monument Mills show a high-ceilinged room with windows on one side. Overhead, a belt system has harnessed the power of the golden river. Down the length of the floor, the squat Jacquard looms churn out bedspreads. And beside the big machines, male workers stand, monitoring. They needed to know how to start and stop the looms. They had to be able to fix minor glitches. But mostly they were attendants, and the main thing they had to learn was how to work at the same unvarying pace as the machinery.

Willie was scared of the children of the mill workers. "Sometimes they called me 'nigger' or tried to attack me." And most of his public school classmates disliked them, too. Instead of common schools ending class antagonism, in Great Barrington anyway, public education had ended up a kind of exclusive club. "I cordially despised the poor Irish and South Germans who slaved in the mills," Willie wrote, "and annexed the rich and well-to-do as my natural companions. Of such is the kingdom of snobs!"

It was a brief, extraordinary annexation: the black boy and his well-to-do white friends joined in and by the public schools. Massachusetts had legally integrated its educational system about a decade before Willie was born. Five years later, the Emancipation Proclamation had passed. The month Willie was born, the era of Reconstruction began. Southern blacks got the vote, successfully ran for office, and demanded equality in, among other things, their education. Coming out of the Civil War, the triumphant Republican Party not only pressed for the passage of a Civil Rights Act but began impeachment proceedings against President Andrew Johnson when he opposed racial equality. Willie would one day call Reconstruction "an extraordinary experiment in democracy."

But by the time he was in the equivalent of fourth grade, the experiment was effectively over. White supremacists had regained control of the South, and "the rich and dominating North," as Willie would put it, ". . . was not only weary of the race problem, but was investing largely in Southern enterprises." It was the end of what the *New York Times* called the era of "moral politics." One day, Willie would eloquently describe the transition: "The slave went free; stood a brief moment in the sun; then moved back again toward slavery."

In the little town of Great Barrington, the Negro boy and his mother were determined that he'd keep moving forward. The question was how. What would he need to know?

In a way, it was obvious. Willie had been on the honor roll since the start of his school career, one of the few students who never missed a day or came late. "Gradually," he would write, "I became conscious that in most of the school work my natural gifts and regular attendance made me rank among the best, so that my promotions were regular and expected." He was climbing the educational ladder, and the promise was that it would be his way out: here he could succeed based not on color or wealth but on an objective measure of his talents.

Trouble was, the ladder had always ended in eighth grade. "I was brought up in a day and state," Willie would write, "where education beyond . . . reading, writing and arithmetic, was considered a private matter." Despite the goal of a single system for all, most of America still had what Willie would call "the English idea of education": you could only go past elementary school if you could pay for it. In Great Barrington, this private education ranged from tutors with a few students in a private home to boarding schools with their own dorms and classrooms. The most prestigious was the Sedgwick Institute, run for the descendants of the prosperous old Dutch and English families and the children of the new lords of the loom. The family that owned the paper mill, for example, sent their children to Sedgwick, paying for it with their "considerable inherited wealth." The academy also accepted, as Willie wrote, "rich young people from out of town," offering them college prep courses. In Willie's view, Sedgwick was educating its students "to become part of the idle rich."

Until the year he was born, the only secondary school options had been private. Then, another way opened. And though it wasn't particularly meant for the Negro boy, it's how Willie planned to slip back into the sunshine. Through a new invention called high school.

Again, it helped that he lived in Massachusetts. At the start of the Civil War, out of some 300 high schools in the country, 103 were in Massachusetts. The first opened in Boston in 1821, and six years later, the legislature passed a law requiring a high school in any town with over five hundred families. Many ducked the requirement. It was, after all, a lot to ask: establish a free high school, open ten months a year, with a mandated syllabus for "all the inhabitants." Especially if not all the inhabitants benefited.

To understand why high school was invented and for whom, it helps to apply the terms Willie had coined to describe the population of Great Barrington. Most of the "mass of Irish peasants" didn't go to high school: not in this town, or the state, or for that matter, the nation. In fact, one argument for extending public school past eighth grade was to counter "the danger to this country . . . in the mass of uneducated people pouring into it from abroad." Immigrants brought "discord, immorality, and poverty." They were either "alien in race and sympathies, or revolutionary in tendencies." Proof of that, some argued, was in the nationwide labor agitation that began in the late 1870s: called "the most violent the country had ever known." High school was designed as the antidote, inoculating decent Americans and keeping them separate from dissenting newcomers. As the United States Commissioner of Education declared in the 1880s: "If you wish property safe from confiscation by a majority composed of communists, you must see to it that the people are educated so each sees the sacredness of property."

The children of the "idle rich" didn't have much to do with high school either. They still went to the academies or, like Louis Russell, were tutored at home. And the kids who were staying on "the farm the farm" didn't need more education; after eighth grade, most of them dropped out to help with agricultural work. In small town Massachusetts the year Willie finished elementary school, less than 20 percent of fifteen- to nineteen-year-olds were still in school. And Massachusetts at least offered the opportunity: nationally, even a decade later, less than 1 percent of the eligible population was enrolled in high school.

No, the institution was invented for a specific and narrow target group: Willie's kingdom of the well-to-do. He remembered there being only some twenty-five students at Great Barrington High; a graduating class of fifteen was large. And he described the kids who went as the children of the town's grocer and jeweler, watchmaker and tinner: his circle of friends. No wonder Great Barrington had been slow to embrace the idea. A quarter century after Massachusetts law required high schools, the state education committee was still marking the town "delinquent." It wasn't till after the Civil War, after the manufacturing economy had taken hold, that Great Barrington approved the funds. Willie was two months old when the town fathers committed an initial two thousand dollars. By the time the high school was finished (only the second brick structure in town), it cost some fifteen thousand.

According to Great Barrington's town historian, its citizens finally approved the high school to end the practice where "boys and girls preparing for college were compelled to do so at their own cost." That's a little misleading. The percentage of town kids interested in going to college was tiny. In fact, across the country, advocates of the high school concept got their budgets approved by arguing that it was an end in itself: all the education most kids would need. Supporters labeled it "the people's college."

The majority of Massachusetts parents remained "uncomprehending and indifferent." It was the middle-class minority—the merchants and well-off farmers—who got behind the idea. A high school degree would differentiate their children, give them status in the newly industrialized world.

Plus, there was the moral argument. Life on the farm, with its reassuring set of values, was disappearing. The apprentice system was all but gone. The result, some thought, was a society on the verge of disintegrating. One educational reformer used the prison population in Massachusetts as evidence. Between 1850 and 1880, it had doubled. You couldn't blame that on "the great number of idle, ignorant, and vicious immigrants," because most of the prisoners were native-born. And you couldn't blame it on illiteracy, since most of the criminals could read and write. Instead, the argument went, the bulging prisons indicated a lack of "moral teaching." Since the days of the Puritans, the "distinguishing mark" of Massachusetts education had been religious and moral instruction. Now, with the industrial revolution permanently changing family structure, the state had to extend that tradition by providing public school for juveniles.

Finally, supporters of the idea of high school appealed to people who wanted to keep things as they were. Great Barrington's grocers and jewelers and watchmakers had succeeded in the American system. For them, anyway, it had been a land of opportunity. If high school was a way of preserving that system, they supported it. The Civil War had torn the country apart. The experiment called Reconstruction had scared both Northern and Southern whites—reconfirming what they saw as "the dangers of unbridled democracy and the political incapacity of the lower orders." As one commentator puts it, extending public education into the high school years was a way to try to ensure "the permanence of our civil, political and religious Institutions."

There were enough votes in town to defeat Ol' Greasy on a regular basis. But even after Great Barrington High got built, a history of the town notes: "[t]he school committees had a constant struggle with reluctant tax-payers to get a fair share of appropriations." Or, as Willie put it, "The high school was not too popular in this rural part of New England." It was, however, where his circle of friends was headed, and Willie was set on joining them. His mother was set on it, too. She insisted he'd be the "first of the clan" to finish high school.

It's hard to know her reasoning, exactly, because Willie never wrote much about her. He mentions his mother's "heavy, kind face," "the impression of infinite patience," and the "curious determination . . . concealed in her softness." He also describes her as "a silent, repressed woman." The small-town aspect of their poverty cut two ways. She was the crippled, impoverished, single mother: a known charity case, even if the charity was unobtrusive. Great Barrington, Willie writes, shared the prevailing American belief that "the poor, on the whole, were themselves to be blamed." In the land of opportunity, where everyone supposedly had an equal chance to succeed, that was a logical conclusion. His mother was to be blamed, then, for never having learned what she needed to know. Well, he would. They both seemed to have agreed on that.

The two of them were now living in some rooms near the back entrance to the Congregational church. They often couldn't meet the rent, and her health was only getting worse. As many of his classmates dropped out of school to work, he stayed on. And unlike grade school, where, he wrote, he'd had "almost no experience of segregation or color discrimination," he now started to "feel the pressure of the 'veil of color'; in little matters at first and then in larger." Still, he stayed on. "I very early got the idea that what I was going to do was prove to the world that Negroes were just like other people." And the proving ground was the school system.

Great Barrington High had two teachers. A couple of years before Willie entered, the school board hired Miss Ida V. Roraback: "a woman of noble Christian character whose highest aim was to serve others." Along with "good scholarship," the board proclaimed, "she added the rarer virtues of untiring enthusiasm and uniform cheerfulness." The concept of high school couldn't have succeeded without women like Miss Roraback. Twenty-four of Great Barrington's twenty-eight teachers were female. Across the state, women accounted for 85 percent of the public school teaching staff. And that wasn't just because of their enthusiasm. Females were typically paid about a third of what male teachers got.

Each day, the cheerful Miss Roraback would keep time with her pointer on the desk while Willie went through his Latin declensions, or recited memorized passages from the English primer, or repeated the laws of algebra. The curriculum was state-mandated and followed the classical model of Boston Latin and the academies. It didn't pretend to be useful in the sense of preparing students to be grocers or farmers. Miss Roraback taught what members of respectable society had traditionally needed to know.

Willie's other teacher was also the principal of the high school: Frank Alvan Hosmer. Descendant of an old New England Congregationalist family, Hosmer had grown up in Woburn, Massachusetts, graduated high school there, and gone on to Amherst College. After teaching a couple of years, the twenty-five-year-old had arrived in Great Barrington in 1878, newly married and on the forefront of the high school movement.

If Miss Roraback was known for her Christian character, Frank Hosmer was described as "popular and progressive." He was in his third year when Willie arrived. Hosmer taught the classics and branched out into theater: Willie would appear in a production of Scott's "Lady of the Lake." But one of the principal's main challenges was to convince the public to support secondary education. Getting appropriations was "a constant struggle." As part of his campaign, he tried to get the Great Barrington High School kids to wear caps with G.B.H.S. on the front. That smacked a little too much of the private-academy approach, and the kids mocked the initials, saying they stood for the "Great Big Hosmer Speculation." A decade and a half after the brick building was completed, the school committee reported: "the high school continues to win favor"—making it sound like an ongoing, uphill battle. In fact, during Willie's junior year, Hosmer would threaten to leave. He was only earning fourteen hundred dollars a year: about average for (male) teachers, but he was also college educated and the principal. The town managed to come up with another hundred dollars and keep him, but it was understood he was staying "at a pecuniary sacrifice."

In the tradition of Horace Mann, the Peabodys, and other school reformers, Hosmer considered himself part of an "educational revival." As one historian writes: "The model for the educational administrator came neither from the business nor the military but from evangelical religion." It's not surprising that after a dozen years at Great Barrington, Hosmer would go on to become president of a missionary college in Hawaii. A liberal Congregationalist, he saw education as a form of enlightenment: a way to bring civilization into darkness. That faith was at the core of his belief in high school—and his belief in Willie.

New England Congregationalists had helped lead the abolitionist movement: Sojourner Truth's advocate, Harriet Beecher Stowe, for example, and her brother the minister Henry Ward Beecher. If that era of moral politics was now over, it wasn't forgotten. "I was born in a community," Willie wrote, "which conceived itself as having put down a wicked rebellion for the purpose of freeing four million slaves." But the community hadn't always seen itself that way—or agreed on the question of freedom. Before the Civil War, abolition had been "the great social issue" among Great Barrington's Congregationalists. Back in 1842, a church committee had debated passing an antislavery resolution—and decided not to. Two years later, when the church hosted an abolitionist meeting, it brought out what was called "the peculiar sensitiveness in the feelings of many on the subject." That sensitiveness no doubt included the town's dependence on slave-produced cotton to feed its mills. And when, in 1847, members of the congregation had called for "some definite and open action" on slavery, the motion was again defeated. At least two people left in protest, declaring that when it came to abolition, the First Congregational Church of Great Barrington seemed "unwilling to consider or permit free discussion." In his defense, the minister said he'd addressed the issue of slavery from the pulpit. But one historian concludes, "The Great Barrington Church seems to have been strangely silent about condemning this evil."

After the Civil War, a new minister, Reverend Evarts Scudder, took over the pulpit, and the church entered what became known as its "Brilliant Era." The brilliance seems to refer to Reverend Scudder's organizing skills. In the almost two decades of his leadership, the congregation grew to include business leaders, the head of the Sedgwick Institute, and Great Barrington's twice-elected state representative, Justin Dewey Jr.–an attorney who would eventually become state supreme court justice. Just after Willie turned fourteen, the church caught fire and burned to the ground; Reverend Scudder started a fund-raising campaign, which led to a stunning new building. While the town's "idle rich" tended to be Episcopalians, in its brilliant era the Congregationalist church was the best attended and, in Willie's view, "the most important."

Its large, influential congregation was all white–except for Willie and his mother. She'd joined back when her son was finishing up his middle-school years. Why? They lived near by, Willie explains, she had "many acquaintances" there, and "because the minister, Scudder, was especially friendly." There was probably more to it. Willie viewed the main "colored" church in town–the Methodist Zion–as being for recently arrived Southern Negroes: a group as outside the town's long-standing community as the Irish. By joining the First Congregational, Willie's mother kept him with his "natural companions": high school classmates like Mary Dewey, the lawyer's daughter. And here, among the families of the well-to-do, Willie had another chance to shine. In Sunday school, he'd often ask probing questions or give "long disquisitions" on the scriptures. "I think I must have been both popular and a little dreaded," he writes, "but I was very happy."

A church historian describes Reverend Scudder as "very much beloved by his congregation . . . conservative . . . dogmatic and unyielding." Like Nabby Smith's father, he always wrote out his sermons, then read them word for word in a firm, unyielding tone. To Reverend Scudder, the fundamental Congregational tenets continued to hold true: man's nature was inherently and essentially sinful; each word of the Bible contained the gospel truth; and while study could improve a man's intellect, no amount of learning would ever change the divine dispensation of his soul.

Congregationalists had a more liberal tradition as well. The lawyer Justin Dewey, for example, not only thought man's soul redeemable but believed the Bible did not "possess equal authority from beginning to end." Man's fate wasn't sealed; progress was possible—in fact, inevitable; and education was the key. When Willie wrote about his "liberal Congregational Sunday School," he was probably talking about Deacon Dewey, who taught it. To Reverend Scudder, Dewey's rationalist approach was no less than blasphemy. A year after Willie's mother joined the congregation, the reverend denounced the deacon from the pulpit. The lawyer resigned rather than change his beliefs, moving over to the town's Episcopal church. While Reverend Scudder was willing to have the Negro woman and her son in his congregation, he wasn't about to preach change or radical experiments in democracy. Instead, as Willie puts it, the congregation "listened once a week to a sermon on doing good as a reasonable duty."

It's telling that Frank Hosmer didn't join Willie's church till the year Reverend Scudder stepped down. It was the liberal side of religion that attracted the principal. And it was the liberal Congregationalists who supported his ongoing crusade for the high school. Justin Dewey, for example, coauthored many of the town's educational reports and sat on the Great Barrington School Committee. That committee summed up its values in a vivid testimonial to Hosmer, written the year they almost lost him to a better-paying job: "The character of the principal of the high school and of teachers in other schools is more important than that of the President and cabinet."

Here's the evangelical public school voice, insisting that democracy began at the local, grassroots level. The point of public education wasn't just to preserve the country's social and civic institutions, but to improve them, to open them up. Willie counted himself a believer. He became the model high school student, taking its rules seriously and playing to win. He led a debate on the question, "Ought the Indians Have Been Driven Out of America?" He had the "honor," he reported, "of being elected president recently of the high school lyceum, of which he is the only colored member." He stood at the top of his class in writing and history and second only to Mary Dewey in math. And with Principal Hosmer's support, this was just the beginning.

Willie was going to become the Negro who went to college.

It was an outlandish goal. For one thing, he'd have to study a different curriculum from his fellow high school students: Greek and higher levels of algebra and Latin. That meant special textbooks, which he couldn't possibly afford. Even a liberal like Justin Dewey thought Willie was reaching too high; he recommended the boy settle for trade school. That, after all, is what Negroes who wanted more education did. But Hosmer encouraged him, "quite as a matter of course," Willie noted. And as the teenager socialized with the well-to-do, visited their homes, listened to their plans for the future, he decided he had to try. His given reason undercuts his idyllic description of Great Barrington as a place where everyone was about the same. "In early years," he writes, "a great bitterness entered my life and kindled a great ambition. I wanted to go to college because others did."

It's a pretty stark admission. He doesn't say he wanted to go to college because of what he'd learn there, or even what he might accomplish after going. In fact, he admitted that for "a young and ambitious colored man," there was no telling "what were the possibilities of employment or of any career after such training." No, he wanted to go, as he describes it here anyway, to prove that he could. To prove that Negroes could be not just like other people, but like the most schooled people in the country. While Willie was at Great Barrington High, less than 2 percent of the nation's eighteen- to twenty-four-year-olds were going to college. And in the history of the nation, only about 650 Negroes had ever graduated from one.

It's a testament to Principal Hosmer's enthusiasm that two out of the thirteen members of Willie's high school class were even considering college. The principal helped convince Mrs. Russell—the mill owner's wife, the mother of Willie's childhood playmate—to pay for the colored boy's college prep books. Willie says he "accepted the offer as something normal and right": part of the town's overseeing custody.

The summer of his third year of high school, he found a different kind of support for his ambition. Willie's 1883 visit to New Bedford was his first extended trip outside Great Barrington, his first time traveling alone, and his first chance to meet anyone from his father's side of the family. He was struck by the landscape at the shore and by a celebration where he got to see thousands of Negroes gathered in one place. But what affected him most was Grandfather Du Bois. The eighty-year-old had never received more than what Willie called "the beginnings of a gentleman's education." Still, here was a model who "held his head high, took no insults, made few friends. He was not a 'Negro,' " Willie wrote, "he was a man!" The "unforgettable" part of the visit was a toast his grandfather raised. A distinguished visitor came by one day, and the boy got to watch his father's father, dressed in a black silk waistcoat, lift a cut-glass decanter off a fine tablecloth, pour two glasses of wine, then murmur a few ceremonial words. The fifteen-year-old "suddenly sensed in my grandfather's parlor what manners meant and how people of breeding behaved."

Back in Great Barrington, Willie's college ambitions soared. According to his calculations, over 80 percent of the Negro college graduates had gone to all-black institutions. The Northern abolitionist movement had funded most of these: "the gift," as Willie put it, "of New England to the freed Negro" and the "finest thing in American history." But growing up in Massachusetts, the teenager could see what people around him thought of as the most prestigious schools. "[W]andering the fields" outside of town, he considered Williams and Amherst, but "I chose the realm of Mind for my territory and planned Harvard and Europe."

Frank Hosmer had known Willie a while now. He'd one day write a letter of recommendation declaring Willie had a "sterling character . . . high scholarship . . . [and] the capacity and the earnest desire to be a man of usefulness in the world." But going to Harvard was out of the question. For one thing, Hosmer admitted that the curriculum at Great Barrington High "was below the standard of Harvard entrance requirements." For another, Willie's mother couldn't possibly afford the tuition. And finally . . . finally, it was just too big a leap. As the local paper noted, Willie's "persistent, industrious effort" had made him "one of the most promising young colored men of the times." A high compliment, but it also kept him in his place: not one of the most promising young men, but young colored men. And there was a prescribed route for young colored men.

Willie's mother died when he was seventeen, the winter after he graduated from high school. A group of the town's Congregationalists—Principal Hosmer, Reverend Scudder, the head of the Sedgwick Institute, and a minister who'd served on the Federal Indian Bureau—chipped in to pay Willie's college tuition. Not to Harvard, but to the all-black Fisk University.

Willie's early education was over. He'd set out to learn what he needed to know to find his way back into the sunshine. The path to follow, he'd decided, was the school system's. But what exactly had his public education taught him?

He wrote about it after he'd grown up to be W. E. B. Du Bois: the renowned sociologist, author of *The Souls of Black Folk*, leading force in the founding of the National Association for the Advancement of Colored People, one of twentieth-century America's great thinkers and activists. "It was to my mind and the minds of most of my teachers a day of Progress with a capital P . . . Inventions and technique were a perpetual marvel and their accomplishment infinite in possibility . . . [E]verywhere wider, bigger, higher, better things were set down as inevitable." Willie was born five years after Henry Ford, and it sure sounds like the same era. It was this sense of advancement, of "Progress," Du Bois wrote, that "dominated education." And it was "especially the economic order [that] determined what the next generation should learn and know."

Looking back, Du Bois saw how much he'd bought into those values. "What the white world was doing, its goals and ideals, I had not doubted were quite right. What was wrong was that I and people like me and thousands of others who might have my ability and aspiration were refused permission to be part of this world. It was as though moving on a rushing express, my main thought was as to my relations with the other passengers on the express, and not to its rate of speed and its destination." He wanted to go that direction because others did. And the educational system would give him his ticket to get on board.

Once he had, his plan was to help others catch a ride. From the days when he was Great Barrington's most promising young colored man, Willie's stated plan had been to join "a group of educated Negroes who from their knowledge and experience would lead the mass." Where? Toward freedom by way of education. One of the key responsibilities of progressive Negro leadership, he'd write, was "supporting the schools."

Not just any kind of school, as his famous debate with Booker T. Washington showed. The issue for his post–Civil War generation was that the nation was suddenly faced, as Du Bois wrote, with "a black man who was not born in slavery. What was he to become?" Washington, founder of the Tuskegee Normal and Industrial Institute, argued that the first thing a freed black man needed was the ability to earn a living. Therefore, he ought to go the same basic route as Judge Dewey had recommended for Willie: trade school. Du Bois's response? "The object of education was not to make men carpenters, but to make carpenters men."

There's some of Principal Hosmer in his voice: the educational reformer as evangelist. And some of his grandfather: the Negro who held his head high. Du Bois thought Washington's insistence on practical training amounted to "adjustment and submission" and "silence as to civil and political rights." As if the most a colored boy could dream of was a chance to operate the Jacquard loom. Yes, they were entering a gilded age dominated by the bigger, higher, better things of industrialism. But, Du Bois wrote, "[I]t is industrialism drunk with its vision of success to imagine that its own work can be accomplished without providing for the training of broadly cultured men and women to teach its own teachers, and to teach the teachers of the public schools."

For Du Bois, the debate with Washington was over "the whole

question as to what the education of Negroes was really aiming at, and, indeed, what was the aim of educating any working class." In the end, he believed, "The Negro race, like all races, is going to be saved by its exceptional men." He called these the "Talented Tenth." Hadn't it been Great Barrington's intellectual elite—men like Principal Hosmer and lawyer Dewey—who had led the town to support a high school? And the aim of the high school, in turn, was to winnow out and reward the "exceptional." Like Willie. Who then had a duty to teach the next generation. "Was there ever a nation on God's fine earth," Du Bois would write, "civilized from the bottom upward? Never; it is, ever was and ever will be from the top downward that culture filters."

For a while, the young man's goal seems to have been to get a gentleman's education: to learn how to offer a civilized toast in a civilized parlor. "Had it not been for the race problem early thrust upon me and enveloping me," Du Bois believed, "I should have probably been an unquestioning worshipper at the shrine of the established social order and of the economic development into which I was born." He'd come sailing out of college, in his words, "blithely European and imperialist in outlook; democratic as democracy was conceived in America." Following his childhood plan, he studied in Europe, then became the first Negro to earn a graduate degree from Harvard: "I had now received more education than most young white men."

What had school trained him for? School. While at Fisk, he'd been a teacher for two summers in a little Tennessee town "where there had been a Negro public school only once since the Civil War." There, among poor rural blacks, he found American education a lot like it had looked a hundred years before. He taught in a log cabin, his students on rough benches, the text "Webster's blue-black spelling book."

After Harvard, he became a professor, which he called "practically my sole chance of earning a living combined with study." He taught history, economics, sociology, looking for "the path to social reform and social uplift." He wrote his first groundbreaking work, *The Philadelphia Negro: A Social Study*, in the belief that if he conducted a scientific investigation of the facts—and then laid them out in the rational way that he'd been taught—the country would begin to see the truth and change. A more racially just society would follow. Like learning a lesson in school.

It didn't work.

The race problem wouldn't fix, and that opened a crack in Du Bois's faith in his education. As he was about to turn forty, in an article he called "The Negro and Socialism," he wrote: "Our natural friends are not the rich but the poor, not the great but the masses, not the employers but the employees." Not the well-to-do, he might have added, but the workers in the cotton mills. Now, as he reviewed his formal schooling, it seemed to have taught him the importance of moral values but "on the whole had avoided economics." And while patriotism and the value of free speech had been part of the curriculum from grade school through Harvard, "in class I do not remember ever hearing Karl Marx mentioned nor socialism discussed."

Around the time he turned fifty, Du Bois writes, Marx hit him like "a beam of new light." By the time of the Great Depression and Roosevelt's New Deal, Du Bois was in his sixties and had come to define the national (and international) challenge as solving the labor problem, "which included the Negro problem." More of his people were going to college, but, he wrote: "The average Negro undergraduate has swallowed hook, line and sinker the dead bait of the white undergraduate who, born in an industrial machine, does not have to think, and does not think." He still saw his Great Barrington childhood in idyllic terms, but he'd come to reject the part of Principal Hosmer's Great Speculation that declared there was "little or no segregation in the North." And he'd also lost faith in the idea that Negroes could overcome prejudice through political agitation and the sheer dint of their accomplishments. "This," Du Bois would write in the 1930s, "is a fable. I once believed it passionately."

Willie had taken the educational system as his way up and out. But what the adult Du Bois concluded was that school hadn't offered the colored boy the tools he'd really needed. Almost since that first walk from the railroad apartment to the school under the chokecherry tree, Du Bois's objective had been to tear down the veil of color. But Marx's beam of light cast the race problem in terms of economics. The abolitionist values that had allowed Willie into school in the first place, the Congregationalist beliefs that had given him the means to continue, the whole glittering invention of high school—all supported democracy as conceived in America. At best, they offered a way to modify the economic system—not change it in any fundamental way. When he realized that, he wrote, "I was astounded and wondered what other areas of learning had been roped off from my mind in the days of my 'broad' education."

Du Bois never gave up on the concept of public school. After all, education had given him the basic skills that had led him to the beam of light. He considered himself proof that students could avoid the dead bait of industrialism. "[W]e who receive education as the dole of the rich," Du Bois wrote in 1931, "have not all become slaves of wealth." But he came to believe that what America lacked was "that sort of public education which will create the intelligent basis of a real democracy." For decades, Du Bois wrestled with the question of what that kind of education might look like. Eventually, he'd decide the litmus test, the crux of the matter, lay in an experience he knew intimately: a black child going to a white school.

Early in the twentieth century, Du Bois was noting how few Negro children were going to school at all: just one in three. "We are today deliberately rearing millions of our children in ignorance." As the decades went by, enrollment grew but the nation's schools also got more segregated. Of the two million Negro children in school by 1935, Du Bois estimated that less than five hundred thousand were in classes with white kids. And those who were experienced what he called "a living hell." They basically faced two possible outcomes. The most likely was repeated failure, eventually producing "the complete ruin of character, gift, and ability." The other possibility, Du Bois wrote, was the child who "triumphs and teaches the school community a lesson." Here, we're getting close to a portrait of Willie. But, Du Bois concluded, even if a Negro climbed that ladder, academic success had the potential of turning the child's "whole life into an effort to win cheap applause."

No, if education is going to produce real democracy, Du Bois declared, kids need to go to schools "where they are wanted." They need the sympathy of their teachers. That, he'd eventually decide, meant racially separate schools. Someday, maybe, the nation would get to the point where interracial, equitable education was a real possibility; he held on to his Great Barrington childhood as a taste of what that might be like. But Du Bois had come to believe that the economic order determined what school taught—and the economic order was pushing public education further and further from his ideal.

Negro children needed Negro schools not only because there they'd have a chance to learn, but because of what they'd learn. "We are the people," he wrote, "whose subtle sense of song has given America its only American music, its only American fairy tales, its only touch of pathos and humor amid its mad money-getting plutocracy." He looked back to the African-American tradition of Sojourner Truth's day—their suffering, their "sorrow songs"—and saw an alternative. By studying and teaching that tradition, there was the possibility of a better system for all. And in the shining world that would result, Du Bois saw schools as "centers of a new and beautiful effort at human education."

HELEN

It's a classic American moment, a classic moment in American education.

Helen Keller and her teacher are standing by the water pump; Helen can't speak, or see, or hear. Teacher (Annie Sullivan) signs W-A-T-E-R, Helen feels the cool flow on her hand, and . . . bang!

"That living word," is how Helen describes it, "awakened my soul, gave it light, hope, joy, set it free!" In Teacher's version: "She . . . stood as one transfixed. A new light came into her face." In both cases, it's light into darkness: the rush of learning.

It's powerful partly because of Helen's handicaps—an against-all-odds awakening—but it's also a gorgeous, condensed version of how education is supposed to work. Learning stripped to its essentials: a teacher, a student, and the need to know. Don't we send kids to school for something like this—maybe a less extreme version, less dramatic, but the same bang as a new world opens? It's a miracle, complete with miracle worker.

Helen was almost seven when it happened, the age of a second grader. She'd been born with all her senses, contracted a fever when she was a year and a half, and then, in her words, "Gradually I got used to the silence and darkness that surrounded me." But she never got used to the frustration. "Nothing," as she described it, "was part of anything." Then, Teacher arrived, and a little over a month later, Helen was out by the pump. "Suddenly I felt a misty consciousness as of something forgotten–a thrill of returning thought; and somehow the mystery of language was revealed to me. Everything had a name and each name gave birth to a new thought."

The miracle is language. It lets her name things. And names let her begin to think, to consider how one thing relates to the next. And that connects her to the world. "As we returned to the house every object which I touched seemed to quiver with life." Teacher says Helen learned thirty words in the next few hours, had a hundred within ten days, four hundred in less than three months. Knowledge pours in.

But wait. The way Helen and her teacher describe it, it's more like knowledge gushes out. She's forgotten what she needs to know; now it wells up from within. Teacher says the speed Helen learns "suggests the waking from a dream."

Before Teacher arrived, Helen had known a few basic signs: mother, father, ice cream, cake. She could communicate, if crudely. Teacher believed language was in the girl, latent but blocked. That's why she saw the moment by the pump as the *second* step in Helen's education. When Anne Sullivan writes a friend, "A miracle has happened! The light of understanding has shone upon my little pupil's mind, and behold, all things are changed!" the letter's dated two weeks *before* W-A-T-E-R.

What's the earlier miracle? Within a week of arriving, Teacher decided that the first thing Helen needed to know was her place. At dinner, the girl was used to circling the table, eating randomly off plates, making a mess. When Sullivan tried to stop her, "She pinched me, and I slapped her every time she did it." While the slapping horrifies the Kellers, Teacher insists their "over-indulgence" is going to make it impossible for Helen to learn. She and her new pupil move into the isolation of a little garden house. Soon, their only other regular contact is with Percy, a black boy, their servant. According to Teacher, Helen's willfulness had to be broken before learning could begin. "[O]bedience is the gateway," Sullivan writes, "through which knowledge and, yes, love, enter the mind of the child."

After about a week of isolation, as Annie Sullivan puts it, "The little savage learned." Civilization arrives. Helen understands and even begins play-acting the teacher-pupil relationship: pretending to spell words to Percy and to the family dog, pretending they've made mistakes and need to be scolded. The first miracle, then, is Helen learning that she must be to Teacher as Percy is to her. Which raises the question of how Annie Sullivan learned that what a savage needs is obedience.

Helen's teacher was what young Willie Du Bois would have called an Irish peasant. The potato famine had driven the Sullivans to America, where Annie was born—outside Springfield, Massachusetts—in 1866. Her mother was tubercular, her father "illiterate and unskilled." Two of Annie's five siblings died young, a brother also had tuberculosis, and Annie got trachoma at age five and started losing her sight. Then, her mother died. In the carriage on the way to the Potter's Field, Annie wanted the window seat, and her father hit her—not for the first or last time. "A fire of hatred blazed up in me," Annie would write, "which burned for many years." At the age blind Helen would be receiving the rush of language, all-but-blind Annie was in a shack on a New England farm trying to keep house for her father. He'd drink and announce, "God put a curse on me for leaving Ireland," then rail against the "landlord" class. After three years of this, Annie, nearly ten, and her younger brother were sent to live at the Tewksbury poorhouse.

She was a ward of the state, and after her brother died, alone. She'd stay at Tewksbury till she was fourteen; we could call it her middle school. She witnessed old women dying penniless, unwanted babies being born; she listened to the stories ex-hookers told and the occasional book read aloud by a "mildly damaged" girl. "I was not shocked, pained, grieved, or troubled," Annie remembered. "Curiosity kept me alert and keen to know everything." She says she came away with the lesson that existence was "primarily cruel and bitter." No subsequent education would ever affect her so deeply. "I doubt if life or for that matter eternity is long enough to erase the terrors and ugly blots scored upon my mind during those dismal years."

It ended when she managed to get transferred from the poorhouse to the Perkins Institute for the Blind in Boston. Perkins had been founded in 1832 by Samuel Gridley Howe, an abolitionist, social reformer, and friend of Horace Mann. Howe had been with Mann during the anti-Catholic riots that had paralyzed Boston and helped inspire the campaign for public education. The Perkins Institute grew out of the same liberal New England impulse. The way to help the less fortunate—the poor, the blind, the Negro—was through various kinds of education. "I would rather have built up the Blind Asylum," Mann wrote, "than have written *Hamlet*, and one day everybody will think so."

The Perkins Institute made its reputation—and did a lot of its fund-raising—based on a single star pupil, Laura Bridgman. When Bridgman arrived at the institute, she couldn't speak, or see, or hear. One day, working with Howe, she suddenly realized that a raised label spelled out the thing it was attached to: a spoon. "[H]er countenance," Howe wrote, "lighted up with a human expression; it was no longer a dog or parrot—it was an immortal spirit." Light into darkness; the awakening of the soul.

Howe was dead by the time Annie Sullivan arrived at Perkins, but Laura Bridgman was still in residence: a middle-aged blind woman selling her crotchet work to visitors and giving demonstrations of how she could thread a needle using her tongue. The institute survived off state aid and private donations. Its new director—Howe's son-in-law, Michael Anagnos—appealed to donors by presenting the blind girls as functioning members of society: polite society. They were always dressed neatly, and they wore green felt masks so visitors wouldn't be offended by their sightless, staring eyes.

Nearly all the two hundred or so students were middle class; Annie described her fellow classmates as "the daughters of ministers and teachers and dentists and druggists." It was like the population in Willie Du Bois's high school, but Annie wasn't interested in making an alliance with the well-to-do. She was large for her age (the other students called her "Big Annie"), way behind in grammar and spelling, and she hadn't even begun to learn Braille. Most important, she was Irish. She knew how the "smug little children" felt about her. "They think having a lot of dead ancestors make them fine folk . . . They seem to forget that everybody must have had a dead grandfather."

Annie fought the Perkins system, from her teachers to her classmates. She was seen as a "radical": pro-Irish, anti–Protestant establishment, more interested in independence than receiving charity. She developed an outright hatred for the founder's widow, Julia Ward Howe. Yes, Mrs. Howe had written the words to "The Battle Hymn of the Republic," the abolitionists' anthem. But Annie had heard her talk about "niggers" and poor Irish with the same upper-class revulsion. To Annie, Mrs. Howe "had the air of one who confers a favor by acknowledging one's existence." The Institute for the Blind confirmed what the "Irish hellion" had learned in the poorhouse: "The men 'nice people' admired rose on the backs of bleeding slaves, black and white, to power and wealth and education."

Her education changed at sixteen when an operation partially restored her sight. Annie began reading Shakespeare—"the noblest and most spiritualizing influence I have ever known"—and going to public speeches and the philharmonic. At the same time, she started, as she put it, to "accept the conventional order of society." She invented what she thought was a cultivated middle name—became Miss Anne Mansfield Sullivan—and ended up valedictorian of her class. Dressed in a borrowed white ball gown, the twenty-year-old spoke of "the great law of our being. God has placed us here to grow, to expand, to progress." Her anger was still there, but she'd learned how to get along.

The problem was that while Perkins had prepared her to enter polite society, it hadn't provided any practical training. She graduated not knowing, as she wrote, "if there was any sort of work I could do to earn my living." Many of the blind went on to make and sell needlework, but she hated sewing. From time spent with Laura Bridgman, she'd learned how to sign the manual alphabet, but it wasn't clear how she could make money doing that. Without family connections or any means of support, she faced the real possibility of ending up back in the poorhouse. Then, Mr. Anagnos announced he might have found her a job as tutor to a young girl.

So, Annie Sullivan came to Helen convinced that the first lesson students had to learn was to accept what she called "the yoke" of authority. As for the subsequent W-A-T-E-R miracle, Teacher claimed she'd simply followed Samuel Howe's method with Laura Bridgman. But after Helen felt all things quivering with language, then what? The twenty-year-old tutor believed her job was "to direct and mold the beautiful intelligence that is beginning to stir in the child-soul." That, not the miracles, was the real work.

Teacher wasn't sure she was up to it. She saw her own mind as still "undisciplined . . . [with] a lot of things huddled together in dark corners." At night, Annie would sneak out of bed and play with Helen's dolls: just one part of the childhood she'd missed. "I need a teacher quite as much as Helen," she wrote and added, "There isn't a living soul in this part of the world to whom I can go for advice on this, or indeed, in any other educational difficulty. The only thing for me to do in a perplexity is to go ahead, and learn by making mistakes."

What is this barren landscape Teacher's ended up in? Pull back from the W-A-T-E-R miracle, and the pump turns out to be in the backyard of a run-down former plantation in the little northern Alabama town of Tuscumbia. No New England reformers here. The education of Helen Keller has to move forward among people Annie's been taught to think of as the enemy.

The first whites had settled near Tuscumbia in 1815, after General Andrew Jackson crushed the southern wing of Tecumseh's Indian Federation. The town was an early embarkation point for the Trail of Tears: lines of Native Americans loaded on keel boats to be shipped down the Tennessee River and west. A land rush followed, with Jackson himself buying up hundreds of acres right across from where Helen Keller would eventually grow up. As president, Jackson would declare it was only right that the Indians were "annihilated or have melted away . . . What good man would prefer a country covered with forests and ranged by a few thousand savages to our extensive Republic?"

Tuscumbia's forests became plantations: cotton fields worked by

African slaves. David Keller, Helen's grandfather, was one of the first settlers. He claimed 640 acres and built Ivy Green, a large "Virginia cottage" that would become Helen's home. The Virginia part was no doubt due to David Keller's wife: great-granddaughter of Virginia's first governor and second cousin to Robert E. Lee. The couple prospered, raising seven sons and three daughters. The Alabama General Assembly appointed Keller to help supervise construction of a road inland, and he later became superintendent of the Tuscumbia and Decatur railroad, the first line west of the Alleghenies.

By the time Helen's father was born in 1836, Tuscumbia had turned into a transportation center. The Tennessee River valley couldn't compete with the incredibly fertile soil and massive plantations farther south in Alabama's Black Belt. Instead, Tuscumbia became a transfer point. Cotton came down the Tennessee, was shifted over to the railroad to avoid the navigational block at Muscle Shoals, then was reloaded onto boats at the Tuscumbia dock. From there, it followed the same route the young Abe Lincoln had: down the Mississippi to the markets in New Orleans. The river town of two thousand emerged as one of the most prosperous in Alabama. The men of Helen's father's generation became merchants and professionals and gentlemen farmers. Helen's uncle went to the University of Louisville and then practiced medicine in Memphis. Her father, Arthur Henley Keller, was tutored in law by a future governor of Alabama before going on to the University of Virginia.

Women, meanwhile, were raised to run the household, a lot like Nabby Smith had been a century earlier. Slavery in the Tennessee River valley wasn't the huge, industrial system of the Black Belt plantations. It was more on the scale that Belle had experienced in upstate New York. As a Tuscumbia historian put it, "The white race, even in the palmy days of slavery, was always in excess of the negroes." Still, slaves were a valuable commodity and one of the main sources of white people's wealth. The year Helen's grandfather died, the Kellers posted an ad in the local newspaper offering a twenty-five-dollar reward for a runaway "negro . . . near six feet high, very dark complexion, and well-formed." Another classified offered "a good bargain" on a "likely Negro Woman, 21 years of age, and her three Children." And the ads for Negro blacksmiths, house servants, and cotton pickers show a society where black people were doing most of the hard labor.

As an infant, Helen Keller had been cared for by her own black nurse. As she'd grown, she'd gotten a "playmate": the daughter of Viney, the cook. "It pleased me," Helen wrote, "to domineer over her." In Teacher's words, Helen "tyrannized the little darkies." After an argument with the cook, the white girl confidently signed to Teacher, "Mother will whip Viney." Not long after the Yankee tutor arrived, Helen's father made it clear that, while Negroes were useful, "We never think of them as human beings." Teacher was faced with a student whose beautiful intelligence had already absorbed some of these values. The day she taught Helen the word *think*, the little girl signed: "My think is white, Viney's think is black."

Teacher came to Tuscumbia three decades after the Civil War, but the South was still a landscape of abandoned plantations, ruined roads, and subsistence farming. A fifth of the Confederacy's white adult population had been killed in the fighting. The net value of Alabama's land had gone from $725 million to $125 million. Many returning soldiers had found, as one Alabama General put it, that "all, all was lost, except my debts." Tuscumbia had been occupied and burned by Union forces. A December 1863 letter from Helen's grandmother described how her slaves had run off, the Yankees had taken her provisions, and corn and pork were almost impossible to come by. "But," she added, "we are not yet subjugated."

After the war, Helen's father had married the daughter of a Memphis merchant and patched together a living doing some legal work, "receiving and forwarding," and, like most of his neighbors, living off whatever he could raise in badly overfarmed soil. Through it all, he'd stoutly maintained that "everything Southern [was] desirable, noble, and eternal." Du Bois had seen Reconstruction as a great experiment in democracy; Captain Keller and his fellow ex-Confederates fought it with all they had. In 1868, claiming they'd uncovered a Unionist plot to set fire to Tuscumbia's Main Street, a mob had promptly and without trial hung three African-Americans from the railroad bridge—and left them there as a reminder: the Confederacy had been defeated, but its values lived on.

Captain Keller was a "simon pure Democrat." In the election of 1874—seen as a referendum on the "Great Issue": "Shall the white man or the negro rule Alabama?"—Keller stood with those who campaigned under the slogans of "White Supremacy" and "Home Rule." On election day, armed whites drove blacks from the polls, and lynchings and assassinations killed thirty-six Republicans statewide. The resulting Democratic victory effectively ended Reconstruction in the state. A month later, Captain Keller bought the *North Alabamian* and began a career as a crusading newspaperman: crusading for the aristocracy and the sharecropping system, against equal rights for Negroes (or for poor whites).

As editor, Keller would run one of the most popular Democratic papers in the state: "[W]henever his sharp blade was raised the enemies of good government went down like ripe grain before the reaper." But that didn't translate into cash. Almost all Captain Keller had was his good name. When his wife died, the forty-one-year-old quickly married Kate Adams, twenty-one, the daughter of a Confederate brigadier general and a descendant of *the* Adams family of Massachusetts. Family legend had it that when their first child was born, the couple couldn't agree on a name, and the baby girl was christened Helen Adams Keller by "mistake." That kept the Captain's Southern pride intact, but the fact remained that he'd given his daughter a Yankee name. It was a near admission that distinguished Confederate roots might no longer be enough.

During Helen's infancy, the Kellers were too poor to move back into Ivy Green; instead they lived in a nearby, one-room annex. But they still considered themselves Southern aristocracy. Though they could have sent Helen to a state school for the deaf and blind, they'd no sooner have done that than sent her "normal" sister to public school. Common schools were just that: for the common people. Carpetbaggers came down and told the Alabama legislature that education was the way to end the region's poverty: "Capital follows the schoolhouse." But men like Captain Keller knew what that was really about: helping the colored. As Du Bois put it, "Public education for all at public expense was, in the South, a Negro idea." While the North institutionalized and expanded its school system, white Southern gentry saw public education as just another way to drag them into a future they didn't want. The "common" values it taught weren't their values. When Helen was growing up, children below the Mason-Dixon Line averaged about as little time in school as the early settlers had: maybe three months a year. And that would remain true into the twentieth century.

Meanwhile, families with money sent their kids to private academies. In Tuscumbia, they'd go to the Deshler Female Institute, which Captain Keller's paper reported was "well-patronized" and "flourishing." Or, there was Miss Anna Pybas's day and boarding school for young ladies: two to five dollars per month for lessons in English, Latin, or French; four dollars for studying piano, organ, or guitar. It was another part of Southern culture that remained rooted in the past: education was largely a private matter that depended on a family's wealth. If a child was struck down, as Helen had been, the solution was to hire a private tutor.

But in 1880, when Helen was born, the Kellers weren't a family with money. Their fortune finally turned four years later, when the Democratic candidate, Grover Cleveland, won the presidency. Republican rule was over, and an observer watched the South celebrate with "guns and pistols, bells and chimes, pots and pans." Captain Keller soon got a patronage job. As the United States marshal for northern Alabama, he'd run the federal courts and be paid on a fee system, so much per subpoena and warrant. He'd also hire deputies and control expenses for court clerks and attorneys. Appointed the summer his daughter turned five, Captain Keller immediately started renovating Ivy Green. After his confirmation the next June, he took Helen to an eye doctor in Baltimore. That led to the Perkins Institute and their Yankee tutor, Miss Sullivan.

Captain and Mrs. Keller expected Teacher to help their daughter with her handicaps—and leave the molding of her intelligence to them. But as Sullivan wrote, she'd come South carrying her "flaming sword of righteousness." She had no intention of letting Helen absorb the hateful "arrogance" of the old Confederacy. The treatment of

Negroes "sickened" Teacher. And then there was the role assigned to women. "It seems to me the heights of a southern woman's ambition to dance well," Sullivan wrote one of her friends. While she admired Mrs. Keller—"a voluminous reader . . . witty, very intelligent . . . interested in politics, agriculture, birds and flowers"—the woman had been educated to be decorative, not practical. As Sullivan's friend and biographer put it, Mrs. Keller had been "carefully nurtured in that witless Southern system by which a woman before marriage was kept entirely ignorant of every form of useful knowledge."

Teacher refused to follow that model. At the same time, the kind of training Annie had received at Perkins would prepare Helen to be what? A blind seamstress? There had to be another way. Five days after w-a-t-e-r had awakened Helen's soul, Teacher wrote north, underlining the sentence: "<u>I have decided not to try to have regular lessons for the present. I am going to treat Helen exactly like a two-year-old child</u>."

The plan was to answer all Helen's questions, spell to her constantly, develop her vocabulary, "but I shall not try to keep her mind fixed on any one thing." The child was "a free and active being," as Sullivan later put it, "whose own spontaneous impulses must be my surest guide." Less than a month after wrestling Helen into obedience, Teacher was letting the blind girl decide her own curriculum.

"She learns because she can't help it," Sullivan writes, two weeks into the experiment, "just as the birds learn to fly." And it was out with the birds that most of the education took place. The twenty-year-old teacher and almost seven-year-old student spent their days wandering through the glories of the Southern spring: smelling flowers, picnicking by the river, investigating the farm with its chickens, horses, and pigs. Teacher's stated goal was to let Helen develop "independent ideas out of actual experiences." Think of it as a two-person variation on the floating school: Helen bubbling with curiosity, touching her way toward knowledge. And Teacher learning, too.

"Indeed, I feel as if I had never seen anything until now," Sullivan writes that spring, "Helen finds so much to ask about." As

Helen skips from word to idea to feeling, Teacher—racing to keep up—lets the whole concept of school fall away. What was a classroom, anyway, but an instructor "digging out of the child what she has put into him?" Two months after arriving in Alabama, Sullivan writes: "I am beginning to suspect all elaborate and special systems of education. They seem to me to be built upon the supposition that every child is a kind of idiot who must be taught to think." Instead, a student ought to be left to follow what Emerson called the private heart. That way, Teacher declares, he will "think more and better, if less showily . . . Let him touch all things and combine his impressions for himself, instead of sitting indoors at a little round table."

Word of the miracle quickly travels north. Less than a month after Teacher writes her first letter back to Mr. Anagnos, there's an article about Helen in the *Boston Herald*. By that winter, the little Southern girl is a celebrity. When she and Teacher visit Memphis, they're "besieged" by what amount to fans. Though Teacher swears, "My beautiful Helen will not be transformed into a prodigy if I can help it," Helen Keller has already become a public figure. Anagnos features her in the Perkins annual report, hailing Helen as the next Laura Bridgman, "a phenomenon." And he paints Annie Sullivan as the miracle worker, having "drunk . . . copiously of the noble spirit of Dr. Howe." Annie didn't think there was anything noble about it: "I came here simply because circumstances make it necessary for me to earn a living." But Anagnos saw both a breakthrough and a publicity bonanza. Soon, Helen, Anne, and Mrs. Keller are visiting President Cleveland at the White House.

Helen had already learned enough to read her first "connected story." Now, the eight-year-old visits the Perkins Institute, where she becomes fascinated by books: *Little Lord Fauntleroy, Swiss Family Robinson, Heidi, Little Women*. Literature will become, as she writes, "my Utopia. Here I am not disenfranchised. No barrier of the senses shuts me out from the sweet, gracious discourse of my book-friends. They talk to me without embarrassment or awkwardness." She's as hungry as the young Lincoln, and the same way he believed that reading was what separated the white man from the savage, Helen feeds on books as the thing that can civilize her. Teacher agrees: she credits reading for the girl's rapid improvement in language.

Perkins is where Helen can get access to a library of Braille books as well as other specialized equipment. By the time Helen's nine, she and Sullivan have become "permanent guests." Plus, Perkins can teach what Annie can't; Helen starts taking French, for example. The agreement Teacher works out with the trustees is that Helen will live and study for free, finishing the equivalent of her elementary education, but won't be formally enrolled. Teacher (whose room and board is also taken care of) remains her private instructor. The two are still running their little floating school, getting the benefit of the institution without following all its restrictions. In return, the Perkins Institute gets to have the nationally famous Helen Keller greet visitors, attend graduations, and help with fund-raisers. As the president of the board puts it after her first visit, "[Helen] belongs to us."

From here on, Helen's formal schooling will take place in the North. If the Kellers worried about that—worried about their daughter being exposed to Yankee values—they couldn't really afford to object. The brief upswing in Captain Keller's fortunes ends with President Cleveland's defeat in 1888. He loses his marshal job and stops paying Annie's wages. In fact, the Kellers can never afford to pay the tutor again.

Teacher and Helen continue to go back to Alabama for summers and holidays. It's becoming part of the New South, led by "brisk men," as Mark Twain puts it, "energetic of movement and speech; the dollar their god, how to get it their religion." A couple miles from Tuscumbia, the town of Sheffield has burst almost overnight into a modern industrial center: five huge pig-iron furnaces mark the new horizon. The local real estate market booms so fiercely that, for a while, Captain Keller runs the *North Alabamian* as a daily, chock full of ads for housing and business opportunities. And Sheffield is just a miniature of what's happening a hundred miles south in Birmingham. There, jobs in the steel mills will help jump the population from three thousand in 1880 to twenty-six thousand a decade later. Northern investors, taking advantage of cheap Southern land and labor, help revitalize the region. Michigan lumbermen, for example, having clear-cut their own forests, buy up Alabama's great piney woods. In the rush, five and a half million acres of public land are sold; by the first decade of the twentieth century, the South will go from producing 10 percent of the nation's lumber to 45 percent.

All of which bypasses Captain Keller. Instead of joining the new class of industrialists, he stays with what historian C. Vann Woodward has called "the romantic cult of the Confederacy." Or, as Teacher put it, his generation ends up "standing between two eras: one dead, the other just born." She and Helen can't afford to wait until that changes. In the North, at Perkins, Helen can find what she needs to know. She's taught how to read lips, for example. As she signs what she "hears" with one hand, the other all but smothers the speaker: a thumb under the nose, a finger over the lips, another stretched down to catch the throat's vibrations. And over at the Horace Mann School for the Deaf, she learns the rudiments of speech. It's an intense training: Helen sometimes has to reach her hand into the teacher's mouth to feel how the tongue shapes specific sounds. She's entered a different phase of education: it's no longer purely spontaneous and joyful. Learning how to talk, as Helen writes, involves "practice, practice, practice. Discouragement and weariness cast me down frequently." And for a long time, only Teacher and a few others can make out what she's trying to say.

Boston not only has the facilities Helen needs, but here she and Teacher have what amounts to a support group. Helen's a celebrity, invited to the homes of the "best people," constantly written up in the papers. It's how she and Teacher survive. Though internationally known and admired, though regularly in the company of the rich and famous, Helen Keller and Annie Sullivan are charity cases. And Teacher, anyway, realizes they probably will be for the foreseeable future. Coming out of the poorhouse, adjusting to the "conventional order of society," Sullivan learned long ago that there were certain skills, certain ways you needed to behave, if you wanted the "nice men" to support you. Part of her responsibility as tutor was to teach Helen those.

At the end of the equivalent of her primary school education,

Mr. Anagnos dedicated over two hundred pages of the Perkins annual report to what he called Helen's "genius." The eleven-year-old
is featured at commencement, playing the piano and spelling an
original essay into Teacher's hand. "Murmurs of 'wonderful, wonderful!' were heard all through the hall." According to Anagnos,
Helen is "of Emersonian temper in the intuitional quality of her
mind." She's unique the way Henry Ford believed all great people
were. The head of Perkins mostly passes over how hard the pretty
Southern girl is working. Instead, he emphasizes how she's learned
from nature: her classroom "the farm the farm," her knowledge innate. And Helen's miracle worker tends to go along with that explanation. "[T]he child has dormant within him when he comes
into the world, all the experiences of the race," Teacher will write.
"These experiences are like photographic negatives, until language
develops them and brings out the memory-images."

"Helen's life is as perfect as a poem," Anagnos writes in the report,
"as pure and sweet as a strain of music." And that's just the start. He
calls Helen "a phenomenal child"; "reverence lends its beautiful halo
to her . . ."; "She is the finest illustration of consecrated, unselfish,
whole-souled devotion that childhood has ever offered to the vision
of men or that of gods." A lot of this is unapologetic fund-raising. The
institute needs to bring in some two hundred thousand dollars annually, plus it's trying to erect a new kindergarten building. Helen's an
active, willing participant. As a twelve-year-old, she hosts a benefit
tea at the mansion of one of Boston's leading philanthropists, John
Spaulding, member of the "Sugar Trust" monopoly. In the newspaper, she calls on the public, "to help me make the lives of little blind
children brighter and happier." The result, according to the *Evening
Transcript*, is an unmitigated success: "All Boston was at Helen Keller's
feet." And the event not only raises money for Perkins. Spaulding
will end up being Helen's leading private benefactor, setting up a
trust to support the teenager and her teacher.

Helen charms people. It's the nature of her personality, but it's
also how she's learned to move through the world: praising it, ex-
cited by its possibilities, deliberately setting out "in my school life . . .

and indeed, in my life," as she'll write in her diary, ". . . to love everybody sincerely." Where Annie Sullivan still has some of her rage, still believes Boston's polite society sees her as a "vulgar upstart," Helen's Southern education is an aristocrat's. She's comfortable with people; she knows—or has learned—how to win them over.

And the idea of Helen Keller appeals to America. There's something angelic about the pretty white girl in her long gown, smiling as she reads lips, communicating with Teacher in what seems like a magic language. A popular poem of the day claimed she could, "hear and see / Things hidden from our kind . . . / 'tis we / Are deaf, are dumb, are blind!" The way her distant relative Reverend Edward Everett Hale framed it, the miracle of Helen Keller was "the great philosophical and religious lesson of the time." He saw modern science reducing man to "a lot of atoms of matter." As the country struggled to recover from the Civil War and to adjust to its new industrial economy, Reverend Hale thought Helen's story proved "the victory of the soul." Helen basically agreed, describing in her autobiography how a voice from "the sacred mountain" told her: "Knowledge is love and light and vision." Alexander Graham Bell saw in the adolescent girl "more of the Divine than has been manifest in anyone I ever met before." Even Mark Twain would compare her to Joan of Arc.

That made it all the more horrifying when she turned out to be a plagiarist.

Anagnos had published one of Helen's short stories in the annual report. It was an idyllic, descriptive piece about King Frost showering the autumn leaves with jewels. But long sections of the fourteen-hundred-word story had been lifted from a published fairy tale. Most people didn't think Helen had deliberately copied it. Instead, the scandal focused on the adults around her. Were they faking her accomplishments? After all, Anagnos and Perkins had a lot to gain from a child genius. So did Annie Sullivan. The nationally publicized incident threatened to ruin all of them.

Friends rallied to Helen and Teacher's defense. Twain argued that "all ideas are secondhand, consciously and unconsciously drawn from a million outside sources." How else would a girl who couldn't see or hear describe the color of autumn leaves except from somebody else's description? Teacher's goal had been for Helen to draw "independent ideas out of actual experience," but that could only go so far. Lots she'd never experience directly. And not all ideas were independent. Wasn't that why children were sent to school? To study other people's ideas? The blind girl may have taken it too far, but wasn't the point of education to learn from what had come before?

Anagnos was worried that the scandal would hurt his institute. He inserted an addendum in the annual report saying Helen's story was "an adaptation, if not a reproduction." And he set up a review committee, which called Helen to testify. The twelve-year-old went before them and defended her innocence, but that night, "wept as I hope few children have wept." Soon, Teacher and pupil retreated to Alabama. Years later, Helen would write how "the thought of those dreadful days" still chilled her heart. She was never again sure that what she wrote (and thought? and felt?) was her own. "I may not be original." And if she wasn't that, what was she?

She and Teacher spent a miserable summer at the Kellers' mountain cabin. Helen sat alone a lot, not writing or reading or signing. Mrs. Keller cooked and tended to a newborn; she didn't have the money for servants. The captain hunted with his friends, campaigned for Cleveland's reelection, and mortgaged whatever he could to stay afloat. "I loaned Captain Keller thirty-five dollars," Teacher wrote, "and this with Helen's thirty-five has, I believe, constituted the family income for the past two months." Cleveland won that fall, but Keller didn't get his marshal's job back. Instead, he had to ask for money from Helen's patron, John Spaulding. That was the other question that rose from her public humiliation: how long would her benefactors keep supporting Helen if she wasn't a pure manifestation of genius?

Helen stayed in Alabama for most of what amounted to her middle school years. Perkins was over. A split with Anagnos had been developing anyway—he thought Teacher had never given the institute enough credit—and the plagiarism incident was the final break.

Still, both Teacher and student assumed their future was in the North. Illiteracy among Southern whites was over 30 percent, for blacks almost 60. Homicide rates below the Mason-Dixon Line were the highest in the nation. Industry was growing, but share-cropping still trapped both black and white.

Plus, Helen had changed. Up until the plagiarism incident, she wrote, "I had lived the unconscious life of a little child." The scandal, her time up North, and entering adolescence all had their effect. Teacher noticed that, among other things, the girl's attitude toward black people had shifted: "how patient and gentle she is with them always." She made an "interesting and touching" visit to a local normal school training Negroes to be public school teachers. But if Helen's values were changing, Tuscumbia's weren't. The spring Helen turns fourteen, for example, there's another lynching. Three blacks are accused of torching a barn owned by the white man who foreclosed on their mortgage. After the men are arrested, masked citizens take them from the town jail (the sheriff is off at a Masonic banquet), hang them from the Tuscumbia bridge, then riddle their bodies with bullets.

Helen and Teacher go north when they can. They accept Alexander Graham Bell's generosity and tour the 1893 World Exposition in Chicago. They accept the offer of a Pennsylvania philanthropist and live on his estate for a while. They accept John Spaulding's gift of a three-hundred-dollar-a-month stipend. And as the reality of the situation hits them, both teacher and student accept that Helen's education has to change.

Up until now, Helen writes, she's studied "in a more or less desultory manner" some ancient and U.S. history, a little French, basic English grammar. Teacher had encouraged the girl to follow her impulses, to be original. Now, they set out to get Helen more standardized schooling. Like Willie Du Bois, Helen will use the educational system to prove she can succeed in the "normal" world. The Pennsylvania philanthropist pays for a tutor to teach what Teacher couldn't because she'd never learned it: Latin, higher math, Tennyson "from a critical point of view." Call it the beginning of Helen's high school education.

Teacher still maintains that Helen's example proves something is "radically wrong" with American schooling: the system "spoils" the enthusiasm "dormant in every human being." During that same summer of 1894 that Helen's being tutored, Annie Sullivan is invited to address a national conference for teachers of the deaf. "[W]e shall never properly develop the higher nature of our little ones," she declares, "while we continue to fill their minds with the so-called rudiments." That fall, Helen enrolls in the private Wright-Humason school in New York City—to learn the rudiments.

It's not as big a contradiction as it seems. Teacher is talking about the beginning stages of education. She continues to believe that little ones learn language like birds learn to fly—and that the classroom only inhibits that. "Language and knowledge are indissolubly connected," she emphasizes; kids will pick up skills at their own pace, led by curiosity and the innate need to think. Training in the rudiments should come later. Teacher's approach (made famous through Helen) preserves early childhood as a time for playing with dolls, not being drilled in spelling and subtraction. Years later, Dr. Maria Montessori would dedicate her book to Keller, "as pupil learns from master," and would apply Teacher's methods to all children, not only the deaf and blind. "Dr. Montessori learned as I learned," Annie responds, "and as every teacher must learn, that only through freedom can individuals develop self-control."

But now Helen has moved to another stage of education. "It was my wish," Teacher wrote, "that she should go to some good school with seeing girls of her own age." By a "good school" she meant a school that would prepare her for college, and Captain Keller had the same ambitions. He was determined to have his daughter start on "a regular Collegiate course . . . when and if I can see my way clear to do so." Trouble was, he never could. John Spaulding would end up paying Helen's and Teacher's expenses at Wright-Humason, a "quite fashionable" new school on Seventy-sixth Street and Central Park West. The private academy specialized in teaching the deaf to speak, but Helen also studied arithmetic, geography, piano, Latin grammar, French and German. She took riding lessons, read *David Copperfield*, discovered one of Teacher's favorites,

Hamlet. And entering a new social circle, she reestablished her reputation for being "pure and sweet."

By the 1890s, New York City had eclipsed Boston as the nation's banking and business capital. It was home to the leading intellectuals—and robber barons—of the Gilded Age. Manhattan socialite Lawrence Hutton took Teacher and Helen under his wing and introduced them to Woodrow Wilson, the naturalist John Burroughs, Standard Oil executive Henry Rogers, the influential editor Mary Mapes Dodge, and the Rockefellers, among others. As the adolescent moved through an even more high-powered society than Boston's, Hutton described her as "a revelation and an inspiration . . . a perfectly clear fresh soul . . . straight from the hand of God."

Teacher helped with the conquest, though she didn't much like New York. Again, she worried her background would be "found out" but remained confident that Helen would carry the day: "[She] was still an Adams," Teacher wrote. "Nothing could change that." Annie also worried that Wright-Humason wasn't actually teaching Helen anything. Its students' "plodding pursuit of knowledge" made Teacher "restive." She understood that Helen needed this training, but, as she wrote a friend, "I was never meant for a schoolmarm."

Helen, meanwhile, was her own kind of restive. She started exploring New York City, and that ended up being the education she valued most. "Taught by religion and a gentle home, nourished with good books . . . I supposed that in our civilization all advances benefited every man." She'd already come to see that wasn't true in the South. Now, she toured the tenements of the Lower East Side and, according to an 1895 article in the *New York Times*, the "pretty and remarkably intelligent blind deaf-and-dumb girl [had] some pointed things to say about those who had great wealth and were content to use it for their own pleasure." She didn't know about Annie Sullivan's time in the poorhouse (Teacher would keep it a secret until they were both middle-aged), but Helen credited Sullivan for her growing anger over how "nice men" made their fortunes.

And then John Spaulding died.

He was Teacher and Helen's main benefactor, and it almost certainly meant the end of private school. Plus, Spaulding's estate wanted Captain Keller to repay the fifteen-thousand-dollar loan he'd received. The captain responded with a mixture of pride and despair. He would use what was left in Helen's education fund to pay the debt. "If this can't be done," he wrote, "I will ask the heirs of Mr. Spaulding to extend this offer long enough to have Helen raise the money by doing what I have always opposed her doing—that is giving the public a chance to see and hear her from the platform."

Captain Keller was serious. He'd gotten an offer from a rapidly growing, multimillion-dollar vaudeville circuit. The relatively new entertainment was eager to appeal to the middle class; amid the jugglers, song-and-dance acts, and all-girl revues, it often sprinkled "legitimate" performers. Helen Keller would be perfect. And she could earn five hundred dollars a week.

"Mother," Helen later recalled, "wrote a heartbroken letter to Teacher declaring that she would die before this happened." It would be a humiliating public display, showing Helen "as you would a monkey." Old and new friends, from Alexander Graham Bell to the Huttons to Mrs. J. Pierpont Morgan, would rally and establish a fund to support the rest of Helen's education. She'd enter the Cambridge School for Young Ladies and then Radcliffe College. Though Helen would describe her experience there as mostly "trivial," her degree would go a long way to legitimatizing her in the public eye. In other words, she'd land on her feet. But the sixteen-year-old had gotten a glimpse into the abyss, and in that way, Spaulding's death marks a kind of end to her innocence and her childhood education.

"What is remarkable in her career is already accomplished." That's how much of the public saw Helen Keller, even as a teenager. Yes, she'd go on to college and, as a sophomore, produce a bestselling autobiography. But if she thought she could make her living as a writer, her audience turned out to be interested in only the one story: her handicaps and how she overcame them. She'd continue to learn from the major issues of her time. She'd support striking mill workers in Lawrence, Massachusetts, join the Wobblies' "one big union," oppose the U.S. entry into World War I. She'd become a leading suffragette and see her education with Teacher as necessarily feminist: "If we women are to learn the fundamental things in life, we must educate ourselves and one another." One measure of her changing political awareness was the letter she attached with a contribution to the NAACP: "The outrages against the colored people," she'd write, "are a denial of Christ." When Du Bois published it in the NAACP's magazine, her fellow Alabamians accused her of being part of "the old Abolition Gang." Eventually, she'd arrive at a perspective a lot like Du Bois's: describing the blind as "only part of a greater problem . . . a million laborers out of work in the United States." And she'd come to view charity—even men like Howe and Spaulding helping people like her and Teacher—as "altruistic, most noble in nature, but . . . not profound . . . They seek cures, and not prevention."

But America had her forever fixed by the water pump, her hand in Teacher's, the light pouring in. The public was more interested in the classic moment—the miracle—than in the education that followed. When supporters fall away and the abyss looms again, Helen and Teacher end up making their living giving lectures cross-country—kind of like Sojourner Truth and Thocmetony. They repeatedly evoke the instant Helen's soul, as she puts it, came "out of bondage." By the time Helen's thirty, they're on a vaudeville tour, two shows a day, the same act each show. Teacher comes out first and describes the W-A-T-E-R miracle. Then Helen demonstrates how she can speak by reciting "Abide with Me" and ends with what she calls her "Message of Happiness." They'll use that basic presentation when Helen, in her mid-forties, becomes spokesperson and principal fund-raiser for the American Foundation for the Blind: a paying job that provides their main income for the rest of their lives.

Helen calls this continuous reenactment of her breakthrough a "beggar's life." Again and again, the little girl returns to the water pump. Again and again, the savage becomes an angel. Meanwhile, with Teacher as her model, Keller continues to fight for a broader definition of learning. For her, the lesson of W-A-T-E-R is that knowledge lets you enter the world, become part of it—and that everyone deserved that right. A decade after Teacher's death, Helen Keller is in the midst of what she calls "the crowning experience of my life": a fact-finding tour visiting crippled World War II soldiers. A reporter asks the blind woman in her mid-sixties what she thinks the veterans expect of their country. "They do not want to be treated as a class apart," she spells out though her interpreter. "They do not want to be treated as heroes. They want to be able to live naturally, and to be treated as human beings."

RACHEL

Rachel was raised on a hilltop in a log cabin without central heating or indoor plumbing. A coal stove sat in each room. The kitchen was a lean-to tacked on the back. From the front porch, she could look over the valley of the Allegheny River into the hills of western Pennsylvania and the twentieth century.

Below the house, Colfax Street followed the hill down to Springdale. It was a river town established on the site of a Native American settlement: first a fort, then the real estate project of a land agent sent by "Philadelphia capitalists," then a way station on the Pennsylvania canal, and after the Civil War, a stop on the West Penn railroad. Rachel Carson would begin her most famous book, *Silent Spring*, with a fable that some took to be about Springdale: "There was once a town in the heart of America where all life seemed to live in harmony with its surroundings." This harmony—with its wildflowers and birds, its "checkerboard of prosperous farms"—is then attacked by a "grim specter" that arrives "almost unnoticed": chemical pollution.

Take the fable as reality, and the outline of Rachel's education seems pretty clear. The girl grows up on a hilltop in the unspoiled harmony of nature; learns to love the outdoors; becomes a writer and a scientist to battle what she'll call "the central problem of our age . . . the contamination of man's total environment." Let's start with that as the basic outline of what Rachel needed to learn, adding one proviso: some or all of it may be made up, a fable.

Her father came to Springdale to be a real estate developer. He was thirty-six, his wife thirty-one, and they had a three-year-old daughter and a one-year-old son. Working as a clerk, Robert Carson had managed to save enough money to sign a mortgage for sixty-four acres, including the cabin and an old apple and pear orchard. It was an investment: he was gambling that Springdale would spread up the hill from the river, and he'd make his killing selling building lots. But it must have seemed like a reasonable gamble. Carson, the son of an Irish carpenter, had grown up across the river from Pittsburgh during a period of extraordinary growth.

Western Pennsylvania sits on a gigantic field of soft, bituminous coal. By the time Andrew Jackson was fighting the Battle of New Orleans, Pittsburgh already had 250 factories. Coal was, as Emerson put it, "power and civilization," and from the 1850s to the 1890s, United States consumption doubled every decade. Fortunes were made. By the time Robert Carson turned ten, Pittsburgh produced half the nation's glass, half the nation's iron, and was a major source of the nation's oil. By the time he was in his twenties, Pittsburgh's Mellon family (to take a prominent example) was worth the equivalent of about $110 million in today's money. Carson, like his contemporary Henry Ford, saw the industrial future just out in front of him. After all, Thomas Mellon, an Ulster Scot, had been a farmer's son who had studied what he called his "secular gospel"—Ben Franklin's autobiography—and ended up parlaying his wife's dowry into an empire of real estate, steel, coal, glass, and railroad lines.

The year Robert Carson bought his land in Springdale, Pittsburgh was at its economic height. It was second only to New York City in the number of new corporations springing up. It was producing ten million tons of steel ingots and castings: a figure that would double in the next five years. In 1901, when J. P. Morgan bought out Andrew Carnegie's Pittsburgh holdings (eventually incorporated with, among other operations, the steel mills in Birmingham), it would result in the largest single company in the world. Just sixteen miles upriver, Springdale was linked to the city by road, water, and rail. Hadn't the Mellons just purchased the electric trolley that ran through town? And weren't they expanding that line even as the Carsons moved in? No doubt about it: Springdale was bound to boom.

Mrs. Carson may have been a little less enthusiastic. Born Maria McLean, she came from a more refined background than her husband's: she was the daughter of a college-educated Presbyterian minister. He'd died when she was eleven, but her mother, Rachel McLean, had moved back home to Washington, Pennsylvania, and managed to enroll Maria in the town's elite female seminary. There, she'd gotten an education in the tradition of the private academy: English grammar, elocution, penmanship, piano, harmony, singing, drawing, and painting—all from women teachers, all of them single and referred to as "Miss." She also took advanced classes with various male reverends and professors and graduated an honors student in Latin. It was the kind of intellectual preparation Nabby Smith had dreamed of getting—but it didn't have much practical application. Maria was qualified to go to college, even to become a college teacher, and the Washington Female Seminary was on the campus of Washington College: site of the nation's first university-level teacher training program. Except the college had been chartered a century earlier for men only—and would remain that way for another century.

Rachel's mother became a teacher despite these obstacles—or, in a sense, because of them. As she graduated from the seminary, the nation had reached the point where it had more children in public high school than in academies. (That despite the fact that Pennsylvania was still almost a decade away from mandatory attendance. And even then, it would require only four months of school—and only for children eight to thirteen.) Public education needed more teachers and, simultaneously, was turning out more female graduates. The result was an expanding, self-perpetuating system. Especially since teaching remained one of the few acceptable ways for an educated, well-bred woman to make a living. While jobs for superintendent and principal still almost always went to men, the majority of the nation's public school teachers were now females.

Like Miss McLean, two thirds of these teachers had no formal training. Instead, many educators across the country followed what was called the Five Formal Steps of Teaching and Learning: 1) preparing the students by recalling old lessons, 2) presenting the new material, 3) associating the new material with the old, 4) generalizing from the lesson, and 5) applying the general idea back to practical examples. Proponents saw this as a scientific way of tying the curriculum together, linking it to experience, and maintaining some standard of instruction. People like Annie Sullivan, on the other hand, saw it as exactly the kind of rote instruction that killed learning. "Lock-step" is how one history of education refers to the method: "[with] the same subjects . . . taught in the same way using the same methods" from coast to coast.

For many women, teaching was a temporary profession. Miss McLean did it for six years, living with and helping to support her widowed mother. At age twenty-four, she met Robert Carson at a choral sing, and they were married by the close of the school year. That ended her career: Pennsylvania–like many states–allowed only single women in the classroom. For the next six years, the couple lived with her mother and tried to save some money. When their second child was born, they decided to find a bigger place.

For Maria Carson, the forty-five-mile move to Springdale meant independence–and isolation. At age thirty-one, she'd be living apart from her mother for the first time. And for the first time, she'd be outside the collegiate, relatively sophisticated, Presbyterian atmosphere of her hometown. Educated to appreciate the arts and culture, Mrs. Carson had her piano toted up the hill and installed in the log cabin.

There, the family settled into a life of dignified but unshakable poverty. Mr. Carson barely paid the mortgage by working as a traveling salesman for an insurance company. Mrs. Carson had a kitchen garden out back, and they kept a few farm animals. Seven years after the move, the building lots were still unsold and still mortgaged to the hilt. Then, the speculative loans that had helped prop up the Gilded Age collapsed. In 1907, a year of bank runs and plummeting stocks, thirty-eight-year-old Maria Carson had her third and last child, a daughter. She named her after a resourceful, independent woman who valued education: the baby's maternal grandmother.

Rachel Carson would grow up to be a private person, rarely speaking in public about her personal history. One of those rare instances was an address she gave to an audience of women after she'd become a bestselling author. "I can remember no time even in earliest infancy," she told them, "when I didn't assume I was going to be a writer. I have no idea why. There were no writers in the family. I read a great deal almost from infancy, and I suppose I must have realized someone wrote the books." That she was reading so young almost certainly means her mother was her teacher. The two were alone together most days, what with Mr. Carson off selling and both older siblings in school. Mrs. Carson didn't make many friends in Springdale; she "kept herself and her family aloof." She read; she played piano; she cooked and cleaned in the cabin on the ridge, her youngest child by her side.

In a letter to a friend, Rachel mentions that she grew up on Beatrix Potter books. Flopsy, Mopsy, Cotton-tail, and Peter Rabbit first appeared in print five years before she was born; a year later came Squirrel Nutkin; and *The Tale of Jemima Puddle-Duck* was published when Rachel was a year old. The stories featured animals dressed up like people, going to the baker's to shop and playing in the finely drawn British woodlands. That fit with her other favorites like *Wind in the Willows*. Though they didn't pose as natural history (it was clear they were fantasy, that "someone wrote the books"), they connected children to nature—encouraged them to observe—and suggested there was a hidden, everyday drama going on right outside.

In that same rare, autobiographical speech, Carson added that she could "remember no time when I wasn't interested in the out-of-doors and the whole world of nature. Those interests, I know, I inherited from my mother and have always shared with her. I was a rather solitary child and spent a great deal of time in woods and besides streams, learning the birds and the insects and flowers." If she wanted to be a writer, her constant reading made sense. But why did she need to know about nature? And how did she learn?

Her earliest connection to the fields above Springdale, she wrote a friend, had nothing to do with facts; it was based on her "sensory impressions of, and emotional response to, the world." Late in life, Carson would write a magazine article that eventually became a slim book called *The Sense of Wonder*. In it, she emphasized exactly this kind of emotional learning. "I sincerely believe that for the child, and for the parent seeking to guide him, it is not half so important to *know* as to *feel*." She describes walking through the woods with her grandnephew (to whom the book is dedicated): "I have made no conscious effort to name plants or animals nor to explain to him, but have just expressed my own pleasure in what we see . . . just going through the woods in the spirit of two friends on an expedition."

That, Carson argues, is how kids learn best. It seems to be how she learned. "Just going through the woods" sounds a lot like Helen and Teacher wandering the Alabama springtime, and Rachel and her mother brought some of the same educational beliefs to the hills of western Pennsylvania. "If a child is to keep alive his inborn sense of wonder," Carson would write, ". . . he needs the companionship of at least one adult who can share it, rediscovering with him the joy, excitement and mystery of the world we live in." The wonder is inborn, to be rediscovered, and the route to knowledge is pleasure. What Carson calls "a diet of facts" is more hindrance than help. And true learning happens one-on-one, with an adult guide: not in school, not with other kids, and not—even for Rachel, the "rather solitary child"—alone.

If Mrs. Carson took it upon herself to teach her daughter about the whole world of nature, at least she had some help. A kind of aid arrived each month: *St. Nicholas* children's magazine. In its first issue, published thirty-five years before Rachel's birth, editor Mary Mapes Dodge had stated the goal: "Let there be no sermonizing . . . no spinning out of facts, no rattling of dry bones . . . The ideal child's magazine is a pleasure ground." It set itself up as the opposite of the Five Formal Steps, its aim to fire up kids' imaginations. Mrs. Dodge had begun by working as an associate editor with Harriet Beecher Stowe, Congregationalist champion of Sojourner

Truth. Her magazine descended from that New England, abolitionist, reform tradition. In New York, Helen Keller had met her in the
circle of wealthy liberals at Lawrence Hutton's.

St. Nicholas aimed to "give clean, genuine fun to children of all
ages . . . to stimulate their ambitions—but along normally progressive lines." Mrs. Dodge solicited work from leading writers of the
day. Twain published *Tom Sawyer Abroad* in *St. Nicholas*; Kipling did
the same with *The Jungle Book*; the magazine inspired Jack London
and accepted some of his first stories. By the time Rachel was reading it, Mrs. Dodge had died, and *St. Nicholas* represented proper,
slightly old-fashioned liberalism. Rachel's mother was still a true
believer. At one point, she'd even set a poem of Mrs. Dodge's to
music, and the magazine had published the result. As the Carsons
struggled to keep the kids in presentable clothes, the former Miss
McLean regularly set aside the money for an annual subscription.

A glance at any issue of *St. Nicholas* makes it clear that it saw its audience as well-behaved, middle-class children—and parents who
wanted their kids to learn those values. So, the frontispiece of
Rachel's July 1914 issue was a gentle, otherworldly painting by fairy-
tale illustrator Arthur Rackham: two well-dressed girls sketched and
read in a quiet garden. The magazine championed the idea that childhood was a time to "get closer to the heart of nature." This couldn't
happen, it argued, by "book-study alone" but only through a "direct
friendship with the woods and fields." The key word is "friendship."
The stories *St. Nicholas* published tended to treat nature like Beatrix
Potter did: the woods were full of little animal friends. Or, going back
to an older tradition, they were stories about tiny spirits, hiding in the
ferns, playing on the toadstools.

So, the year after Rachel was born, the magazine carried a piece
by sixteen-year-old Edna St. Vincent Millay describing a "fairy
wind." When Rachel was four, it published thirteen-year-old Stephen
Vincent Benét's "A Song of the Woods" with a "tricksy sprite" dancing around a fairy ring. And when Rachel was seven, among the articles about baseball and water turbines, her summer issue included
a poem called "The Fairy Steeple" with an illustration of a little
winged girl riding a bumblebee. "Up the Fairy Steeple / The Fairy

Ringers climbed, / And out o'er all the country, / The Bluebell Music chimed!" Forty-five years later, Carson would write that she'd always loved lichens "because they have a quality of fairyland." And she'd describe an unseen insect as "the fairy bell ringer," its call "exactly the sound that should come from a bell held in the hand of the tiniest elf."

Around when Rachel entered first grade, the Carson children posed for a photo that could have fit into the gentle pages of *St. Nicholas*. It's a family outing, a swim, in what appears to be the Allegheny River. Sitting on a boulder by the shore, seventeen-year-old Marian looks pretty in her bathing suit and bandanna, fifteen-year-old Robert Carson manly in a fedora and long pants. Seven-year-old Rachel is scowling slightly, turned away from the camera, her bathing cap an odd-shaped thing, her feet muddy from exploring the shore. Behind them, milk cows drink from the river. It's an idyllic, pastoral American scene—if you look past Rachel's expression. And if you don't ask what's happening to the river and the landscape beyond it.

There's no sign of Springdale in the picture; the Carsons probably walked upstream to swim. For one thing, there was a marsh in town that bred fierce mosquitoes. But worse than that was the smell. Springdale's shoreline was dominated—and had been for the past thirty years—by the Franklin Glue Works. One of the largest factories of its kind in the nation, the big brick buildings held a hundred employees, its adhesive used in emery and sandpaper. Most people's first impression when they stepped off the Springdale train was the god-awful stink of boiling animal parts: ears, tails, hides, bones. The carcasses arrived regularly at the factory, were dumped into vats of lime, then cooked over long periods at high temperatures until the bits of animal had been reduced to a jelly. Franklin was an appropriate name: the Glue Works was a modern version of Ben Franklin's "noxious trade": the same greasy stench of rendered animal fat, only on an industrial scale. Years later, Rachel Carson would write how "the sense of smell, almost more than any other, has the power to recall memories." She was talking about nature and more delicate scents, but the smell from Franklin Glue Works might explain why she'd always remember Springdale as a dreary, uninspiring, oppressive place. The factory also produced tankage: a fertilizer made from the animal residue. And it dumped a steady stream of yellow-brown waste back into the Allegheny.

The other, even larger industry on Springdale's shoreline was the Heidenkamp Plate Glass Company. It employed some three hundred men, and above its sprawling two-story buildings, hung gray clouds of smoke. They came from the mix of ground silica, soda, and lime that the workers melted under enormous heat: some three thousand degrees Fahrenheit. The molten glass was then skimmed for impurities, cooled, ground to the desired thickness, and polished. Again, river water fed and flushed the process, which also released fumes, acids, and fine-particulate glass dust.

The idyllic photo of the Carson kids wasn't a lie. Rachel could find a place to swim, the same way she could go off into the woods behind her house and get closer to nature. But it was a deliberate act: a careful kind of editing. To discover the "joy, excitement and mystery of the world"—the natural world—she had to turn her back on Springdale and the future it promised. The town had a population of twelve hundred, with four hundred of its jobs thanks to the Glue Works and the glass factory.

And the same story was being told all through the Allegheny Valley. Heidenkamp's was small compared with Pittsburgh Plate Glass, which had a fifty-building, six-thousand-employee factory in the next town of Creighton. Just around the bend from Springdale, in Natrona, a salt company had been operating since before the Civil War. Its mines kept filling up with a dark liquid its owner had originally disposed of by bottling as digestive medicine. Then he'd discovered that the stuff worked as fuel for lamps. Eventually, Natrona was recognized as the birthplace of America's oil industry. By Rachel's childhood, Pennsylvania was producing half the world's supply of petroleum.

As the Carson kids sat for the photograph by the riverbank, a report had already appeared describing the discharges from Allegheny's oil refineries as "simply amazing." For thirty miles, there was "not a mussel, not a crawfish, nor a fish able to live." And the seven-year-old with muddy feet could find evidence of the industrial revolution wherever she looked. Three miles upriver from Springdale was the Alcoa aluminum works, which the Mellon family had helped start and which had grown until New Kensington was triple the size of Rachel's hometown. Alcoa prospered thanks to a breakthrough method of smelting bauxite. The process emitted various fluorides known to kill fish and cattle and suspected of harming humans. Starting at the Natrona salt mills, then, and climaxing at the confluence with the Monongahela River in Pittsburgh, the region by 1909 contained "possibly the greatest variety of pollution of any of the streams in the state." Or, for that matter, the nation.

Isolated on the ridge, spending a lot of her time in the woods, Rachel could almost avoid all this. But once she was school-age, her three-fifths-of-a-mile walk each morning brought her out of nature and down into industrial reality. First, she passed her father's building lots: the fields sectioned off and waiting for buyers. Realtors advertised Springdale as a "Big Money Making Development" about to happen: "Only 38 minutes by train to the heart of Pittsburgh, and just a few minutes to New Kensington." All across the area, citizens were eager to turn their woods into suburbia. Years later, Rachel would call this sort of wholesale development "the destruction of beauty and the suppression of human individuality." At the end of the Carson property, Rachel took a shortcut across the neighbor's. Here, the hills were being systematically dug up and hauled away to provide sand for the glass factory.

Her walk ended at School Street, where she entered what looked like a cross between a factory and a church. One of the first brick structures in Springdale, the two-story building had the massive construction and narrow windows of a manufacturing site—with a steeple and bell up top. The architecture was fairly common—towns across the country had put up almost identical buildings—and a source of pride. It connected Springdale to progress, to the future. It showed the town cared about its kids.

The Mellon family had donated the land twenty-five years earlier. Built to house grades one through eight, the school was overcrowded by the time Rachel entered in 1913. (Two years later, the district would add six rooms and an auditorium.) A class portrait from that time shows a young woman teacher in charge of forty-one first graders. They're a neatly dressed, serious group: the boys all in white shirts and black pants, the girls in skirts with bows in their short hair. A few may have been the children of Polish and Hungarian factory workers: "foreigners," as Springdale referred to them, who lived in company-built houses on what was known as Yellow Row. But judging by their names—Smith, Brown, McQuaid, Stewart—Rachel's classmates were mostly "Americans": probably from the brick houses owned by shopkeepers and the factory foremen. Despite how poor her family was, Rachel managed to fit in: a photograph shows her in the right kind of skirt and short hair, hands crossed obediently in her lap just like the other kids.

On the surface anyway, it's a portrait of Horace Mann's dream: the common school education. Not that everyone shared common interests or skills, of course. Classrooms like this included kids who didn't much enjoy learning from books and weren't very good at it. Once they might have stayed on the farm or learned a trade in town, but school was now mandatory. The system responded by offering what was called an industrial education: "useful Knowledge" in Ben Franklin's terms. But that raised the question of which kids should be in those programs, how that would be determined, and whether everyone would still be getting an equal education. It was like the Booker T. Washington–W. E. B. Du Bois debate over practical training, but played out in all-white towns like Springdale. Or, to put it in Henry Ford's terms, didn't public schools need to give kids an industrial education to prepare them for the jobs that wouldn't ask them to think?

Philosopher and educational reformer John Dewey thought that was the wrong way to ask the question. In 1899, Dewey was exclaiming, "How many of the employed are today mere appendages to the machines they operate! This . . . is certainly due in large part to the fact that the worker has had no opportunity to develop his imagination." Dewey argued that schools like Rachel's should be replacing what industrialism had helped destroy. "The good old days of children's modesty, reverence and implicit obedience" were gone. Boys and girls no longer grew up on the farm, did chores with their parents, learned shared values firsthand. In Springdale, for example, the Carsons split up each morning: Mr. went off to sell, Mrs. stayed home and did the chores, the kids walked down the hill and spent their day on School Street. Society, as Dewey defined it, "is a number of people held together because they are working along common lines, in a common spirit, and with reference to common ends." He believed the responsibility for creating that community now fell, to a large part, on the big brick building with the bell up top.

Whichever side you took on these issues, as Rachel entered the system all seemed to agree that public education had become a central tool for shaping the nation, for "realizing the promise of American life," as one historian puts it. That, in turn, called for the kind of "joint effort" that fit Lincoln's definition of what government was for. In many places, public education was passing out of the control of locals. Pennsylvania, for example, had created a state Board of Ed for regulating the curriculum, fixing minimum salaries, and setting teacher qualifications across the state. Hand in hand came a new emphasis on standardized testing and grades.

Rachel doesn't seem to have paid much attention. She did fine, getting As and Bs, but School Street doesn't come up when she describes how she learned what she needed to know. And her mother, the ex-teacher, seems to have agreed. Whether Mrs. Carson thought the Springdale public schools didn't measure up to the Washington Female Seminary, or simply liked having her youngest home, she let Rachel skip school. Often. In the first three months of second grade, Rachel only made it in a total of about three weeks. Sometimes she was sick; sometimes there was the chance she might get sick; sometimes it was just more fun to stay home. The absences continued through third and fourth grade.

Her alternative education–her hilltop education–was with her mother: playing outside, reading, writing stories. In third grade, she composed a *St. Nicholas*–style tale called "The Little Brown House," where Mr. and Mrs. Wren search for and finally find a "dear little brown house with a green roof . . . that is just what we need." In fourth grade, "The Sleeping Rabbit" was her version of Beatrix Potter: Rachel's bunny snoozes beside a copy of *Peter Rabbit*. Meanwhile, downhill in the brick building, her class was working its way through a standard, four-hundred-page reader: a collection of essays and exercises with numbered paragraphs, pronunciation keys, and vocabulary lists.

The Carson family valued education. Though the Springdale schools ended in eighth grade, the district offered optional tutoring through tenth, and both Rachel's older siblings were sent. Mr. Carson's income remained spotty; Mrs. Carson had begun to offer piano lessons to supplement it; they could have used whatever extra cash a working teenager might have brought in. But keeping the kids in school was worth the sacrifice if it gave them a chance to get ahead.

Rachel's big sister finished tenth grade and then got a job as a stenographer in town. A year later, underage, she married a man from New Kensington; the couple moved in with the Carsons, where nine-year-old Rachel watched the marriage quickly fall apart. About the time it did, Rachel's brother completed tenth grade, and he found work in a local radio repair shop. Stenography and radio repair were relatively good jobs: skilled work with a future tied to the booming American economy. As the United States entered World War I, demand for manufactured goods soared, and the Allegheny Valley cranked up its production of steel, aluminum, and oil. Her sister's wages rose, her brother joined the military, and the war helped make Rachel a published writer.

Each month, Mrs. Carson's favorite magazine devoted a section to what it called the St. Nicholas League: writing by young authors from age five to eighteen. During Rachel's childhood, the league's badge winners included the young e.e. cummings, William Faulkner, F. Scott Fitzgerald, and Samuel Eliot Morrison. The league's stated goal was to "stimulate them to strive toward higher ideals both in thought and in living, to protect the oppressed, to grow in understanding of all forms of nature." With the war on, it also championed "intelligent patriotism"; almost every page of the magazine had an inspirational story about America's fighting men. Rachel submitted one about "a famous aviator . . . [as] told to me by my brother, who is a soldier." She'd left the fairy-tale world of "A Sleeping Bunny" behind. At the same time, her description of a pilot crawling out onto the wing of his damaged plane was still imaginary: far from Springdale and the day-to-day life of a fifth grader.

Springdale's population would almost triple during the decade that included World War I. A large part of that had to do with military buildup, which accelerated an already growing demand for electricity. About the time Rachel's aviator piece ran in *St. Nicholas*, the West Penn Power Company bought a lot on Springdale's riverfront and began constructing a giant plant. Back when the Carsons had first moved to town, local competition to provide electricity had been intense: some 150 companies existed in the Allegheny Valley, each building its own generators and hanging its own lines. But since then, conglomerates had bought up and consolidated the industry. West Penn Power was a combine of 53 smaller companies, including some the Mellon family had once owned. It now controlled the production of electricity for most of southwest Pennsylvania—and it, in turn, was a subsidiary of American Water Works and Electric out of New York. The parent company's monopoly extended over five states. If the building on School Street had once been the town's symbol of progress, the West Penn power station would soon dwarf it—and everything else in Springdale.

West Penn Power taught a blunt, daily lesson: nature was there to be used. The power plant needed coal and water: to make steam, to turn the blades of its twenty-five-thousand-kilowatt generators, to produce electricity. Springdale had the water: not only the Allegheny but an underground stream that ran some two hundred feet below the river. The stream provided "soft" water, filtered by rock and silt, which meant less corrosion for the generators. And coal was everywhere. The infamous Harwick mine was back over the ridge from the Carsons' home. There, four years after the family moved in, 177 men had died when trapped gas exploded in an unventilated shaft. Rachel regularly passed the mass grave next to Springdale's Lutheran church. Over in New Kensington, Alcoa had dug a thousand-acre coal mine under an old bathing beach, and next door in Creighton, the plate glass factories had their own mines. The West Penn plant actually got its fuel from across the river. The company had drilled two transportation tunnels under the Allegheny. In one, loaded coal cars rumbled toward Springdale, where a rotary dumper flipped and emptied them; meanwhile, a long line of empties was rattling back in the other. No wonder Rachel's father kept worrying that his building lots were honeycombed by illegal mines. Almost everywhere the Carsons looked, the landscape was being turned inside out: the underground pulled to the surface, transported, and burned.

Armistice was declared in November 1918. When Rachel's brother returned from serving in Europe, he found a changed town. West Penn had put up rows of bunkhouses for its workers. High-voltage lines were being strung. Duquesne Light Company, which controlled the supply of electricity for the city of Pittsburgh, would soon break ground on its own power plant—also on the Springdale shoreline, this one straight downhill from the Carsons. Known as a "mine mouth" plant, the Colfax station would have its own private railroad running back and forth to the Harwick mine behind the Carsons' cabin.

Though peace had come, Rachel kept turning out war stories. In January of her sixth-grade year, her St. Nicholas League entry was about a lone American soldier killing "Huns." In February, she published a piece called "A Message to the Front," and that August, she went back into military history for "A Famous Sea-Fight" about Admiral Dewey and the Spanish-American War. Looking back, Carson would say she became a professional author at age eleven. By seventh grade, she'd published four stories in a national magazine, all of them wartime adventures. Like the young Ben Franklin, she'd learned how to write for a paying market: in her case, nonfiction recreations of a world far from Springfield and Pennsylvania. It was a craft she practiced outside school, as part of her solitary life, and her success must have felt like proof that her ridgetop education was the one that counted.

By now, Springdale had started to call itself "Power City." Rachel's sister had become an accountant for West Penn. Her brother had become an electrician's assistant, also for the power company. Before long, Rachel's father would take part-time work as a night supervisor at West Penn's switching yard. While he hadn't entirely given up on his land development, times had changed. The postwar newspapers were still filled with rags-to-riches stories, especially Henry Ford's—now selling a million Model Ts a year. But if Springdale was any indication, the average Joe (or Jill) was far more likely to end up working for a giant corporation than starting one. Many of the kids in the local school found jobs with West Penn or Duquesne Light: in John Dewey's terms, that had become the town's common end. And that was the practical reason for going on past eighth grade. Judging by Rachel's siblings, anyway, it worked: you ended up at a desk, or as an electrician, instead of digging coal out of the dark.

But as the red and white Duquesne stack rose into the Carsons' view, Rachel quite literally looked past the local economic reality. She wasn't continuing into ninth grade to get an industrial education. And she also wasn't keen about the regular curriculum, especially given the role it assigned to girls. The summer after Rachel turned thirteen, the long battle of the suffragette movement was finally won. With the passage of the Nineteenth Amendment, women could vote, and the 1920s offered new possibilities of female independence, from Nobel Prize winners like Marie Curie to national heroines like Amelia Earhart. But most girls were still expected to settle down with a man and raise a family. That was the model put forward in text books and readers. And it was part of the unofficial curriculum, too. In the days of agricultural America, lots of the pairing-off happened at rural gatherings: hoedowns and church socials. Now that teenagers spent their days in high school, that became the place you passed notes and learned to flirt.

Rachel Carson doesn't mention having a boyfriend in either elementary or high school. She'd go to her college prom with a man, but her description of the evening would dwell on the outfit worn by her biology instructor, a woman. Most of her biographers make a point of saying there's no evidence Carson ever had a sexual relationship with a woman: a disclaimer that seems to be necessary partly because her most passionate private correspondence is with a female. Addressed to "Darling" and signed, "I love you so dearly– Rachel," they're letters of pleasure and longing, written in middle age. "[Y]ou were always with me when I wakened in the night . . . and always the sense of your presence, and of your sweet tenderness, and love was very real to me." Carson would never marry, have children, or live with another woman. Instead, she remained single, sharing a home with her mother until Mrs. Carson's death, when Rachel was fifty-one.

What she didn't learn in high school, then–what she rejected– was the idea that she would function as a second-class citizen in a man's world. She could and would be an equal. And somewhere in these years she also discovered that female society offered her an alternative: companionship, encouragement, support for her sense of wonder.

In the summer between ninth and tenth grade, Rachel published her last piece in *St. Nicholas*. The fifteen-year-old had moved past war stories and, for that matter, stories "as told to." She's still writing on assignment, so to speak–to fit the magazine's suggested topic of "My Favorite Recreation"–but her article offers a first-person glimpse into her private hilltop education.

The teenager and her dog, Pal, leave the Carson house an hour after sunrise on a May morning. They wander uphill toward her "discovery," the "deeper woodland" of a pine forest: "the sort of place that awes you by its majestic silence, interrupted only by the rustling breeze and the distant tinkle of water." Notebook and camera in hand, she's doing what she calls "bird-nesting–in the most approved fashion" and goes on to list what she finds. As she heads home at dusk, "gloriously tired, gloriously happy!" the essay ends as a hymn to nature.

St. Nicholas published it as nonfiction; it's also an act of imagination.

From her description, it sounds like Rachel's discovery is a stand of old-growth forest, probably Eastern hemlock. If so, it was one of the few remaining pockets in the Allegheny Valley. By this May day in 1921, clear-cut lumbering was so widespread that locals had taken to calling their forest the "Allegheny Brush-patch." Starting in 1890, wood chemical plants had found uses for "nearly every accessible tree," leaving "the once vast forests," in the words of the U.S. Forest Service, "barren hillsides as far as the eye could see." By the time Rachel was thirteen, only .06 percent of the original woods was left, and the Allegheny watershed was the scene of constant erosion and flooding.

As Rachel composed "My Favorite Recreation," the four blast furnaces of Springdale's plate glass company were turning out their daily, two-thousand-square-foot quota. The glue factory was boiling animal parts to jelly. Two generating units of the six-million-dollar West Penn power station were up, its coal cars shuttling under the Allegheny. And when Rachel came home that May evening, gloriously happy, she was greeted by the stack of Duquesne Light Company, billowing clouds of dense smoke.

By this time, there had already been nearly a decade of medical studies linking that smoke to various illnesses, including pneumonia. Industrial pollution was killing not only the poor, one Pittsburgh report stated, but "many of our most useful business men . . . on whom most had been spent on education." In response, over seventy-five cities had passed smoke-abatement ordinances. While businesses had resisted and most newspapers ridiculed the laws, they'd passed thanks to a fledgling environmental movement: an environmental movement often led by females. "All around the nation, middle-class and upper-middle-class women with the leisure to devote to activism joined civic clubs like the Ladies Health Protective Association of Pittsburgh and the Wednesday Club of St. Louis." Smoke abatement was just part of their agenda: sewage disposal, solid waste removal, clean water—all had become issues that women addressed as "keepers of the house and protectors of morality."

By bird-nesting in the approved fashion, Rachel signaled that she'd already joined the movement. National magazines were encouraging young women to get out of their sooty, coal-heated homes and take "healthful rambles over the country." As well as "restful relaxation," the rambles were seen as educational, part of a nationwide curriculum called "Nature Study." Rachel's essay fit right in. Her description of "the oriole's aerial cradle" could have been in response to Anna Botsford Comstock's *Handbook of Nature Study*: Lesson 31, The Oriole. Ms. Comstock advised parents and teachers to give out the questions "during the first week in May." Question number one began, "Where did you find the nest?" Number two: "What is the shape of the nest?"

The *Handbook of Nature Study* had been developed in response to the industrial revolution; think of it as a kind of by-product. In the late nineteenth century, New York City charity workers had begun noticing that more and more of their indigent children came from the country. It was one thing for city tenements to fill up with immigrant kids; public education could help teach them America's core values. But if kids were driven off "the farm the farm," those very values were threatened. There didn't seem to be any way to save East Coast agriculture from the lethal combination of depleted soil, competition from the Midwest, and the promise of a better life in the city. But there was education. Even if kids didn't live on the farm anymore, they could be taught its values. The New York State Assembly funded a Nature Study program at the Cornell College of Agriculture.

The guides produced at Cornell were aimed at the "intelligent child of twelve." They had an imaginative, fairy-tale approach a lot like *St. Nicholas*. In fact, John Dewey opposed them for not being based enough in science. But the program had begun to catch on back when Rachel's mom was teaching; and by the time Rachel was in school, Nature Study courses were part of almost every state's curriculum. Though produced at an agricultural college, they focused more on cultivating "a love of the beautiful" than learning how to plow. Nature Study, as one author puts it, was seen as "the great remedy for the alienation of man from the land and from his neighbor." There was a national consensus that children of the industrial age needed what Rachel learned on her daylong ramble.

As well as developing observational skills and a love of the beautiful, Nature Study offered schools a way to integrate their curriculum. When a child found an oriole's nest, for example, Comstock's outline would help answer questions about migration, protective coloring, animal architecture. In the process, the student might also learn some math, spelling, even history. One textbook suggested that if a student brought in a piece of coal, the discussion could go from geological composition to the mining industry to the history of the state of Pennsylvania.

Like the Peabody sisters' earlier crusade, the movement tried to separate itself from formal schooling. "Nature study is not elementary science," Comstock declared: not a way of learning biology or classifi-cations, not a lesson at all. "When it is properly taught, the child is unconscious of mental effort or that he is suffering the act of teach-ing." It was supposed to be indirect learning—Abe Lincoln–style—and fun. The same applied to nature writing. An adult shouldn't ask a stu-dent to keep a journal of her rambles with the ulterior motive of teach-ing English composition; that was "sickening to the honest spirit." An adult ought to ask, Comstock emphasized, "*because she wished to know what he had discovered*." The writing would then be straightforward, in-formative. It was a kind of anti-school-curriculum, pro the outdoors and direct experience. As one of the patriarchs of the movement, nat-uralist Louis Agassiz, advised a group of Massachusetts teachers: "Study nature, not books."

What Comstock wrote was, of course, a *handbook*—and that was just one of the contradictions of this back-to-nature movement in an industrial age. "We have adapted ourselves to our physical environ-ment by stripping our land of its forests, our air of its birds, our wa-ters of their fish," one Nature Study text declared. "Nature has been our slave, from whom we could take anything, to whom we owed nothing." The slave had to be set free. Except the nation derived its wealth from this slavery: from seeing trees as logs waiting to be split, forests as fields waiting to be developed. Nature couldn't be set totally free. Instead, the realization had grown—among industrialists as well as reformers—that for it to work, it had to renew. When Rachel was sixteen, a presidential proclamation established the half-million-acre Allegheny National Forest. The "Brush-patch" would still work for mankind, but from now on, the Forest Service de-clared, it would make sure trees were lumbered and coal mined "in a sustainable way."

The newly named conservation movement looked for some model to show Americans how to live in harmony with nature. More and more, it taught young bird-nesters like Rachel to look to the American Indian. Not Indians like Sarah Winnemucca, who had learned English and tried to adapt to modern culture. But Tecumseh, who had fought the settlers and all they stood for. He was "the great Redman, the personal embodiment of all that was good in the Red race." Nature Study explicitly connected appreciation of the outdoors with childhood, innocence, the savage *before* civilization. As school reformer Francis Parker phrased it, "A little child is a little 'Injun' . . . He begins with the same natural love and instinct . . . the wrong comes later." Elementary students learned Indian crafts; new organizations like the Boy Scouts and Campfire Girls taught what Teddy Roosevelt called "the barbarian virtues." A director of a Nature Study program in Los Angeles expanded the theme in *Popular Science Monthly*: kids on field trips ought to hear "the stories and songs of negroes and Indians [because] these more primitive people are but grown children, living in closer touch with nature." Again, this definition didn't include Sojourner Truth with her web of scars, or W. E. B. Du Bois, the Harvard graduate. The emphasis was on the uneducated, the noble, the pure.

At the same time, Rachel was determined to get even more education than her sister and brother had. She was going to continue past tenth grade, which meant she had to walk down into town each morning and catch a trolley upriver and across the bridge to New Kensington. The eleventh-grade class she entered at Parnassus High was huge: forty-four students. Its form of education was as industrial in its own way as the town's Alcoa plant. New Kensington's air was smoggy with fly ash and sulfate particles, its river full of mercury and other carcinogens. H. L. Mencken, traveling through the region at the time, described it as "the boast and pride of the richest and grandest nation ever seen on earth"—and "so dreadfully hideous, so intolerably bleak and forlorn that it reduced the whole aspiration of man to a macabre and depressing joke."

The bleakness seemed to steel Rachel's resolve. She'd changed from a kid who skipped school whenever possible to one whose high school honors thesis lectured against "intellectual dissipation." Each day, she commuted to New Kensington like it was a job. And it's true that public education had become big business. During Rachel's senior year, for example, her father finally sold some of his real estate. The town of Springdale bought it as a site for a new elementary school, and a few years later, would buy more to build Springdale Senior High. For Mr. Carson, public education provided a way (finally) to turn a profit. For Rachel, it offered a job that would someday help her leave the Allegheny landscape behind. Meanwhile, her alternative, interior, private education continued: looking for birds' nests, writing her stories, spending hours imagining distant places.

Rachel goes on to graduate first in her class—and then she's gone. First, to an all-female Christian college in Pittsburgh; then to the eastern seaboard. Never again to live in the Allegheny Valley. She would become one of the few female biologists in the country and take a job at the U.S. Bureau of Fisheries: one of only two women there. The fisheries job would support her, her mother, and members of her extended family for over fifteen years. It was government work, often bureaucratic, more like high school than her ridgetop education. "I had given up writing forever, I thought."

Her job was to read the latest scientific research and turn it into informational bulletins for the general public. She became a kind of translator, explaining nature to her audience the way *St. Nicholas* and the Nature Study movement had for theirs. Her main subject was the ocean, which seemed an unlikely match given her landlocked early education. But she'd been studying the subject for years. "Even as a child," Carson wrote, "—long before I had ever seen it—I used to imagine what it would look like, and what the surf sounded like." She'd read poetry about the ocean, studied photographs, sat on the hill writing fiction set on the shore. She hadn't actually experienced the sea, but she'd hardly ever experienced the "majestic silence" of a wilderness either. She studied them both the same way: extrapolating from what she could see, relying on her sense of wonder, believing in the mystery as much as the science. Even after she finally got there, the ocean remained an unknown. That was part of its appeal. "To understand the shore," she wrote, "it is not enough to catalog its life." Instead, "True understanding demands intuitive comprehension."

Three books would result, including her first major success, *The Sea Around Us*. In each, Carson's prose owes as much to nineteenth-century romantic literature as it does scientific writing. She's evoking an unseen and unseeable world. Describing the ocean floor, for example, she writes: "Mysterious and eerie are the immense areas, especially in the north Pacific, carpeted with a soft, red sediment in which there are no organic remains except sharks' teeth and the ear bones of whales." It's a landscape she hadn't witnessed and never would: an imagined landscape, almost a fairy tale.

Nature, as Carson defined it, offered the human race "inner contentment" and "reserves of strength"; there was "something infinitely healing" about it. She'd come to see it that way not from a childhood amid pure, unspoiled beauty but in comparison with the stink of town, the gash of the coal mine. When she's a famous author and tells President Kennedy's Science Advisory Committee that America's children are growing up in a "sea of carcinogens," she could have been describing Springfield and the Allegheny Valley. And wasn't part of her evidence—a part she kept secret—that even as she gave her testimony she was dying of breast cancer? In her last book, *Silent Spring*, Carson asked "whether any civilization can wage relentless war on life without destroying itself, and without losing the right to be called civilized." It was a rhetorical question. She'd learned the answer long ago.

JACK

He'd need to know what a mucker was.

There was the Carl Sandburg poem, published the year before Jack was born:

> Twenty men stand watching the muckers.
>> Stabbing the sides of the ditch
>> Where clay gleams yellow,
>> Driving the blades of their shovels
>> Deeper and deeper for the new gas mains
>> Wiping sweat off their faces
>>> With red bandanas
> The muckers work on . . . pausing . . . to pull
> Their boots out of suckholes where they slosh.
>
> Of the twenty looking on
> Ten murmer, "O, it's a hell of a job,"
> Ten others, "Jesus, I wish I had the job."

By this definition, there hadn't been a true mucker on either side of Jack's family for two generations. At fourteen, Grandfather Kennedy had left school to be a stevedore on the Boston docks. But by his mid-twenties, he'd bought his own business: a saloon by the Haymarket, followed by another and then a third. Soon, he had a whiskey importing business, then was elected to the Massachusetts Lower House, then the State Senate. By the time he was thirty, he was at the Democratic Convention seconding the nomination of Captain Keller's hero, Grover Cleveland, for president. That was the year Jack's father, Joe, was born—into a well-off family with considerable political clout.

On Jack's mother's side, Grandfather Fitzgerald had gone to Boston Latin: the same public school that, almost two hundred years after Ben Franklin, was still preparing students for Harvard. Honey Fitz (as he came to be known) entered Harvard Medical School after graduating from the Jesuit-run Boston College. When his father died, he dropped out and became a Customs House clerk, which led to a job with the ward boss of the North End. By the time his first child—Jack's mother, Rose—was a year old, Honey Fitz had been elected to the city council. And by the time his daughter was four, he'd become a congressman: one of only three Catholics in the House and the only Democrat from the proudly Republican state of Massachusetts.

The city of Boston was by this time one third Irish and rife with prejudice. The years Annie Sullivan was rebelling against the Protestant establishment at the Perkins Institute, each of Jack's grandfathers was establishing a political base in an Irish neighborhood. Working-class muckers were their source of power and wealth, but they made sure their children—Jack's parents—grew up a long ways from ditch digging.

Joe Kennedy was born in a town house in East Boston. Running for office years later, Jack would declare that his father proved the American dream: "He started out without any resources, and he has done extremely well." But according to Joe Kennedy's sister, they grew up with "servants and teams of horses, lovely clothing, and European travel." Joe went to private Catholic schools till he was thirteen, then transferred to Boston Latin for seventh grade. Academically, he was awful: failed physics, French, and advanced Latin; got Ds in English, history, and geometry; had to repeat his junior year. But the redheaded Irish boy ended up a star baseball player and the president of his senior class. As far as he was concerned, it wasn't the education that mattered but the fact of going to Latin. "[It] somehow seemed to make us all feel that if we could stick it out, we were made of just a little bit better stuff than the fellows our age who were attending what we always thought were easier schools." It separated you from the muckers and most everyone else. Despite his grades, Joe was accepted at Harvard in 1908. It didn't hurt that his father was the founder of two banks and the patronage boss of Boston's second ward, that he was a pretty good ballplayer, and that he had a diploma from Boston Latin.

Honey Fitz, meanwhile, had moved his family out to suburban Concord. They lived in what Rose remembered as "a big old rambling . . . wonderfully comfortable house" and drove around in an elegant horse and carriage. The break from the city included Rose going to public school. The year she was born, the church had issued a "command" that "Catholic schools are the only places for Catholic children." Many of Boston's Irish obeyed, preferring their children be taught in the faith than Americanized in public schools. But Honey Fitz wanted Rose in the mainstream, and she attended West Concord Grammar. By then, Fitz had left Congress to run a weekly newspaper: bought for five hundred dollars, and with his political ties helping to sell ads, now bringing in a reported twenty-five thousand dollars a year. When Rose was fourteen, the Fitzgeralds moved into a fifteen-room mansion in Dorchester. She went to high school there, as well as taking private lessons in French, dancing, piano, and voice. Dorchester offered "fresh air and open spaces," as Rose put it, but had also been incorporated into the city, which allowed Honey Fitz to enter and win the 1905 mayoral race. As Joe Kennedy was starting his junior year at Latin, and Rose was being accepted at prestigious Wellesley College, her father became the first mayor of Boston to be born of Irish immigrants.

But instead of going to Wellesley, Rose ended up at the Convent of the Sacred Heart. At age ninety she'd call the decision her "greatest regret," but it wasn't actually her decision. Her father, the mayor, was facing corruption charges, and one way to appease his political base was to have his daughter get a Catholic education. Meanwhile, she was being courted by Joe Kennedy, the son of another prominent

Irish political family. Though it doesn't seem to have been an arranged marriage, it would be a marriage made comfortable by arrangements. After graduating from Harvard at age twenty-four, Joe was given a job in his father's bank, and soon Honey Fitz was helping him become one of Boston's youngest bank examiners. As an examiner, he got a tip about a planned takeover of the Kennedy bank, helped block it, and eighteen months after joining the business became its president. His rapid success had as much to do with family ties as having "better stuff."

Which is how Jack Kennedy came to be born even further from the life of a mucker than his parents had been. When the bank president married the ex-mayor's daughter, they put two thousand dollars down on a two-and-a-half-story house in the Brookline suburbs. "It was not as luxurious as any of my friend's houses," Rose recalled, "but it was very compact and comfortable . . . One of my friends sent me her maid—a gay neat Irish girl who cooked and served & made the beds." According to a survey published in 1917, the year of Jack's birth, Brookline was one of the wealthiest towns in the country: 170 of its citizens were listed in *Who's Who*. Most of the men were professionals who commuted to Boston for work, raising their children in the six-square-mile town "because of the superior advantage afforded as regards health, beauty, morals, and social contact." Social contact was key. Brookline had begun as the favorite resort of Boston's merchant princes. It's where the Peabody sisters had launched their progressive girls' school. Though subdivision had started in the 1880s, by the twentieth century it was still home to the textile manufacturer Augustus Lowell, the landscape designer Frederick Law Olmsted, the inventor of the Gillette safety razor, Harvard professors, judges on the Massachusetts Supreme Court, industrialists, and bankers.

The Kennedy home was a smaller version of the kind of Boston town house Joe had been born in. It sat on a detached lot with room for a lawn, a porch, and a garden. Though 30 percent of Brookline was foreign-born by 1910—and half of those Irish—the tree-lined streets tended to disguise differences. What mattered was that you could afford to live there. Or, as one architectural historian puts it, Brookline's unifying principal was "segregation by income." There was no manufacturing in town. And the commercial center, a few blocks from the Kennedy house, hid its storefronts behind a mock-Tudor facade. It was supposed to look like a quaint British village. As if work, labor, the crass making of money didn't exist.

Joe Kennedy, meanwhile, drove his new Model T into the city each morning to make his fortune. The day Jack was born, his father was named trustee of the Massachusetts Electrical Company: a way, Joe purportedly said, "to meet people like the Saltonstalls." He avoided serving in World War I (and boosted his career) by having Honey Fitz get him a white-collar job at a shipyard. After the war, a member of the electric board offered him a position as a stockbroker. In the unregulated, postwar market of insider trading and stock pools, a man with access to better information could make a killing. Soon, the Kennedys had moved up to a Rolls-Royce and a larger, fourteen-room house. By then, Rose had five children under six years old. The two oldest, Joe Jr. and Jack, were ready for school. That, too, would be segregated by income.

"If Joe wouldn't accept a Catholic school," Rose later said, "I thought they should go to public school, where they'd meet the grocer's son and the plumber's son as well as the minister's son and the banker's son. They could have seen that some of these boys were even brighter than they were." So, at four and a half, Jack entered kindergarten at Edward Devotion Grammar, the neighborhood school. Except the nature of the neighborhood guaranteed he wouldn't meet the plumber's son.

The idea of egalitarian, democratic public education supposed that all classes of Americans lived together—and sent their kids to public school. But that hadn't been true since Franklin's time, and income-segregated suburbs like Brookline now made it even less likely. Edward Devotion served some of the town's wealthiest blocks. Situated on "ample grounds" off Harvard Avenue, Devotion paid its teachers top salaries and had recently built a large addition that included a first-floor auditorium and the latest in hygiene: porcelain toilets. Jack attended kindergarten from nine till noon: thirty children of the well-to-do playing with the latest in modern educational toys and supervised by two "cultivated, well-educated" women.

According to his mother, Jack was a "natural reader" who'd learned before entering kindergarten. Rose Kennedy had hired a former schoolteacher as governess and made a point of choosing the children's books for their "educational and inspirational values": *St. Nicholas*–approved material like Kipling's *Jungle Book* and *King Arthur and the Round Table*. But Jack, she said, "gobbled books—not necessarily the ones I had so thoughtfully chosen." Meanwhile, though he liked school, he didn't take it very seriously or understand why it was supposed to be so important. "You know I am getting on all right," Jack declared in second grade, "and if you study too much, you're liable to go crazy." It was cute enough for his mother to jot down in her diary. But it had to have been a little worrisome, too. The Kennedys decided to forget about meeting the plumber's son and ended Jack's public school education after third grade. By then, he was a millionaire's son.

Joe Kennedy's first big haul had come from a tip that Henry Ford was about to buy a certain coal company. Kennedy scooped up fifteen thousand shares and nine months later had almost tripled his investment. With that, he'd left the brokerage firm to set up his own office. His fortune would come from these kinds of transactions: not making things, like Ford, but making money. He spent the spring of Jack's second-grade year in New York City, using a five-million-dollar pool to manipulate stock prices. And rumor had it that, with Prohibition on, he was bringing in a lot of extra cash through his connections with bootleggers. What drove Joe Kennedy, his wife later said, was "the desire for the freedom which money provides, the freedom to come and go where he pleased, when he pleased and how he pleased."

Education helped you make connections; connections were how you made money; money bought freedom. The place for his sons to make the right connections was Noble and Greenough, a small private academy just a few blocks from the Kennedys' new house. It was where not only the Saltonstalls but the Bundys and the Storrows sent their boys: Social Register families, old money, Boston aristocracy. "One of the lessons of my life," Rose Kennedy later declared, "is that people have a better time . . . if they stay with friends who have similar backgrounds, interests, and resources." While the Kennedy boys had a different background from the other Noble and Greenough students—"We were probably the first and only ones who were Catholic," according to Jack—their resources compared. Eight-year-old Jack and his big brother arrived each morning in a chauffeur-driven limousine. And they learned to have similar interests, blending in with the other students, all dressed in the required crimson jerseys, crimson knickers, and crimson stockings.

Noble and Greenough's school colors deliberately mimicked Harvard's; it had been preparing kids to go there since its founding just after the Civil War. The all-female staff emphasized math and grammar: "very drill, drill, all the time," as one of Jack's fellow students put it. At the eight-fifteen assembly, the whole school would recite memorized selections from the Bible or uplifting passages from English literature. Mrs. Kennedy approved. And as the mother (by now) of six, she appreciated that private school ran three hours longer than public. When Noble and Greenough decided to move its upper school campus, Jack's father was instrumental in keeping the lower school (renamed Dexter) in Brookline and ended up on its board.

Dexter provided all the amenities, including an organized fourth-grade football team; Jack was captain. It also offered a kind of protection. The conflicts that had been part of the industrial revolution since before Henry Ford had only grown fiercer in the 1920s. After World War I, as wages dropped, a hundred and twenty thousand New England textile workers went on strike, demanding an eight-hour workday. The union movement spread to the region's telephone operators and then to the Boston police force, which had staged a walkout as part of its demand to organize. The riots that followed had the *Wall Street Journal* declaring, "Lenin and Trotsky are on their way." That was part of the fear behind the Red Scare of the early twenties: that the Russian Revolution would be imported from overseas. The resurgent Ku Klux

Klan targeted the fourteen and a half million immigrants who had entered the country since the turn of the century. The federal government set quotas to keep out undesirables: especially Russians and dark-skinned southern-European Catholics.

Jack grew up in the midst of the agitation—and carefully separated from it. The year he entered kindergarten, two Italians had been arrested fifteen miles from Brookline. They were accused of committing murder during the robbery of a shoe factory, and though they had no criminal records, their affiliation with anarchist groups all but guaranteed a quick conviction. Through Jack's second year at Dexter, there were appeals for a new trial, and the case of Nicola Sacco and Bartolomeo Vanzetti drew international attention. Protesters converged on the Boston area. Americans from John Dewey to Helen Keller argued that the U.S. justice system was being blinded by racial and political prejudice. The week that the last appeal failed, Joe Kennedy was telegramming Jack good luck in his fifth-grade baseball game. That summer, not six miles from the Dexter campus, huge crowds surrounded the Charleston Prison as Sacco and Vanzetti were executed.

If private schools insulated their students from these sorts of issues, public schools—faced with a flood of new immigrants—looked for ways to stop what was being called "the deterioration of American intelligence." During World War I, the army had started giving soldiers a new kind of test, designed to sort officer material from muckers. The results fit neatly with long-held assumptions: "Nordics" came out on top, southern Europeans scored low, and Negroes were ranked at the bottom. After the war, IQ tests became a popular educational tool. According to a 1923 ad, a school could buy a series of five tests for $1.45, administer them in thirty minutes, and find them "immediately useful for classifying children in grades 3 to 8." Critics pointed out that intelligence wasn't a single, quantifiable thing—that there was no accurate way to assign it a number—that the IQ test didn't measure an actual quantity but was "fundamentally an instrument for classifying a group of people." But classification was exactly what its supporters wanted. The tests promised a scientific, businesslike way not only to identify and weed out potential troublemakers (those with low intelligence), but also to improve the educational system by tracking the gifted. "[They] will be elected the rulers of the realm," one of the inventors of the tests dreamed, "and then will come perfect government—Aristocracy in Democracy."

Jack's was the first generation to be sorted. The Brookline schools gave intelligence tests "to all the children very early," as Rose Kennedy recalled. She was shocked when Jack scored higher than his older, harder-working brother. The results would stick with him all through his schooling, as teachers and administrators kept insisting Jack wasn't living up to his IQ. But even as the public system turned more and more to testing—to determine everything from who took honors curriculum to which kids got an "industrial education"—the Kennedys had opted out. If the grocer's son wanted to compete with the plumber's son, fine. But Joe and Rose knew it was where you went to school that determined the better stuff. And they could buy that for Jack.

Joe Kennedy purchased it with movie money. If, as Jack claimed, his father had achieved the American dream, it had started to shift from Henry Ford's man-plus-machine to man-plus-entertainment. The business model in this new consumer society was the holding company. So, Joe Kennedy snapped up Pathé Film (which made newsreels), an independent distribution network, and a nationwide chain of theaters (the same that had once tried to book Helen Keller in vaudeville). It meant he was soon getting paid a hundred thousand dollars annually by three different companies, doubling his estimated worth of two million dollars. For Jack, it meant his tenth birthday featured the exclusive showing of a brand-new Tom Mix cowboy movie. And for the family, it meant a move. Joe Kennedy was now spending most of his time in Hollywood or New York. Though Rose worried that switching schools would be "disquieting" for the children, the Kennedys rented a twenty-room mansion in Riverdale, overlooking the Hudson. The day after arriving, Joe Jr. and Jack were enrolled in the Riverdale Country School.

Rose, separated for the first time from extended family and friends, called the move a "blow to the stomach," but the kids adjusted quickly. Though Jack was attending his third school in three years, Riverdale Country turned out to be not all that different from Dexter. Founded in 1907 by Frank Hackett, all-boy Riverdale catered to the sons of rich New Yorkers. Hackett—who liked to be called "the Duke"—was an Irish scholarship boy who'd worked his way through Columbia University. He didn't care for the term "private school"; he preferred "independent." "Private" implied the motive was "individual financial profit," and he argued that the real goal of non-public education was the "public good." In a speech delivered the year before the Kennedy boys arrived, Hackett pointed out that less than 5 percent of high school students applied to college; so, public schools "quite properly" geared their curriculum to kids who weren't going on. The job of independent schools, on the other hand, was to pour "into our colleges, and later into our professional and business life, a constant stream of students imbued with high patriotic purpose and unusually well trained to become leaders for the best." Aristocracy in democracy.

Was that what Jack—a skinny, freckle-faced ten-year-old—was supposed to be learning: how to become a leader? According to the Duke, the "genius" of a country school education was combining "scholarly, intimate teaching" with "abundant play in the open" and "a home-like atmosphere." Riverdale wasn't "the farm the farm"; fifteen miles outside New York City, it was designed to look more like a country estate. No industrial brick schoolhouses here; the campus featured "colonial style" quarried stone and classrooms built around leafy courtyards. It was homelike if your home was a Park Avenue brownstone or a suburban mansion, and the setting reassured parents that their children were being instilled with the proper values. Jack's day started with nine A.M. chapel. After a prayer and a hymn, the boys would listen to Hackett read from the morning *New York Times*, complete with his editorial comments on current events. The Duke had proudly volunteered to speak out against unions during the Red Scare and supported what he called the "unified attack on communism." After setting the boys straight on the latest news, he often ended chapel with a poem. A favorite was Angela Morgan's "Work":

Work!
Thank God for the might of it,
The ardor, the urge, the delight of it . . .

Then, the boys would hurry off to a morning of small classes, study, and recitation. Lunch was followed by a good two hours of sports, then a late-afternoon study period to end the long day.

If his marks were the measure, Jack did well. In sixth grade, he was getting nineties in history and winning the school prize for best composition. But as the Duke put it, "Learning from books is but one small part in the educational process." Riverdale's schedule emphasized sports almost as much as studies, and that meshed with Joe Kennedy's values. "After all, the first requisite of a successful . . . education," he'd later write Jack, "[is] learning how to meet people and getting along with them." A team sport was the traditional way to do that, and Riverdale's high tuition guaranteed who would be on Jack's teams. Seven hours a day, five days a week, he was with the sons of bank presidents, attorneys, business leaders. "It isn't what you learn," is how Harvard's president characterized private school life, "but the friends you make that matters."

The Duke and other supporters of the independent school system recognized that much of America saw this as "undemocratic." But private schools, they argued, developed innovative practices later picked up by public education. The longer day, for example. And the longer school career: by now, a third of the nation's fourteen- to seventeen-year-olds were staying on into high school. More and more, public school followed the private school model of keeping kids separated from the adult world, and for that matter, divided by age. That kind of control made it easier, the argument went, to teach appropriate material at the appropriate time—and instill appropriate values.

Like many independent schools, Riverdale was run by a board of trustees. That helped financially: even with high tuitions, most private schools needed donations to survive, and the board helped lead the fund-raising. But it also helped shape the atmosphere of the place. Having the headmaster answerable to a board of alumni and parents was a way of checking to make sure the school reflected the right values. Educational experts argued that public education needed to take the same route. Under the control of political bosses like Honey Fitz, many of the big-city schools had become part of the patronage system: jobs and policies were dictated by politics. To counter that—and to ensure that children were being taught good American morals—public schools needed to be overseen by citizen boards. The boards ought to be democratically elected, the experts suggested, but the odds were that only relatively well-off citizens would have the time and inclination to run. Or for that matter, to vote. While the elections would be public, for all intents and purposes they'd function as private affairs, more likely to be influenced by bankers than ditch diggers. It worked. A 1916 survey found that 75 percent of the school board members in the country's larger city systems were either businessmen or professionals. Public schools, like private ones, made sure only the right people were in charge of building character.

The independent school was, as one author puts it, "the most important agency for transmitting the traditions of the upper social classes, and regulating the admission of new wealth and talent." The Kennedy parents supported that transmission. Jack was, in his words, "constantly drilled" to succeed. "Well, I grew up in a very strict house, and one where there was no—there were no free riders and everyone was expected to do, give their best to what they did." Joe Kennedy was more succinct. "We don't want any losers around here. In this family we want winners." Rose's term was "effective"; she wanted her children to develop into effective people. "[T]he fact was," Rose wrote, "[meals] were about the only times for Joe and me to talk with the children," and she made sure they weren't wasted on what she called "pointless chatter." She hung a bulletin board outside the dining room and posted newspaper clippings so the children could discuss "the topics of the day."

Picture a dinner in May 1929, the month Jack turned twelve. The Kennedys have moved a few miles from Riverdale to Bronxville, where Joe has spent a quarter million dollars on a mansion he's renamed Crownlands. Described as one of the area's most magnificent homes, it features a two-story, semicircular portico entrance, a three-car garage with chauffer's quarters, a basement Joe had remodeled to include a billiard room and movie theater, and acres of rolling land. In the dining room, Jack sits with his parents, his teenage brother, and his three oldest sisters, while a governess copes with the three youngest siblings. A uniformed staff serves, quietly clearing the soup course, refilling water glasses. Joe Kennedy sits at the head of the big table. For the last decade, he's moved, as one magazine put it, in "the intense, secretive circles of operators in the wildest stock market in history, with routine plots and pools, inside information and wild guesses." By merging his movie holdings into a conglomerate called RKO, he's made some five million dollars in the past year. Just this month, he's gotten a hunch—or a tip—that the good times aren't going to last through the year, and he's begun liquidating most of his stocks.

None of this is discussed.

"Money," Jack's younger brother Bobby will recall, "was a subject that was taboo." According to Rose, it wasn't "forbidden . . . but simply didn't meet the criterion [of] . . . interesting." Joe Kennedy was more adamant: "I have never discussed money with my wife and children, and I never will." The kids are given "normal" allowances to teach them the value of a buck, forcing Jack at one point to write his father a mock plea for a raise. Meanwhile, the source of all that's around them—the reason they're eating like this and living in a twenty-one-room house and going to private school—is never brought to the table.

Instead, they might discuss school or current events. But the way Jack recalls it, "We didn't have opinions in those days . . . It was mostly talk about some of the personalities that my father ran into." Joe Kennedy is making movies with Gloria Swanson, working with the director Eric von Stroheim, mingling with the Hollywood elite as well as political power brokers. It must have been a heady conversation—or monologue. What is the seventh grader supposed to learn from this? That money doesn't matter? Or that things that do matter aren't to be discussed? That personality is what counts: people more important than ideas? Or is Jack supposed to learn that what he needs to know is, somehow, elsewhere? The Kennedys insisted that all the children attend meals and arrive on time; Bobby once hurled himself through a piece of plate glass in his rush to get to dinner. But Jack became known for sliding in late, after the first course, then eating out back afterward with the kitchen staff.

That May of 1929, Jack's father has already decided the two oldest boys need to go away to boarding school. Bronxville—a mile square with a few thousand residents—has a per capita income, Rose notes, "among the highest in the country." It's exclusive enough that the younger Kennedy children all go to its well-funded public schools, nationally recognized for appealing to "curiosity and understanding" instead of "drilling facts into the helpless students' heads." Social life in Bronxville—a planned, Victorian-style community—revolves around country clubs, at-home teas, elegant formal parties. There's been some subdivision: the decade before the Kennedys arrived, roads were widened, estates cut up to build Tudor-style homes, and there was an influx of "the stock market crowd." Still, Bronxville only allowed certain kinds of new money. It made a point of keeping out "the other," as a village historian explains, "which might have been defined as black, Catholic, or Jew." Despite their religion, the Kennedys had managed to buy their way in; now they embraced the exclusivity. "Restrictions?" asks a 1925 ad in *House and Garden*—then proudly answers: "Yes! Bronxville has always been carefully guarded in its development . . . [T]o be able to call Bronxville one's home," it goes on, "is to have one's social status definitely and pleasantly established."

So why send the boys away? Riverdale Country was in that elite circle of preparatory schools that could all but guarantee Ivy League admission. Up until 1900, Harvard, Yale, and Princeton had each had its own entrance exam. When the Ivy League switched to a shared test called the College Boards, the private school curriculum followed suit. Three hours long, graded by outside examiners (including prep school teachers), the Boards followed the European model of ranking applicants based on extended essays. So private schools made sure their students were prepared, down to having them read the kind of novels that would look good on the English essay. Public schools, meanwhile, paid next to no attention. The result amounted to a monopoly. The year Jack was born, about 50 percent of Harvard's students came out of private school, 70 percent of Yale's, and 80 percent of Princeton's. Though this would change some by the time Jack took the test twenty years later, Princeton's percentage would still be at 85, with two private schools accounting for more of its incoming freshmen than all the nation's public schools combined. Once you got into prep school, as Jack's Dexter classmate, McGeorge Bundy, remarked: "If you weren't a notorious and incorrigibly stupid or lazy person you could go to any college you wanted. You really could." Riverdale was one of those prep schools. Yet Joe Jr. was sent off to Choate in the fall of 1929 and Jack to Canterbury a year later.

Canterbury satisfied Rose's dream of having a son educated in the faith: it was one of only two Catholic prep schools in the country. It also got its kids into the Ivy League. The year Jack entered, seven out of twenty-one seniors went to Yale, seven to Princeton, and one to Harvard. A small school, with fewer than a hundred students, Canterbury was run by a priest and emphasized discipline. It required Jack to wear a dark suit, white shirt, black shoes (shined), and a "four-in-hand" neatly tied. "It's a pretty good place," the thirteen-year-old gamely wrote his parents, but he also admitted being "pretty homesick." He took history, grammar, an introduction to science, first-year Latin and first-year algebra. The school also taught morals, doctrine, and liturgy. "[Y]ou have a whole lot of religion," is how Jack put it, and added: "The place is freezing at night and pretty cold in the daytime."

While he made honor roll first semester, a teacher found Jack "highly reserved and somewhat on the defensive, not quite certain of himself." Maybe what he wasn't certain about was why he was there. He was eager to please. "[T]hough I may not be able to remember material things such as tickets, gloves and so on," he wrote home that fall, "I can remember things like *Ivanhoe* and the last time we had an exam on it I got a ninety eight." In another letter, he asked for a newspaper subscription, or "the Litary Digest because I did not know about the Market Slump until a long time after" And, he adds, he also needed some golf balls. But which had he been sent away to learn? Had the teenager been packed off so he could become a better Catholic? A better golfer? To study Latin, or current events?

If he wasn't sure about the end goal, the means were clear. He was allowed occasional trips back to Bronxville and could be visited on prescribed weekends, but the main difference between Riverdale Country School and Canterbury was the isolation. Boarding school meant living almost totally apart from the general public. Jack ate, slept, and exercised on campus; going downtown was a rescindable privilege. There aren't that many parallels in American education. Military schools isolated their students; so did schools for the blind like Perkins. And then there were the state-run boarding schools that Sarah Winnemucca had resisted: places like Carlisle where Native American children were sent to break them of tribal traditions.

For an indication of the world Jack had entered, note his passing mention that he'd only just heard about the market slump in the fall of 1930. That would seem impossible. But thirty years later, while running for president, he'd confirm it: "I have no first-hand knowledge of the depression," he told an interviewer. "I really did not learn about the depression until I read about it at Harvard." Back in the fall of Jack's last year in the Riverdale school, the stock market had been booming. More and more trading was done on credit, which meant even the muckers were able to get in on the profit taking. Joe Kennedy later claimed that this had been his signal. "When the time comes that a shoeshine boy knows as much as I do about what is going on in the stock market . . . it's time for me to get out." Within a month of Black Thursday, the value of equities had dropped an estimated thirty-two billion dollars. Within three months, unemployment had gone from fewer than half a million Americans to more than four million.

Even if he had been reading the newspaper, Jack might not have known the extent of the collapse. Most stories followed the reassuring line of President Hoover and his secretary of the Treasury, Andrew

Mellon: the economy was fundamentally sound. During Jack's first month at Canterbury, when thousands marched on Manhattan's City Hall, the *New York Times* declared it a riot and said only communists would call it a demonstration. But if Jack had been getting the paper—and had turned to the business section—he could have read about that taboo subject: Kennedy money. A *Times* article reported that Joe Kennedy was selling Pathé Film to RKO for five million dollars. That is, selling a company he owned to a conglomerate he controlled. As he entered the annual meeting where he'd complete the deal, he was greeted by "epithets from minority stockholders." They "questioned and heckled him," shouting that Pathé was worth five times that much—that this was insider trading and another example of the rich profiting off the crash. As "heavily armed private detectives . . . succeed[ed] in preventing physical violence," Kennedy pushed the sale through.

Jack left Canterbury in the spring of 1931 to have an emergency appendectomy. By then, eight million people were out of work. When he traveled home to spend the rest of the term recovering, did he somehow miss the lines of unemployed, the drifters in the railroad stations? Even back in Bronxville, a startling number of "Going Out of Business" signs had appeared on storefronts. That summer, as Jack was being tutored in Latin, Henry Ford was cutting his workforce from 137,000 to 37,000. And by that fall, another million people had joined the nation's unemployed. If Jack still wasn't aware of the Depression—still hadn't heard a mucker murmur, "Jesus, I wish I had the job"—it was deliberate: he'd been taught not to notice.

Joe Kennedy decided Canterbury had wasted a year of Jack's life, but he blamed the institution, not the concept of boarding school. He transferred Jack to Choate, where Joe Jr. was flourishing. Choate was five times larger than Canterbury, Christian but not Catholic, more like Riverdale Country. It, too, had developed under a charismatic leader. George St. John was a private school teacher who'd married the daughter of the head of admissions at Yale. He'd arrived at Choate's Wallingford, Connecticut, campus the year after the Duke founded Riverdale. Since then, he'd boosted enrollment from fifty to five hundred boys, enlarging the physical plant to match. All this, St. John claimed, though he was "a child" when it came to economics. "I doubt if I had ever read a financial page, studied the ways of banks or the stock market, seen a copy of the *Wall Street Journal.*"

Like the population he served, St. John didn't discuss money—and spent a good deal of time chasing it. While the stock market boomed, he'd raised funds for a chapel, then gotten the Mellon family to donate a library (Paul Mellon went to Choate), received the capital for a new infirmary from the mother of another student, and in 1929 was able to build a dining hall, again thanks to a single wealthy donor. The year Jack arrived, the Depression had cut prep school enrollment by 25 percent and revenues by 40 percent. Still, in the depths of hard times, St. John managed to buy more land, construct a track and athletic fields, and erect a winter exercise building.

With one of every seven Americans out of work, Choate improved its sports facilities. Headmaster St. John believed they were at the core of the school's values. When he wrote the Kennedys that Joe Jr. was "one of the most worthwhile people in the world," he was prompted not only by the boy's academic success but his positions on the varsity football and hockey teams. According to St. John, Choate's job was to create "an aristocracy of the mind and the heart." He saw education "as a moral and spiritual force, its first job is to inspire." That's why chapel was compulsory; running a school without one, the headmaster said, was "like running a line for light and power without a powerhouse." And that's also why he had the boys memorize and recite the Kipling poem that began, "Our school it is a garden," and ended, "half a proper gardener's work is done upon his knees." Latin grades mattered, of course, but the ultimate goal, St. John said, was "to instill the work habit and high motives." That's how you could tell a Choate student: he had just a little bit better stuff.

Jack didn't have it.

He tried. His first year, he went out for football, baseball, basketball, crew, and golf. Trouble was, he weighed all of 117 pounds and kept getting sick. He was in the infirmary by November, back in January, and three months later had swollen glands and a bad cold. Plus, the school knew about his high IQ, and his grades didn't match. Within a month of arriving, Jack was in academic trouble. The problem, St. John wrote Joe Kennedy, was "one of application." The father agreed: "Jack has a great deal of natural ability, but is careless in applying it." As Rose Kennedy put it, the grades weren't as troubling as Jack's "lack of diligence in his studies; or, let us say, lack of 'fight.'" Here was the real, the awful character flaw: he didn't seem to give a damn.

Choate's reaction was to press harder. His housemaster required Jack to meet with him daily: "I have him repeat his French and Latin vocabularies to me every night. He is not allowed to leave his room during study period. I have worked with him in algebra." His room was inspected twice daily because the boy littered the floor with shirts, suits, assignment sheets, as if he didn't care about them either. He was establishing a reputation. "Jack Kennedy has a high IQ," wrote Choate's director of studies, "and is one of the most undependable boys in the Third Form." By the end of the year, it was clear he'd fail his language courses and would have to go to summer school. "What makes the whole problem difficult," his housemaster added, "is Jack's winning smile and charming personality . . . It is an inescapable fact that his actions are *really* amusing and evoke real hilarity."

Jack was fourteen; Choate was his fifth school. As his mother saw it, he "couldn't or wouldn't conform." But in some ways his behavior fit what one writer has called the "arranged acquaintanceships" of boarding school. While his brother was winning the school's Harvard Trophy for combined academic and athletic excellence, Jack was pelting his classmates with oranges thrown from an upstairs window, stuffing one kid's room so full of pillows he could barely open the door, and generally exhibiting a tendency, as his second-year housemaster put it, "to foster a gang spirit."

St. John kept reassuring the Kennedys that Choate could straighten their son out. When it came to discipline, the headmaster described himself as "a square guy." Of course, it was in the school's interest to keep Joe Kennedy happy. It was true that some educational experts had started lambasting the family's source of income—the movies—as morally degrading. One 1928 study went so far as to call Hollywood "in effect, an institution of informal education, socially uncontrolled and wholly unsupervised." What moviegoers learned in the dark was the very opposite of the code American schools were trying to teach. But Joe Kennedy had already helped Choate get a state-of-the-art movie projector. And he'd contributed to the scholarship fund. Plus, Kennedy had become a leading adviser and donor to Franklin Delano Roosevelt, the presidential candidate who personified prep school–Ivy League culture. When FDR won the election at the start of Jack's tenth-grade year, the *New York Times* list of his informal cabinet included Joe Kennedy, "fiery Boston and New York financier."

Fiery he was. After visiting his son that fall, Kennedy wrote St. John a furious letter. "I can't tell you how unhappy I felt in seeing and talking with Jack. He seems to lack entirely a sense of responsibility. His happy-go-lucky manner with a degree of indifference does not portend well for his future development." The boy, Kennedy added, was "at a very critical stage in his career." He could either "go ahead and be very much worthwhile or else slide off and get in with a group which regarded everything as a matter of fact."

It was a pretty accurate read of the sixteen-year-old. Except the slide had already started. Jack had seen what worthwhile looked like and wasn't interested.

He was still sickly, and unable to gain weight, he'd end up in a New Haven hospital that winter, then be sent to his family's new Florida estate to recuperate. PALM BEACH ROUND OF PARTIES, the *New York Times* reported on its society page: "John Kennedy and His Sisters Entertain." When he returned to school that spring of 1934, he wrote an essay for English class that whacked away at Choate's values. Justice, he'd been taught, was "always . . . linked with God." The worthwhile were ultimately rewarded; the irresponsible punished. Everyone got treated the same because everyone was equally capable of doing the right thing. "But," the seventeen-year-old asked, "how much better chance has [the] boy born with a silver spoon in his mouth of being good than the boy who from birth is surrounded by rottenness and filth. This even to the most religious of us can hardly seem a 'square deal.'"

It's a declaration. And the implications ran from the God of his mother's church to that "square guy," Headmaster St. John. Jack may have been insulated from the breadlines and protests, from the fifteen million now unemployed, but in the world he did know—the carefully protected world of his private education—he'd reached the conclusion that being good was . . . well, it was bullshit. Convenient bullshit.

When Jack returned to Choate for his senior year, he wrote his father that he was going to "stop fooling around" and admitted, "I have been bluffing myself about how much real work I have been doing." But soon St. John was describing Jack as "the most childish, irresponsible" senior in his residence. "All methods of coercion fail," his housemaster reported, including appealing to school spirit; Jack was "a complete individualist in theory and practice." The Christmas report added, "Unfortunately, it must be all for Jack or he won't play."

Particularly galling was the growing evidence that these very qualities were helping make him a student leader. He was living over the dining hall, and kids regularly gathered in his room, including some of the school's star athletes. So many came that Jack decided to restrict the group to a dozen or so: a kind of club. St. John got wind of it and was furious. A year at Choate now cost as much as the average American family's annual income. Enrollment was dropping as the Depression dragged on, and one of Choate's main selling points was its ability to instill character. Here was what the headmaster called "a colossally selfish, pleasure loving, unperceptive group—in general opposed to the hardworking, solid people in the school, whether masters or boys." In an angry speech in morning assembly, St. John denounced Jack and his friends as "muckers."

Perfect.

The headmaster used the word as a kind of all-purpose criticism: those who mucked up the Choate program. They didn't delight in the ardor of hard work. They didn't have the fight, the spirit, the better stuff. Was there also a hint of anti-Irish prejudice? Was part of the word's edge its implication of commonness, of sweaty hands-on labor?

Jack embraced it. He had thirteen gold emblems made in the shape of tiny shovels and emblazoned on each, "The Muckers Club." The gold shovel proudly proclaimed that a mucker was a bullshitter and a bullshit detector. Rumors started that at the spring dance the Muckers were going to cover the floor with horse manure. According to Jack's roommate: "Hell, the worst things we did were to sneak out for milkshakes and to play our radio when we weren't supposed to." As Jack described it in his scrapbook, the purpose of the club was to "put over festivities in our own little way and to buck the system more effectively."

That's exactly what got to St. John. Per one witness, "When he heard the name of the club—he saw red." At lunch, in front of the whole school, the headmaster denounced the group as "public enemies" of the Choate community, then pulled them into his office and expelled all thirteen.

Trouble was, Choate couldn't afford multiple expulsions—especially of star athletes. It might lead to a drop in applications, and worse, in fund-raising. The headmaster reversed himself. But he cabled the father of "the chief mover of the group" that there had to be a meeting that weekend.

FDR had appointed Joe Kennedy chairman of the new Securities Exchange Commission, his job to regulate fair trade in the stock market. "It takes a thief," the president had reportedly said, "to catch a thief." So, Jack's father got the cable at the thirty-three-room mansion he was renting near Washington and telegraphed St. John he'd be on the next sleeper train to Connecticut. The face-off came Sunday at noon, and according to St. John, they "held nothing back." The headmaster "reduced Jack's conceit, if it was conceit, and childishness, to considerable sorrow." Meanwhile, the chairman of the Securities Exchange Commission looked on, "supporting the school completely," per St. John. "I've always been very grateful to him."

Except when St. John left to take a call, father whispered to son, "If that crazy Muckers Club had been mine, you can be sure it wouldn't have started with an *M*."

Call it Jack's unofficial graduation. His father didn't quite get it—calling it the Fuckers Club would have been less effective—but the old man approved. His boy was a leader. And his target was old-money, old-school pretension. The Kennedys didn't have to worry that Jack sided with—or even knew much about—muckers. A psychologist reassured Jack's parents: "He does not define himself as a left winger." And the boy would follow the prescribed route from Choate to Princeton and then Harvard: getting in, like his father, more through influence than grades.

"Education," President Kennedy would one day proclaim, "is both the foundation and the unifying force of our democratic way of life—it is the mainspring of our economic and social progress—it is the highest expression of achievement in our society, ennobling and enriching human life." Maybe so, but not his education. Far from unifying him with the democratic masses, Jack's schooling set him apart and above. The achievements it valued tended to be on the ballfield—and the Muckers cheerfully proclaimed that even those didn't really matter. The little gold shovels signaled what they thought of being worthwhile, of the work habit and high motives.

Jack's mother believed that what she called this "silly episode" was "a turning point in his life . . . leading to adult maturity and perspective." It's true he didn't end up a rebel or a juvenile delinquent. But his adult style can be seen as a continuation of what had made him a Mucker: that happy-go-lucky, matter-of-fact, unworthwhile approach—which successfully fostered a gang spirit. Despite his mediocre school achievements and maybe because it would infuriate St. John, his Choate classmates voted him "most likely to succeed." There's a photograph of Jack on his official graduation day. He's facing the camera, his hair neatly parted, and he's wearing the proper black gown that covers him almost to the ground. There, peeking out from beneath, is a pair of two-tone saddle shoes, dirty.

ELVIS

Through the generations of nation-building, of exploration and settlement and industrialization, his ancestors stayed almost invisible. White against the white planks of weathered shacks, white against the constant landscape of cotton, they seemed to disappear. As if they didn't count, left no marks. As if they were nothing.

In the Revolutionary War, at the Battle of Hanging Rock, while the young Andy Jackson stood in the shade tending to the soldiers' horses, John Presley fought. Then, after the war, he moved between the newly opened frontiers of North Carolina and Tennessee. But he doesn't seem to have owned any land, and neither would his son. Then again, in eastern Tennessee, most families didn't. Almost three fifths of the frontier households were tenants. The richest sixth of the population—the class that hired the grown-up Andrew Jackson as a lawyer—ended up owning more than half the available real estate.

In the next generation, Dunnan Presley Jr., fought in the war against Mexico and was issued 160 acres in Tennessee. But by the time he'd enlisted for the Civil War, his family was in Mississippi, and the farm was gone. At his death, his estate consisted of household property worth twenty-five dollars and a cow. His daughter (who never married) spent her life farming other people's black Mississippi land, "sharing" most of her crop with various landlords, raising her nine children in tenant shacks. Her son Jesse went to school a few months of the year but spent most of the time planting, weeding, and picking cotton. He dropped out when he was eleven, married at seventeen, and was the father of two boys by the time he was twenty. His second son, Vernon Elvis, was born in the country outside Tupelo, Mississippi. By the time Vernon was a teenager, the family had moved into East Tupelo: five unpaved streets on the wrong side of the tracks. His uncle ran the grocery store and was mayor, but his father still worked shares. A local dairy farmer held their fifteen-hundred-dollar mortgage—which would never get paid off.

As history stripped the Presleys, left them landless through generations of debt, it worked the Mansells in almost exactly the same way. William Mansell fought under Colonel and then Major General Andrew Jackson, driving Native Americans out of the South. Like Jackson, Mansell was Ulster-Scotch, and like Jackson, claimed land in the newly opened territory. He settled along the Alabama-Mississippi border, where, again, most of the real estate went to speculators: three men alone ended up with two million acres. While Mansell managed to secure a farm, his eldest son, John, would lose it. And John's children ended up homesteading near Saltillo, north of Tupelo, trying to secure a piece of property in a landscape that didn't seem to allow it. They lived isolated lives, rarely getting into town, living on other people's farms. White Mansell's daughter married her first cousin, and their child, Gladys Smith, grew up spending eight to nine months of the year in the fields. The family worked shares, always in debt, moving every couple of years when it got to be too much. In March, they'd borrow money to plow and plant cotton; through the summer, anyone in the family old enough to walk helped weed and thin; in late August, they were all out under the sun, each picking 100, 150 pounds of cotton a day. And then come October, it was time to settle with the landlord. Year after year, it came out the same: they had nothing. They were nothing.

The Presley and the Mansell families orbited within a twenty-mile radius of Tupelo, a cotton trading center. It had sprung up, just before the Civil War, as a stop on the Mobile railroad line. Two decades later, town fathers managed to lure the Memphis-to-Birmingham track as well. But at the start of the twentieth century, with the land ravaged by erosion, cotton prices plummeted. Tupelo had avoided the industrialization that Helen Keller's family had seen in Alabama, but now the town's leading citizens recognized the need to diversify. As a first step, they proposed a mill to process cotton locally instead of shipping it north to places like Lawrence and Lowell. Landowners protested. Factory jobs would draw sharecroppers off the land and ruin the tenant system. Tupelo went ahead and built a five-hundred-spindle mill, but it made sure to protect the status quo.

First, the mill was segregated. Negroes would still have only one option: working in the fields at the lowest possible wages. Second, the mill would assign two thirds of the sewing, dying, and cutting jobs to women. Since they got paid less than men, that would help the mill's profits. Plus, it meant white males would still be tied to the tenant farming system. Finally, while some families would live in company housing down by the tracks, the mill would mostly hire single girls. Factory work would only be a temporary thing, until they got married. Each evening, the girls rode chartered buses back into the country, continuing to live on the farms where they'd eventually settle. By 1920, the Tupelo cotton mill employed 450 people, and other garment factories had grown around it: one turned out smocks, another work shirts, another baby clothes. The town of four thousand floated a bond and built the first concrete roads in Mississippi, securing its place as a commercial center. In 1927, a Carnation milk plant moved in: diversification now included some local farmers switching over to dairy. But sharecropping remained, and the invisible stayed invisible.

Gladys Smith made the shift to factory work in late 1932. Her father had recently died; two of her uncles were already living in East Tupelo; she knew how to run a sewing machine; and the Tupelo Garment Center would pay her two dollars for a nine-hour day. It was the midst of the Depression. The spring before, on a single April day, a quarter of all Mississippi's real property had been auctioned off to pay delinquent taxes. Some forty thousand farms went under the hammer. When presidential candidate Franklin Roosevelt passed through Tupelo that year, he saw what he called "a scarcity of raiment" and "a lack of food." But what "made the tears come to my eyes," he recalled, was the lack of hope.

Vernon Presley, two years younger than Gladys, had already

moved to town. He'd quit school around eighth grade and was picking up work where he could: day laborer, milkman, carpenter, sometimes in the cotton fields. On Sundays, he'd attend Pentecostal services in a tent on a vacant lot in East Tupelo. The co-pastor was Gains Mansell, Gladys's uncle, and that's where Vernon and Gladys met. They eloped six months after she got to town; a year later, she was pregnant. In the world of sharecropping, where children were workers, twenty-two-year-old Gladys was late starting a family. But maybe that's why she'd waited: because she had other dreams for herself and for her children.

The newly elected FDR came back through the area when Gladys was seven months pregnant. A crowd of seventy-five thousand— more than double the county's population—streamed into town to hear the president speak. He declared a "change in the looks on people's faces." Tupelo had become the first city in the nation to get electricity from the Tennessee Valley Authority (TVA), and the president promised that "the number of new refrigerators that had been put in . . . [means more than] just plain dollars and cents. It means," he announced, "a greater human happiness."

Roosevelt would declare the tenant system amounted to "generations of unthinking exploitation." The solution lay with the refrigerator, the paved highways, the electric lines cutting the horizon. The Presleys were starting in debt. Their first home was heavily mortgaged to Orville Bean, the same dairy farmer who held Vernon's father's note. The young couple had to borrow money to pay the doctor in January 1935 when Elvis Aaron was born. And the shotgun shack that Vernon built wasn't even tied into the electric grid. But to have gotten out of the cotton fields and to be living in town was to see the flickering possibility of FDR's future.

A tornado tore through Tupelo when Elvis was fifteen months old, killing over two hundred people, destroying homes and businesses. Rebuilding and modernizing began immediately. Around the same time, Roosevelt's agricultural department initiated a "plow-up": paying landowners to destroy their cotton crops in order to boost prices. Because it had already begun the process of diversifying its economy, New Deal policy makers saw Tupelo as a model for the New South.

In that model, people like the Presleys and Mansells would stop being nothing, would rise with the rest of the country. The question was whether the landowners and business leaders would permit that change. Whether the generations of exploitation really had been unthinking. The answer came when Elvis was still a toddler, but it helped determine what he'd need to know.

By 1937, there were almost half a million workers in the Southern garment industry. They were non-union and, according to a Tupelo newspaper editor, paid starvation wages. The Congress of Industrial Organizations (CIO) saw the potential for the single largest organized labor force in the country. If garment workers could be unionized, it would fundamentally change the balance of power in the South. It would challenge the aristocracy that Captain Keller had fought so hard to maintain and that still ruled the region. Even more, as CIO organizer and tactician Myles Horton put it, a successful Southern union might open the door for a nationwide "democratic, radical, social movement." W. E. B. Du Bois's dream of a shining world.

One of the first CIO actions was at Tupelo's cotton mill. Workers occupied the building, calling for a raise from ten to fifteen dollars a week—and for the work week to be shortened from forty-five to forty hours. The owners' response would become a standard tactic across the South. First, they refused to negotiate. Then, they got the state government to call in the National Guard. With the strike a week old, the troops marched onto a baseball field near the mill and began firing their weapons. The National Guard claimed it was just a "practice drill," but the strikers charged out carrying wrenches and hunks of metal and forced the troops to retreat. Next, the governor arrived and tried to broker a settlement. Finally, when the strike had gone on for three weeks, the owners decided to solve the problem: they closed the mill. Permanently. Four hundred people lost their jobs, and Tupelo lost a key part of its economy, but the town stayed union-free. In case the message wasn't clear enough, a female organizer was dragged down the steps of her hotel and run out of town. Another local "agitator" (as the paper called him) was abducted off a downtown street, taken out into the country, tied by a noose to the axle of a car, then beaten.

Looking back on the Depression era, Myles Horton realized he'd believed "capitalism was on its last legs." He'd hoped that Roosevelt was going to help change the system. But the message from places like Tupelo was just the opposite: Horton ended up realizing that capitalism "wasn't even limping, that Roosevelt's job was to make it work." New Deal programs like the TVA and the cotton plow-up were part of what would be called the "Southern Enclosure" movement: designed to bring some relief to the cotton-dominated economy without disturbing the sharecropping system.

A poor man caught in that enclosure had few choices. It was the winter after the strike that Vernon Presley was arrested for forgery. He changed the value on a four-dollar check written by Orville Bean. Holding their mortgage, doling out day-work to Vernon, Bean's control over his tenants amounted to an in-town version of sharecropping. While the stolen dollars couldn't have meant that much to the landlord, people said Bean wanted to teach Vernon and his other tenants a lesson. It was the same lesson the strike had taught: people like the Presleys needed to know their place. Vernon got three years at the infamous Parchman prison, where, in the midst of the Depression, some 60 percent of the prisoners were in for burglary and robbery: "crimes of hunger," as one analyst put it, "not honor."

Gladys and their three-year-old ended up staying with cousins in downtown Tupelo. Gladys was "on commodities"–living off government-issued cheese, sugar, and beans–and finding occasional work at a laundry. "We never had any luxuries," her son would recall, "but we never went hungry. Of course that's something to be thankful for . . . because there's so many people who don't." That was the lesson he was supposed to learn, starting young: to be thankful for what he got. He was. Well, he tried to be. But the disparity between the promised refrigerator future and how little they actually had was explosive. And one of the only places they were allowed to explode was church.

By this time, Gladys's uncle was the sole preacher at the Assembly of God. He'd managed to put up a wooden building for his congregation of sixty, most of them relatives and friends. "When Elvis was just a little fellow, no more than two years old," Gladys would later recall, "he would slide down off my lap, run into the aisle and scramble up to the platform. There he would stand looking at the choir and trying to sing with them. He was too little to know the words . . . but he could carry the tune and he would watch their faces and try to do as they did." Asked as a grown-up how he got into gospel music, Elvis answered, "We grew up with it."

The Assembly of God was a poor man's denomination, a sharecropper's religion. Its congregants started with the knowledge that they didn't count, and on this earth, probably never would. "You must feel your need," the preacher would call out. "Is your life barren of power?" Then, he'd quote Acts 1:8: "But ye shall receive power, after that the Holy Ghost is come upon you." Early-twentieth-century Pentecostals were outcasts, many of them displaced by modern industrialism. The more established denominations didn't want much to do with them, and the feeling was mutual. In the heat of their awakening, Pentecostals often rejected the need for any set order of service, a church building, or even a preacher. Believers saw it as a revival of "primitive Christianity," where everyone was equal and all that counted was direct contact with the Spirit. That occurred miraculously, unexpectedly, democratically. "[It] fell upon me and filled me," is how an early convert described it, ". . . seemed to lift me up, and instantly I began to speak in another language. I could not have been more surprised if at the same moment someone had handed me a million dollars."

This speaking in another language was considered a spontaneous, miraculous baptism worth more than money. Believers traced it back to the original Pentecost, when Christ's apostles spoke with "tongues like as of fire." It's why Gladys and the boy and the other Mansells and Presleys gathered in the East Tupelo church: for the possibility that the Holy Ghost would manifest, burst forth in someone's mortal body. Then the shouting, stomping congregant became proof that His was the only true power, that all this would pass, that the end was near. It was an impossible response to an impossible situation: being trapped on earth.

Music was there to help. The Assembly of God allowed instruments that older denominations frowned on: tambourines, guitars, drums, whatever it took to break through to ecstasy. The driving clamor was a lot like Sojourner Truth's ring shouts, although by now much of the Methodist Church had grown conservative and saw Assembly of God singing as anarchy. Pentecostals often couldn't afford hymnals. Some practiced shape-note singing—a leader setting the key and teaching the words as they went—but the church also recognized "singing in the spirit." A believer could just launch into song. If people ended up on different beats, harmonies clashing, words lost or made up or repeated, well, that was the angelic choir. Sometimes it "rolled . . . over the entire company," as one witness wrote, ". . . rising and swelling . . . rolling and sinking . . . [like the] waves of the ocean." The singers were guided by the divine. "It did not at all appear like human voices," as another put it. "When the last quivering note died away, a hush fell upon all . . . [W]e were loath to open our eyes or come back to earth again."

One of the founders of modern Pentecostalism would come to denounce these behaviors as "negroisms." The accusation was that they were "noises as practiced by the Negroes of the Southland pawned off on people all over the world as the working of the Holy Spirit." But that was years later. In the beginning, the Pentecostal movement had been noticeably, radically integrated. "The color line," as one witness put it, "was washed away by the blood." In the beginning of the twentieth century, as the revival swept through the South, it brought white tenant farmers together with black: they were both penniless, hungry for hope, trapped in the same enclosure. From outside, who could tell whether the screams of joy, the waves of release, were inspired by "negroisms," or the old Methodist Love Feasts? And from the inside, who cared? It was the Spirit that counted.

By World War I, the revival had cooled some, as Pentecostals realized they'd have to deal with this world until the next. Racial distinctions reappeared. The Assembly of God split off and became a "white man's church," so that Gladys's little boy, staring into the choir, only saw faces like his own. But the rapture—the thing he needed to know—was a lot like what the black Pentecostals found across town. And in both places, when the shouting, testifying believers finally came back to earth, they were still trapped.

Vernon was let out of prison after nine months and not much later was trying to get out of Tupelo. The governor of Mississippi, citing an "acute economic emergency," had launched a series of bonds to support new industry. One analyst has called it "a state-subsidized affirmative action program for unemployed White male workers." Its major achievement was helping a Birmingham industrialist finance a shipyard on the Gulf Coast. Vernon and one of his cousins moved down with their families. For a half year or so, they formed a kind of forward wing of the Presley family: shipworkers, members of the modern labor force, on the verge of being able to afford that refrigerator. But the shift was apparently too sudden, the situation too foreign. The cousins decided they missed East Tupelo, and the Presleys followed them back, Gladys explaining, "We're not staying down there alone."

Still, they kept trying to unlock the future. One key, everybody kept saying, was education. When it came to its public school system, Mississippi was playing catch-up: in 1936, its per-student spending was less than a third the national average. By 1941, when Elvis entered first grade at East Tupelo Consolidated, the state was in the middle of a six-million-dollar funding increase, had extended the school term to eight months (for white kids), and had passed a law providing free textbooks for grades one through eight. The wood-frame building where Elvis went was fifteen years old and serviced some seven hundred students, grades one through twelve: two grades to a room until you reached fifth. Still, the poorest white neighborhood in town had its own school complete with electricity, indoor plumbing, and heating: a "shared source of pride and joy." Gladys often walked her son the half mile across Highway 78. Part of that was protective: "My mama never let me out of her sight." School, after all, took her only child out into the larger, modern world and promised (or threatened) to make that move permanent. The other part was probably to make sure he went.

A few months after the boy started, the United States entered World War II. From then till fourth grade, his father was away more than he was home. As military expenditures pumped the Southern economy, Vernon joined the local carpenter's union, then got work about ninety miles west in Como, Mississippi, building a prisoner-of-war camp. After that, he found a job at a munitions plant up in Memphis. By war's end, he'd managed to save two hundred dollars to put down on a house. But the Tupelo economy still worked the same way. The house was once again heavily mortgaged to Orville Bean. "There weren't any old plantation owners," claimed the heir to one of the town's garment factories. But he went on to describe postwar Tupelo in near feudal terms: the population was "mostly hill farmers and yeomen." Factory jobs were still almost all for women; the few open to men were going to returning vets. It was the same trap. In less than a year, the Presleys lost the house and had to move into a rental on Mulberry Alley in "Shake Rag," the black part of Tupelo.

By then, their eleven-year-old was already performing. Two years earlier, he'd started singing on a children's talent show broadcast over local radio. His voice was good enough for his fifth grade teacher—Orville Bean's daughter—to arrange to have him perform the country weeper "Old Shep" at the state fair. According to one researcher, over the next two and a half years he was on the radio ten times, singing hymns, show tunes, country-western and patriotic songs. His parents managed to buy him a cheap guitar. "I took the guitar, and I watched people, and I learned to play a little bit," he recalled. His uncle taught him chords, as did his preacher and a local country performer. "But I would never sing in public. I was very shy about it, you know."

Maybe that was true. Or maybe, looking back after he'd become well-known, he didn't want to reveal how hard he'd worked to learn what he needed to know. As one of his cousins recalled, "[O]ur entertainment [was] gathering at each other's house and singing and having a good time." That wasn't the paying public, but piece together all the recollections about where he sang—at school, in church, on the radio, to friends, girls, the crowd at the state fair—and he doesn't seem to have been shy about his voice. That, not the guitar, was his prime instrument, and he worked at it, studied.

"[T]he Grand Ole Opry is the first thing I ever heard, probably. But I liked the blues," he recalled, "and I liked the gospel music . . . gospel quartets and all that." The church was a regular chance for him to sing. Their new, nineteen-year-old pastor would ask him to take part in the special performing portion of the service. "[W]e might have someone do a Blackwood Brothers type of quartet number, different ones in the church would get up or maybe somebody visiting would sing," the pastor recalled. "[Elvis] sang quite a few times and he was liked." To be liked at a Pentecostal service meant more than having a good voice. A singer had to manifest the Spirit, move the audience toward God, make music drenched in emotion.

The boy followed quartet music closely. The Blackwood Brothers, for example, were so popular by the late 1940s that they had to put together a second group to cover all the concert requests. Some Pentecostals didn't approve of their kind of gospel boogie: "We warn God's people . . . Fun, froth, and religious frolic are indicative of shallow-pan Christianity." The worry was that the Blackwoods' clean-cut harmonies were too worldly, more about entertainment than speaking in tongues. But the "shallow-pan" quartets helped make Pentecostalism presentable. The Blackwoods appeared in crisp suits and ties, traveled in a big tour bus, and broadcast three times a day over a five-thousand-watt Iowa station that reached twenty-seven states and three Canadian provinces.

If Elvis learned at church, he also studied at Joe Kennedy's "institution of informal education": the movies. He loved Gene Autry, Roy Rogers, and shoot-'em-ups in general. Snapshots from the period show him in his holster, practicing his draw. As a measure of how popular the films were, the fall Elvis entered Tupelo Junior High, the editor of a local paper showed Wild West movies to gather a crowd for a lecture series on "Cotton's Future"—and got a thousand people to attend. The Assembly of God condemned this kind of popular culture, too. As did the public schools. Movies distracted youth, led to juvenile delinquency, and, according to one censor, offered "a liberal education in the art of loving." Elvis went as often as he could.

The Presleys' move to Shake Rag put them in a section of Tupelo "out of sight," as one study of the town put it, "of much of the white community." Blacks accounted for about 40 percent of the population, but, the study went on, the two societies "intersect only at a limited number of points." It seems fair to call Elvis Presley one of those points. He went to an all-white middle school (getting through the first two years with Cs in reading and Ds in arithmetic). His family continued to attend the all-white Assembly of God in East Tupelo (Vernon was now a deacon). But for the next year and a half, the twelve-year-old came home to the black slum on the mud flats east of the railroad.

Poverty had pushed them across the color line. "There were times we had nothing to eat but cornbread and water," Vernon remembered, "but we always had compassion for people. Poor we were, I'll never deny that. But trash we weren't." And he concluded, "We never had any prejudice. Neither did Elvis." That doesn't sound possible: the air was as thick with prejudice as the cotton lint that blew off the fields. But even as cleaned-up, revisionist history, it's a statement the father didn't need to make. The Presleys could have left the stereotype alone—that poor Southern whites defined themselves by what they weren't: black. Instead, the parents seem to have learned—and taught their son—a different lesson. They weren't crusaders; they didn't fight segregation. But they weren't trash either. Sitting down to cornbread and water didn't mean you had to find some way to feel superior to the folks over there, eating the same. Some fifteen years after he'd moved out of Shake Rag, Elvis was asked what one lesson he'd pass on to *his* son. "I think my biggest thing would be consideration . . . consideration for other people's feelings." Why? "To keep yourself from being hardened."

"When I grow up," his mother remembered the boy saying, "I'm going to buy you a fine house and pay everything you owe at the grocery store and get two Cadillacs—one for you and Daddy, and one for me." That was the American dream, the kind of thing that happened in the movies. But in Shake Rag, they were having a hard enough time paying the twenty-one-dollar milk bill. Vernon had gone from working at a lumberyard to driving the delivery truck for a grocery store. "My father was a common laborer," is how Elvis would put it. "He didn't have a trade." Gladys sometimes brought in extra money by working at the laundry. The town leaders, meanwhile, had launched a campaign that called for increased production: "Per Person, Per Acre, Per Animal Unit." The effort, now formally known as the Tupelo model, promoted better education and higher wages not as rights (the town was still actively, violently anti-union), but because its businessmen were convinced that "uneducated, unorganized people [were] a liability."

For many, it was too little too late. Over the next decade, 20 percent of Mississippi's population would leave the state. In early November 1948, the Presleys headed for Tennessee. "Dad packed all our belongings in boxes and put them on top and in the trunk of a 1939 Plymouth," is how their son remembered it. "We left Tupelo over night. We were broke, man, broke." Gladys recalled it as more thought-out than that. They'd been talking it over for a while, and one of her brothers and his family had agreed to come along. Either way, the move to Memphis was the next logical step in the long migration: off the farm and into the future.

Elvis's education was already more urban than rural. He'd grown up in a place where the trains stopped, where people worked in factories, where he could walk to the movies. What he'd learned so far—in school and out—depended on a city mix of people and influences: more like Ben Franklin's Boston than Abe Lincoln's log cabin. Sure, he's in overalls for his first Tupelo Junior High picture. But he didn't pick cotton or lead a mule; his parents had worked hard to make sure of that. He's probably the first Presley or Mansell to spend eight months of the year in a classroom. And by the time he's a teenager and headed for Memphis, he's posing in a suit and a shirt with a collar.

The family moved into a boardinghouse: a big Victorian from the city's grand past, now cut up into sixteen small rooms. Vernon found work at the same munitions plant that had employed him during the war; Gladys ran a sewing machine. While it was a big change from Tupelo, population eleven thousand, to Memphis, closer to four hundred thousand, the parents were doing much the same kind of work. And the boy was continuing at school. The move had interrupted his eighth-grade year, and he could have used the excuse to drop out. He'd now gotten as far as Vernon ever had, and in the working-class neighborhood where they'd landed, an eighth-grade education was about average. But he finished the year at a downtown middle school. And would go on to Humes High. Coming to Memphis, after all, was about trying to enter the New South.

The city the Presleys now called home had been run for the past forty years by one of the country's most powerful bosses, Edward Crump. Crump kept Memphis strictly segregated. The city was 40 percent black, and he wooed Negro voters by handing out certain city jobs: mail carrier, garbage collector. He allowed blues clubs on Beale Street, a Negro League baseball team, black doctors and lawyers. At the same time, Crump's police commissioner had proudly announced, "[T]his is a white man's country and always will be and any Negro who doesn't agree to this had better move on." The displaced white sharecroppers who poured into Memphis lived, prayed, and went to school almost entirely among their own. Around the time the Presleys came to town, Boss Crump swore he'd go to jail for "the balance of my life" rather than obey President Truman's order to integrate military facilities like the Memphis Defense Depot.

Crump's political machine ran on jobs. As the *Washington Post* put it, Memphis citizens "lick the boots of their notorious tyrant not because they have to . . . [but] because it pays." In 1924, Henry Ford's Model T assembly plant had become the city's first symbol of "industrial civilization." In 1938, Firestone had bought eighty-five acres and set up an enormous tire and rubber factory. By the time the Presleys arrived, Kimberly-Clark was producing paper products, and International Harvester had a sizable farm machine factory. Tennessee had aggressively courted Northern industry, taking Mississippi's idea of bonds for business and issuing three times as many. In 1949, executives asked why they'd moved their businesses to the South cited the weather, the availability of raw materials, and the region's growing consumer market. What they avoided mentioning was cheap, non-union labor. Or the segregation that helped produce it. Blacks at Firestone and other factories routinely did the hardest work and got the lowest wages. The CIO called prejudice a way for employers to "create false contests between Negro and white workers." Attempts to organize across racial lines—on the Memphis docks, for example, in the late thirties—were crushed, often violently. Although wages in the South had almost doubled since the start of World War II, pitting black against white helped keep them 15 percent below the going rate in the Northeast.

Early in 1949, Vernon found a new job at a paint factory. It only brought in about nineteen hundred dollars a year, below the city's median of twenty-three hundred. On the other hand, that meant the Presleys qualified for public housing.

They moved into the Lauderdale Courts as Elvis was entering high school: both considered steps up and out. Back in 1937, under FDR's Housing Act, Memphis had razed twenty-six acres of Market Square slums. It replaced them with the Courts: a low-income complex with one-, two-, and three-story group houses built around a central mall. A strict set of rules monitored who was allowed to live there and how they had to behave once they got in. It wasn't hard to be poor enough: the median income in Memphis qualified you. Yet almost none of the 315 families who had been living in Market Square were accepted. Instead, the housing authority wanted poor people who were "very nice and deserving"—which is how a home service worker described the Presleys.

Once you got a place in the Courts, you entered a self-contained world. One of the expressed goals of its modernist design was to provide "desirable privacy from residential areas." In other words, it kept the deserving poor separate from the undeserving. That way, residents could be educated. The Courts set out to teach middle-class behavior, monitoring everything from drinking habits to housekeeping. Gladys, for example, got special mention for always having her floors nicely waxed. The Memphis Housing Authority viewed the project as a gateway: "From slums to public housing to private ownership."

The modern high school embraced a lot of the same goals. Humes High was big: sixteen hundred students, all white, grades seven through twelve. According to one of Elvis's classmates, they came from "a wide range of income levels from high middle to extremely low," with the Presleys at the bottom. It's true Vernon didn't make much, but his factory job brought in more than many people at the Courts. On his first day at school, Elvis was "so nervous he was bug-eyed," but soon blended in. In fact, freshman and sophomore years, hardly anyone seems to have noticed him. Which was part of the point, wasn't it? High school took kids from all kinds of backgrounds and taught them how to conform to agreed-upon standards.

At Humes, the goal was to prepare kids for the New South: a job on the assembly line, a house in one of the subdivisions sprouting up at the city limits. Elvis followed the agenda, getting Bs in science, English, and math. He also received some practical training: boys at Humes routinely took wood shop the same way girls took home ec. Central to the curriculum was instilling the proper values. Teachers taught personal appearance, health, how to behave on a date. Students were expected to show school spirit at pep rallies and were encouraged to participate in after-school clubs: Elvis belonged to the Speech Club, English Club, History Club, and Biology Club. And beginning sophomore year, he got what might be called a patriotic education by joining a junior version of the Reserve Officers Training Corps, the ROTC.

Since the First World War, America's public education system had been inviting the army to teach students "the value of citizenship, service to the United States, personal responsibility, and a sense of accomplishment." From the military's point of view, the ROTC helped identify potential officers, a lot like the original IQ tests. At the start of the 1950s, when Elvis joined, the program's popularity had jumped dramatically thanks to the cold war heating up. U.S. troops were fighting Communists in North Korea, and at home, a new Red Scare had critics screening textbooks and teachers for subversive leanings. Some saw John Dewey's theory of building community as more than a little suspicious; as one pamphlet put it, "Progressive Education Increases Juvenile Delinquency." In response, public schools used the ROTC program as a way of reassuring taxpayers that kids were being taught to be patriots. At Humes, the junior officers learned how to fire rifles, marched in the Veteran's Day parade, and joined the King and Queen's Honor Guard for the city's annual, strictly segregated Cotton Carnival.

Elvis, by all reports, wore his uniform proudly. In fact, he seems to have gone along with his school program in general. Sure, in his part-time job as a movie usher he studied the greased pompadour of Tony

Curtis and Marlon Brando's sexy rebellion. And he brought some of their style into high school—although judging by photos of his friends, he wasn't alone in that. If he was a little "different," as some classmates later claimed, he didn't stick out much, and there's no sign of his being a rebel. In fact, he'd end up graduating with a good-conduct certificate. For the Presleys and Mansells, after all, being seen as a little different had too often meant countrified, ignorant, no account. The modern high school was in the business of smoothing out those differences. The summer after he turned sixteen, he took a job at Precision Tool, the same munitions manufacturer that had employed his father and three of his uncles. He may have had more oil in his hair come junior year, but he also tried out for the football team and volunteered at the school library: buying into the system even if it mostly seemed to bore him. "I had no idea what the teacher was saying," a friend quotes him, ". . . I was dreaming." He drifted along beneath the surface of high school, carried toward its postwar promise of something like security.

Meanwhile, his education outside school had broadened and deepened. Memphis offered more radio stations, more records at the local store, and more chances to hear a wider variety of live music. Rhythm and blues artists from a young B. B. King to Ruth Brown performed on Beale Street, and there was a whole other scene that included country music just across the Mississippi in West Memphis clubs. Whether you were an ambitious businessman, like the owner of the Memphis Recording Service, or a kid who harmonized with his buddies at the Lauderdale Courts, you could hear the possibilities: a sort of upswelling, as the mix of sounds and styles brought the invisible to the surface.

Back during Elvis's freshman year, the son of an Alabama tenant farmer had taken a show tune called "Lovesick Blues" and made it the most popular country song in the nation. Hank Williams had then gone on to become a Grand Ole Opry regular and was not only making a couple hundred thousand dollars a year, but had signed a five-year movie contract. The mainstream appeal of white performers from the South had been reinforced by singers like Eddy Arnold, a smooth-voiced pop star, and songs like "Tennessee Waltz," which sold almost five million copies in 1951. So-called country-western singers mostly dressed in spangly duds, sang with a drawl, and had a pedal-steel guitar moaning in the background. But they didn't do cowboy songs much anymore. Instead, they sang about regular working folks: in and out of love, drinking, trying to hold on to a job. To the high school boy, that must have been one of the more amazing lessons: that people across the country would pay to hear about guys like the ones at Precision Tool, or the women over at St. Joseph's Hospital, where Gladys now had a job as a nurse's aide.

The phenomenon included religious music. Hank Williams sang gospel narratives as Luke the Drifter. The country star who'd hit with "Old Shep," Red Foley, went on to score nationally with "Just a Closer Walk with Thee" and 1951's "Peace in the Valley," credited as the first million-selling gospel record. Meanwhile, the Blackwood Brothers had moved to Memphis the fall of Elvis's second year at Humes. They'd begun broadcasting their peppy, Pentecostal harmonies over a local radio station and performing at Ellis Auditorium. "[T]hey would sing all night," Elvis recalled, "and I would stay there all night." By his junior year, they'd signed with a major label, RCA, and had a national hit, "Rock My Soul."

If he dreamed of someday being part of all this, he had to know it was an outrageous dream and dangerous. New Year's Day 1953, the twenty-nine-year-old Hank Williams died from drugs and drink and all the contradictions of his rise. That week, the Presleys were forced out of Lauderdale Courts. The catch in the Memphis Housing Authority's plan was that a deserving family couldn't be too successful. The combined incomes of Gladys and Vernon had put them over the Courts' limit, never mind that they still couldn't reach that goal of "private ownership." Instead, they had to move back into a boarding-house, then a rented apartment. Elvis, meanwhile, appeared in the annual Humes High talent show. The trappings couldn't have been more Old South. An interlocutor opened, and the school band played in blackface: a minstrel show. Elvis did a midtempo ballad. "Nobody knew I even sang," is how he recalled it some twenty years later. "It was amazing how popular I became after that. Then I went on through high school and I graduated." Maybe he did become popular for the last two months of his senior year. The day after graduation, he started work on the assembly line.

He was soon back at Precision Tool, where, with overtime, he brought in more than sixty dollars a week: as much as any adult in his family had ever earned. Still, it was a job he could have landed without a diploma—and he remembers being ambitious for more. "At one time, when I got out of school, I thought I wanted to be a doctor or something in the medical profession . . . but I didn't have money to go to college." A couple months after graduation, he was down at the Memphis Recording Service, home to the new Sun record label. He paid to cut two sides, backing himself with his childhood guitar. Then, at the start of the new year, he cut another two, all slow ballads. These private recordings were so his mother could hear him sing, and the people at the label, and so he could hear himself. It was a first chance to study his voice and to figure out the specific skills not just of singing but of recording. Legend has it that when the assistant at Sun asked him who he sounded like, he answered, "I don't sound like nobody." But on those first sides, he sounds like all kinds of people—and not sure how to fit the pieces together.

"Little by little I gain experience." That's how Elvis would later describe his learning style. He started going to a new Assembly of God church over on East McLemore. It was a ways from his neighborhood, but the Blackwoods were members and sang there when they were in town. The pastor, Reverend James Hamill, knew the same Mississippi the Presleys had come from. "We were poor people," he proclaimed, "that the poor people called poor." He, too, had promised his mother he'd make "some real money" and was now building his Memphis congregation through no-nonsense preaching and canny use of the media. Newspaper ads and radio broadcasts helped; and the Reverend Hamill would soon start a television ministry that became a model of modern evangelical outreach. The Blackwoods drew people, too, and the reverend came out in defense of quartet singing as "simple songs that carry a message, done well and done under the anointing of the Holy Spirit." If the Tupelo church had taught separation from and disdain for this world, the First Assembly of God, Memphis, borrowed marketing strategies from big business. It was okay to advertise your faith, to shake your stuff. In fact, it helped spread the Word.

Elvis was soon spending time with Cecil Blackwood, younger brother of the group's baritone singer and a resident of the Lauderdale Courts. He and Jimmy Hamill, the reverend's son, had started a teen quartet: a sort of minor league Blackwoods that appeared regularly on the radio. Elvis auditioned for the group, but, as Cecil recalled, "[W]e didn't have an opening." On top of trying to break into the quartet scene, making private recordings, and hanging out at the record store to learn the latest hits, Elvis also followed what was known as race music: what Du Bois had once called his people's "subtle sense of song."

A few blocks south of the Assembly of God and across the Memphis color line was East Trigg Baptist Church. Its pastor, Reverend W. H. Brewster, was an extraordinary, nationally known songwriter who presided over an extraordinary, nationally known choir. The year the Presleys moved to Memphis, the singer Mahalia Jackson had a major gospel hit with Brewster's "Move on Up a Little Higher"—which Brewster called a response to "the fight for rights here in Memphis." Mahalia had carefully studied the phrasing of East Trigg's lead singer, Queen C. Anderson: how she soared through an uptempo number, playing off the background singers, ending each phrase with a rising burst of confidence and power. Now, in a special section set aside for whites, Elvis studied there, too, as did visitors from Sun Records, James Blackwood, and others.

Elvis's chance to move on up was actually three chances in quick succession. First, he got a job driving truck at Crown Electric. It meant a pay cut from Precision Tool and still didn't seem to have anything to do with his high school diploma: the boy was making deliveries like his father had back in Tupelo. Except this was actually the beginning of an apprenticeship: the entry-level job for becoming a licensed electrician. It meant he was on his way to having a trade—and that refrigerator. He worried he was too "absentminded" for the work, might "blow somebody's house up." But in the landscape of the New South, this was the eighteen-year-old's chance to follow those electric lines into the future.

A couple months after Elvis started at Crown, a plane carrying two members of the Blackwoods crashed, killing both. Elvis attended the standing-room-only funeral at the city auditorium. When Cecil Blackwood was called up to replace his older brother, it left an opening in the teen quartet. As Cecil recalled it, Elvis filled in "for several weeks." He was on the verge of being a full-time member of the farm team for one of the leading gospel quartets in the country. From there, who knew?

Sun Records gave him his third option. Impressed by his recordings (and persistence), they called and arranged to have the teenager woodshed with a pair of older musicians to see if they could come up with a commercial number. Eight days after the Blackwoods' plane crash, the three of them—the apprentice electrician, a guitar player who worked at a dry cleaners, and a bass player with a day job at the Firestone tire factory—were in the studio trying out various ballads. At one point, they jammed on an old and fairly obscure rhythm and blues tune, "That's All Right (Mama)," released back when Elvis lived in Shake Rag. The label owner thought they might have something.

And there we have to leave him. A photo from that July shows him in a bow tie, white shirt, and country-western jacket, his hair in a spiky flattop, a slight smile on his lips. His education is over. In the simplest terms, he's found a voice. "I just landed upon it accidentally," he tells an early interviewer. "More or less. I'm a pretty close follower of religious quartets, and they do a lot of rockin' spirituals. And so that's where I got the idea from, is religious quartets." Religious quartets, blues singers, pop crooners, country-western and gospel stars—all had their influence. That it was an accident may be—more or less—true. He'd say elsewhere that he relied a lot on instinct, "going by impulse and just what I feel on the spur of the moment." But he'd been raised to be modest. And a haphazard self-education fit in that American tradition of the guy who just stumbles on knowledge. Truth is, he'd worked at it. He'd followed the quartets and then, in his own words, "got an idea."

What idea? Early in his career, an interviewer suggests his style—especially his jittery hip thrusts onstage—came from the Presleys' "holy roller" background. It's one of the few times Elvis gets angry in public. "That's not it! That's not it at all! . . . My religion has nothin' to do with what I do now, because the type of stuff I do now is not religious music." More, he rejects the term "holy roller": "I have never used that expression." To call him that was to continue the dismissal, the erasure, that had haunted the Presleys and Mansells for generations. It made them, to use Vernon's terms, "trash." But the young man's voice testifies to just the opposite. One of the things that's so startling about Presley, from "That's All Right (Mama)" on, is how confident he sounds. Like a man who knows who he is, who's declaring himself.

And isn't that, finally, what he's learned? If his style came partly from groups like the Blackwoods, the idea behind it has to do with the right to have a voice at all. And in that sense, it *is* the sound of someone singing in the spirit. Not singing religious songs and not the Holy Spirit of the Assembly of God. But something related: an inspired, goofy, freed spirit where, suddenly, anything's possible. "Every dream I ever dreamed has come true a hundred times," he'd proclaim late in his life. By then, his sound had brought him staggering amounts of fame and wealth. And though that was part of what he'd been after—the American dream of hitting the jackpot, of buying his parents a Cadillac—they were the results, not the idea itself.

The idea was that he could rock the world, shake clear of the enclosure, go beyond even those electric lines that caged the horizon. The idea was that a person could declare himself in such a way that he stood apart from the landscape of cotton fields and weathered shacks—that he challenged the very notion of being, or not being, "white." People like him were supposed to harden into a category, to disappear. Instead, in an explosion of contradictions, he finds hope. His sudden appearance isn't actually sudden: it rises out of a long history. And so does this idea, this hope: that we can learn what we need to know.

EPILOGUE: THE PRESENT

And so we come back to the present.

We enter the period of our own educations—somewhere between the moment Elvis stepped out into the world and today.

And we ask ourselves Henry Adams's question: What part turned out to be useful and what not?

Our answers are going to depend on when we grew up and where, what was happening to the country, which schools we went to, and a lot of other factors. Including how these questions have been answered in the past.

Whatever the particular circumstances, an American education is going to bear the marks of rebellion: the one that spurred Ben Franklin and created the country. It will be shaped by the promises of that independence: the hidden current that Adams's great-grandmother, Nabby Smith, touched—the electric current that called to Elvis. How we understand our land will be affected by how our ancestors understood it: from the pioneers clearing forest to the smokestack in front of Rachel Carson's house. And no matter when and where we get our education, it's going to carry the reminders of Belle's school, slavery.

The flow of this history has cut certain channels, certain accepted possibilities of learning. We live in a country where a person can buy an education like Jack Kennedy's, or be trapped between cultures like Thocmetony. We've inherited the repercussions of what school offered Willie Du Bois. And have absorbed—maybe without even knowing it—the value of the nonchalant, unschooled style that Lincoln studied.

These voices talk back and forth, argue with each other, argue with us. Don't we still face some of the choices Andy Jackson did: how to proceed in a landscape defined by war? Don't we still have to decide if Henry Ford was right: that great men are born and that most people don't want to think? Aren't we still wondering if school can transform the savage, the foreigner, the blind girl?

The story that all these stories tell is of people trying to find their way to knowledge. Trying to find what they'll need to know. We add our history to the ones we've already heard. And then we come back to the question of how to prepare for the future. We listen for what's next.

That sound in the distance? Kids' voices.

Imagine a playground at dusk.

NOTES

PROLOGUE

2   **"What part of education"** Henry Adams, *Education of Henry Adams*, ix.
2   **"intelligent silence"** Ibid., 13–14.
2   **"time thrown away"** Ibid., 38.
2   **"wasted"** Ibid., 59.
2   **"The man of sixty"** Ibid., 38.
2   **"After God had carried us"** Spring, *American School*, 16.

BEN

4   **Not quite eighteen** Unless otherwise noted, the chronology of Franklin's life is taken from Franklin, *Autobiography*.
5   **"particular in this Description"** Ibid., 75.
5   **"self-help book"** Edward S. Morgan in his introduction to Franklin, *Autobiography*.
5   **"fit to be imitated"** Franklin, *Autobiography* 43.
5   **"early Readiness"** Ibid., 54.
5   **Ben's great-grandfather** Isaacson, *American Life*, 7.
5   **Ben's mother, Abiah** Tourtellot, *Shaping of Genius*. 98–107.
6   **constantly reading** Samuel Eliot Morison, *Builders of the Bay Colony*, (Boston: Northwestern University Press, 1981), 184.
6   **"[W]ithout Knowledge"** Ibid., 117, 119.
6   **one university graduate** Tourtellot, Shaping of Genius, 158.
6   **about six thousand people** Ibid., 50–51.
7   **The infant mortality rate was** Warden, *Boston*, 18.
7   **"My elder Brothers"** Franklin, *Autobiography*, 52.

7   **Under English law** Rorabaugh, *Craft Apprentice*, 3–4.

8   **"hovered on the edge"** Ibid., 5.

8   **Merchants were the wealthiest** Ibid.

8   **"ability to read and understand"** Homes, *Tercentenary History*, 4–7.

8   **"ye true sense"** Ibid., 8.

8   **four Rs** Pulliam and Van Patten, *History of Education in America*, 33.

9   **"enclining to Fatness"** Rorabuagh, *Craft Apprentice*, 150.

9   **student's first three years** Homes, *Tercentenary History*, 258.

9   **"put our class"** Ibid., 315.

9   **"if their capacities allow"** Ibid., 258–59.

9   **"Tutors be strict"** Morison, *Builders of the Bay Colony*, 185.

9   **"Tedious and burthensome"** Ibid., 151.

9   **"hookey"** Homes, *Tercentenary History*, 83.

9   **"so full of play"** Ibid., 77–78.

9   **"the Expence of a College Education"** Franklin, *Autobiography*, 53.

10   **"piety"** Tourtellot, *Shaping of Genius*, 156.

10   **"generally a Leader"** Franklin, *Autobiography*, 54.

10   **"mild encouraging"** Ibid., 53.

11   **"At Ten Years Old"** Ibid.

11   **noxious trade** Tourtellot, *Shaping of Genius*, 199.

11   For tallow making, see Sinclair A. Sheers, "How to Render Tallow," http://www.suite101.com/article.cfm/soapmaking/79078, and "Making Tallow for Soap," www.salaam.co.uk/lifestyle/homeinfo.php?ann_id=310.

11   **Ebenezer** Tourtellot, *Shaping of Genius*, 113.

11   For apprentice work, see Franklin, *Autobiography*, 53.

12   **"and always took care"** Ibid., 55.

12   **"clear pleasing Voice"** Ibid., 54.

12   **"Saving of time"** Tourtellot, *Shaping of Genius*, 156.

12   **taught himself geography** Ibid., 128.

12   **"It has ever since"** Franklin, *Autobiography*, 57.

12   For craft hierarchy, see Rorabaugh, *Craft Apprentice*, 5.

12   For Boston economy, see Warden, 70–81.

13   **"Almost every problem"** Ibid., 80.

13   **"You have no rights"** Ibid., 57–59.

13   **"solid Judgment"** Franklin, *Autobiography*, 54.

13   **"I was taken home"** Ibid., 57.

13   **"wonders, rareties"** Ibid., 58.

13   **"relative luxury"** Warden, *Boston*, 17.

14   **"Bookish Inclination"** Franklin, *Autobiography*, 58.

14   **"I stood out"** Ibid.

14   **"without pay"** Ibid., 58–59. In the last year of his apprenticeship, he was due "Journeyman's wages."

14   For a printing apprentice's duties, see Oswald, *History of Printing*, especially 354.

14   **boil lampback** Rorabaugh, *Craft Apprentice*, 10–14.

15   **by watching** Ibid., 10.
15   **"often beaten me"** Franklin, *Autobiography*, 68, 70.
15   **"his lawful commands"** Oswald, *History of Printing*, 355.
15   **"a useful Hand"** Franklin, *Autobiography*, 59.
15   **"a tolerable English writer"** Ibid., 62.
15   **"Prose Writing"** Ibid., 60.
16   **"flatter'd"** Ibid.
16   **"the humble Enquirer"** Ibid., 64.
17   **"evading"** Ibid., 63.
17   **John Locke** Ibid., 63–64.
17   **"natural reason"** Tourtellot, *Shaping of Genius*, 218.
17   For the smallpox epidemic, see Ibid., 240.
18   For Elisha Cooke, see Warden, *Boston*, 91–96.
18   **"Hell-Fire Club"** Tourtellot, *Shaping of Genius*, 258.
18   **Modeling themselves on** Ibid., 89.
18   **"would object to printing"** Franklin, *Autobiography*, 67.
19   **"Jack Modish"** Tourtellot, *Shaping of Genius*, 330.
19   **"*poor* or *rich*"** Franklin, *Writings*, 5.
19   **"exquisite Pleasure"** Franklin, *Autobiography*, 68.
19   **"learned languages"** Franklin, *Writings*, 8.
20   **class of forty** Tourtellot, *Shaping of Genius*, 348.
20   **"famous Seminary"** Ibid., 10.
20   **"little more"** Franklin, *Writings*, 13.
20   **"Dunces"** Ibid., 11.
20   **"Performances"** Franklin, *Autobiography*, 68.
20   **"write their Names"** Franklin, *Writings*, 16.
20   **Puritan Pride . . . "garnish"** Ibid., 22.
21   **"blind Zealots"** Ibid., 40.
21   **"His Majesty's Government"** Tourtellot, *Shaping of Genius*, 401.
21   **"Freedom of Thought"** Franklin, *Writings*, 24.
21   **"ruin their Country"** Ibid., 27.
21   **"their Virginity"** Ibid., 34.
21   **"liberal Education"** Ibid., 37.
21   **"a High Affront"** Tourtellot, *Shaping of Genius*, 424.
21   **"I began to be considered"** Franklin, *Autobiography*, 68.
21   **"Rules"** Recent scholarship attributes this piece, once thought to be James Franklin's, as Benjamin's work. See Franklin, *Writings*, 1,497–499.
21   **"inoffensive"** Ibid., 47.
22   **"State" with "Steeple"** From a poem attributed to James Franklin, Tourtellot, *Shaping of Genius*, 411.
22   **"very flimsy"** Franklin, *Autobiography*, 70.
22   **"the traditional institutions"** Warden, *Boston*, 99.
22   **"scarce any Accomplishment"** Tourtellot, *Shaping of Genius*, 313.
23   **"Rulers some Rubs"** Franklin, *Autobiography*, 69.
23   **"*self-education*"** Ibid., 136.

23 **"Proposals Relating to"** Written in 1749. See the University of Pennsylvania's University Archives and Records Center, http://www.archives.upenn
.edu/primdocs/1749proposals.html.
24 **"gloomy Soul"** Franklin, *Writings*, 54.
24 **"A TRADESMAN"** Franklin, *Autobiography*, 183.
25 **only irritated** Withey, *Dearest Friend*, 101.
25 **"His whole life"** Chernow, *Alexander Hamilton*, 518.
25 **"A learned blockhead"** Franklin, *Writings*, 1,194.

NABBY

26 **"Every assistance and advantage"** Abigail Adams and John Adams, *Book of Abigail and John*, 3.
27 For Smith family history, see Nagel, *Adams Women*, especially 8–10.
27 **intellectual ambition** Withey, *Dearest Friend*, 1–5.
27 **Weymouth** Ibid., 2.
27 **"Inactivity"** Gelles, *Portia*, 111.
27 **He'd remain there** Nagel, *Adams Women*, 9.
27 For Quincy family history, see Abigail Adams, *Letters of Mrs. Adams*, xxii.
28 **"the most noted"** Nagel, *Adams Women*, quoting Charles Francis Adams, 8.
28 **thin and frail** Withey, *Dearest Friend*, 8.
28 **"volatile, giddy"** Ibid., 10.
28 For Great Awakening, see Ibid., 6.
29 **"totally secluded"** Nagel, *Adams Women*, 8.
29 For colonial women's farmwork, see Jane Kamensky, "The Colonial Mosaic: 1600–1760," in Cott, *No Small Courage*, 63.
29 For cloth and clothing, see Edwin Tunis, *Colonial Living* (Cleveland and New York: World Publishing Co., 1957), 47–48.
29 **weaving in America** Laurel Thatcher Ulrich, "Sheep in the Parlor, Wheels on the Common: Pastoralism and Poverty in Eighteenth Century Boston," in *Inequality in Early America*, ed. Carla Gardina Pestana and Sharon V. Salinger (Hanover and London: University Press of New England, 1999, 190–91.
30 **three yards** Ibid., 50–52.
30 **"Teach her"** Volo and Volo, *Family Life*, 248.
30 **Girls brought up** Alice Morse Earle, *Child Life in Colonial Days*, Stockbridge, MA: (1899; Berkshire House, 1993), 306.
30 **about half the white women** Kamensky, "Colonial Mosaic," 65.
31 **"Wives are"** Volo and Volo, 176.
31 **financial merger** Kamensky, "Colonial Mosaic," 67.
31 **"I begin to think"** Abigail Adams and John Adams, *Book of Abigail and John*, 136.
31 **herb baths** Abigail Adams, *New Letters* 45.
31 **"No man"** Nagel, *Adams Women*, 76.
32 **"Kindness"** Abigail Adams and John Adams, *Book of Abigail and John*, 32.
32 **"women, in general"** Abigail Adams, *Letters of Mrs. Adams*, 339.

32 **"too much sensibility"** Abigail Adams and John Adams, *Book of Abigail and John*, 330.

32 For New England population and farm size, see Kamensky, "Colonial Mosaic," 102.

32 **"mined the land"** Tunis, *Colonial Living*, 104.

33 For Smith's farms, see Withey, *Dearest Friend*, 5.

33 **"as a family member"** Nagel, *Adams Women*, 47.

33 **"fight ourselves"** Withey, *Dearest Friend*, 60.

33 **"very clever"** Abigail Adams, *New Letters*, 70.

33 **"immensely rich"** Abigail Adams, *Letters of Mrs. Adams*, 50.

33 **one out of every six** Billy G. Smith, "Black Women Who Stole Themselves in Eighteenth Century America," in Pestana and Salinger, *Inequality in Early America*, 135.

33 **"a clever Girl"** Abigail Adams and John Adams, *Book of Abigail and John*, 44.

33 **black maid** Withey, *Dearest Friend*, 21.

33 **"pretty good Housekeeper"** Abigail Adams, *New Letters*, 33.

33 **"We should never wait"** Nagel, *Adams Women*, 12.

34 **"The poorer sort"** Abigail Adams and John Adams, *Book of Abigail and John*. 152.

34 **"I was never sent"** James M. Volo and Dorothy Dennen Volo, *Family Life*, 249.

34 **"I regret"** Abigail Adams and John Adams, *Book of Abigail and John*, 218.

34 For the dame's school, see Earle, *Child Life* 128–38.

34 **"scenes of dissipation"** Nagel, *Adams Women*, 12.

34 **"unacquaintedness"** Abigail Adams and John Adams, *Book of Abigail and John*, 28.

34 **"corrupt the purity"** Ibid., 73–74.

35 **"more durable impression"** Abigail Adams, *Letters of Mrs. Adams*, xxv.

35 **"wise and just"** Nagel, *Adams Women*, 11.

35 **"Wild colts"** Withey, *Dearest Friend*, 10.

35 **"happy method"** Abigail Adams, *Letters of Mrs. Adams*, xxvi.

35 **"Little Tom . . . learns"** Abigail Adams and John Adams, *Book of Abigail and John*, 274.

35 **"a peculiar easy manner"** Ibid., 153.

35 **"little smattering"** Abigail Adams, *Letters of Mrs. Adams*, 211.

36 **"valuable ideas"** Nagel, *Adams Women*, 11.

36 **"the raptures"** Ibid., 14.

36 **"exterior form"** Ibid., 12–14.

36 **"Milton, Pope"** Gelles, *Portia*, 115.

36 **"passionately fond"** Abigail Adams, *Letters of Mrs. Adams*, 262.

37 **raised the possibility** Bober, *Abigail Adams*, 9–10.

37 **Cotton Tufts** Nagel, *Adams Women*, 14.

37 **"Unkle Tufts"** *Adams Family Correspondence*, vol. 1, ed. L. H. Butterfield and Marc Friedlaender (Cambridge, MA: Belknap Press, Harvard University, 1963), 13.

37   **"Calliope . . . Diana"** Abigail Adams, *Letters of Mrs. Adams*, xxviii.
37   ***King Lear*** Abigail Adams and John Adams, *Book of Abigail and John*, 38.
37   **"lines of Dryden"** Ibid., 92.
37   **"Extremity is"** Nagel, *Adams Women*, 55.
37   **"insipid"** Gelles, *Portia*, 115.
37   **"whatever I possest"** Abigail Adams, *Letters of Mrs. Adams*, 262.
38   **"God is"** Abigail Adams and John Adams, *Book of Abigail and John*, 90.
38   **her wit** Ibid., 17.
38   **"middle class"** Charles Francis Adams, in Abigail Adams, *Letters of Mrs. Adams*, xxix.
38   **"Are fondness and Wit"** John Adams's diary 3, 32.
38   **their kisses** Abigail Adams, *Letters of Mrs. Adams*, 19, 17.
39   **"Habit of Reading"** Ibid., 42.
39   **"Eyes of Lysander"** Ibid., 43.
39   **"most dangerous thing"** Nagel, *Adams Women*, 79.
39   **"Latin and Greek"** Withey, *Dearest Friend*, 81.
39   **"I hope your Attention"** Abigail Adams and John Adams, *Book of Abigail and John*, 247.
40   **"a continual Scaene"** Ibid., 57.
40   **"*Style* I never studied"** Abigail Adams, *Letters of Mrs. Adams*, xxi, xxii.
40   **"natural ease"** Ibid., 260.
40   **"[T]'is a pleasure"** Abigail Adams and John Adams, *Book of Abigail and John*, 33.
40   **"great restraint"** Abigail Adams, *Letters of Mrs. Adams*, 41.
40   **"a relief to my mind"** Ibid., 204.
41   **"not any ambition"** Ibid., xxxi.
41   **"call my own"** Ibid., 159.
41   **"a harder mettle"** Ibid., 21.
41   **"Remember the Ladies"** Ibid., 121.
41   **"mortifying"** Gelles, *Abigail Adams*, 20.
42   **"the deepest root"** Abigail Adams and John Adams, *Book of Abigail and John*, 153.
42   **"Nature has assigned"** Gelles, *Portia*, 26.
42   **creek mud and dung** Abigail Adams and John Adams, *Book of Abigail and John*, 56.
43   **"the Family, the stock"** Ibid., 59.
43   **"a Mothers care"** Abigail Adams, *Letters of Mrs. Adams*, 276.
43   **"private affairs"** Ibid., 119.
43   **"the best care"** Ibid.
43   **"our little farm"** Ibid., 38.
43   **closed all schools** Ibid., 221.
43   **"driven away"** Ibid., 63.
43   **"liable every hour"** Earle, *Child Life*, 171.
43   **"Hermitta"** Abigail Adams, *Letters of Mrs. Adams*, 128–29.
44   **"Farmeriss"** Ibid.

44 **stillborn** Abigail Adams and John Adams, *Book of Abigail and John*, 180.
44 **"not more than half"** Ibid., 186.
44 **"Sensibility"** Ibid., 245.
44 **"More tender"** Ibid., 313.
44 **"Our Boys"** Ibid., 183.
45 **"Debts are"** Abigail Adams, *Letters of Mrs. Adams*, 221.
45 **"Pray keep me"** Ibid., 125.
45 **"an excessive love"** Ibid., 67.
46 **"Politicks and War"** Ibid., 260.

ANDY

47 **ignorant, vengeful** Wilentz, *Andrew Jackson*, 152.
47 **only regular reading** Remini, *American Empire*, 7.
47 **"The planter, the farmer"** Ibid.
47 **"the moneyed interest"** Ibid., 155.
47 **surprisingly elegant** See Schlesinger, *Age of Jackson*, 36–46.
47 For Jackson family and Lowlander Scots history, see Booraem, *Young Hickory*, 4.
48 **the first wave** Lefler and Newsome, *North Carolina*, 76.
48 **quarter million** Wilentz, *Andrew Jackson*, 14.
48 **"substantial people"** Lefler and Newsome, *North Carolina*, 77.
48 **ten times more** Wright, *South Carolina*, 59.
49 **120,000 acres** Lefler and Newsome, *North Carolina*, 77.
49 **elimination of the Cherokee** Wright, *South Carolina*, 92–93.
49 **"scarce any history"** Lefler and Newsome, *North Carolina*, 78.
49 **"ignorant, mean, worthless"** Charles Woodmason, quoted in Wright, *South Carolina*, 97.
49 **"an inconsiderable place"** Lefler and Newsome, *North Carolina*, 101.
49 **sixty families** Robinson, *William R. Davie*, 11.
49 **Hutchinson sister** Booraem, *Young Hickory*, 8–9.
50 **two hundred acres** Remini, *Andrew Jackson*, 15.
50 **considerable spread** Lefler and Newsome, *North Carolina*, 113–14.
50 **James Crawford had his own skills** Booraem, *Young Hickory*, 16.
50 **"motley national origins"** Commager and Morris, *Spirit of 'Seventy-six*, 1,062.
51 **plantation owners and merchants** See Fox, *Charleston Story*, 73–75.
51 **or ten slaves** Wright, *South Carolina*, 109.
51 **less than 5 percent** Lefler and Newsome, *North Carolina*, 107–8.
51 **"Criminals and Vagabonds"** Ibid., 150.
51 **Four thousand residents** Wright, *South Carolina*, 98.
51 **"literary evenings"** Robinson, *William R. Davie*, 14.
51 **Westminster Larger Catechism** Booraem, *Young Hickory*, 21.
51 For catechism questions, see the Center for Reformed Theology and Apologetics, http://www.reformed.org/documents/index.html?mainframe=http://www.reformed.org/documents/larger1.html.

52 **Between 70 and 80 percent** Booraem, *Young Hickory*, 22, note on 223.

52 **the reverend's skull** Ibid., 21.

53 For James Crawford's farm, see ibid., 14–16.

53 For stills, See Ibid., 39–40.

53 **"free and independent"** Lefler and Newsome, *North Carolina*, 188, 192.

53 **referred to only as Joe** Robinson, *William R. Davie*, 27.

54 For school description, see Booraem, *Young Hickory*, 31–32.

54 **"dead languages"** Remini, *Andrew Jackson*, 16.

54 **"grotesque"** Ibid.

54 **inland for safety** Booraem, *Young Hickory*, 33.

55 **a foot soldier** Ibid., 16.

55 **"Travelers with"** Elkanah Watson quoted in Lefler and Newsome, *North Carolina*, 111.

55 **by Crawford's slaves** Booraem, *Young Hickory*, 16.

55 **hoop skirts** Lefler and Newsome, *North Carolina*, 110.

55 **"Pickle Beef Cut"** Booraem, *Young Hickory,* 43.

56 **Stono Ferry** Robinson, *William R. Davie*, 32.

56 **largest single American loss** Commager and Morris, *Spirit of 'Seventy-six*, 1,099.

56 **"within a hundred yards"** Booraem, *Young Hickory*, 49.

56 **"horrid yells"** Commager and Morris, *Spirit of 'Seventy-six*, 1,112.

56 **"I have cut 170"** Booraem, *Young Hickory*, 50.

57 **"thirteen gashes"** Ibid.

57 **"romantic partisan warfare"** Lefler and Newsome, *North Carolina*, 230.

57 **"written protections"** Booraem, *Young Hickory*, note on 235.

57 **"more hostile"** Commager and Morris, *Spirit of 'Seventy-six*, 1,139.

58 For Hanging Rock, see ibid., 1,121.

58 **Davie's eighty men** Robinson, *William R. Davie*, 44.

58 **"not distinguishable"** Commager and Morris, *Spirit of 'Seventy-six*, 1,123.

58 **"the poor Tories"** James P. Collins, *Autobiography of a Revolutionary Soldier*, quoted in Commager and Morris, *Spirit of 'Seventy-six*, 1,145.

58 **Blame fell** Ibid., 1,132.

58 **"full-scale invasion"** Ibid., 1,135.

59 **"fattening his Horses"** Ibid., 76–77, and Robinson, *William R. Davie*, 69.

59 **"uniformly"** Commager and Morris, *Spirit of 'Seventy-six*, 1,138.

59 **"many of the plantations"** Robinson, *William R. Davie*, 66.

59 **"Where you from?"** Remini, *American Empire*, 19.

59 **"The enemy seems"** Commager and Morris, *Spirit of 'Seventy-six*, 1,151.

59 **"bold and daring"** Ibid., 1,152.

60 **"Whigs and Tories"** Ibid.

60 **"not sufficient"** Robinson, *William R. Davie*, 87.

60 **"hunted like deer"** Booraem, *Young Hickory*, 89.

60 **clean his boots** Remini, *Andrew Jackson*, 21.

60 **"The sword"** Ibid., note on 429.

61 **"harshly"** Remini, *American Empire*, 21.

61 **"I frequently heard"** Ibid., 22.

61 **nine hundred loyalists** Commager and Morris, *Spirit of 'Seventy-six*, 1,177.

61 **the local militia held** Ibid., 1,175.

61 **kill his brother Robert** Remini, *Andrew Jackson*, 19.

62 **reminded him of lessons** Brands, *Andrew Jackson*, 31–32.

62 **"I, at first"** Wilentz, *Andrew Jackson*, 17.

62 **"became rich"** Booraem, *Young Hickory*, 107.

62 **household of eleven** from 1790 census "Heads of Families" South Carolina http://www.census.gov/prodz/decennial/documents/1790k=02.pdf.

62 **"I forget now what"** Booraem, *Young Hickory*, 113, and Brands, *Andrew Jackson*, 33.

63 **"at the age"** Booraem, *Young Hickory*, 113.

63 **"pretty good saddler"** Ibid., 115.

63 **"and swore"** Ibid., 116.

63 **the city's wealthy** Remini, *Andrew Jackson*, 20–21.

63 **"addicted"** Lefler and Newsome, *North Carolina*, 112.

63 **"Instead of Politics"** Robinson, *William R. Davie*, 145.

64 **controlled 75 percent of the wealth** Frazer, *Charleston! Charleston!* 135.

64 **"whom they call Tories"** Ibid., 169.

64 **"bitter class antagonism"** Ibid., 172.

64 **Andy probably took part** Booraem, *Young Hickory*, 124.

64 **"My calculation"** Remini, *Andrew Jackson*, 28.

65 **"Dislocated whites"** Burstein, *Passion of Andrew Jackson*, 10.

65 **the Federalist Party** Lefler and Newsome, *North Carolina*, 240–41.

65 **Princeton** Robinson, *William R. Davie*, 31.

65 **"one of those cool"** Ibid., 45.

66 For Davie's political career, see Ibid.

67 For Macay's history, see Booraem, *Young Hickory*, 168.

67 **"Aw, I was a raw lad"** Ibid., 166.

67 **"aspeedy redress"** Burstein, *Passion of Andrew Jackson*, 18.

68 **"one of the biggest"** Booraem, *Young Hickory*, 193.

68 **political reputation** For a good brief summation of Jackson's career, see Wilentz, *Andrew Jackson*.

68 **"their inquiries"** Remini, *American Empire*, 27.

68 **first female slave** Remini, *Andrew Jackson*, 27.

BELLE

69 **a huge patent** LeFevre, *History of New Paltz*, 455–56.

69 **owned several miles** Ibid., 461–63.

69 **"faithfulness, docility"** Sojourner Truth, *Narrative*, 9.

70 **Northern Dutch slavery** See Douglas Harper, "Slavery in New York," http://www.slavenorth.com/author.htm.

70 **On average** Mabee, *Sojourner Truth*, 1.

70 **"Despite their unequal"** McManus, *Negro Slavery in New York*, 12.

70   **"Every other white man"** Zimm et al., *Southeastern New York*, 26.
70   **"Life was leisurely"** Ibid., 28.
70   **number of blacks in New York** McManus, *Negro Slavery in New York*, 12.
70   **Most of these** Williams-Myers, *Long Hammering*, 21.
71   **two thousand slaves in Ulster** Ibid., 27.
71   **between 1750 and 1770** McManus, *Negro Slavery in New York*, 30.
71   **Blacks soon made up** Gellman and Quigley, *Jim Crow New York*, 14.
71   **never seem to have** See Sojourner Truth, *Narrative*.
71   **"it was customary to give"** See Roth, *"Society of Negroes Unsettled,"* and the Hardenbergh family genealogy, http://www.hardenbergh.org/irene/hardee007 .htm#id2474.
71   **In the cellar** Sojourner Truth, *Narrative*, 11.
72   **children a kind of flaw** McManus, *Negro Slavery in New York*, 43.
72   **"overstocked hives"** Ibid., 45.
72   **Low Dutch** Van Buren, *History of Ulster County*, 55.
72   ***grootje*** Dilliard, *Album of New Netherland*, 55.
72   **Homes in Ulster County** Ibid., 86.
73   **"Astonishing"** Williams-Myers, *Long Hammering*, 57.
73   **"half-freedom"** Ibid., 15.
73   **went to the kids** Sojourner Truth, *Narrative*, 9.
73   **"memorizing the Heidelberg Catechism"** Fabend, *Zion on the Hudson*, 179–80.
73   **Society for the Propagation** See Williams-Myers, *Long Hammering*, chapter 4.
74   **"[T]here is a God"** Sojourner Truth, *Narrative*, 12.
74   **"terrible auction"** Ibid., 13.
74   **"more critics than buyers"** McManus, *Negro Slavery in New York*, 171.
74   **"fight ourselves"** Withey, *Dearest Friend*, 60.
75   **Thirty years before Belle** McManus, *Negro Slavery in New York*, 161.
75   **a dozen years** Ibid., 167.
75   **another decade** See Harper, "Slavery in New York."
75   **erased slowly** See McManus, *Negro Slavery in New York*.
75   For New York state manumission laws and slave population, see ibid., especially 176.
76   For Belle's sale, see Sojourner Truth, *Narrative*.
76   **A good wagon** See Roth, *"Society of Negroes Unsettled."*
76   For Webster in Newburgh, see Unger, *Noah Webster*, 44.
76   **"extreme depression"** Ibid.
76   **"*Now* is the time"** Ibid., 54.
76   **soon replaced the *New England Primer*** Spring, *American School*, 59.
76   **bestselling** Unger, *Noah Webster*, 227.
77   **"Begin with the infant"** Ibid., 81.
77   **"In our American republic"** Ibid., 142.
77   **finally authorized state money** Folts, *State Education Department*.
77   **"The Dutch"** Unger, *Noah Webster*, 110.
77   **legislature reversed course** Folts, *State Education Department*.

77   **"a singular machinery"** Spring, *American School*, 61.

78   **"Federal Catechism"** Ibid., 62.

78   **the governor of New York** Clinton, "Address on Monitorial Education."

78   **"evil must be corrected"** Ibid.

78   **Their method of instruction** Katz, *Class, Bureaucracy, and Schools*, 10.

78   **"a blessing"** See Clinton, "Address on Monitorial Education."

78   **"of either acknowledging the rights"** Unger, *Noah Webster*, 81.

78   **New York Manumission Society** Berlin and Harris, *Slavery in New York*, 119.

79   **"rescue the minds"** Ibid., 189.

79   **fewer than five hundred** African American Registry, "African Free School Opens."

79   **"*Now the war*"** Sojourner Truth, *Narrative*, 18.

79   **"If they sent me"** Ibid.

79   **no learning** Mabee, *Sojourner Truth*, 4.

79   **"I have got my answer ready"** Ibid.

79   **livestock** Sojourner Truth, *Narrative*, 10.

79   **"slavery was the wickedest thing"** Ibid., 91.

80   **"Simple and artless"** Painter, *Sojourner Truth*, 147.

80   **"I don't read such"** Ibid., 230.

80   **"beg God"** Sojourner Truth, *Narrative*, 19.

80   **how communication worked** See Gutman, *Black Family in Slavery and Freedom*, 342.

80   **six of her ten** Sojourner Truth, *Narrative*, 11.

80   **"answer to her prayer"** Ibid., 19.

80   **sideways** Mabee, *Sojourner Truth*, 4.

80   **With the Hardenberghs** Williams-Myers, *Long Hammering*, 53.

80   **"terribly—terribly"** Ibid., 18.

80   **"rude, uneducated"** Sojourner Truth, *Narrative*, 20.

81   **"wild, out-of-door"** Ibid.

81   **carry the day's catch** Ibid.

81   **Kingston was no longer** Zimm et al., *Southeastern New York*, 113, 189.

81   **curse and smoke and drink** Painter, *Sojourner Truth*, 27.

81   **"Washington's Ball"** See http://www.americanrevolution.org/washington-smusic.html and "Patriotic Songs and Hymns" *The Cambridge History of English and American Literature* in 18 volumes (1907–21) at http://www.bartleby.com/228/0303.html.

81   **"three or four times"** Sojourner Truth, *Narrative*, 14.

81   **as they aged** Ibid., 14–16.

82   **farm overlooking the Hudson** Mabee, *Sojourner Truth*, 5.

82   **"isolated, conservative, tightly-knit"** see Roth, "*Society of Negroes Unsettled*."

82   **It consisted of** LeFevre, *History of New Paltz*, 199.

82   **more female slaves** Heidgerd, *Black History of New Paltz*, 15.

82   **Belle's new owner, John Dumont** Sojourner Truth, *Narrative*, 22.

82   **two white servants** Mabee, *Sojourner Truth*, 8, 248.

82   **"*That* wench"** Sojourner Truth, *Narrative*, 23.

82   **"New York passed a statute"** Mabee, *Sojourner Truth*, 10.

82   **"[I]t seemed almost impossible"** Ibid.

82   **"with much difficulty"** Ibid., 5.

82   **"the labor of slaves"** Unger, *Noah Webster*, 174.

83   ***"grind her down"*** Sojourner Truth, *Narrative*, 22.

83   **As slavery in New York** McManus, *Negro Slavery in New York*, 183.

83   **"muttered something"** Sojourner Truth, *Narrative*, 23.

83   **"Oh, yes, he sometimes"** Ibid., 24.

83   **"her fellow slaves taunted"** Ibid, 23–24.

83   **"It made me true"** Ibid.

83   **"it helped form in her"** See the interpretation of Olive Gilbert, the author-transcriber of Sojourner Truth, *Narrative*, on 24 and throughout.

83   **tend the dying** Painter, *Sojourner Truth*, 17–18.

84   **"Lord, Lord, I can"** Sojourner Truth, *Narrative*, 117.

84   **never heard a preacher** Ibid.

84   **by 1800** Lincoln, *Black Experience in Religion*, 9.

84   **on a small island** Sojourner Truth, *Narrative*, 44.

84   **"pay him"** Ibid., 45.

84   **"yielded to all"** Ibid.

84   **let her go a year early** Ibid., 28.

85   **"back into Egypt"** Ibid., 47.

85   **food booths, applejack** Williams-Meyers, *Long Hammering*, 90.

85   **"the original Congo dances"** Gutman, *Black Family in Slavery and Freedom*, 333.

85   **James Fenimore Cooper** Ibid., 334.

85   **the shakedown** Williams-Meyers, *Long Hammering*, 92, 98.

85   **"boisterous rioting"** Ibid., 96.

85   **Society of Negroes Unsettled** Roth, *"Society of Negroes Unsettled."*

86   **The Pinkster King** Ibid., 90.

86   **"most effective means"** Sojourner Truth, *Narrative*, 46.

86   **proudly African-American** See discussion in Gutman, *Black Family in Slavery and Freedom*, 335.

86   **"an excellent dancer"** Painter, *Sojourner Truth*, 43.

86   **Robert was owned by** Mabee, *Sojourner Truth*, 6.

86   **Robert was eventually** Sojourner Truth, *Narrative*, 25, and Painter, *Sojourner Truth*, 18–19.

86   **"a poor old man"** Sojourner Truth, *Narrative*, 15.

86   **She never saw him** Ibid., 16.

87   **she married another** And for possible unhappiness of marriage, Painter, *Sojourner Truth*, 296, footnote 24.

87   **"Tom's version"** Mabee, *Sojourner Truth*, 7.

87   **a legal marriage** Sojourner Truth, *Narrative*, 26.

87   **Five years earlier** McManus, *Negro Slavery in New York*, 178.

87   **never could take** Mabee, *Sojourner Truth*, 15.

87   **Opposition was** Fabend, *Zion on the Hudson*, 2, and Gellman and Quigley, *Jim Crow New York*, 30.

87 **technically freed** Gellman and Quigley, *Jim Crow New York*, 14.

87 **"used to sit"** Painter, *Sojourner Truth*, 20.

88 **"I did not *run*"** Sojourner Truth, *Narrative*, 31.

88 **"the life of Indians"** Williams-Myers, *Long Hammering* 117.

88 **to the poorhouse** Roth, "*Society of Negroes Unsettled*."

89 **"spirituals"** C. Eric Lincoln, ed., *The Black Experience in Religion* (Garden City, NY: Anchor Books, 1974), 56, quoting from Eileen Southern's *The Music of Black America: A History*.

89 **By this time New York City** Gellman and Quigley, *Jim Crow New York*, 77.

89 **"Methodist perfectionists"** Painter, *Sojourner Truth*, 41.

89 **then briefly joined** Ibid., 50, and Sojourner Truth, *Narrative*, 67.

89 **"What happened"** McManus, *Negro Slavery in New York*, 195.

89 **"came to the conclusion"** Sojourner Truth, *Narrative*, 72.

89 **"With the exception of her children"** Painter, *Sojourner Truth*, 181.

90 **"a genuine specimen"** Ibid., 98.

90 **"remarkable talent for singing"** Sojourner Truth, *Narrative*, 83–84.

90 **So, the tune of** Mabee, *Sojourner Truth*, 229.

90 **"She sang with the strong"** Sojourner Truth, *Narrative*, 119.

90 **pay off the mortgage** Mabee, *Sojourner Truth*, 53.

90 **would finally reunite** Painter, *Sojourner Truth*, 100, and Mabee, *Sojourner Truth*, 93.

91 **"grandly formed"** Sojourner Truth, *Narrative*, 124.

91 **"the great and good"** Painter, *Sojourner Truth*, 206.

91 **"washerwoman"** Ibid., 207.

ABE

92 **"the legend"** Donald, *Lincoln*, 21.

92 **"Owing to my father"** Lincoln, *Speeches and Writings*, 178.

92 **Trace back how** Donald, *Lincoln*, 20.

93 **the classic, early American pioneer** Winkle, *Young Eagle*, 2.

93 **"yearning for the wilderness"** Beveridge, *Abraham Lincoln*, 9.

93 **The British had designated** Gilbert, *God Gave Us This Country*, 56.

93 **"not an American interest"** Ibid., 58.

94 **"more frequent than I"** Ibid., 62.

94 **forests were huge** Federal Writers' Project, *Kentucky*, 22.

94 **were used to planting** Harden County History Museum, The History of Hardin County, http://www.hardinkyhistory.org/history.htm.

94 **"Forest Wars"** Gilbert, *God Gave Us This Country*, 29.

94 **massive land purchases** Ibid., 98, and Federal Writers' Project, *Kentucky*, 39.

94 **George Washington** Gilbert, *God Gave Us This Country*, 58.

94 **"waste and unappropriated lands"** McClure, *Two Centuries*, 6.

94 **Grandfather Lincoln** bought Winkle, *Young Eagle*, 6, and Warren, *Lincoln's Youth*, 33.

94 **about to intensify** Warren, *Lincoln's Youth*, 4.

94   **"great discomfort"** Winkle, *Young Eagle*, 7.

94   **war of small raids** Gilbert, *God Gave Us This Country*, 56.

95   **"a gloomy thing"** John T. Christian, "The Baptists in Kentucky," www .geocities.com/baptist_documents/kent.bapt.hist.christian.html, quoting John Taylor's *A History of Ten Baptist Churches,* 1823.

95   **some two thousand** Gilbert, *God Gave Us This Country*, 133.

95   **238-acre farm** Warren, *Lincoln's Youth*, 5.

95   **"a wandering laboring boy"** Ibid., 4.

95   **trade that brought in** Federal Writers' Project, *Kentucky*, 42.

95   **serve on juries** Ibid., 299, and Warren, *Lincoln's Youth*, 5.

95   **two building lots** Warren, *Lincoln's Youth*, 9.

95   **350 acres** Winkle, *Young Eagle*, note on 319.

95   **top 15th percentile** Donald, *Lincoln*, 22.

95   **she'd been raised from the age of seven** Warren, *Lincoln's Youth*, 8.

96   **"went to school together"** Ibid.

96   **One biographer says** Herndon and Weik, *Herndon's Life of Lincoln*, 12.

96   **"highly intellectual"** Ibid., 14.

96   **church had been founded** Baptist Encyclopedia, *Kentucky Baptists*, 650.

96   **"strong gestures and tears"** James H. Sightler, *The Separate Baptist Revival and Its Influence in the South* (Sightler Publications, 2004), http:// sightlerpublications.com/Baptisthistory/Separate%20Baptist.html.

96   **three of the eighteen** see Christian, "Baptists in Kentucky," and Baptist Encyclopedia, *Kentucky Baptists*.

96   **read the Bible aloud** Warren, *Lincoln's Youth*, 30.

97   **functioning public school system** Ibid., 11, and Federal Writers' Project, *Kentucky*, 84–85.

97   **"cluster of cabins"** Federal Writers' Project, *Kentucky*, 83.

97   **neighbor and fellow parishioner** Warren, *Lincoln's Youth*, 11.

97   **revised speller** i.e., Dilworth's speller; see Ibid., 29.

97   **Even two decades later** Federal Writers' Project, *Kentucky*, 85.

97   **at least two teachers** Warren, *Lincoln's Youth*, 11.

97   For Kentucky population, see Beveridge, *Abraham Lincoln*, 33.

97   **ended up in litigation** Warren, *Lincoln's Youth*, 10, 12.

97   **Lincolns weren't alone** Winkle, *Young Eagle*, 11.

97   **legal center** Beveridge, *Abraham Lincoln*, 18, and Federal Writers' Project, *Kentucky*, 299.

98   **became senators** Federal Writers' Project, *Kentucky*, 299, and Hardin County History Museum, "History of Hardin County."

98   **"all working for the rich"** Donald, *Lincoln*, 24.

98   **Now he was losing** Warren, *Lincoln's Youth*, 13.

98   **On Abe's seventh birthday** Beveridge, *Abraham Lincoln*, 35.

98   **"This removal was partly"** Lincoln's campaign biography, John L. Scripps, *Chicago Press and Tribune*, June 1860, http://showcase.netins.net/web/ creative/lincoln/speeches/autobiog.htm [Scripps bio].

98   **almost as many slaves** Donald, *Lincoln*, 24.

98   **"Slave states"** Hofstadter, *American Political Tradition,* 110.

99   **"You are continually driving"** Gilbert, *God Gave Us This Country,* 257.

99   **"first American civil war"** Ibid, 1, 3.

99   **for two dollars an acre** Winkle, *Young Eagle,* 11.

100   **the surveyor** Warren, *Lincoln's Youth,* 20.

100   **"vast forest"** Beveridge, *Abraham Lincoln,* 38–40.

100   **one traveler found it depressing** Warren, *Lincoln's Youth,* 38.

100   **"a wild region"** Lincoln autobiography sent to Jesse Fell, December 20, 1859, http://showcase.netins.net/web/creative/lincoln/speeches/autobiog.htm [Fell bio].

100   **"that most useful instrument"** Scripps bio.

100   **"the clearing away of surplus"** Federal Writers' Project, *Indiana,* 117.

101   **opened six acres** Winkle, *Young Eagle,* 12.

101   **seven other families** Donald, *Lincoln,* 25.

101   **By the Lincolns' second winter** Wilson, *Indiana,* 87.

101   **supposed to be a system** Federal Writers' Project, *Indiana,* 97.

101   **There wouldn't be any free schools** Ibid.

101   **"enclave of transplanted Kentuckians"** Winkle, *Young Eagle,* 12, and Warren, *Lincoln's Youth,* 86, 114.

101   **Hanging Rock** *History of Warrick,* 279.

101   **They kept cows** Winkle, *Young Eagle,* 12–13.

101   **"apparently killed"** Scripps bio.

101   **"the greatest pleasure"** Herndon and Weik, *Herndon's Life of Lincoln,* 25.

102   **"half hunters"** Beveridge, *Abraham Lincoln,* 38.

102   **"A few days before"** Scripps bio.

102   **That spring of 1818** *History of Warrick,* 288.

103   **hardest in the boy's life** Donald, *Lincoln,* 26.

103   **"We lived the same as"** Federal Writers' Project, *Indiana,* 117.

103   **included bedclothes** Warren, *Lincoln's Youth,* 65.

103   **run the Hardin County jail** Ibid., 60.

103   **substantial background** Winkle, *Young Eagle,* 18.

103   **"desolate region"** Ibid., and Beveridge, *Abraham Lincoln,* 70.

103   **growth spurt** Herndon and Weik, *Herndon's Life of Lincoln,* 25, and Winkle, *Young Eagle,* 64.

103   **"made a way for him"** Herndon and Weik, *Herndon's Life of Lincoln,* 30.

104   **Typically these had** *History of Warrick,* 399, 413.

104   **couple of dollars** Ibid., 399.

104   **taught etiquette** Warren, *Lincoln's Youth,* 81–82.

104   **now nine families** Ibid., 98.

104   **"fifty families"** Ibid., 98–99.

104   **"Spencer County replaced"** *History of Warrick,* 280.

104   **about forty acres** Winkle, *Young Eagle,* 19.

104   **"we owe everything"** Wills, *Lincoln at Gettysburg,* 154.

104   **"Diligent for knowledge"** Douglas L. Wilson, *Honor's Voice,* 57.

104   **"Abe was not Energetic"** Ibid.

104   **"Lincoln was lazy"** Ibid.

105 **"could read a little"** Warren, *Lincoln's Youth*, 133.

105 **"I induced my husband"** Herndon and Weik, *Herndon's Life of Lincoln*, 33.

105 **"What . . . has your education been?"** Warren, *Lincoln's Youth*, 245, footnote 43.

105 **"I can say this"** This quotation, through page 106, is continuous in the original source; see ibid.

106 **new teacher** Ibid., 102.

106 **"made speeches such as"** Ibid., 80.

106 **"promoting piety and virtue"** Ibid., 77, 106.

106 **Abe was a sexton** Ibid., 121.

106 **"the revelation of God"** Herndon and Weik, *Herndon's Life of Lincoln*, xxx.

106 **"word for word"** Ibid., 55, and Warren, *Lincoln's Youth*, 121.

107 **"tasteless stories"** Wilson, *Honor's Voice*, 69.

107 **"Governor Tickner"** Ibid., 68.

107 **"training by the Hanks boys"** Ibid., 69.

107 **"a democratic muse"** Wills, *Lincoln at Gettysburg*, 27.

107 **"I was raised to farm work"** Winkle, *Young Eagle*, 20.

107 **"horse high"** Warren, *Lincoln's Youth*, 143–44.

107 **"awful lazy"** Herndon and Weif, *Herndon's Life of Lincoln*, 38.

107 **"Abs father"** Wilson, *Honor's Voice*, 56.

108 **"always bringing them to me"** Herndon and Weif, *Herndon's Life of Lincoln*, 39.

108 **"I catch the idea"** Hofstadter, *American Political Tradition*, 95.

108 **"He must understand everything"** Donald, *Lincoln*, 29.

108 **Azel Dorsey** Warren, *Lincoln's Youth*, 129–131.

108 **"did not amount to"** Scripps bio.

108 **"a small stock of goods"** *History of Warrick*, 365–66, and Wilson, *Honor's Voice*, 62.

108 **sixteen newspapers** Warren, *Lincoln's Youth*, 168.

109 **overwhelming favorite** Federal Writers' Project, *Indiana*, 61.

109 **"an engine for the support"** Schlesinger, *Age of Jackson*, 46.

109 **"almost entirely a newspaper one"** Herndon quoted in Wilson, *Indiana*, 62.

109 **"What can you do in Missouri?"** Lincoln, *Writings*, 256.

109 **"the public utility of"** Ibid., 1.

109 **"a combination of the people"** Winkle, *Young Eagle*, 185.

110 **"the most important subject"** Lincoln, *Writings*, 4.

110 **"the roughest work"** Donald, *Lincoln*, 34.

110 **"read *The Revised Laws*"** Warren, *Lincoln's Youth*, 201.

110 **"Noah Webster's"** Ibid., 70.

110 **"I recollect thinking then"** Donald, *Lincoln*, 31.

110 **"I could scarcely believe my"** Ibid., 34, and Gilbert, *God Gave Us This Country*, 333.

111 **"Every school boy"** Gilbert, *God Gave Us This Country*, 333.

111 **"no chance of ever rising"** Weems, *Life of Washington*, 24.

112   **"defective"** The autobiography Lincoln sent to Charles Lanman, June 1858, http://showcase.netins.net/web/creative/lincoln/speeches/autobiog.htm.

112   **"some schools, so called"** Fell bio.

112   **"a performance"** Hofstadter, *American Political Tradition*, 55.

112   **"such restricted and unpromising"** Herndon and Weif, *Herndon's Life of Lincoln*, 37.

112   **"log cabin myth"** See Edward Pessen, *The Log Cabin Myth* (New Haven, CT: Yale University Press, 1984).

112   **"but a government like ours"** Winkle, *Young Eagle*, ix.

112   **"plain, simple backwoodsman"** Gilbert, *God Gave Us This Country*, 328.

112   **"a great piece of folly"** Herndon and Weif, *Herndon's Life of Lincoln*, 1–2.

113   **"He was never in college"** Scripps bio.

113   **"as I have never seen them"** Hofstadter, *American Political Tradition*, 106.

113   **"is universally admitted"** David G. Vanderstel, "Native Americans in Indiana: Resistance and Removal," Conner Prairie Interpreter Resource Manual, http://www.connerprairie.org/HistoryOnline/indnam.html.

113   **"Numerous skeletons"** *History of Warrick*, 256.

THOCMETONY

114   **When she says "up"** Zanjani, *Sarah Winnemucca*, 267.

114   **"the last survivor"** Ibid., 237.

114   **Peabody who had arranged** Canfield, *Sarah Winnemucca of the Northern Paiutes*, 201.

114   **"Oh, for shame"** Hopkins, *Life Among the Piutes*, 207.

115   **"her equally distinguished sister"** The third Peabody sister, Sophia, married Nathaniel Hawthorn.

115   **"In the history of"** Canfield, *Sarah Winnemucca of the Northern Paiutes*, 222.

115   **"A few years ago"** Zanjani, *Sarah Winnemucca*, 266–67.

115   **"steam-engine system"** Marshall, *Peabody Sisters*, 315.

115   **"the great equalizer"** Spring, *American School*, 113.

115   **Huge linen mills . . . by some 30 percent** Katz, *Irony of Early School Reform*, 6.

116   **"a proletariat"** Ibid., 7.

116   **"a riot"** Spring, *American School*, 109.

116   **"common virtues"** Ibid., 112.

116   **"a higher and better state"** Katz, *Irony of Early School Reform*, 88.

116   **half the states in the union** Pulliam, *History of Education*, 5th ed., 66.

116   **"*Train up a child*"** Spring, *American School*, 110.

116   **"When a child"** Unitarian Universalist Historical Society, http://www.uua.org/uuhs/duub/articles/peabodysisters.html.

117   **"I attribute the success"** Zanjani, *Sarah Winnemucca*, 266.

117   **For Great Basin ecology,** see Knack and Stewart, *As Long as the River Shall Run*, 1–9.

117 **Thocmetony's band its name** Zanjani, *Sarah Winnemucca*, 8.

118 **two boys and a girl** Canfield, *Sarah Winnemucca of the Northern Paiutes*, 3.

118 **sun-dry the rest** Wheat, *Survival Arts*, 11.

118 **owl demon's baskets** Ibid., 11–12.

118 **"the Indian believed"** Ibid., 13.

118 **willow cradle** Ibid., 98.

119 **a thousand pounds of pine nuts** Knack and Stewart, *As Long as the River Shall Run*, 20.

119 **thick, nutritious soup** Wheat, *Survival Arts*, 29–39.

119 **"a hundred skins"** Ibid., 77.

119 For winter and spring hunting, etc., see Wheat, *Survival Arts*, especially 9 and 11.

120 **for some three thousand years** Knack and Stewart, *As Long as the River Shall Run*, 13.

121 **"women worked with plants"** Ibid., 23.

121 **most of what you had was disposable** Wheat, *Survival Arts*, 91.

121 **"They not only take care"** Hopkins, *Life Among the Piutes*, 53.

121 **only one war dance** Ibid., 51.

122 **not an enemy** Knack and Stewart, *As Long as the River Shall Run*, 26–27.

122 **Families bet against families** Wheat, *Survival Arts*, 13.

122 **Winners were never** Ibid.

122 **"made arrangements to collect information"** Federal Writers' Program, *Nevada*, 32.

122 **killed fourteen more** Zanjani, *Sarah Winnemucca*, 13.

122 **"a groupe of the lowest"** Euler, *Paiute People*, 27–28.

123 **"broke upon our eyes"** Chaffin, *Pathfinder*, 204–5.

123 **"poor-looking Indians"** Ibid., 37–38, 206.

123 **Kit Carson** Euler, *Paiute People*, 39.

123 **"Asiatic" Indian bands** Chaffin, *Pathfinder*, 237–38.

123 **"fixed determination"** Kirsch and Murphy, *West of the West*, 243.

123 **"awful piles"** Stewart, *California Trail*, 50.

123 **"Indolent and degraded . . ."** Stewart, *California Trail*, 67.

123 **"guide and hostage"** Ibid., 68.

124 **"fear and respect"** Kirsch and Murphy, *West of the West*, 226–27.

124 **"I looked North and South"** Hopkins, *Life Among the Piutes*, 14.

124 **Donner's Pass** Murphy, *Across the Plains*, xiii.

125 **"hair on their faces"** Hopkins, *Life Among the Piutes*, 20.

125 **"Let us bury our girls"** Ibid., 11.

125 **had been trained to** Paiute women on their long searches for food often hid their children; Euler, *Paiute People*, 38.

125 **"Oh, can anyone imagine"** Hopkins, *Life Among the Piutes*, 12.

125 **A third of New York City's** Zinn, *People's History*, 220.

125 **no effective federal brake** Schlesinger, *Age of Jackson*, 218.

125 **About two thousand people** Federal Writers' Program, *Nevada*, 34, 36.

126 **"and 953 graves"** Gary A. Horton, "Carson River Chronology."

126 **"go back to father"** Hopkins, *Life Among the Piutes*, 26.

126 **"his sweetheart"** Ibid., 22.

126 **"Oh, mother"** Ibid., 25.

126 **first steamboat** Zanjani, *Sarah Winnemucca*, 31.

126 **"voice like an angel"** Hopkins, *Life Among the Piutes*, 31–33.

127 **"how to work and cook"** Ibid., 34.

127 **"men whom my grandpa called"** Ibid., 36.

127 **"They are not people"** Ibid., 37.

127 **Asiatic cholera** Zanjani, *Sarah Winnemucca*, 40.

127 **The epidemic would cut** Ibid., 43.

127 **"will not believe"** Hopkins, *Life Among the Piutes*, 42.

128 **romantic notion** Ibid., note on 52.

128 **Mormon Station became** Federal Writers' Program, *Nevada*, 37.

128 **"Emigrant"** Zanjani, *Sarah Winnemucca*, 43.

128 **two hundred white residents** Knack and Stewart, *As Long as the River Shall Run*, 43–44.

128 **negotiate a treaty** Zanjani, *Sarah Winnemucca*, 43.

129 **"playmates"** Hopkins, *Life Among the Piutes*, 58.

129 **"best servants"** Knack and Stewart, *As Long as the River Shall Run*, 62, and Zanjani, *Sarah Winnemucca*, 47.

129 **William Ormsby, was** Michael Sutton, "Ormsby Origins," 1999, http://www.ormsby.org/genie/Branches/John_S.html.

129 **"Olive Cynthia Ormsby"** Hal Schindler, "History Etched in Stone," *Salt Lake Tribune*, August 29, 1993, http://historytogo.utah.gov/salt_lake_tribune/in_another_time/082933.html.

129 **an oil portrait** Canfield, *Sarah Winnemucca of the Northern Paiutes*, 12.

129 **"learned the English language"** Hopkins, *Life Among the Piutes*, 58.

130 **"make up the set"** Zanjani, *Sarah Winnemucca*, 52.

130 **"Paiute Princess"** Ibid., 52.

130 **When Sarah protested** Ibid., 49–50.

130 **"some geographical explorations"** *Northern Paiute Nation, et al., v. United States of America* (February 16, 1972), http://digital.library.okstate.edu/icc/v27/iccv27p039.pdf.

130 **"Indians are begging"** Euler, *Paiute People*, 80–81.

130 **right across from it** Scott Schrantz, "The Two Houses of Ormsby," May 6, 2006, http://aroundcarson.com/thenandnow/17.

130 **The winter of 1868** Gary A. Horton, "Carson River Chronology," and Hopkins, *Life Among the Piutes*, 64.

131 **five miles wide** Hinckle and Hobbs, *Richest Place on Earth*, 31, and Gary A. Horton, "Carson River Chronology."

131 **"a general stampede"** Canfield, *Sarah Winnemucca of the Northern Paiutes*, 19–20.

131 **dotted with smokestacks** Federal Writers' Program, *Nevada*, 273, Hinckle and Hobbs, *Richest Place on Earth*, 49.

131 **"freezing and starving"** Zanjani, *Sarah Winnemucca*, 53.

131 **"portrayed white men"** Knack and Stewart, *As Long as the River Shall Run*, 42.
131 **"I would rather be with"** Zanjani, *Sarah Winnemucca*, 229.
131 **"She ate breakfast with me"** Canfield, *Sarah Winnemucca of the Northern Paiutes*, 20.
132 **six thousand white people** Knack and Stewart, *As Long as the River Shall Run*, 45.
132 **sawdust clogged** Gary A. Horton, "Carson River Chronology."
132 **Two little girls** Hopkins, *Life Among the Piutes*, 71.
132 **"badly mutilated"** Sutton, quoting a letter from Dr. J. S. Ormsby to Mrs. W. M. Ormsby, June 3, 1806.
132 Depending on the source see Gary A. Horton, "Carson River Chronology," and Knack and Stewart, *As Long as the River Shall Run*, 72.
133 For Truckee's death, see Hopkins, *Life Among the Piutes*, 69.
134 **the minstrel act** Zanjani, *Sarah Winnemucca*, 75.
134 **"eloquent"** Canfield, *Sarah Winnemucca of the Northern Paiutes*, 164.
134 **"listless dependency"** . . . "If this is the kind" Zanjani, *Sarah Winnemucca*, 101, 103.
134 **"only ashamed"** Hopkins, *Life Among the Paiutes*, 225.
134 **"devoid of conscience"** Canfield, *Sarah Winnemucca of the Northern Paiutes*, 224.
134 **"are not disposed"** Ibid., 231.
135 **Carlisle commencement speaker** Zanjani, *Sarah Winnemucca*, 265.
135 **These are the days** Canfield, *Sarah Winnemucca of the Northern Paiutes*, 245.
135 **"rudely stare"** Zanjani, *Sarah Winnemucca*, 272.
135 **absconds with** Canfield, *Sarah Winnemucca of the Northern Paiutes*, 251.
136 **the ghost dance** Zanjani, *Sarah Winnemucca*, 284–85.

HENRY

137 **"[F]rom seven on . . . put him *out*"** For Ford's notes, see Olson, *Young Henry Ford*, 20.
138 **"a time in every man's education"** Emerson, *Selected Writings*, 267.
138 **"simply by tinkering"** Ford, *My Life and Work*, 23.
138 **Some biographers say"** Nevins, *Ford*, 42.
138 **Others say it was** Olson, *Young Henry Ford*, 8.
138 **Twenty-fourth Michigan Regiment** See "Turning Points in Detroit History," http://www.michiganhistorymagazine.com/detroit/pdf/nd00tur.pdf.
139 **greatest industrial surge** Bogart, *Economic History of the American People*, 553.
139 For Ford family history, see Olson, *Young Henry Ford*, and Collier and Horowitz, *Fords*.
139 **"the great miracle of America"** Watts, *People's Tycoon*, 18.
139 **"We children"** Nevins, *Ford*, 35.
139 **Patrick O'Hearn"** Olson, *Young Henry Ford*, 10.
140 **ninety-one-acre farm** Nevins, *Ford*, 40–41.
140 **"The farm the farm"** Emerson, *Selected Writings*, 60.
140 **"for sanity"** Watts, *People's Tycoon*, 312.

140   **ten thousand more miles** Dunbar, *Michigan*, 484.

140   **Lumber helped** For an overview, see Catton, *Michigan*, 108–43.

141   **sixty million board feet** Catton, *Michigan*, 130.

141   **leading source of lumber** Maria Quinlan, "Lumbering in Michigan," http://www.michigan.gov/hal/O,1607,7-160-17451_18793-53133–,00.html.

141   **manufactured the first freight cars** Babson, *Working Detroit*, 5.

141   **Michigan Car Company** Teaford, *Cities of the Heartland*, 53.

141   **Detroit's biggest export** Jacobs, *Economy of Cities*, 124.

141   **largest smelter** Babson, *Working Detroit*, 5.

141   **more than doubled** Catton, *Michigan*, 123.

141   **massive iron ore boats** "Detroit Dry Dock Building," part of the Detroit Web page developed by Reynolds Farley and Judy Mullin for Professor Farley's courses at the University of Michigan, http://detroit1701.org/Dry %20Dock.html.

141   **"My mother always said"** Olson, *Young Henry Ford*, 20.

141   **duties as a housewife** Ibid., 15.

142   **"My mother taught me"** For Mary Ford's teachings, see Watts, *People's Tycoon*, 8–10.

142   **"couldn't be happy here"** Olson, *Young Henry Ford*, 17.

142   **"I went to Sunday school"** Ibid., 31.

142   **"I have tried to live my life"** Watts, *People's Tycoon*, 8.

142   **"Could read all the first reader"** Nevins, *Ford*, 43.

142   **"pedagogical conservative"** Westerhoff, *McGuffey and His Readers*, 18.

142   **"aimed to combine"** Ibid., 62.

142   **one hundred twenty million copies** Ibid., 14.

143   **"single teacher supervised"** See "Scotch Settlement School," Dearborn Michigan History Web site, 2000, http://www.geocities.com/histmich/ dearborn.html.

143   **"The day began"** Nevins, *Ford*, 45.

143   **"wasn't any set schedule"** Ibid., 45.

143   **"Religion, morality and knowledge"** Matthew J. Brouillette, "A Brief History of Government Education in Michigan," from Mackinac Center for Public Policy, School Choice in Michigan.

143   **Its 1835 constitution** Dunbar, *Michigan*, 393.

143   **a centralized system** Ibid., 398.

143   **"If children, as is generally"** Brouillette, "Brief History."

143   **"as late as 1850"** Clarence M. Burton, "When Detroit Was Young," http:// www.historydetroit.com./stats.asp

143   **"democratic conception"** Ford, *My Life and Work*, 10.

143   **four thousand school districts** Dunbar, *Michigan*, 402.

143   **Michigan Supreme Court** Cremin, *American Education*, 162–63.

144   **"the influence of McGuffey"** Westerhoff, *McGuffey and His Readers*, 16.

144   **"a lit-tle boy"** *McGuffey's Pictorial Eclectic Primer*, Lesson LXXXIX (Cincinnati: Wilson, Hinkle & Co., 1857; reprinted by Henry Ford, 1939).

144   *Second Reader* Lindberg, *Annotated McGuffey*, 59.

144 **"common sense and common honesty"** Watts, *People's Tycoon*, 12.

144 **"industry and morality"** Ibid.

145 **"extra discipline"** Olson, *Young Henry Ford*, 16.

145 **" 'mourners bench' "** Nevins, *Ford*, 45–46.

145 **he begins a letter** Ibid., 107.

145 **"I don't like to read"** Watts, *People's Tycoon*, ix.

145 **Tommy Garrett** Olson, *Young Henry Ford*, 20.

146 **jewelry shop** Ibid., 20–21.

146 **"I was always tinkering"** Ibid., 20.

146 **Philadelphia Centennial** Nevins, *Ford*, 62.

146 **"laziest bugger"** Watts, *People's Tycoon*, 14.

146 **"watch a threshing machine"** Ibid.

147 **"drudgery"** Ibid.

147 **"too much work"** Ford, *My Life and Work*, 22.

147 **"Power is utilized"** Ibid., 15.

147 **panic of 1837** Babson, *Working Detroit*, 5.

147 **Eighteen thousand businesses** "People and Events: The Panic of 1873," *American Experience*, PBS, new content 1999–2001, http://www.pbs.org/wgbh/ amex/grant/peopleevents/e_panic.html.

147 **protests and work stoppages** See Brecher, *Strike!*, 1–22.

147 **Three hundred policemen** Zinn, *People's History*, teaching edition, 179.

147 **"a breakdown in character"** Boyer and Morais, *Labor's Untold Story*, 41.

147 **"a pocket full of"** Ford, *My Life and Work*, 24.

148 **sister Margaret claimed** Olson, *Young Henry Ford*, 22.

148 **"without a mainspring"** Watts, *People's Tycoon*, 16.

148 **"10 H.P. N&S"** Olson, *Young Henry Ford*, 23.

148 **"Mr Reden Let me"** Ibid.

149 **"I draw a plan"** Ford, *My Life and Work*, 32.

149 **"He walked around"** Watts, *People's Tycoon*, 35.

149 **"the 'expert' state of mind"** Ford, *My Life and Work*, 90.

149 **"this primary wisdom"** Emerson, *Selected Writings*, 277.

149 **"first watch I fixed"** Olson, *Young Henry Ford*, 22.

149 **a single factory in New Haven** Hounshell, *American System to Mass Production*, 60.

150 **The watch ran** Olson, *Young Henry Ford*, 21–22.

150 **behind his textbook** Watts, *People's Tycoon*, 20.

150 **"Machines are to mechanics"** Nevins, *Ford*, 58.

150 **"I really did not know"** Olson, *Young Henry Ford*, 22.

150 **"a bit of solder"** Ibid.

150 **"rude, simple"** Ford, *My Life and Work*, 229.

151 **"could do almost anything"** Ibid., 22.

151 **"a Sunday without work"** Olson, *Young Henry Ford*, 32.

151 **"for 1/2 Hr"** Ibid., 21.

151 **right back in** Nevins, *Ford*, 71–72.

151 **some appreciation for** Ford, *My Life and Work*, 97.

151 **"An educated man"** Ibid., 256.

151 **"true education"** Ibid., 257.

151 **"Modern industry"** Ibid., 220.

152 **a kind of rebel** Ibid., 24, and Olson, *Young Henry Ford*, 26.

152 **"Henry worries me"** Watts, *People's Tycoon*, 21.

152 **an aunt's house** Nevins, *Ford*, 78.

152 **"any particular love"** Ibid., 72–73.

152 **starts at $1.10 a day** Ibid., 79, and Babson, *Working Detroit*, 6.

152 **"Who's in charge"** Olson, *Young Henry Ford*, 53.

152 **"I went to Detroit"** Nevins, *Ford*, 80.

152 For babitting, see Magonolia Metal Company, *Magnolia Metal Bearing Book*.

153 **nine hundred manufacturing enterprises** Nevins, *Ford*, 76.

153 **almost doubled their production** Bogart, *Economic History of the American People*, 571.

153 **"FIRE HYDRANT"** "A Retired Machinist," Thomas Flower obituary, *Evening News*, September 30, 1901, http://www.rootsweb.com/~miwayne/detnews1901.htm.

153 **"every description"** See Flower newspaper ad, http://www.photostogo.com/store/Chubby.asp?ImageNumber=772953.

153 **"They manufactured everything"** Quoted in Watts, *People's Tycoon*, 24.

153 **had been disappearing** Rorabaugh, *Craft Apprentice*, 208.

154 **about 60 percent more** See Nelson, *Managers and Workers*, 96, and Oestricher, *Solidarity and Fragmentation*, 10.

154 **"little or no instruction"** Nelson, *Managers and Workers*, 96.

154 **putting hexagons on** Olson, *Young Henry Ford*, 27.

154 **"The master had become"** Rorabaugh, *Craft Apprentice*, 206.

154 **"an inferno"** Nelson, *Managers and Workers*, 28.

154 **"awfully hot"** Olson, *Young Henry Ford*, 27.

154 **"how to do a few things"** Watts, *People's Tycoon*, 24.

154 **"a farmboy"** Hounshell, *American System to Mass Production*, 221.

154 **balance wheel cast at a third** Watts, *People's Tycoon*, 39.

155 **contracted out** Ibid., 86.

155 **makes it look like** Ford, *My Life and Work*, 24.

155 **the climax of his schooling** Olson, *Young Henry Ford*, 30.

155 **an industrial strip** Zunz, *Making America Corporate*, 29–30; see also Farmer, *History of Detroit*

155 **"Particular attention"** Thomas A. Klug, "Historic American Engineering Record: Dry Dock Engine Works," 2002, 8, http://www.marygrove.edu/ids/papers/Dry_Dock_Engine_Works.doc.

155 **A decade later** Ibid., 5.

155 **A two-cylinder engine** Ibid., 9.

155 **more than half these** Ibid., 11.

155 **"in the history of Detroit"** Drutchas, "The Man with a Capital Design."

156 **all were designed** "Frank E. Kirby," a leaflet given to passengers on a Port Huron cruise, 1990, http://www.boblosteamers.com/kirby.html [Kirby].

156   **arranged for the fifteen-year-old** Farley and Mullin, "Detroit Dry Dock Company/Globe Trading Building," and Kirby.

156   **also designed tugboats** Kirby, 14.

156   **single largest stockholder** Klug, "Historic American Engineering Record," 14.

156   **also bought shares** Ibid., 13.

157   **"a new combination"** Watts, *People's Tycoon*, 44.

157   **"natural mechanic"** Ibid., 33.

157   **"Almost anyone can"** Ford, *My Life and Work*, 3.

157   **and, yes, Kirby** Olson, *Young Henry Ford*, 30–31.

157   **A photograph shows** Ibid., 29.

157   **"were encouraged to think"** Rorabaugh, *Craft Apprentice*, 209.

157   **ten-hour shifts** Babson, *Working Detroit*, 7.

157   **"80 percent"** Ibid., 9.

157   **German and British** Oestricher, *Solidarity and Fragmentation*, 33.

157   **about 90 percent** Klug, "Historic American Engineering Record," 17.

157   **the *Socialist*** Oestricher, *Solidarity and Fragmentation*, 82.

157   **Workingmen's Party** Ibid., 80.

158   **elected one of its members** Babson, *Working Detroit*, 10.

158   **fifteen hundred members** Ibid., 10, 11.

158   **"An injury to one"** Brecher, *Strike!*, 28.

158   **"No wage worker ever"** Oestricher, *Solidarity and Fragmentation*, 22.

158   **" 'labor-saving' machinery"** Ibid, 87.

158   **"Man minus the machine"** Collier and Horowitz, *Fords*, 80.

158   **"He is not less"** Babson, *Working Detroit*, 10.

158   **"vast majority of men"** Ford, *My Life and Work*, 103.

158   **"self-evident that"** Ibid., 80.

159   **"lifting the worker"** Ibid., 191.

159   **"something sacred"** Ibid., 273.

159   **"larger men"** Ibid., 5, 10.

159   **"Where is the master"** Emerson, *Selected Writings*, 289.

159   **"To believe your own thought"** Ibid., 266.

159   **"universal car"** Ford, *My Life and Work*, 67.

159   **"one serves"** Ibid., 12–13.

159   **"repetitive labor"** Ibid., 107.

160   **"most certainly all men"** Ibid., 10.

WILLIE

161   **"unobtrusive charity"** Du Bois, *Autobiography*, 95.

161   **"I was not hungry"** Ibid., 73.

161   **"overseeing custody"** Ibid.

161   **"middle-class people"** Ibid., 78, 75.

161   **"of my colored kin"** Ibid., 75.

162   **its first schoolhouse** Taylor, *History of Great Barrington*, 347, 352.

162 **"each day, five days a week"** Du Bois, *Autobiography*, 76.

162 **"We learned the alphabet"** Ibid., 77.

162 **"inevitably white"** Ibid.

162 **without even basic skills** Ibid., 109.

162 **"an equal chance for earning"** Mann, "Twelth Annual Report."

162 **twice as much of its budget** Taylor, *History of Great Barrington*, 553.

163 **"his name in connection"** *Report of a Committee of the Town of Great Barrington upon the subject of abolishing School Districts, and establishing a Town School System*, 7, 13 [*Report of a Committee*].

163 **"lower and ruder"** Ibid.; see 1864–65 School Committee Report, page 5.

163 **"inevitably white American"** Du Bois, *Autobiography*, 76.

163 **"education according to the preconceptions"** Du Bois, *Against Racism*, 250.

163 **"glibly and usually correctly"** Du Bois, *Autobiography*, 76.

163 **"some fixed habits"** *Report of a Committee*; see 1864–65 School Committee Report, page 3.

163 **"became deeply grounded"** Du Bois, *Against Racism*, 250.

163 **twenty-one buildings** "Selectman Annual Report" for Great Barrington, March 1, 1876, found in *Report of a Committee*.

163 **"fat and greasy"** Du Bois, "Socialism and the American Negro," in *Against Racism*, 303.

164 **"a mighty family"** Du Bois, *Darkwater*, 6.

164 **"The bits of land"** Ibid.

164 **By 1873** Foner, *Reconstruction*, 482.

164 For Lowell information, see "Lowell's Southern Connection," from the the Lowell National Historical Park Web site, www.nps.gov/lowe/2002/loweweb/lowe_history/lowe_handbook/connect.htm.

165 **"lords of the lash"** Ibid.

165 **"a golden river"** Du Bois, *Darkwater*, 6.

165 For Monument Mills, see Drew, *History of Monument Mills*, 1984 (not paginated).

165 **Parley Russell** Cooke, *Historic Homes*, 171–72.

165 **Louis Russell** Du Bois, *Autobiography*, 86–87.

165 **"a mass of Irish"** Ibid., 82.

165 **"set aside"** Ibid., 83.

165 **state law** Foner, *Reconstruction*, 482.

166 **Jacquard looms** See Drew, *History of Monument Mills*.

166 **Photographs of Monument Mills** Ibid.

166 **"called me 'nigger'"** Du Bois, *Autobiography*, 82.

166 **"I cordially despised"** Du Bois, *Darkwater*, 10.

167 **about a decade before** Spring, *American School*, 96.

167 **"an extraordinary experiment"** Du Bois, *Autobiography*, 61.

167 **"not only weary of"** from Du Bois, *The Souls of Black Folk*, "Of Mr. Booker T. Washington and Others," in *Seventh Son*, vol. I, 360.

167 **"moral politics"** Foner, *Reconstruction*, 527.

167 **"The slave went free"** Ibid., 602.

167 **"I became conscious"** Du Bois, *Autobiography*, 76.

167 **"in a day and state"** Du Bois, *Education of Black People*, 129.

167 **"the English idea"** Ibid., 130.

168 **private education ranged** Taylor, *History of Great Barrington*, 354–55.

168 **"inherited wealth . . . idle rich"** Du Bois, *Autobiography*, 86.

168 **103 were** Katz, *Class Bureaucracy and Schools*, 34.

168 **over five hundred families** Ibid.

168 **"all the inhabitants"** Inglis, *Rise of the High School*, 36.

168 **"danger to this country . . . in tendencies"** Krug, *Shaping of the American High School*, 11.

168 **"most violent"** Foner, *Reconstruction*, 585.

169 **"wish property safe"** Krug, *Shaping of the American High School*, 23.

169 **less than 20 percent** Kaestle and Vinovskis, *Education and Social Change*, 260.

169 **even a decade later** Krug, *Shaping of the American High School*, 11.

169 **some twenty-five students** Du Bois, "Socialism and the American Negro," in *Against Racism*, 303.

169 **fifteen was large** Lewis, *W. E. B. Du Bois*, 50.

169 **grocer and jeweler** Du Bois, *Autobiography*, 84.

169 **"delinquent"** Inglis, *Rise of the High School*, 43.

169 **fifteen thousand** Taylor, *History of Great Barrington*, 355.

169 **"boys and girls"** Ibid., 454.

170 **"the people's college"** Krug, *Shaping of the American High School*, 6.

170 **"uncomprehending and indifferent"** Katz, *Irony of Early School Reform*, 47.

170 **"idle, ignorant, and vicious"** George R. Stetson, "Literacy and Crime in Massachusetts," from the *Andover Review*, December 1884, 2.

170 **"dangers of unbridled"** Foner, *Reconstruction*, 497.

170 **"permanence of our"** George R. Stetson, "The Necessity for Moral and Industrial Training in the Public Schools," *Andover Review*, October 1886, 15–24.

171 **"a constant struggle"** Taylor, *History of Great Barrington*, 455.

171 **"not too popular"** Du Bois, *Autobiography*, 92.

171 **"first of the clan"** Ibid., 63.

171 **"heavy, kind face"** Du Bois, *Darkwater*, 6.

171 **"silent, repressed"** Du Bois, *Autobiography*, 65.

171 **"poor, on the whole"** Ibid., 80.

171 **"to feel the pressure"** Ibid., 83.

171 **"prove to the world"** Lewis, *W. E. B. Du Bois*, 32.

171 **"of noble Christian character"** Taylor, *History of Great Barrington*, 454.

172 **about a third** Kaestle and Vinovskis, *Education and Social Change*, 264.

172 **would keep time** Lewis, *W. E. B. Du Bois*, 37.

172 **members of respectable society** See Katz, *Irony of Early School Reform*.

172 For Hosmer biography, see Amherst yearbook 1896, http://distantcousin/ Yearbooks/MA/Amherst/Bio1871_1896/Page/060.jpg.

172 **"popular and progressive"** Taylor, *History of Great Barrington*, 455.

172 **G.B.H.S.** Du Bois, *Autobiography*, 85.

172 **"continues to win"** Taylor, *History of Great Barrington*, 455.

173 **"a pecuniary sacrifice"** Ibid.

173 **"educational revival . . . evangelical religion"** Katz, *Class, Bureaucracy, and Schools*, 44.

173 **"I was born in a community"** Du Bois, *Autobiography*, 100.

173 For Barrington Congregationalist history, see Conn, *First Congregational Church*, 27–28.

174 **"strangely silent"** Ibid., 27.

174 For Reverend Scudder, see ibid. 52.

174 **"most important"** Du Bois, *Autobiography*, 88.

174 **"many acquaintances"** Ibid.

174 **Methodist Zion** Ibid., 83.

174 **"a little dreaded"** Ibid., 89.

174 **"very much beloved"** Conn, *First Congregational Church*, 37–38.

175 **man's nature** Ibid., 39.

175 **"equal authority"** Ibid.

175 **"liberal Congregational"** Du Bois, "A Soliloquy on Viewing My Life from the Last Decade of Its First Century," in *Seventh Son*, vol. II, 733.

175 **"a reasonable duty"** Ibid.

175 **"character of the principal"** Taylor, *History of Great Barrington*, 455.

176 **"Ought the Indians"** Lewis, *W. E. B. Du Bois*, 39.

176 **"high school lyceum"** Du Bois column in the *New York Globe*, from *Seventh Son*, vol. I, 168.

176 **settle for trade school** Lewis, *W. E. B. Du Bois*, 34.

176 **"as a matter of course"** Du Bois, *Autobiography*, 101.

176 **"a great bitterness"** Du Bois, *Against Racism*, 17.

176 **"young and ambitious"** Du Bois, *Autobiography*, 102.

176 **less than 2 percent** Andrew Delbanco, "Colleges: An Endangered Species?" *New York Review of Books*, vol. 52, no. 4, March 10, 2005 http://www.nybooks.com/articles/17777.

176 **"only about 650"** Du Bois, "The Talented Tenth," in *Seventh Son*, vol. I, 392.

177 **"normal and right"** Du Bois, *Autobiography*, 101.

177 **"a gentleman's education"** Ibid., 66.

177 **"held his head high"** Ibid., 71.

177 **"how people of breeding"** Ibid., 98.

177 **over 80 percent** Du Bois, "The Talented Tenth," in *Seventh Son*, vol. I, 392.

177 **"to the freed Negro"** W. E. B. Du Bois, *The Souls of Black Folk*, 1903, http://www.bartleby.com/114/6.html.

177 **"[w]andering the fields"** Du Bois, *Against Racism*, 29.

177 **"sterling character"** Ibid., 5.

178 **"below the standard"** Du Bois, *Autobiography*, 102.

178 **"one of the most promising"** Lewis, *W. E. B. Du Bois*, 53.

178 **chipped in** Ibid., 55.

178 **"to my mind"** Du Bois, *Autobiography*, 154–55.

178 **"the economic order"** Ibid.

179 **"on a rushing express"** Ibid., 156.

179 **"group of educated Negroes"** Ibid., 123.

179 **"supporting the schools"** Du Bois, "The Philadelphia Negro," in *Seventh Son*, vol. I, 222.

179 **"not born in slavery"** Du Bois, "Education and Work," in *Seventh Son*, vol. I, 558.

179 **to earn a living** Du Bois, *Education of Black People*, 11.

179 **"make men carpenters"** Du Bois, "Education and Work," in *Seventh Son*, vol. I, 560.

179 **"adjustment and submission"** Du Bois, "Of Mr. Booker T. Washington and Others," in *Seventh Son*, vol. I, 355.

179 **"drunk with its vision"** Du Bois, "The Talented Tenth," in *Seventh Son*, vol. I, 397.

179 **"the whole question"** Du Bois, "Education and Work," in *Seventh Son*, vol. I, 559.

180 **"its exceptional men"** Du Bois, "The Talented Tenth," in *Seventh Son*, vol. I, 385.

180 **"from the bottom upward"** Ibid., 390.

180 **"Had it not been"** Du Bois, *Autobiography*, 154–55.

180 **"blithely European"** Ibid., 126.

180 **"received more education"** Ibid., 148.

180 **"since the Civil War"** Ibid., 118.

180 **"practically my sole chance"** Ibid., 148.

180 **"path to social reform"** Ibid., 289.

181 **"Our natural friends"** Du Bois, "The Negro and Socialism," in *Seventh Son*, vol. I, 427.

181 **"Karl Marx mentioned"** Ibid., 126.

181 **"a beam of new light"** Ibid., 289.

181 **"included the Negro problem"** Ibid., 305.

181 **"The average Negro undergraduate"** Du Bois, *Seventh Son*, vol. I, 563.

181 **"believed it passionately"** Du Bois, "Segregation in the North," in *Seventh Son*, vol. II, 242.

182 **"I was astounded"** Du Bois, *Autobiography*, 289.

182 **"dole of the rich"** Du Bois, "The Negro and Communism," in *Seventh Son*, vol. II, 282.

182 **"a real democracy"** Du Bois, "Does the Negro Need Separate Schools?" in *Seventh Son*, vol. II, 409.

182 **"deliberately rearing millions"** Du Bois, "The Talented Tenth," in *Seventh Son*, vol. I, 399.

182 **Of the two million** Du Bois, "Does the Negro Need Separate Schools?" in *Seventh Son*, vol. II, 408.

183 **"cheap applause"** Ibid., 411.

183 **"American fairy tales"** Du Bois, "The Conservation of Races," in *Seventh Son*, vol. I, 183.

183   **"new and beautiful"** Du Bois, "Does the Negro Need Separate Schools?" in *Seventh Son*, vol. II, 417.

HELEN

184   **"That living word"** Helen Keller, *My Life*. 36.
184   **"A new light"** Ibid., 257.
184   **"used to the silence"** Ibid., 26.
184   **"Nothing"** Lash, *Helen and Teacher*, 46.
185   **"Suddenly I felt"** Helen Keller, *My Life*, 37.
185   **"returned to the house"** Lash, *Helen and Teacher*, 55.
185   **"waking from a dream"** Ibid., 75.
185   **"A miracle has happened"** Helen Keller, *My Life*, 252.
185   **"She pinched me"** Braddy, *Anne Sullivan Macy*, 121.
185   **"[O]bedience is the gateway"** Helen Keller, *My Life*, 249.
186   **"The little savage"** Ibid., 253.
186   **"illiterate and unskilled"** Lash, *Helen and Teacher*, 5.
186   **"fire of hatred"** Ibid.
186   **"God put a curse"** Ibid.
186   **"I was not shocked"** Ibid., 10.
186   **"I doubt if life"** Ibid., 13.
187   **"rather have built up"** Ibid., 17.
187   **"[H]er countenance"** Ibid.
187   **"the daughters of ministers"** Braddy, *Anne Sullivan Macy*, 68.
187   **"smug little children"** Lash, *Helen and Teacher*, 28.
188   **"radical"** Ibid., 29.
188   **"the air of one"** Ibid., 34.
188   **"The men 'nice people' admired"** Ibid., 28.
188   **"noblest and most spiritualizing"** Braddy, *Anne Sullivan Macy*, 70.
188   **"conventional order of society"** Lash, *Helen and Teacher*, 30.
188   **"great law of our being"** Ibid., 37.
188   **"to earn my living"** Braddy, *Anne Sullivan Macy*, 95.
189   **"the yoke"** Lash, *Helen and Teacher*, 54.
189   **"direct and mold"** Ibid.
189   **"dark corners"** Helen Keller, *My Life*, 26.
189   **"isn't a living soul"** Ibid., 273.
189   **Tuscumbia in 1815** Captain A. H. Keller, "Colbert County, Alabama."
189   **"What good man would prefer"** Andrew Jackson's Second Annual Message, in James D. Richardson, *A Compilation of the Messages and Papers of the Presidents 1789–1908*, vol. 2, published by Bureau of National Literature and Art, 1908, and quoted at the PBS "Africans in America" Web site, http://www.pbs.org/wgbh/aia/part4/4h3437t.html.
190   **David Keller** James, "Colbertians,"
190   **later became superintendent** Captain A. H. Keller, "Colbert County."
190   **couldn't compete with** Federal Writers' Program, *Alabama*, 76.

190   **river town of two thousand** *Memorial Record of Alabama*, 202.

190   **Helen's uncle went** William Atkinson, ed., *Physicians and Surgeons of the United States*, (Philadelphia; Charles Robson, 1878), 443.

190   **Arthur Henley Keller** Captain A. H. Keller, "Colbert County."

190   **"The white race, even in"** *Memorial Record of Alabama*, 223.

190   **"negro . . . near six feet high"** Ad in the *North Alabamian*, Tuscumbia, May 26, 1838, http://www.rootsweb.aneestry.com/~alcorlber/aa-runaways.htm.

190   **Another classified** Ads in the *North Alabamian*, 1836 and 1837, http://www.ferris.edu/jimcrow/links/misclink/moulton.

191   **"It pleased me"** Helen Keller, *My Life*, 28.

191   **"tyrannized"** Ibid., 249.

191   **"Mother will whip"** Ibid., 270.

191   **"We never think of them"** Lash, *Helen and Teacher*, 45.

191   **"My think is white"** Helen Keller, *My Life*, 276.

191   **a fifth of the Confederacy's white adult** Foner, *Reconstruction*, 125.

191   **$725 million** Federal Writers' Program, *Alabama*, 65.

191   ***all, all* was lost"** Foner, *Reconstruction*, 125.

191   **"not yet subjugated"** "Inventory of the Charles Campbell Papers 1743–1896," http://ead.lib.virginia.edu/vivead/published/wm/viw00063.component.

191   **"receiving and forwarding"** Lash, *Helen and Teacher*, 45.

191   **like most of his neighbors** Federal Writers' Program, *Alabama*, 76.

191   **"everything Southern"** Braddy, *Anne Sullivan Macy*, 131.

191   **mob had promptly** Harry E. Wallace, "Tuscumbia on the Move," in the *Times Daily* newspaper, Florence, Muscle Shoals, Sheffield, Tuscumbia, and Northwestern Alabama, February 25, 1999, http://www.rootsweb.com/~allauder/historyshoals2.htm.

192   **"simon pure democrat"** *Memphis Avalanche*, quoted in Lash, *Helen and Teacher*, 45.

192   **"Shall the white man . . ."** *Moulton Advertiser*, August 15, 1873, http://www.ferris.edu/jimcrow/links/misclink/moulton.

192   **White Supremacy and home rule** Vann Woodward, *Origins of the New South*, 9.

192   **On election day** Foner, *Reconstruction*, 552–53, and Wallace, "Tuscumbia on the Move."

192   **bought the *North Alabamian*** Lash, *Helen and Teacher*, 45, and Paul Horton, "The Assassination of Rev. James Madison Pickens and the Persistence of Anti-Bourbon Activism in North Alabama," *Alabama Review*, April 2004, http://www.findarticles.com/p/articles/mi_qa3880/is_200404/ai_n9363929.

192   **"his sharp blade"** *Memorial Record of Alabama*, 203, and Colbert County, Alabama Biographies, "The Keller Family of Colbert County, Al.," newspaper accounts, compiled and submitted by Lee Freeman, http://www.rootsweb.com/~alcolber/bio-keller-family-nwspr.htm.

192   **Helen Adams Keller by "mistake"** Helen Keller, *My Life*, 25.

192   **"Capital follows"** See the Southern Education Foundation's timeline, "1875–1895: Disenfranchisement," http://www.sefatl.org/1878.asp.

192 **"Public education for all"** Spring, *American School*, 220.
193 **into the twentieth century** Vann Woodward, *Origins of the New South*, 61–65.
193 **"well-patronized"** Captain A. H. Keller, "Colbert County."
193 **Miss Anna Pybas's** Wallace, "Tuscumbia on the Move," and Tennessee Valley Historical Society, "The Journal of Muscle Shoals History," vol. 9, 1981, 7.
193 **"guns and pistols"** Ayers, *Promise of the New South*, 47.
193 **patronage job** "The Keller Family of Colbert County, Al."
193 **As the United States marshal** See http://www.usmarshals.gov/history/index.html.
193 **"flaming sword of righteousness"** Lash, *Helen and Teacher*, 71.
194 **"sickened"** Herrmann, *Helen Keller*, 61.
194 **"heights of a southern woman's"** Ibid.
194 **"voluminous reader"** Ibid., 59–60.
194 **"carefully nurtured"** Braddy, *Anne Sullivan Macy*, 101.
194 **"I have decided not"** Helen Keller, *My Life*, 258.
194 **"to keep her mind fixed"** Ibid.
194 **"spontaneous impulses"** Ibid., 307.
194 **"just as the birds"** Ibid., 258.
194 **"independent ideas"** Ibid., 260.
194 **"never seen anything"** Ibid.
195 **"digging out of the child"** Ibid.
195 **"I am beginning to suspect"** Ibid.
195 **"besieged"** Lash, *Helen and Teacher*, 84.
195 **"My beautiful Helen"** Helen Keller, *My Life,* 266.
195 **"of the noble spirit"** Lash, *Helen and Teacher*, 80.
195 **"I came here"** Ibid.
195 **"my Utopia"** Helen Keller, *My Life*, 100.
196 **she credits reading for** Lash, *Helen and Teacher*, 129.
196 **"permanent guests"** Ibid., 109.
196 **"belongs to us"** Perkins Institute and Massachusetts School for the Blind "Fifty-eighth Annual Report of the Trustees," 85 [Perkins, Fifty-eighth Annual].
196 **"brisk men"** Vann Woodward, *Origins of the New South*, 153.
196 **as a daily** *Memorial Records of Alabama*, 203.
196 **south in Birmingham** Ayers, *Promise of the New South*, 56.
197 **five and a half million acres** Ibid., 124.
197 **"the romantic cult"** Vann Woodward, *Origins of the New South*, 14.
197 **"between two eras"** Braddy, *Anne Sullivan Macy*, 131.
197 **"practice, practice, practice"** Helen Keller, *My Life*, 61.
197 **homes of the "best people"** Perkins Institute and Massachusetts School for the Blind, "Sixtieth Annual Report of the Trustees," 110 [Perkins, Sixtieth Annual].
198 **" 'wonderful, wonderful.' "** Ibid., 57.
198 **"Emersonian temper"** Ibid., 68.

198   **"child has dormant"** Lash, *Helen and Teacher*, 66.
198   **"as perfect as"** Perkins, Sixtieth Annual, 58.
198   **two hundred thousand dollars** Perkins, Fifty-eighth Annual, 90.
198   **"All Boston was"** Lash, *Helen and Teacher*, 153.
199   **"to love everybody"** Helen Keller, *My Life*, 237.
199   **"vulgar upstart"** Lash, *Helen and Teacher*, 116.
199   **popular poem** by Edmund Clarence Steadman, quoted in Ibid., 100.
199   **"the victory of the soul"** For Hale's perspective, see Perkins Institute and Massachusetts School for the Blind, "Sixty-first Annual Report of the Trustees," 202–23.
199   **"Knowledge is love"** Helen Keller, *My Life*, 34.
199   **"more of the Divine"** Lash, *Helen and Teacher*, 172.
199   **Twain argued** Ibid., 146.
200   **an addendum** Perkins, Sixtieth Annual, 95.
200   **"wept as I hope"** Lash, *Helen and Teacher*, 140.
200   **"dreadful days"** Helen Keller, *My Life*, 62.
200   **"not be original"** Ibid., 68.
200   **"I loaned Captain"** Lash, *Helen and Teacher*, 159.
201   **Illiteracy among Southern whites** See the Southern Education Foundation's timeline, "1875–1895: Disenfranchisement," http://www.sefatl.org/1878.asp.
201   **Homicide rates below** Ayers, *Promise of the New South*, 155.
201   **"the unconscious life"** Helen Keller, *My Life*, 70.
201   **attitude toward black people** Lash, *Helen and Teacher*, 165.
201   **local normal school** Ibid., 182.
201   **another lynching** *Leighton News*, April 27, 1894, http://www.ferris.edu/jimcrow/links/misclink/moulton.
201   **"more or less desultory"** Helen Keller, *My Life*, 73.
202   **"radically wrong"** Lash, *Helen and Teacher*, 420.
202   **"shall never properly"** Helen Keller, *My Life*, 317–18.
202   **"*Language* and *knowledge*"** Ibid., 317.
202   **"as pupil learns from master"** Lash, *Helen and Teacher*, 418.
202   **"Dr. Montessori learned"** Ibid.
202   **"It was my wish"** Ibid., 178.
202   **"a regular Collegiate course"** Ibid., 182.
203   **"socialite Lawrence Hutton"** Ibid., 193.
203   **"a revelation"** Ibid., 192.
203   **"still an Adams"** Braddy, *Anne Sullivan Macy*, 174.
203   **"plodding pursuit"** Herrmann, *Helen Keller*, 100.
203   **"I supposed that in our civilization"** Helen Keller, *Out of the Dark*, 8, 9.
203   **"remarkably intelligent blind"** *New York Times*, January 6, 1895, 17, col. 1; and Lash, *Helen and Teacher*, 187.
204   **"If this can't be done"** Lash, *Helen and Teacher*, 196.
204   **"legitimate" performers** Kobylak, "Primer on the History of American Juggling."

204 **five hundred dollars a week** Lash, *Helen and Teacher*, 196.
204 **"wrote a heartbroken letter"** Ibid., 196.
204 **"you would a monkey"** Ibid.
204 **mostly "trivial"** Helen Keller, *Out of the Dark*, 41.
204 **"remarkable in her career"** Helen Keller, *My Life*, 223.
204 **only the one story** Koestler, *Unseen Minority*, 55.
205 **"If we women are to learn"** Helen Keller, *Out of the Dark*, 42.
205 **"outrages against the colored people . . ."** Lash, *Helen and Teacher*, 454.
205 **"Abolition Gang"** Ibid.
205 **"part of a greater problem"** Ibid., 370.
205 **"cures, and not prevention"** Ibid., 373.
205 **"out of bondage"** Helen Keller, *My Life*, 60.
205 **a paying job** see Koestler, *Unseen Minority*, 59–69.
206 **"the crowning experience"** Lash, *Helen and Teacher*, 685.
206 **"a class apart"** Ibid., 684.

RACHEL

207 **first a fort** Ross and Andorf, *Springdale* (not paginated).
207 **"There was once a town"** Carson, *Silent Spring*, 13.
207 **"a grim specter"** Ibid., 14.
207 **"the central problem"** Ibid., 18.
208 **He was thirty-six** Lear, *Rachel Carson*, 11.
208 **son of an Irish carpenter** Ibid., 9.
208 **soft, bituminous coal** Pennsylvania Environmental Council, "Three Rivers Conservation Plan," March 2004, chapter 2, http://www.dcnr.state.pa.us/brc/rivers/riversconservation/registry/62chap2.pdf.
208 **"power and civilization"** Freese, *Coal*, 9.
208 **Pittsburgh's Mellon family** Cannadine, *Mellon*, 94.
208 **"secular gospel"** Ibid., 13.
208 **second only to** Ibid., 161.
208 **ten million tons** Lorant, *Pittsburgh*, 275.
208 **largest single company** Cannadine, *Mellon*, 161.
209 **Maria McLean** See Lear, *Rachel Carson*, 11.
209 **Washington College** Crumrine, *History of Washington County*, 455–58; see the Historic Pittsburgh, University of Pittsburgh's Digital Research Library, http://digital.library.pitt.edu/cgi-bin/t/text/text-idx?idno=00hc17099m;view=toc;c=pitttext.
209 **for men only** Pulliam, *History of Education*, 5th ed., 103.
209 **more children in public** Ibid., 90.
209 **only four months** Pennsylvania State Archives, "Records of the Department of Education: Agency History," http://www.phmc.state.pa.us/bah/DAM/rg/rg22ahr.htm.
210 **two thirds of these teachers** Pulliam, *History of Education*, 5th ed., 102.
210 **Five Formal Steps** Ibid., 105–6.

210   **"a scientific way of tying"** Ibid. see Hoyt, *History of Modern Education.*

210   **"Lock-step"** Pulliam, *History of Education*, 5th ed., 106.

210   **At age twenty-four** Lear, *Rachel Carson*, 10–11.

210   **the Gilded Age collapsed** Bogart, *Economic History of the American People*, 693–94.

211   **"I can remember no"** Carson, *Lost Woods*, 148.

211   **"her family aloof"** Lear, *Rachel Carson*, 13.

211   **letter to a friend** Carson to Dorothy Freeman, in *Always, Rachel*, 7.

211   **"learning the birds and the insects"** Carson, *Lost Woods*, 148.

212   **"sensory impressions"** Carson and Freeman, *Always, Rachel*, 7.

212   **"I sincerely believe"** Carson, *Sense of Wonder*, 45.

212   **"just going through the woods"** Ibid., 18.

212   **"inborn sense of wonder"** Ibid., 45.

212   **"diet of facts"** Ibid.

212   **"no sermonizing"** Cornelia Meigs, ed., *A Critical History of Children's Literature: A Survey of Children's Books in English*, rev. ed. (London: Macmillan Company, 1969), 257.

212   **kids' imaginations** Ibid.

213   **"clean, genuine fun"** Linda Young and James Young, "Tribute to St. Nicholas."

213   **Twain published** Ibid.

213   **even set a poem** Sterling, *Sea and Earth*, 28.

213   **July 1914 issue** *St. Nicholas*, July 1914, vol. 61, no. 9, author's collection.

213   **"the heart of nature"** Frye, *St. Nicholas Anthology*, 407.

213   **Millay . . . "fairy wind"** Frye, *St. Nicholas Anthology*, 416, 421.

213   **"The Fairy Steeple"** *St. Nicholas*, July 1914, vol. 61, no. 9, author's collection.

214   **"a quality of fairyland"** Carson, *Sense of Wonder*, 39.

214   **"exactly the sound"** Ibid., 79.

214   **Franklin Glue Works** See Ross and Andorf, *Springdale.*

214   **"the sense of smell"** Carson, *Sense of Wonder*, 66.

215   **"dreary, uninspiring"** Lear, *Rachel Carson*, 9.

215   **tankage "Glue,"** How Products Are Made: vol. 5, http://www.madehow .com/Volume-5/Glue.html.

215   **even larger industry** Ross and Andorf, *Springdale.*

215   **The molten glass** Armstrong County Genealogy Project, *History of Armstrong County.*

215   **Creighton** Toker, *Pittsburgh.*

215   **half the world's supply** Paleontological Research Institution, "Story of Oil in Pennsylvania."

215   **"not a mussel, not a crawfish"** Pennsylvania Environmental Council "The Watershed Atlas of the Allegheny River," http://www.watershedatlas .org/timeline/fs_timeline.html [PEC, "Watershed Atlas"].

216   **smelting bauxite** *Pittsburgh Tribune-Review*, "Aluminum's Long History in Steel City," http://www.pittsburghlive.com/x/pittsburghtrib/print_430000.html; and G. L. Waldbott, A. W. Burgstahler, and H. L. McKinney, *Fluoridation:*

The Great Dilemma (Lawrence, KA: Coronado Press, 1978), 295–305, http://www.flouridealert.org/industry.htm.

216 **"the greatest variety of pollution"** PEC, "Watershed Atlas."
216 **"Big Money Making Development"** Ross and Andorf, *Springdale*.
216 **"the destruction of beauty"** Carson, *Lost Woods*, 161.
216 **dug up and hauled away** Ross and Andorf, *Springdale*, and Sterling, *Sea and Earth*, 30.
216 **The Mellon family . . . Two years later . . . class portrait** Ross and Andoy, *Springdale*.
217 **industrial education** Cremin, *Transformation of the School*, 50.
217 **In 1899, Dewey . . . "common ends"** Spring, *American School*, 244.
218 **"the promise of American life"** Cremin, *Transformation of the School*, 88.
218 **state Board of Ed** Pennsylvania Department of Education, "Records."
218 **a new emphasis** Cremin, *Transformation of the School*, 188–89.
218 **total of about three weeks** Sterling, *Sea and Earth*, 16.
218 **"The Little Brown House"** Lear, *Rachel Carson*, 17.
219 **vocabulary lists** Sterling, *Sea and Earth*, 19.
219 **Rachel's big sister** Lear, *Rachel Carson*, 22.
219 **league's stated goal** Meigs, *Critical History of Children's Literature*, 260.
219 **"intelligent patriotism"** Linda Young and James Young, "Tribute to St. Nicholas."
220 **"about a famous aviator"** Sterling, *Sea and Earth*, 25.
220 **Springdale's population** Ibid., 30.
220 **West Penn Power** Answers.com, "Dusquesne Light Holdings, Inc.," International Directory of Company Histories, Gale Group, http://www.answers.com/topic/duquesne-light-holdings-inc.
220 **American Water Works** Answers.com "Allegheny Energy, Inc.," International Directory of Company Histories Gale Group, http://www.answers.com/allegheny-energy-inc%20Power, and Ross and Andorf, *Springdale*.
220 **underground stream** Ross and Andorf, *Springdale*.
220 **infamous Harwick mine** See Washlaski, "Tribute to the Coal Miners."
220 **the mass grave** Report of the Department of Mines of Pennsylvania, Fourteenth Bituminous District, 1904 (Harrisburg, PA: Harrisburg Publishing Co., 1905), at http://freepages.genealogy.rootsweb.ancestry.com/~njm1/21harwk1.htm.
220 **Over in New Kensington** Allegheny Foothills Historical Society, *Where Wild Plum Trees Grew: Bicentennial Edition of Plum Borough History, 1788–1988*; 1988, at Bridges and Tunnels of Allegheny County Pennsylvania, http://pghbridges.com/newkenW/0604-4488/logansferrymine_tun.htm.
221 **No wonder Rachel's father** Sterling, *Sea and Earth*, 33.
221 **High-voltage lines** Ross and Andorf, *Springdale*.
221 **turning out war stories** Lear, *Rachel Carson*, 19.
221 **"Power City"** Ross and Andorf, *Springdale*.
222 **part-time work as** Lear, *Rachel Carson*, 21–23.
222 **her description of the evening** Ibid., 44.

223 **passionate private correspondence** See Carson and Freeman, *Always, Rachel.*

223 **"when I wakened in the night"** Ibid., 15.

223 **"My Favorite Recreation"** Carson, *Lost Woods*, 13.

223 **clear-cut lumbering** U.S. Department of Agriculture, Forest Service, "History of the Allegheny National Forest," http://www.fs.fed.us/r9/forests/allegheny/about/history.

224 **"barren hillsides"** Ibid.

224 **only .06 percent** PEC, "Watershed Atlas."

224 **two-thousand-square-foot quota** Ross and Andorf, *Springdale.*

224 **one Pittsburgh report** Freese, *Coal*, 153.

224 **"All around the nation"** Ibid., 150.

224 **"keepers of the house"** Ibid.

224 **"healthful rambles"** Lutts, *Nature Fakers*, 70.

225 **"Where did you find"** Comstock, *Handbook of Nature Study*, 122–23.

225 **in response to the industrial revolution** Ibid., xi–xii.

225 **"intelligent child of twelve"** Ibid., xiii.

225 **almost every state's curriculum** Kevin C. Armitage, " 'The Child Is Born a Naturalist': Nature Study, Woodcraft Indians, and the Theory of Recapitulation," in *Journal of Gilded Age and Progressive Era*, vol. 6, issue 1; the History Cooperative, http://www.historycooperative.org/journalis/jga/6.1/armitage.html.

225 **"love of the beautiful"** Comstock, *Handbook of Nature Study*, 1–2.

225 **"the great remedy"** Cremin, *Transformation of the School*, 77.

225 **integrate their curriculum** See Tolley, *Science Education of American Girls*, chapter 6, "Study Nature, Not Books."

226 **One textbook suggested** Lutts, *Nature Fakers*, 27.

226 **"not elementary science"** Comstock, *Handbook of Nature Study*, 5.

226 **"the child is unconscious"** Ibid., 6.

226 **"*because she wished to know*"** Ibid., 16.

226 **"Study nature"** Tolley, *Science Education of American Girls*, 2.

226 **"Nature has been our slave"** Armitage, "Child Is Born a Naturalist."

226 **Allegheny National Forest** PEC, "The Watershed Atlas of the Allegheny River."

226 **"a sustainable way"** U.S. Department of Agriculture, "History of the Allegheny National Forest."

227 **"the great Redman"** Armitage, "Child Is Born a Naturalist."

227 **"a little 'Injun' "** Ibid.

227 **"barbarian virtues"** Ibid.

227 **"negroes and Indians"** Ibid.

227 **Parnassus High** Lear, *Rachel Carson*, 23–24.

227 **Alcoa plant** Freese, *Coal*, 168–71, and Roy A. Hunt, "The Aluminum Pioneers," speech delivered April 26, 1951, http://www.rahuntfdn.org/images/History/AlumPioneers.pdf.

227 **"macabre and depressing"** Lorant, *Pittsburgh*, 327–28.

228 **Springdale bought it** Ross and Andorf, *Springdale*.
228 **first in her class** Lear, *Rachel Carson*, 24–25.
228 **"I had given up"** Ibid., 80.
228 **"Even as a child"** Carson, *Lost Woods*, 54.
229 **"True understanding"** Carson, *Edge of the Sea*, vii–viii.
229 **"Mysterious and eerie"** Carson, *Sea Around Us*, 105.
229 **"infinitely healing"** Carson, *Sense of Wonder*, 88.
229 **"sea of carcinogens"** Carson, *Silent Spring*, 213.
229 **"whether any civilization"** Ibid., 95.

JACK

230 **Carl Sandburg poem** Sandburg, "Muckers," in *Chicago Poems*, http://poetry
      .eserver.org/chicago-poems.txt.
230 **Grandfather Kennedy** Dallek, *Unfinished Life*, 9.
231 **Honey Fitz** Ibid., 10.
231 **one third Irish and rife** Kessler, *Sins of the Father*, 9.
231 **"without any resources"** "Presidential Countdown–Mr. Kennedy: a Pro-
      file," the Honorable John F. Kennedy interviewed by Walter Cronkite, as
      broadcast over the CBS television network, September 20, 1960; transcript
      at http://www.jfklink.com/speeches/joint/joint190960_kennedyprofile.html.
231 **"servants and teams of"** Kessler, *Sins of the Father*, 12.
231 **he was awful** Ibid., 17.
232 **"if we could stick it out"** Dallek, *Unfinished Life*, 16.
232 **Joe was accepted at** Kessler, *Sins of the Father*, 17.
232 **founder of two banks** Ibid., 12, and Dallek, *Unfinished Life*, 8.
232 **"big old rambling"** Dallek, *Unfinished Life*, 11.
232 **issued a "command"** Goodwin, *Fitzgeralds and the Kennedys*, 104.
232 **twenty-five thousand dollars** Ibid., 110.
232 **private lessons in French** Dallek, *Unfinished Life*, 12.
232 **"fresh air and open spaces"** Rose Fitzgerald Kennedy, *Times to Remem-
      ber*, 23.
232 **incorporated into the city** Tucci, *Built in Boston*, 74.
232 **"greatest regret"** Goodwin, *Fitzgeralds and the Kennedys*, 143–44.
233 **Honey Fitz was helping** Ibid., 239.
233 **got a tip** Hamilton, *J.F.K.*, 23.
233 **"not as luxurious as"** *Letters of Joseph P. Kennedy*, 14.
233 **one of the wealthiest towns** Van Sickle, *Public Schools of Brookline,* 1, 35.
233 **"morals, and social contact"** Ibid., 27.
233 **Brookline had begun** Tucci, *Built in Boston*, 74; Curtis, *History of the Town of
      Brookline*.317; and Denehy, *History of Brookline*.
233 **Though 30 percent** Van Sickle, *Public Schools of Brookline*, 31.
234 **Brookline's unifying principal** Tucci, *Built in Barton*, 84.
234 **no manufacturing** Denehy, *History of Brookline*, 5.
234 **"like the Saltonstalls"** Hamilton, *J.F.K.*, 34.

234   **white-collar job** Kessler, *Sins of the Father*, 32–33.

234   **up to a Rolls-Royce** Hamilton, *J.F.K.*, 42.

234   **"wouldn't accept a Catholic school"** Goodwin, *Fitzgeralds and the Kennedys*, 457.

234   **Edward Devotion served** Van Sickle, *Public Schools of Brookline*, 82–167.

234   **top salaries** Ibid., 62.

235   **"cultivated, well-educated"** Ibid., 181, 264–46.

235   **"natural reader"** Rose Fitzgerald Kennedy, *Times to Remember*, 110.

235   **"not necessarily the ones"** Ibid., 111.

235   **"I am getting on all right"** *Letters of Joseph P. Kennedy*, 40.

235   **tripled his investment** Kessler, *Sins of the Father*, 34.

235   **five-million-dollar pool** Goodwin, *Fitzgeralds and the Kennedys*, 330–36.

235   **bootleggers** Kessler, *Sins of the Father*, 35–38.

235   **"desire for the freedom"** Goodwin, *Fitzgeralds and the Kennedys*, 331.

235   **Social Register families** Dallek, *Unfinished Life*, 27.

236   **"people have a better time"** Hamilton, *J.F.K.*, 34.

236   **chauffeur-driven limousine** Ibid., 55.

236   **"crimson knickers"** Ibid., 53.

236   **Noble and Greenough's** Sharon Cummins "A Noble Pursuit," *Log*, Kennebunkport Historical Society, http://www.mykennebunks.com/a_noble _pursuit.htm.

236   **"very drill, drill"** Hamilton, *J.F.K.*, 56.

236   **on its board** Goodwin, *Fitzgeralds and the Kennedys*, 368.

236   **textile workers went out on strike** Brecher, *Strike!*, 115.

236   **"Lenin and Trotsky"** Ibid., 116.

236   **resurgent Ku Klux Klan** See Zinn's *People's History*, and Richard O. Boyer and Herbert M. Morais, *Labor's Untold Story*, 222–23.

237   **set quotas** See Spring, *American School*, 297, and Gould, *Mismeasure of Man*, 261.

237   For Sacco and Vanzetti, see Russell, *Sacco and Vanzetti*.

237   **"the deterioration of"** Gould, *Mismeasure of Man*, 260.

237   **long-held assumptions** Spring, *American School*, 301.

237   **"immediately useful"** Gould, *Mismeasure of Man*, 211.

237   **"fundamentally an instrument"** N. J. Block and Gerald Dworkin, eds., *The I.Q. Controversy* (New York: Pantheon Books, 1976), 11.

238   **"rulers of the realm"** Spring, *American School*, 300.

238   **"all the children very early"** Rose Fitzgerald Kennedy, *Times to Remember*, 152.

238   **She was shocked** Hamilton, *J.F.K.*, 50.

238   **a hundred thousand dollars annually** Kessler, *Sins of the Father*, 56.

238   **Tom Mix** Hamilton, *J.F.K.*, 61.

238   **"disquieting"** Ibid., 61–62.

238   **"blow to the stomach"** Dallek, *Unfinished Life*, 29.

239   **Frank Hackett** Hackett, *Quickened Spirit*, 6–24.

239   **preferred "independent"** Ibid., 188.

239 **"into our colleges"** Ibid., 190.

239 **"home-like atmosphere"** Ibid., 64.

239 **his editorial comments** Ibid., 85.

239 **"unified attack"** Ibid., 118.

240 **"Work!"** Ibid., 89.

240 **best composition** Hamilton, *J.F.K.*, 75.

240 **"Learning from books"** Powell, *Lessons from Privilege*, 126.

240 **"the first requisite"** Goodwin, *Fitzgeralds and the Kennedys*, 478.

240 **sons of bank presidents** Hackett, *Quickened Spirit*, 69.

240 **"isn't what you learn"** Powell, *Lessons from Privilege*, 45.

240 **"undemocratic"** Sargent, *Brief Guide to Schools*, 8–9.

240 **a third of the nation's** Pulliam, *History of Education*, 5th ed., 121.

241 **"A 1916 survey"** Spring, *American School*, 292.

241 **"for transmitting the traditions"** C. Wright Mills, *The Power Elite*, quoted in Cookson and Persell, *Preparing for Power*, 18.

241 **"constantly drilled"** John F. Kennedy in "Presidential Countdown," the CBS Cronkite interview, 1960.

241 **"don't want any losers"** Rose Fitzgerald Kennedy, *Times to Remember*, 143.

241 **"effective"** Ibid., 107.

241 **"about the only times"** Ibid., 102, 105.

241 **"topics of the day"** Ibid., 104.

241 **Crownlands** Bronxville Centennial Celebration, *Building a Suburban Village*, 314–16.

242 **"intense, secretive circles"** Burns, *John Kennedy*, 16.

242 **RKO** Hamilton, *J.F.K.*, 69–70.

242 **"taboo"** Kessler, *Sins of the Father*, 47.

242 **"simply didn't meet"** Rose Fitzgerald Kennedy, *Times to Remember*, 116.

242 **"I have never discussed money"** Burns, *John Kennedy*, 20.

242 **a mock plea** Lieberson, *John Fitzgerald Kennedy*, 6, and Rose Fitzgerald Kennedy, *Times to Remember*, 113.

242 **never brought to the table** Kessler, *Sins of the Father*, 81.

242 **"We didn't have opinions"** Ibid., 43.

243 **sliding in late** Rose Fitzgerald Kennedy, *Times to Remember*, 102.

243 **"among the highest in the country"** Ibid., 166.

243 **"drilling facts"** Richard M. Perdew, "A Community School," in Bronxville Diamond Jubilee Committee, *Bronxville*, 71–73.

243 **country clubs, at-home teas** Dorée Smedley, "The Early Nineteen Hundreds," in Bronxville Diamond Jubilee Committee, *Bronxville*, 47.

243 **"the stock market crowd"** Ibid., 93.

243 **"black, Catholic, or Jew"** Bronxville Centennial Celebration, *Building a Suburban Village*, 18.

243 **"Restrictions"** Ibid.

243 **private school curriculum followed** Powell, *Lessons from Privilege*, 139.

244 **on the English essay** Ibid., 130.

244 **about 50 percent of Harvard students** Ibid., 127.

244 **twenty years later** Ibid.
244 **McGeorge Bundy** Ibid., 136.
244 **seven out of twenty-one seniors** Dallek, *Unfinished Life*, 30.
244 **"a pretty good place"** Ibid.
244 **He took history, grammar** Lieberson, *John Fitzgerald Kennedy*, 10.
244 **also taught morals** Stossel, *Sarge*, 26.
244 **"a whole lot of religion"** Dallek, *Unfinished Life*, 30.
244 **"highly reserved"** Stossel, *Sarge*, 21.
244 **"things like *Ivanhoe*"** Burns, *John Kennedy*, 24.
245 **"the Market Slump"** Ibid., 25.
245 **while running for president** Dallek, *Unfinished Life*, 31.
245 **trading was done on credit** Phillips, *From the Crash to the Blitz*, 16–27.
245 **"a shoeshine boy"** Goodwin, *Fitzgeralds and the Kennedys*, 421.
245 **value of equities** Phillips, *From the Crash to the Blitz*, 32.
245 **fewer than half a million** Piven and Cloward, *Poor People's Movements*, 46.
246 **"declared it a riot"** Ibid., 51–52.
246 *Times* **article reported** "Pathe Sale Voted at Stormy Meeting," *New York Times*, January 6, 1931, 26.
246 **this was insider trading** "Writ Asked to Stop Pathe Sale to R.K.O.," *New York Times*, January 25, 1931, 23.
246 **eight million people** Piven and Cloward, *Poor People's Movements*, 46.
246 **Even back in Bronxville** Hamilton, *J.F.K.*, 87.
246 **Henry Ford was cutting** Piven and Cloward, *Poor People's Movements*, 46.
246 **another million people** Ibid.
246 **wasted a year** *Letters of Joseph P. Kennedy*, 142.
246 **For George St. John,** see St. John, *Forty Years at School*.
247 **"a child"** Ibid., 83.
247 **funds for a chapel** Ibid., 114–26.
247 **the Depression had cut** Powell, *Lessons from Privilege*, 65.
247 **managed to buy more land** Phillips, *From the Crash to the Blitz*, 35, and St. John, *Forty Years at School*, 127–31.
247 **"one of the most worthwhile"** Goodwin, *Fitzgeralds and the Kennedys*, 459.
247 **varsity football and** Ibid., 459–60.
247 **"an aristocracy of the mind"** St. John, *Forty Years at School*, 146.
247 **"moral and spiritual force"** Ibid., 143.
247 **"like running a line for light"** Ibid., 101.
247 **Kipling poem** Ibid., 144.
247 **"instill the work habit"** Sargent, *Brid Guide to Schools*, 71.
247 **first year, he went out for** Goodwin, *Fitzgeralds and the Kennedys*, 462.
248 **in the infirmary by November** Dallek, *Unfinished Life*, 34.
248 **his high I.Q.** Lieberson, *John Fitzgerald Kennedy*, 15.
248 **"but is careless"** Hamilton, *J.F.K.*, 90–91.
248 **"lack of diligence"** Rose Fitzgerald Kennedy, *Times to Remember*, 177.
248 **"repeat his French and Latin"** Hamilton, *J.F.K.*, 93.
248 **His room was inspected** Ibid., 95

248 **"one of the most undependable"** Ibid.

248 **"Jack's winning smile"** Ibid., 93.

248 **"couldn't or wouldn't"** Rose Fitzgerald Kennedy, *Times to Remember*, 177.

248 **"arranged acquaintanceships"** Powell, *Lessons from Privilege*, 44.

248 **"a gang spirit"** Hamilton, *J.F.K.*, 98.

248 **"a square guy"** St. John, *Forty Years at School*, 12.

249 **One 1928 study** Spring, *American School*, 340.

249 **"fiery Boston and"** "The 'Cabinet' Mr. Roosevelt Already Has," *New York Times*, November 20, 1932, xx2.

249 **"can't tell you how unhappy"** *Letters of Joseph P. Kennedy*, 120.

249 **New Haven hospital** Dallek, *Unfinished Life*, 35.

249 **on its society** page "Palm Beach Has Round of Parties," *New York Times*, March 27, 1934, 18.

249 **an essay for English class** *Letters of Joseph P. Kennedy*, 133.

250 **"stop fooling around"** Burns, *John Kennedy*, 27.

250 **"the most childish"** Hamilton, *J.F.K.*, 121.

250 **"methods of coercion"** Ibid., 106, 117.

250 **"all for Jack"** Ibid., 120.

250 **A year at Choate now cost** Phillips, *From the Crash to the Blitz*, 34, and Sargent, *Brief Guide to Schools*, 71.

250 **"colossally selfish"** Hamilton, *J.F.K.*, 124.

251 **"the worst things we did"** Goodwin, *Fitzgeralds and the Kennedys*, 487.

251 **"to buck the system"** Ibid., 486.

251 **"he saw red"** Rose Fitzgerald Kennedy, *Times to Remember*, 181.

251 **"public enemies"** Hamilton, *J.F.K.*, 125.

251 **"the chief mover"** Rose Fitzgerald Kennedy, *Times to Remember*, 182.

251 **"to catch a thief"** Hamilton, *J.F.K.*, 109.

251 **the next sleeper train** Kessler, *Sins of the Father*, 119.

251 **"reduced Jack's conceit"** Lieberson, *John Fitzgerald Kennedy*, 17.

251 **"that crazy Muckers Club"** Goodwin, *Fitzgeralds and the Kennedys*, 488.

252 **"He does not define himself"** Hamilton, *J.F.K.*, 130.

252 **"both the foundation and"** John F. Kennedy, *Wisdom of JFK*, 40.

252 **"silly episode"** Rose Fitzgerald Kennedy, *Times to Remember*, 183.

252 **There's a photograph** Lieberson, *John Fitzgerald Kennedy*, 20.

ELVIS

253 **John Presley** See Dundy, *Elvis and Gladys*, 59–61, and Donald W. Presley and Edwin C. Dunn, *The Rhineland to Graceland: The Story of the Presley Family and Their German Heritage Revealed*, http://freepages.genealogy.rootsweb.ancestry .com/~eddunn/book/toc.html.

254 **into East Tupelo** Guralnick, *Last Train to Memphis*, 11; Dundy, *Elvis and Gladys*, 61; and the 1930 federal census as reproduced at http://www .familytreeexpert.com/1930census/1930presleycensus.htm.

254 **it worked the Mansells** Dundy, *Elvis and Gladys*, 14–24.

254   **three men alone** Grisham, *Tupelo*, 22.

254   **eight to nine months of the year** Dundy, *Elvis and Gladys*, 32.

254   **picking 100, 150 pounds** Maharidge and Williamson, *And Their Children After Them*, 28.

254   **a stop on the Mobile railroad** Grisham, *Tupelo*, 28.

254   **erosion, cotton prices** Federal Writers' Project, *Mississippi*, 434.

255   **five-hundred-spindle mill** Grisham, *Tupelo*, 47, and Strickland, *A History of Cotton Mills*.

255   **By 1920** Federal Writers' Project, *Mississippi*, 255.

255   **floated a bond** Grisham, *Tupelo*, 46–50.

255   **Carnation milk** Ibid., 83.

255   **Gladys Smith made the shift** Dundy, *Elvis and Gladys*, 41–48.

255   **on a single April day** McCarty, *Depression and Hard Times*.

255   **Franklin Roosevelt passed through** Tobey, *Technology as Freedom*.

256   **He'd quit school** Guralnick, *Last Train to Memphis*, 12.

256   **"change in the looks"** Tobey, *Technology as Freedom*.

256   **"generations of unthinking exploitation"** Maharidge and Williamson, *And Their Children After Them*, 15.

256   **the shotgun shack** Guralnick, *Last Train to Memphis*, 12.

256   **A tornado** Grisham, *Tupelo*, 87.

257   **starvation wages** Ibid., 105.

257   **organizer Myles Horton** Glen, *Highlander*, 84.

257   **from ten to fifteen dollars** Grisham, *Tupelo*, 105.

257   **across the South** Tindall, *Emergence of the New South*, 520.

257   For the Tupelo strike, see Strickland, *History of Cotton Mills*.

257   **a female organizer** Tindall, *Emergence of the New South*, 525.

257   **Another local agitator** Grisham, *Tupelo*, 106.

258   **"capitalism was on its"** *Autobiography of Myles Horton*, 81.

258   **Southern enclosure movement** Woods, *Development Arrested*, 122–31.

258   **doling out day-work** Clayton and Heard, *Elvis Up Close*, 11.

258   **Bean wanted to teach Vernon** Guralnick, *Last Train to Memphis*, 14.

258   **"crimes of hunger"** Oshinsky, *Worse Than Slavery*, 164.

258   **on commodities . . . work at a laundry** Guralnick, *Last Train to Memphis*, 14, and Clayton and Heard, *Elvis Up Close*, 12.

258   **"never had any luxuries"** Osborne, *Elvis Word for Word*, 17.

258   **put up a wooden building** Dundy, *Elvis and Gladys*, 73.

258   **"just a little fellow"** Guralnick, *Last Train to Memphis*, 14.

259   **"grew up with it"** Osborne, *Elvis Word for Word*, 243.

259   **Acts 1:8** Stanley M. Horton, *Azusa Street Mission*.

259   For early-twentieth-century Pentecostals, see Blumhofer, *Restoring the Faith*, especially 11.

259   **"fell upon me and filled me"** McGee, *William J. Seymour*.

259   **"like as of fire"** Acts 2; see Robert Mapes Anderson, *Vision of the Disinherited: The Making of American Pentecostalism* (New York: Oxford University Press, 1979), 20–22.

260 **singing as anarchy** Anderson, *Vision of the Disinherited*, 37.

260 **"rising and swelling"** Riss, *Singing in the Spirit*.

260 **"last quivering note"** Aimee Semple McPherson, 1918, quoted in Riss, *Singing in the Spirit*.

260 **"negroisms"** Blumhofer, *Restoring the Faith*, 56.

260 **"The color line"** Bartleman, *Azusa Street*, xviii, quoted in McGee, *William J. Seymour*.

260 **revival swept through** Maharidge and Williamson, *And Their Children After Them*, 13.

260 **By World War I** Blumhofer, *Restoring the Faith*, 134.

260 **"white man's church"** Anderson, *Vision of the Disinherited*, 168, 190.

261 **"state-subsidized affirmative action"** Woods, *Development Arrested*, 142.

261 **a shipyard on the Gulf Coast** Farrell, *Not Just Farms Anymore*.

261 **"We're not staying"** Dundy, *Elvis and Gladys*, 87.

261 **six-million-dollar funding increase** Kinsey, *Giving a Voice*.

261 **The wood-frame building** Clayton and Heard, *Elvis Up Close*, 24.

261 **"shared source of pride"** Dundy, *Elvis and Gladys*, 90.

261 **"My mama never let me"** Guralnick, *Last Train to Memphis*, 13.

261 **joined the local carpenter's union** *Elvis: The Official Auction Featuring Items from the Archives of Graceland*, Guernsy's, Harry N. Abrams, New York, 1999, 35 [*Auction*].

262 **"weren't any old plantation owners"** Willey, *Bitter Roots and Sweet Faith*, 4.

262 **going to returning vets** Ibid.

262 **talent show broadcast** Boussiron, *Elvis*, 28.

262 **on the radio ten times** Ibid., 30–33.

262 **"I took the guitar"** Guralnick, *Last Train to Memphis*, 23.

262 **"gathering at each other's house"** Clayton and Heard, *Elvis Up Close*, 15.

262 **"the first thing I ever heard"** Osborne, *Elvis Word for Word*, 224.

263 **"a Blackwood Brothers type"** Guralnick, *Last Train to Memphis*, 20.

263 **"followed quartet music"** Osborne, *Elvis Word for Word*, 243.

263 **put together a second group** Terrell, *Music Men*, 107.

263 **"We warn God's people"** James R. Goff Jr., *Southern Gospel's Preacher Boys: Remembering the Couriers*, AG Heritage, 2007, http://ifphc.org/Uploads/Heritage/An_01_02.pdf.

263 **broadcast three times a day** Terrell, *Music Men*, 106.

263 **loved Gene Autry** Clayton and Heard, *Elvis Up Close*, 27.

263 **showed Wild West movies** Willey, *Bitter Roots and Sweet Faith*, 12.

263 **according to one censor** Spring, *American School*, 341.

263 **"out of sight . . . intersect only"** Grisham, *Tupelo*, 139.

263 **about 40 percent** Federal Writers' Project, *Mississippi*, 262.

264 **"Cs in reading"** *Auction*, 35.

264 **"There were times"** Guralnick, *Last Train to Memphis*, 29.

264 **"consideration for other people's"** Osborne, *Elvis Word for Word*, 192.

264 **"When I grow up"** Guralnick, *Last Train to Memphis*, 16.

264 **twenty-one-dollar milk bill** *Auction*, 35.

264 **"a common laborer"** Dundy, *Elvis and Gladys*, 10.

264 **"Per Person, Per Acre"** Grisham, *Tupelo*, 91.

265 **Tupelo Model** Ibid., 93–99.

265 **"20 percent of Mississippi's"** Ibid., 100.

265 **"Dad packed"** Dundy, *Elvis and Gladys*, 132.

265 **The family moved into** Guralnick, *Last Train to Memphis*, 32.

265 **an eighth-grade education was** U.S. Census Bureau, *Census Tract Statistics, Memphis Tennessee*, 1950 Population Census Report, vol. 3, ch. 30 (Washington, DC: Government Printing Office, 1952), www2.census.gov/prod2/decennial/documents/41557421v3p2ch09.pdf [Census Bureau, *Memphis*].

265 **finished the year** Dundy, *Elvis and Gladys*, 135.

266 **Edward Crump** Tucker, *Memphis Since Crump*, 17.

266 **"a white man's country"** Ibid., 19.

266 **"the balance of my life"** Ibid., 57.

266 **"lick the boots"** Ibid., 39.

266 **Henry Ford's Model T** Johnson, *Art of Architecture*.

266 **Kimberly-Clark** Tindall, *Emergence of the New South*, 694.

266 **aggressively courted** Cobb, *Selling of the South*, 35.

266 **In 1949, executives** National Planning Association study, cited in ibid., 210–11.

266 **routinely did the hardest.** See Honey, *Power of Remembering*.

266 **Although wages in the South** Cobb, *Selling of the South*, 114, 210.

267 **nineteen hundred dollars a year** Guralnick, *Last Train to Memphis*, 33.

267 **Lauderdale Courts** See Johnson, *Art of Architecture*.

267 **wasn't hard to be poor enough** Guralnick, *Last Train to Memphis*, 33, and Census Bureau, *Memphis*.

267 **almost none of** Johnson, *Art of Architecture*.

267 **"nice and deserving"** Guralnick, *Last Train to Memphis*, 33.

267 **"desirable privacy"** Johnson, *Art of Architecture*.

267 **got special mention** Guralnick, *Last Train to Memphis*, 33.

267 **"From slums to"** Ibid.

267 **sixteen hundred students** Dundy, *Elvis and Gladys*, 135.

267 **"a wide range of income"** T. Don Sage, Humes Class of 1953 fiftieth reunion, http://humeshighclassof53.com/looking_back.htm.

267 **more than many people at the Courts** Census Bureau, *Memphis*.

267 **freshman and sophomore years** Guralnick, *Last Train to Memphis*, 8, 36.

268 **one of the subdivisions** Johnson, *Arts of Architecture*.

268 **took wood shop** Guralnick, *Last Train to Memphis*, 36.

268 **"belonged to the Speech Club."** Dundy, *Elvis and Gladys*, 135.

268 **"the value of citizenship"** Title 10, U.S. Code, cited in Arthur T. Coumbe and Lee S. Harford, *U.S. Army Cadet Command*, U.S. Army Cadet Command, Fort Monroe, Virginia, 1996, https://www.usarmyjrotc.com/jrotc/dt2_History/history.html.

268 **program's popularity had jumped** *ROTC History (Unofficial)*, extracted from Coumbe, http://academic.udayton.edu/rotc/hist-rotc.htm.

268   **as one pamphlet put it** Spring, *American School*, 365.

268   **Honor Guard** Sage, Humes Class of 1953 fiftieth reunion.

269   **good-conduct certificate** Dundy, *Elvis and Gladys*, 135.

269   **same munitions manufacturer** Guralnick, *Last Train to Memphis*, 43.

269   **"I had no idea"** Clayton and Heard, *Elvis Up Close*, 44.

269   **Hank Williams** Malone, *Country Music USA*, 236.

269   **"Tennessee Waltz"** Ibid., 231.

270   **"Red Foley"** "Red Foley" liner notes by John W. Rumble, on *Red Foley*, MCAD-10084, produced by the Country Music Hall of Fame and Museum, 1994.

270   **over a local radio station** Guralnick, *Last Train to Memphis*, 46.

270   **"would sing all night"** Osborne, *Elvis Word for Word*, 244.

270   **New Year's Day 1953** Malone, *Country Music U.S.A.*, 237.

270   **combined incomes** Guralnick, *Last Train to Memphis*, 49.

270   **in blackface** Sage, Humes Class of 1953 fiftieth reunion.

270   **"amazing how popular I became"** Guralnick, *Last Train to Memphis*, 53.

271   **The day after graduation** *Auction*, 38.

271   **sixty dollars a week** Ibid., 39.

271   **"wanted to be a doctor"** Osborne, *Elvis Word for Word*, 187.

271   **"I don't sound like"** Guralnick, *Last Train to Memphis*, 63.

271   **"Little by little"** Osborne, *Elvis Word for Word*, 190.

271   **"poor people called poor"** Elvis's radio interview with James E. Hamill, Flower Pentecostal Heritage Center, http://odeo.com/audio/8094773/view.

271   **"simple songs"** Goff, *Southern Gospel's Preacher Boys*.

272   **"didn't have an opening"** *Blackwood Brothers and Elvis*, http://www.biwa.ne.jp/~presley/elnews-Blackwoods.htm.

272   **East Trigg Baptist** Guralnick, *Last Train to Memphis*, 46–52.

272   **"the fight for rights"** Reagon, *We'll Understand It Better By and By*, 201.

272   **Mahalia had carefully studied** Horace Clarence Boyer and Lloyd Yearwood, *How Sweet the Sound*, 89.

272   **"absentminded"** Guralnick, *Last Train to Memphis*, 84.

273   **"for several weeks"** *Blackwood Brothers and Elvis*.

273   **spiky flattop** Guralnick, *Last Train to Memphis*, 88.

273   **"More or less"** Osborne, *Elvis Word for Word*, 30.

273   **"going by impulse"** Ibid., 192.

274   **"That's not it"** Ibid., 53.

274   **"I have never used that"** Ibid., 52.

274   **"Every dream I ever"** Ibid., 232.

SELECTED BIBLIOGRAPHY

Adams, Abigail. *New Letters of Abigail Adams: 1788–1801*. Edited and with an introduction by Stewart Mitchell. Boston: Houghton Mifflin, 1947.

——. *Letters of Mrs. Adams, the Wife of John Adams*. With an introduction by her grandson, Charles Francis Adams. Boston: Wilkins, Carter, and Company, 1848.

Adams, Abigail, and John Adams. *The Book of Abigail and John: Selected Letters of the Adams Family, 1762–84*. Edited by L. H. Butterfield, Marc Friedlaender, and Mary-Jo Kline. Cambridge, MA: Harvard University Press, 1975.

Adams, Henry. *The Education of Henry Adams*. Boston: Houghton Mifflin, 1918.

Adams, John. diary 3, 1759, *Adams Family Papers: An Electronic Archive*, Massachusetts Historical Society, http://masshist.org/digitaladams/aea/cfm/doc.cfm?id=D3.

African American Registry. "The African Free School Opens." http://www.aaregistry .com/african_american_history/425/The_African_Free_School_opens.

Anderson, Robert Mapes. *Vision of the Disinherited: The Making of American Pentecostalism*. New York: Oxford University Press, 1979.

Ayers, Edward L. *The Promise of the New South: Life After Reconstruction*. New York: Oxford University Press, 1992.

Babson, Steve, with Ron Alpern, Dave Elsila, and John Revitte. *Working Detroit: The Making of a Union Town*. New York: Adama Books, 1984.

Bartleman, Frank. *Azusa Street*. South Plainfield, NJ: Bridge Publishing, 1980 (from newspaper articles, 1906).

Berlin, Ira, and Leslie M. Harris, eds. *Slavery in New York*. New York: New Press, 2005.

Beveridge, Albert J. *Abraham Lincoln: 1809–1858*, vol. 1. Boston: Houghton Mifflin, 1928. Reprint, St. Clair Shores, MI: Scholarly Press, 1971.

Block, N. J., and Gerald Dworkin, eds. *The I.Q. Controversy*. New York: Pantheon Books, 1976.

Blumhofer, Edith L. *Restoring the Faith: The Assemblies of God, Pentecostalism, and American Culture*. Urbana and Chicago: University of Illinois Press, 1993.

Bober, Natalie S. *Abigail Adams: Witness to a Revolution.* New York: Atheneum, 1995.

Bogart, Ernest Ludlow. *Economic History of the American People.* New York: Longmans, Green and Company, 1937.

Booraem, Hendrik. *Young Hickory: The Making of Andrew Jackson.* Dallas: Taylor Trade Publishing, 2001.

Boussiron, Richard. *Elvis: A Musical Inventory, 1939–55.* York, England: Music Mentor Books, 2004.

Boyer, Horace Clarence, and Lloyd Yearwood. *How Sweet the Sound: The Golden Age of Gospel.* Washington, DC: Elliot and Clark, 1995.

Boyer, Richard O., and Herbert M. Morais. *Labor's Untold Story.* New York: United Electrical, Radio and Machine Workers of America, 1955 (5th ed., 1972).

Braddy, Nella. *Anne Sullivan Macy: The Story Behind Helen Keller.* Garden City, NY: Doubleday, Doran and Company, 1933.

Brands, H. W. *Andrew Jackson: His Life and Times.* New York: Doubleday, 2005.

Brecher, Jeremy. *Strike!* San Francisco: Straight Arrow Books, 1972.

Bronxville Centennial Celebration. *Building a Suburban Village: Bronxville, New York, 1898–1998.* Bronxville, NY: Bronxville Centennial Celebration, 1998.

Bronxville Diamond Jubilee Committee. *Bronxville: Views and Vignettes, 1898–1973.* Bronxville, NY: Bronxville Diamond Jubilee Committee, 1974.

Burns, James MacGregor. *John Kennedy: A Political Profile.* New York: Harcourt, Brace and World, 1961.

Burstein, Andrew. *The Passion of Andrew Jackson.* New York: Alfred A. Knopf, 2003.

Canfield, Gae Whitney. *Sarah Winnemucca of the Northern Paiutes.* Norman, OK: University of Oklahoma Press, 1983.

Cannadine, David. *Mellon: An American Life.* New York: Alfred A. Knopf, 2006.

Carson, Rachel. *The Edge of the Sea.* Cambridge, MA: Riverside Press, 1955.

———. *Lost Woods: The Discovered Writings of Rachel Carson.* Edited by Linda Lear. Boston: Beacon Press, 1998.

———. *The Sea Around Us.* New York: Oxford University Press, 1950–51; illustrated commemorative edition, 2003.

———. *The Sense of Wonder.* New York: Harper & Row, copyright 1956, published 1965.

———. *Silent Spring.* New York: Crest Book, 1964.

Carson, Rachel, and Dorothy Freeman. *Always, Rachel: The Letters of Rachel Carson and Dorothy Freeman, 1952–1964.* Edited by Martha Freeman. Boston: Beach Press, 1995.

Catton, Bruce. *Michigan: A Bicentennial History,* New York: W. W. Norton and Company, 1976.

Chaffin, Tom. *Pathfinder: John Charles Frémont and the Course of American Empire.* New York: Farrar, Straus and Giroux / Hill and Wang, 2002.

Chernow, Ron. *Alexander Hamilton.* New York: Penguin Press, 2004.

Clayton, Rose, and Dick Heard, eds. *Elvis Up Close: In the Words of Those Who Knew Him Best.* Atlanta: Turner Publishing, 1994.

Clinton, Governor DeWitt. "Address on Monitorial Education." 1809. In William

Bourne, *History of the Public School Society of the City of New York.* 1870. http://www
.constitution.org/lanc/dewitt_clinton.htm.

Cobb, James C. *The Selling of the South: The Southern Crusade for Industrial Development,
1936–1990.* Urbana and Chicago: University of Illinois Press, 1993.

Collier, Peter, and David Horowitz. *The Fords: An American Epic.* New York: Summit
Books, 1987.

Commager, Henry Steele, and Richard B. Morris. *The Spirit of 'Seventy-Six: The Story
of the American Revolution as Told by Participants.* Indianapolis and New York: Bobbs-
Merrill, 1958.

Comstock, Anna Botsford. *Handbook of Nature Study.* Ithaca, NY: Comstock Publishing, Cornell University Press, 1911, revised edition 1939.

Conn, Howard J. *The First Congregational Church of Great Barrington: 1743–1943: A
History.* Great Barrington, MA: Berkshire Courier, 1943.

Cooke, Robin Hillyer, ed. *Historic Homes and Institutions and Genealogical and Personal
Memories of Berkshire County, Massachusetts.* New York: Lewis Publishing, 1906.

Cookson, Peter W., and Caroline Hughes Persell. *Preparing for Power: America's Elite
Boarding Schools.* New York: Basic Books, 1985.

Cott, Nancy, ed. *No Small Courage: A History of Women in the United States.* New York:
Oxford University Press, 2000.

Cremin, Lawrence A. *American Education: The National Experience, 1783–1876.* New
York: Harper & Row, 1980.

———. *The Transformation of the School: Progressivism in American Education, 1876–1957.*
New York: Vintage Books, 1961.

Crumine, Boyd, ed. *History of Washington County, Pennsylvania with Biographical Sketches
of Many of Its Pioneers and Prominent Men.* Philadelphia: L. H. Everts and Co., 1882.

Curtis, John Gould. *History of the Town of Brookline, Massachusetts.* Boston: Houghton
Mifflin, 1933.

Dallek, Robert. *An Unfinished Life: John F. Kennedy, 1917–1963.* Boston: Little,
Brown and Company, 2003.

Denehy, John William. *A History of Brookline, Massachusetts: From the First Settlement of
Muddy River Until the Present Time, 1630–1906.* Brookline, MA: Brookline Press,
1906.

Dilliard, Maud Esther. *An Album of New Netherland: Dutch Colonial Antiques and Architecture.* New York: Bramhall House, 1963.

Donald, David Herbert. *Lincoln.* New York: Simon & Schuster, 1995.

Drew, Donna. *A History of Monument Mills, Housatonic, Ma.* Great Barrington, MA:
Attic Revival Press, 1984.

Drutchas, Geoffrey G. "The Man with a Capital Design," *Michigan History,* March-
April 2002. http://www.michiganhistorymagazine.com/extra/politics/drutchas2002
.pdf.

Du Bois, W. E. B. *Against Racism: Unpublished Essays, Papers, Addresses, 1887–1961.*
Edited by Herbert Aptheker. Amherst: University of Massachusetts Press,
1985.

———. *The Autobiography of W. E. B. Du Bois.* International Publishers, 1968.

——. *Darkwater: Voices from Within the Veil.* New York: Harcourt, Brace and Howe, 1920.

——. *The Education of Black People: Ten Critiques, 1906–1960.* Amherst: University of Massachusetts Press, 1973.

——. *The Seventh Son: The Thoughts and Writings of W. E. B. Du Bois.* 2 vols. New York: Random House, 1971.

Dunbar, Willis Frederick. *Michigan: A History of the Wolverine State.* Grand Rapids, MI: William B. Eerdmans Publishing, 1965.

Dundy, Elaine. *Elvis and Gladys.* New York: Macmillan, 1985.

Elvis: The Official Auction Featuring Items from the Archives of Graceland, Guernsy's, New York: Harry N. Abrams, 1999.

Emerson, Ralph Waldo. *Selected Writings of Ralph Waldo Emerson.* New York: New American Library, 1965.

Euler, Robert C. *The Paiute People.* Phoenix: Indian Tribal Series, 1972.

Fabend, Firth Haring. *Zion on the Hudson: Dutch New York and New Jersey in the Age of Revivals.* New Brunswick, NJ: Rutgers University Press, 2000.

Farley, Reynolds, and Judy Mullin. "Detroit Dry Dock Company/Globe Trading Building." University of Michigan. http://detroit1701.org/Dry%20Dock.html.

Farmer, Silas. *History of Detroit and Wayne County and Early Michigan: A Chronological Cyclopedia of the Past and Present.* Detroit: Silas Farmer & Co., 1890.

Farrell, Sean. *Not Just Farms Anymore: The Effects of World War II on Mississippi's Economy.* Mississippi History Now, an online publication of the Mississippi Historical Society, September 2001. http://mshistory.k12.ms.us/index.php?id-247.

Federal Writers' Program. *Alabama: A Guide to the Deep South.* Work Projects Administration, American Guide Series. New York: Richard R. Smith, 1941 (republished 1973).

Federal Writers' Program. *Nevada: The Silver State.* Work Projects Administration, American Guide Series. Portland, OR: Binfords & Mott, 1940.

Federal Writers' Project. *Indiana: A Guide to the Hoosier State.* Works Progress Administration. New York: Oxford University Press, 1941.

Federal Writers' Project, *Kentucky: A Guide to the Bluegrass State.* Works Progress Administration. New York: Hastings House, 1954 (first published 1939).

Federal Writers' Project. *Mississippi: A Guide to the Magnolia State.* Works Progress Administration. New York: Hastings House, 1938.

Folts, James D. *History of the University of the State of New York and the State Education Department,* 1996, http://www.nysl.nysed.gov/edoc/education/sedhist.htm.

Foner, Eric. *Reconstruction: 1863–77.* Boston: Harper and Row, 1988.

Ford, Henry. *My Life and Work.* With Samuel Crowther. Mumbai, India: Wilco Publishing House, 2005 (originally published 1922).

Fox, John Marion. *The Charleston Story: Scenes from a City's History.* Harrisburg, PA: Stackpole Books, 1978.

Franklin, Benjamin. *The Autobiography of Benjamin Franklin.* New Haven, CT: Yale University Press, 1964.

——. *Writings.* New York: Library of America, 1987.

Frazer, Walter J. Jr. *Charleston! Charleston! The History of a Southern City.* Columbia, University of South Carolina Press, 1989.

Freese, Barbara. *Coal: A Human History.* Cambridge, MA: Perseus Publishing, 2003.

Frye, Burton C., ed. *A St. Nicholas Anthology: The Early Years.* New York: Meredith Press, 1969.

Gelles, Edith B. *Abigail Adams: A Writing Life.* New York: Routledge, 2002.

——. *Portia: The World of Abigail Adams.* Bloomington and Indianapolis: Indiana University Press, 1992.

Gellman, David L., and David Quigley, eds. *Jim Crow New York: A Documentary History of Race and Citizenship, 1777–1877.* New York and London: New York University Press, 2003.

Gilbert, Bil. *God Gave Us This Country: Tekamthi and the First American Civil War.* New York: Atheneum, 1989.

Glen, John M. *Highlander: No Ordinary School.* Knoxville: University of Tennessee Press, 1996.

Goodwin, Doris Kearns. *The Fitzgeralds and the Kennedys: An American Saga.* New York: Simon and Schuster, 1987.

Gould, Stephen Jay. *The Mismeasure of Man.* New York: W. W. Norton, 1981.

Grisham, Vaughn L. Jr. *Tupelo: The Evolution of a Community.* Dayton, OH: Kettering Foundation Press, 1999.

Guralnick, Peter. *Last Train to Memphis: The Rise of Elvis Presley.* Boston: Little, Brown and Company, 1994.

Gutman, Herbert G. *The Black Family in Slavery and Freedom: 1750–1925.* New York: Vintage Books, 1976.

Hackett, Allen. *Quickened Spirit: A Biography of Frank Sutliff Hackett.* Riverdale, NY: Riverdale Country School, 1957.

Hamilton, Nigel. *J.F.K.: Reckless Youth.* New York: Random House, 1992.

Hardin County History Museum. "The History of Hardin County." http://www .hardinkyhistory.org/history.htm.

Heidgerd, William. *Black History of New Paltz.* New Paltz, NY: Haviland-Heidgerd Historical Collection, Elting Memorial Library, 1986.

Herndon, William H., and Jesse W. Weik. *Herndon's Life of Lincoln.* New York: Da Capo, 1983 (originally published 1942).

Herrmann, Dorothy. *Helen Keller: A Life.* New York: Alfred A. Knopf, 1998.

Hinckle, Warren, and Frederic Hobbs. *The Richest Place on Earth: The Story of Virginia City and the Heyday of the Comstock Lode.* Boston: Houghton Mifflin, 1978.

The History of Armstrong County Pa: Her People, Past and Present, volume 1, chapter 12: Ford City Borough, Armstrong County Genealogy Project, http://www.paroots .com/~armstrong/beersproject/history/chapter13.html.

History of Warrick, Spencer and Perry Counties, Indiana. Chicago: Goodspeed Bros. & Co., 1885.

Hofstadter, Richard. *The American Political Tradition and the Men Who Made It.* New York: Alfred A. Knopf, 1949.

Homes, Pauline. *A Tercentenary History of the Boston Public Latin School: 1635–1935.* Cambridge, MA: Harvard University Press, 1935.

Honey, Michael. *The Power of Remembering: Black Factory Workers and Union Organizing in the Jim Crow Era.* Organization of American Historians. http://www.oah.org/meetings/2001/honey.html.

Hopkins, Sarah Winnemucca. *Life Among the Piutes: Their Wrongs and Claims.* Reno and Las Vegas: University of Nevada Press, 1994 (originally published 1883).

Horton, Gary A. "Carson River Chronology." Nevada Department of Conservation and Natural Resources, Division of Water Resources. http://water.nv.gov/WaterPlanning/carson/carson2.htm.

Horton, Myles. *The Long Haul: An Autobiography of Myles Horton.* With Judith Kohl and Herbert Kohl. New York: Anchor Books/Doubleday, 1990.

Horton, Stanley M. "A Typical Day at the Azusa Street Mission." *Enrichment Journal,* General Council of the Assemblies of God, reprinted from *Heritage,* Fall 1982. http://www.ag.org/enrichmentjournal/199904/034_typical_day.cfm.

Hounshell, David A. *From the American System to Mass Production: The Development of Manufacturing Technologies in the United States, 1800–1932.* Baltimore: Johns Hopkins University Press, 1984.

Hoyt, Charles Oliver. *Studies in the History of Modern Education.* New York: Silver, Burdett and Co., 1908.

Inglis, Alexander James. *The Rise of the High School in Massachusetts.* New York: Teachers College of Columbia University, 1911.

Isaacson, Walter. *Benjamin Franklin: An American Life.* New York: Simon & Schuster, 2003.

Jacobs, Jane. *The Economy of Cities.* New York: Vintage Books, 1969.

James, R. L. "The Colbertians: A History of Colbert County, Alabama, and Some of Its Pioneer Citizens Before 1875." Originally published in the *Alabama Historical Quarterly,* 1945; reprinted by the Natchez Trace Genealogical Society, Florence, AL, 1980. http://archiver.rootsweb.com/th/read/ALCOLBER/1999-02/0919895548.

Johnson, Judith. *The Art of Architecture: Modernism in Memphis, 1890–1980.* Memphis Heritage. http://www.memphisheritage.org/mhihost/Read-ModernismInMemphis.html.

Kaestle, Carl F., and Maris A. Vinovskis. *Education and Social Change in Nineteenth-Century Massachusetts.* New York: Cambridge University Press, 1980.

Katz, Michael B. *Class, Bureaucracy, and Schools: The Illusion of Educational Change in America.* New York: Praeger Publishers, 1975.

——. *The Irony of Early School Reform: Educational Innovation in Mid-Nineteenth Century Massachusetts.* Cambridge, MA: Harvard University Press, 1968.

Keller, Captain A. H. "Colbert County, Alabama; History: Tuscumbia." *Northern Alabama Historical and Biographical Illustrated.* Birmingham, AL: Smith & Deland, 1888. http://www.rootsweb.ancestry.com/~alcolber/hist-tuscumbia.htm.

Keller, Helen. *Out of the Dark: Essays, Letters, and Addresses on Physical and Social Issues.* Doubleday, Garden City, NY: Page and Company, 1913.

——. *The Story of My Life.* Garden City, NY: Doubleday, 1905 (1954 edition).

Kennedy, John F. *The Wisdom of JFK.* Edited by T. S. Settel. New York: E. P. Dutton and Co., 1965.

Kennedy, Joseph P. *Hostage to Fortune: The Letters of Joseph P. Kennedy.* Edited by Amanda Smith. New York: Viking, 2001.

Kennedy, Rose Fitzgerald. *Times to Remember.* Garden City, NY: Doubleday, 1974.

Kennedy, Rose, Joseph P. Kennedy, Jacqueline Rouzier Kennedy, Robert F. Kennedy, and Eunice Kennedy Shrines. *John Fitzgerald Kennedy . . . As We Remember Him.* Edited by Goddard Lieberson. New York: Atheneum, 1965.

"Kentucky Baptists," Baptist Encyclopedia, 1881. www.geocities.com/baptist _documents/kentucky.baptists.tbe1881.html.

Kinsey, James. *Giving a Voice to a Shared Past: Public Education and (De)segregation in Mississippi, 1868–2000.* Department of History and Philosophy, Jackson State University. http://www.jsums.edu/~history/Voices/Voices_From_A_Shared_Past_ Sustaining%20the%20Infrastructure%20of%20Public%20Education.html.

Kirsch, Robert, and William S. Murphy. *West of the West.* New York: E. P. Dutton, 1967.

Kessler, Ronald. *The Sins of the Father: Joseph P. Kennedy and the Dynasty He Founded.* New York: Warner Books, 1996.

Knack, Martha C, and Omer C. Stewart. *As Long as the River Shall Run: An Ethnology of Pyramid Lake Indian Reservation.* Reno and Las Vegas: University of Nevada Press, 1984 (paperback edition 1999).

Kobylak, Wes. "A Primer on the History of American Juggling." *Juggler's World* 39, no. 2. http://www.juggling.org/jw/87/2/vaudeville.html.

Koestler, Frances A. *The Unseen Minority: A Social History of Blindness in the United States.* New York: David McKay Company, 1976.

Krug, Edward A. *The Shaping of the American High School: 1880–1920.* Madison and Milwaukee: University of Wisconsin Press, 1969.

Lash, Joseph P. *Helen and Teacher: The Story of Helen Keller and Anne Sullivan Macy.* New York: Delacorte Press/Seymour Lawrence, 1980.

Lear, Linda. *Rachel Carson: Witness for Nature.* New York: Henry Holt and Company, 1997.

Lefler, Hugh Talmadge, and Albert Ray Newsome. *North Carolina: The History of a Southern State.* Chapel Hill: University of North Carolina Press, 1963.

LeFevre, Ralph. *History of New Paltz, New York and Its Old Families.* Baltimore: Genealogical Publishing Co., 1973.

Lewis, David Levering. *W.E.B. Du Bois: Biography of a Race: 1868–1919.* New York: Henry Holt and Co., 1993.

Lincoln, Abraham. *Abraham Lincoln: Speeches and Writings, 1832–1858.* New York: Library of America, 1989.

Lincoln, C. Eric, ed. *The Black Experience in Religion.* Garden City, NY: Anchor Books, 1974.

Lindberg, Stanley W. *The Annotated McGuffey: Selections from the McGuffey Eclectic Readers, 1836–1920.* New York: Van Norstrand Reinhold, 1976.

Lorant, Stefan. *Pittsburgh: The Story of an American City.* Garden City, NY: Doubleday, 1964.

Lutts, Ralph H. *The Nature Fakers: Wildlife, Science and Sentiment.* Golden, CO: Fulcrum Publishing, 1990.

Mabee, Carleton, with Susan Mabee Newhouse. *Sojourner Truth: Slave, Prophet, Legend.* New York: New York University Press, 1993.

Mackinac Center for Public Policy. "School Choice in Michigan: A Primer for Freedom in Education." Midland, MI: Mackinac Center for Public Policy, 1999. http://www.mackinac.org/article.aspix?ID=2032.

Magnolia Metal Company. *The Magnolia Metal Bearing Book.* New York: Magonolia Metal Company, 1927. http://www.metalwebnews.org/ftp/bearing-book.pdf.

Maharidge, Dale, and Michael Williamson. *And Their Children After Them.* New York: Pantheon Books, 1989.

Malone, Bill C. *Country Music USA: A Fifty-Year History.* Published for the American Folklore Society by the University of Texas Press, Austin, 1968.

Mann, Horace. "Twelfth Annual Report of Horace Mann as Secretary of the Massachusetts State Board of Education." 1848. http://www.tncrimlaw.com/civil_bible/horace_mann.htm.

Marsh, Dave. *Elvis.* New York: Times Books, 1982.

Marshall, Megan. *The Peabody Sisters: Three Women Who Ignited American Romanticism.* Boston: Houghton Mifflin, 2005.

McCarty, Kenneth G. *Depression and Hard Times in Mississippi: Letters from the William M. Colmer Papers.* Mississippi History Now, an online publication of the Mississippi Historical Society, December 2000. http://mshistory.k12.ms.us/features/feature11/hardtimes.html.

McClure, Daniel E. *Two Centuries in Elizabethtown and Hardin County, Kentucky.* Hardin County Historical Society, 1979.

McGee, Gary B. "William J. Seymour and the Azusa Street Revival." *Enrichment Journal,* General Council of the Assemblies of God. http://enrichmentjournal.ag.org/199904/026_azusa.cfm.

McManus, Edgar J. *A History of Negro Slavery in New York.* Syracuse, NY: Syracuse University Press, 1966.

Meigs, Cornelia, ed. *A Critical History of Children's Literature: A Survey of Children's Books in English.* London: Macmillan, 1969.

Memorial Record of Alabama, Vol. 1. Madison, WI: Brant and Fuller, 1893.

Murphy, Virginia Reed. *Across the Plains in the Donner Party.* New Haven, CT: Linnet Books, 1996.

Nagel, Paul C. *The Adams Women.* New York: Oxford University Press, 1987.

Nelson, Daniel. *Managers and Workers: Origins of the New Factory System in the United States, 1880–1920.* Madison: University of Wisconsin Press, 1975.

Nevins, Allan, with Frank Ernest Hill. *Ford: The Times, the Man, the Company.* New York: Charles Scribner's Sons, 1954.

Oestricher, Richard Jules. *Solidarity and Fragmentation: Working People and Class Consciousness in Detroit, 1875–1900.* Urbana and Chicago: University of Illinois Press, 1986.

Olson, Sidney. *Young Henry Ford: A Picture History of the First Forty Years.* Detroit: Wayne State University Press, 1963.

Osborne, Jerry. *Elvis Word for Word.* New York: Harmony Books, 1999–2000.

Oshinsky, David M. *Worse Than Slavery: Parchman and the Ordeal of Jim Crow Justice.* New York: Free Press/Simon & Schuster, 1996.

Oswald, John Clyde D. *A History of Printing: Its Development Through Five Hundred Years.* New York: Appleton and Company, 1928.

Painter, Nell Irvin. *Sojourner Truth: A Life, A Symbol.* New York: W. W. Norton, 1996.

Paleontological Research Institution. "The Story of Oil in Pennsylvania". http://www.priweb.org/ed/pgws/history/pennsylvania/pennsylvania.html.

Pennsylvania Department of Education. "Records of the Department of Education: Agency History." Pennsylvania State Archives. http://www.phmc.state.pa.us/bah/DAM/rg/rg22ahr.htm.

Perkins Institute and Massachusetts School for the Blind. "Annual Report of the Trustees" 58, 60, 61st editions. Boston: Wright and Potter Printing Co., 1890, 1892, 1893.

Pestana, Carla Gardina, and Sharon V. Salinger, eds. *Inequality in Early America.* Hanover, NH: University Press of New England, 1999.

Phillips, Cabell. *From the Crash to the Blitz: 1929–1939.* London: Macmillan, 1969.

Piven, Frances Fox, and Richard A. Cloward. *Poor People's Movements: Why They Succeed, How They Fail.* New York: Pantheon Books, 1977.

Powell, Arthur G. *Lessons from Privilege: The American Prep School Tradition.* Cambridge, MA: Harvard University Press, 1996.

Pulliam, John D. *History of Education in America.* New York: Merrill, fifth edition, 1991.

Pulliam, John D., and James Van Patten. *History of Education in America.* Merrill, Englewood Cliffs, NJ: Merrill, sixth edition, 1995.

Reagon, Bernice Johnson. *We'll Understand It Better By and By: Pioneering African American Gospel Composers.* Washington, DC: Smithsonian Institution Press, 1992.

Remini, Robert V. *Andrew Jackson.* New York: Twayne Publishers, 1966.

——. *Andrew Jackson and the Course of American Empire, 1767–1824.* New York: Harper & Row, 1977.

Report of a Committee of the Town of Great Barrington upon the Subject of Abolishing School Districts, and Establishing a Town School System. J. A. Royce, printer. Lee, MA: 1865.

Riss, Richard M. *Singing in the Spirit in the Holiness, Pentecostal, Latter Rain and Charismatic Movements.* Paper delivered at Orlando '95, July 29, 1995. http://www.pctii.org/arc/riss.html.

Robinson, Blackwell P. *William R. Davie.* Chapel Hill: University of North Carolina Press, 1957.

Rorabaugh, W. J. *The Craft Apprentice: From Franklin to the Machine Age in America.* New York: Oxford University Press, 1986.

Ross, Lynn Mo., and Ellarose Andorf, eds. *Springdale: A Walk down Memory Lane: From Indian Village to Power City.* Springdale, PA: Springdale Book Committee, 1981.

Roth, Eric J. *"The Society of Negroes Unsettled": The History of Slavery in New Paltz,* New York. Hugenot Historical Society Library and Archives, May 2001. http://www.locustlawn.org/library_archives/exhibits_research/african_american/slavery.html.

Russell, Francis. *Sacco and Vanzetti: The Case Resolved.* New York: Harper & Row, 1986.

Sandburg, Carl. *Chicago Poems.* New York: Henry Holt, 1916.

Sargent, Porter. *A Brief Guide to Schools: Boarding and Residential.* Boston: Porter Sargent, 1936.

Schlesinger, Arthur M. Jr. *The Age of Jackson.* Boston: Little, Brown and Company, 1945.

Sheers, Sinclair A. "Soapmaking." www.suite101.com/article.cfn/soapmaking.

Spring, Joel. *The American School: 1642–2000.* New York: McGraw Hill Higher Education, fifth edition, 2001.

St. John, George Henry. *Forty Years at School.* New York: Holt and Company, 1959.

Sterling, Philip. *Sea and Earth: The Life of Rachel Carson.* New York: Thomas Y. Crowell, 1970.

Stewart, George R. *The California Trail: An Epic with Many Heroes.* New York: McGraw-Hill, 1962.

Stossel, Scott. *Sarge: The Life and Times of Sargent Shriver.* Washington, DC: Smithsonian Books, 2004.

Strickland, Narvell. "A History of Cotton Mills and the Industrial Revolution." 2001 http://narvellstrickland1.tripod.com/cottonmillhistory2/index1.html

Taylor, Charles J. *History of Great Barrington.* Great Barrington, MA: Clark W. Bryan, 1882.

Teaford, Jon C. *Cities of the Heartland: The Rise and Fall of the Industrial Midwest.* Bloomington and Indianapolis: Indiana University Press, 1993.

Terrell, Bob. *The Music Men: The Story of Professional Quartet Singing.* Asheville, NC: Bob Terrell Publisher, 1990.

Tindall, George B. *The Emergence of the New South: 1913–1945*, vol. 10 of *A History of the South.* Louisiana State University Press and Littlefield Fund for Southern History of the University of Texas, 1967.

Tobey, Ronald C. *Technology as Freedom: The New Deal and the Electrical Modernization of the American Home.* Berkeley: University of California Press, 1996.

Toker, Franklin. *Pittsburgh: An Urban Portrait.* University Park: Pennsylvania State University Press, 1986.

Tolley, Kim. *The Science Education of American Girls: A Historical Perspective.* New York: RoutledgeFalmer, 2003.

Tourtellot, Arthur Bernon. *Benjamin Franklin: The Shaping of Genius: The Boston Years.* New York: Doubleday, 1977.

Truth, Sojourner. *Narrative of Sojourner Truth*, with "Book of Life" and "A Memorial Chapter." New York: Barnes and Noble Classics, 2005 (based on memorial edition, 1878).

Tucci, Douglas Shand. *Built in Boston: City and Suburbs, 1800–1950.* Boston: New York Graphic Society, 1978.

Tucker, David M. *Memphis Since Crump: Bossism, Blacks, and Civic Reformers, 1948–68.* Knoxville: University of Tennessee Press, 1980.

Unger, Harlow Giles. *Noah Webster: The Life and Times of an American Patriot.* New York: John Wiley and Sons, 1998.

Van Buren, Augustus. *A History of Ulster County Under the Dominion of the Dutch*. Astoria, New York: J. C. and A. L. Fawcett, 1989 (first edition 1923).

Van Sickle, James Hixon. *Educational Survey of the Public Schools of Brookline, Mass.* Brookline, MA: Brookline School Committee, 1917.

Vann Woodward, C. *Origins of the New South: 1877–1913*. Vol. 9 in *A History of the South*. Louisiana State University Press and the Littlefield Fund for Southern History of the University of Texas, 1951.

Volo, James M., and Dorothy Denneen Volo. *Family Life in 17th- and 18th-Century America*. Westport, CT: Greenwood Press, 2006.

Waldbott, G. L., A. W. Burgstahler, and H. L. McKinney. *Fluoridation: The Great Dilemma*. Lawrence, KA: Coronado Press, 1978.

Warden, G. B. *Boston: 1689–1776*. Boston: Little, Brown and Company, 1970.

Warren, Louis A. *Lincoln's Youth: Indiana Years: Seven to Twenty-one: 1816–1830*. New York: Appleton Century, Crofts, 1959.

Washlaski, Raymond A. "A Tribute to the Coal Miners that Mined the Bituminous Coal Seams of the Harwick Mine, Allegheny County, Pennsylvania, U.S.A." from "The Old Miner." Updated December 19, 2006. http://patheoldminer.rootsweb.com/allharwick.html.

Watts, Stephen. *The People's Tycoon: Henry Ford and the American Century*. New York: Alfred A. Knopf, 2005.

Weems, Mason L. *The Life of Washington*. Edited by Marcus Cunliffe. Cambridge, MA: Belknap Press of Harvard University, 1962 (first edition 1800).

Westerhoff, John H. III. *McGuffey and His Readers: Piety, Morality and Education in Nineteenth Century America*. Milford, MI: Mott Media, 1992 (originally published 1978).

Wheat, Margaret M. *Survival Arts of the Primitive Paiutes*. Reno: University of Nevada Press, 1967.

Where Wild Plum Trees Grew: Bicentennial Edition of Plum Borough History, 1788–1988. Allegheny Foothills Historical Society, 1988, Bridges and Tunnels of Allegheny County Pennsylvania. http://pghbridges.com/newkenW/0604-4488/logansferrymine_tun.htm.

Wilentz, Sean. *Andrew Jackson*. New York: Times Books/Henry Holt, 2005.

Willey, Susan. *Bitter Roots and Sweet Faith: Tupelo Conversations and Memories*. Dayton, OH: Charles F. Kettering Foundation, 1999.

Williams-Myers, A. J. *Long Hammering: Essays on the Forging of an African American Presence in the Hudson River Valley to the Early Twentieth Century*. Trenton, NJ: Africa World Press, 1994.

Wills, Garry. *Lincoln at Gettysburg: The Words That Remade America*. New York: Simon & Schuster, 1992.

Wilson, Douglas L. *Honor's Voice: The Transformation of Abraham Lincoln*. New York: Alfred A. Knopf, 1998.

Wilson, William E. *Indiana: A History*. Bloomington: Indiana University Press, 1966.

Winkle, Kenneth J. *The Young Eagle: The Rise of Abraham Lincoln*. Dallas: Taylor Trade Publishing, 2001.

Withey, Lynne. *Dearest Friend: A Life of Abigail Adams*. New York: Free Press, 1981.

Woods, Clyde. *Development Arrested: The Blues and Plantation Power in the Mississippi Delta.* London: Verson, 1998.

Wright, Louis B. *South Carolina: A Bicentennial History.* New York: W. W. Norton, 1976.

Young, Linda, and James. "A Tribute to St. Nicholas: A Magazine for Young Folks." http://flyingdreams.home.mindspring,com/nick.htm.

Zanjani, Sally. *Sarah Winnemucca.* Lincoln: University of Nebraska Press, 2001.

Zimm, Louise Hasbrouck, Joseph W. Emsley, Rev. A. Elwood Corning, and Willitt C. Jewell, eds. *Southeastern New York: A History of the Counties of Ulster, Dutchess, Orange, Rockland and Putnam.* New York: Lewis Historical Publishing, Volume 1, 1946.

Zinn, Howard. *A People's History of the United States.* New York: Harper & Row, paperback edition 1980.

———. *A People's History of the United States, a Teaching Edition.* New York: New Press, 1997.

Zunz, Olivier. *Making America Corporate: 1870–1920.* Chicago: University of Chicago Press, 1990.

INDEX

A NOTE ON THE AUTHOR

Daniel Wolff is the author of *4th of July, Asbury Park*, picked as an Editor's Choice in the *New York Times Book Review*. He has written for publications from *Vogue* to *Wooden Boat* to *Education Weekly*. His other books include *You Send Me: The Life and Times of Sam Cooke*, two volumes of poetry, and collaborations with the photographers Ernest Withers, Eric Meola, and Danny Lyon. He is currently producing a documentary project on New Orleans, *Right to Return*, with director Jonathan Demme.